Emerging Technologies for Securing the Cloud and IoT

Amina Ahmed Nacer
University of Lorraine, France

Mohammed Riyadh Abdmeziem
Ecole Nationale Supérieure d'Informatique, Algeria

A volume in the Advances in Information Security, Privacy, and Ethics (AISPE) Book Series

IGI Global
PUBLISHER of TIMELY KNOWLEDGE

Published in the United States of America by
IGI Global
Information Science Reference (an imprint of IGI Global)
701 E. Chocolate Avenue
Hershey PA, USA 17033
Tel: 717-533-8845
Fax: 717-533-8661
E-mail: cust@igi-global.com
Web site: http://www.igi-global.com

Library of Congress Cataloging-in-Publication Data

CIP Data in progress

This book is published in the IGI Global book series Advances in Information Security, Privacy, and Ethics (AISPE) (ISSN: 1948-9730; eISSN: 1948-9749)

British Cataloguing in Publication Data
A Cataloguing in Publication record for this book is available from the British Library.

All work contributed to this book is new, previously-unpublished material.
The views expressed in this book are those of the authors, but not necessarily of the publisher.

For electronic access to this publication, please contact: eresources@igi-global.com.

Advances in Information Security, Privacy, and Ethics (AISPE) Book Series

ISSN:1948-9730
EISSN:1948-9749

Editor-in-Chief: Manish Gupta, State University of New York, USA

MISSION

As digital technologies become more pervasive in everyday life and the Internet is utilized in ever increasing ways by both private and public entities, concern over digital threats becomes more prevalent.

The **Advances in Information Security, Privacy, & Ethics (AISPE) Book Series** provides cutting-edge research on the protection and misuse of information and technology across various industries and settings. Comprised of scholarly research on topics such as identity management, cryptography, system security, authentication, and data protection, this book series is ideal for reference by IT professionals, academicians, and upper-level students.

COVERAGE

- Network Security Services
- Privacy Issues of Social Networking
- Security Information Management
- Data Storage of Minors
- Tracking Cookies
- Cyberethics
- Security Classifications
- Access Control
- Risk Management
- Information Security Standards

IGI Global is currently accepting manuscripts for publication within this series. To submit a proposal for a volume in this series, please contact our Acquisition Editors at Acquisitions@igi-global.com or visit: http://www.igi-global.com/publish/.

The Advances in Information Security, Privacy, and Ethics (AISPE) Book Series (ISSN 1948-9730) is published by IGI Global, 701 E. Chocolate Avenue, Hershey, PA 17033-1240, USA, www.igi-global.com. This series is composed of titles available for purchase individually; each title is edited to be contextually exclusive from any other title within the series. For pricing and ordering information please visit http://www.igi-global.com/book-series/advances-information-security-privacy-ethics/37157. Postmaster: Send all address changes to above address.

Titles in this Series

For a list of additional titles in this series, please visit:
http://www.igi-global.com/book-series/advances-information-security-privacy-ethics/37157

Investigating and Combating Gender-Related Victimization
Gabriela Mesquita Borges (University of Lusíada, Portugal) Ana Guerreiro (University of Maia, Portugal & School of Criminology, Faculty of Law, University of Porto, Portugal) and Miriam Pina (School of Criminology, Faculty of Law, University of Porto, Portugal & Faculté de Droit, des Sciences Criminelles et d'administration Publique, Université de Lausanne, Switzerland)
Information Science Reference • copyright 2024 • 279pp • H/C (ISBN: 9798369354360) • US $265.00 (our price)

Navigating Cyber Threats and Cybersecurity in the Logistics Industry
Noor Zaman Jhanjhi (School of Computing Science, Taylor's University, Malaysia) and Imdad Ali Shah (School of Computing Science, Taylor's University, Malaysia)
Information Science Reference • copyright 2024 • 448pp • H/C (ISBN: 9798369338162) • US $295.00 (our price)

Analyzing and Mitigating Security Risks in Cloud Computing
Pawan Kumar Goel (Raj Kumar Goel Institute of Technology, India) Hari Mohan Pandey (Bournemouth University, UK) Amit Singhal (Raj Kumar Goel Institute of Technology, India) and Sanyam Agarwal (ACE Group of Colleges, India)
Engineering Science Reference • copyright 2024 • 270pp • H/C (ISBN: 9798369332498) • US $290.00 (our price)

Cybersecurity Issues and Challenges in the Drone Industry
Imdad Ali Shah (School of Computing Science, Taylor's University, Malaysia) and Noor Zaman Jhanjhi (School of Computing Science, Taylor's University, Malaysia)
Information Science Reference • copyright 2024 • 573pp • H/C (ISBN: 9798369307748) • US $275.00 (our price)

Emerging Technologies and Security in Cloud Computing

For an entire list of titles in this series, please visit:
http://www.igi-global.com/book-series/advances-information-security-privacy-ethics/37157

IGI Global
PUBLISHER of TIMELY KNOWLEDGE

701 East Chocolate Avenue, Hershey, PA 17033, USA
Tel: 717-533-8845 x100 • Fax: 717-533-8661
E-Mail: cust@igi-global.com • www.igi-global.com

To Katia…

Table of Contents

Detailed Table of Contents

The internet of things (IoT) has recently received a lot of attention, and it is an appealing technology that allows for the inclusion of intelligence in many applications by allowing communication between things, machines, and all things with people. It enables the exchange of environmental information with people via systems and software in a variety of human-related issues. IoT offers intelligent solutions to various issues such as smart energy, network monitoring, transportation, and waste management. The processes for processing enormous amounts of data, storage, and resource and energy management are the most significant problems. However, future IoT developments promise to provide many applications that are more complicated and intelligent than the usage of artificial intelligence approaches. In this chapter, we'll give a brief overview of IoT technologies, explore how they're used in different contexts, and explain why it's a good and promising technology. Additionally, we will examine a number of potential IoT applications while taking into account the difficulties they will encounter and upcoming trends.

The current surge in interconnected devices, which includes the Internet of Things (IoT) devices and the continually expanding cloud infrastructure, marks a new era of digital transformation and convenience. This transformative wave is reshaping industries, ushering in the age of smart cities, autonomous vehicles, and effortless remote collaboration. Yet, the growing complexity and reach of these technologies bring an accompanying increase in potential vulnerabilities and security risks. Thus, this study delves into the convergence of artificial intelligence (AI), cloud computing, and IoT security. It investigates how these state-of-the-art technologies can be leveraged to protect networks, data, and devices, presenting inventive solutions to address the ever-evolving threat landscape. Additionally, it sheds light on the challenges posed by AI-powered techniques and offers insights into future trends, making it a valuable resource for researchers, students, and cybersecurity professionals.

The term internet of things (IoT) denotes the advanced phase of the internet, wherein a worldwide communication infrastructure is established between individuals and machines. The IoT is now being developed as a worldwide infrastructure that has the potential to significantly transform various aspects of human life. Nevertheless, the interconnected nature of IoT systems and the involvement of other disciplines in their implementation have presented novel security obstacles. However, the utilization of deep learning techniques holds significant importance in enhancing the security of IoT systems. This transformation goes beyond the facilitation of secure communication between devices, as it enables the development of intelligent systems that prioritize security. In this chapter, the basic architecture of IoT has been discussed with its applications and security challenges. Different deep-learning techniques for securing IoT devices with their strengths and weaknesses have also been explored.

Sharing data and facts rather than the content of a website is what the semantic web is all about. Sir Tim Berners-Lee proposed the semantic web concept in 2001. The semantic web assists in the development of a technological stack that supports a "web of data" rather of a "web of documents." The ultimate goal of the web of data is to provide computers the ability to do more meaningful jobs and to create systems that can enable trustworthy network connections. Different data interchange formats (e.g. Turtle, RDF/XML, N3, NTriples), query languages (SPARQL, DL query), ontologies, and notations (e.g. RDF Schema and Web Ontology Language (OWL)) are all used in semantic web technologies (SWTs) to provide a formal description of entities and correspondences within a given knowledge domain. These technologies are useful in accomplishing the semantic web's ultimate goal. Linked data is at the core of the semantic web since it allows for large-scale data integration and reasoning. SPARQL, RDF, OWL, and SKOS are among the technologies that have made linked data more powerful; however, there are many difficulties that have been detailed in different publications.

This chapter delves into the integration of artificial intelligence of things (AIoT) with cloud computing environments, facilitated by semantic web control models. It explores how leveraging semantic technologies can enhance the interoperability, intelligence, and efficiency of AIoT systems within cloud infrastructures. The chapter begins by elucidating the foundational concepts of AIoT, cloud computing, and the Semantic Web. It then discusses the challenges associated with integrating AIoT devices and cloud platforms, such as data heterogeneity, interoperability issues, and security concerns. Next, it presents various semantic web control models and their applicability in AIoT-cloud integration, including ontology-based reasoning, knowledge representation, and semantic interoperability standards. Furthermore, the chapter analyzes case studies and practical implementations showcasing the benefits of employing Semantic Web control models in AIoT-cloud environments. Lastly, it outlines future research directions and potential advancements in this burgeoning field.

The proliferation of internet of things (IoT) devices has resulted in an unprecedented influx of data, leading to heightened concerns regarding the privacy and security of sensitive information in cloud environments. Privacy-preserving machine learning techniques have emerged as essential tools for ensuring the confidentiality of IoT data while facilitating meaningful analysis. This chapter provides an overview of the key principles and methodologies employed in privacy-preserving machine learning for IoT data in cloud environments. Key considerations encompass data anonymization, secure transmission, and adherence to stringent data protection regulations such as the General Data Protection Regulation (GDPR). Robust encryption and access control mechanisms are implemented to safeguard data integrity while allowing for effective analysis. Techniques like homomorphic encryption and secure multi-party computation enable secure computations on encrypted data, ensuring privacy while maintaining the utility of the data.

According to Pew Research Center, eight-in-ten Americans acquire news from digital devices, favoring mobile devices over desktops and laptops. News is therefore spread faster, wider, and easier. However, many of these mobile messages are at risk of being incorrect or even distorted on purpose. This research aims to mitigate this problem by identifying mobile text misinformation to allow mobile users to accurately judge the messages they receive. The proposed method uses various mobile data mining technologies including ChatGPT and several ensemble learning methods (including recurrent neural networks (RNN) and bagging, boosting, stacking, & voting means) to identify mobile misinformation. In addition, sentiment and emotional analyses are discussed in comparison. Experiment results show the ensemble learning methods provide higher accuracy than standalone ChatGPT or RNN model. Nevertheless, the problem, misinformation identification, is intrinsically difficult. Further refinements are needed before it is put into practical use.

Internet security has been a problem for businesses around the world. Encryption, authentication, and virtual private networks have been used to safeguard the network infrastructure and communications over the whole process of data protection. Intrusion detection systems (IDSs) are an advancement in network security that safeguards organizational data. System detecting intrusions into computer networks is known as IDS. Throughout their life, information cannot be guaranteed to be secured. An IDS's task is to find if there is any danger or security breach. The IDS identifies deliberate attempts by authorized users or by third parties to take advantage of security flaws as well as actual abuse. In this study, the authors used classifiers such as decision trees, support vector machines, Naive Bayes, random forests, and logistic regression. The authors also used machine learning algorithms to calculate accuracy, precision, recall, and false positives. They can conclude that this model suggested decision trees with the highest accuracy of 82.3%.

Secure communication protocols are paramount in ensuring the integrity, confidentiality, and availability of data in the interconnected landscapes of cloud computing and the internet of things (IoT). This comprehensive review explores the significance of these protocols, beginning with an introduction to cloud computing, IoT, and the challenges they pose to security. The exploration of security threats in both ecosystems lays the foundation for in-depth discussions on communication protocols tailored for Cloud and IoT environments. The review provides an exhaustive analysis of communication protocols for cloud security, including TLS/SSL and IPsec, unraveling their strengths, weaknesses, and use cases. Transitioning to IoT, the exploration delves into protocols such as MQTT and CoAP, evaluating their suitability across diverse IoT scenarios. Integration challenges in Cloud and IoT environments, real-world case studies, and emerging technologies like blockchain further enrich the discussion. Looking to the future, trends such as zero trust architecture and edge computing are examined, along with the potential impact of blockchain on security. Practical recommendations for implementing secure communication protocols and best practices for ongoing security in Cloud and IoT systems are presented. The conclusion underscores the critical role of secure communication protocols in navigating the evolving digital landscape.

Preface

As we stand at the intersection of technological innovation and connectivity, the realms of cloud computing and the Internet of Things (IoT) have emerged as transformative forces, reshaping the landscape of our digital existence. The profound convenience and connectivity offered by these technologies come hand-in-hand with unprecedented challenges, especially in the domain of security.

The collaborative effort of Amina Ahmed Nacer from the University of Lorraine, France, and Mohammed Riyadh Abdmeziem from Ecole nationale Supérieure d'Informatique, Algeria, brings forth this edited reference book on *Emerging Technologies for Securing the Cloud and IoT*. This compilation aims to be a guiding beacon for researchers, students, professionals, and policymakers navigating the intricate landscape of securing cloud-based IoT systems.

The rapid adoption of cloud services and the proliferation of IoT devices have accentuated the need for robust security measures. Our book endeavors to delve into the multifaceted dimensions of this imperative, encompassing authentication and access control, data protection, privacy preservation, threat detection and prevention, secure communication protocols, risk assessment, and key management.

The chapters within this volume span a wide spectrum, including practical approaches, case studies, experimental evaluations, and theoretical frameworks. Our goal is to provide practical guidance and in-depth analysis of the latest trends in securing the Cloud and IoT ecosystems.

The thematic areas covered in this book include security frameworks, blockchain applications, artificial intelligence, machine learning, threat modeling, risk analysis, identity and access management, data protection, intrusion detection and prevention, secure communication protocols, forensics, incident response, security standards, regulations, and compliance, as well as key management protocols addressing cloud-based IoT specificities.

We believe that the collective wisdom shared in these pages will not only contribute to the academic discourse but will also offer valuable insights to practitioners and policymakers. This compilation stands as a testament to the collaborative efforts required to navigate the intricate challenges posed by the confluence of cloud computing and the Internet of Things. We extend our gratitude to the contributors who have shared their knowledge, making this reference book a valuable resource for understanding the advancements and challenges in securing the Cloud and IoT. May it serve as a catalyst for further exploration and innovation in this dynamic field.

CHAPTER 1: SMART APPLICATIONS BASED ON IoT: CHALLENGES AND EMERGING TRENDS LANDSCAPE

Coming from Red Sea University in Sudan and Taif University in Saudi Arabia, Elmustafa Sayed Ali Ahmed, Abdolsamed A. Bakhit, and Rashid Saeed contribute a chapter that spotlights the burgeoning attention IoT has garnered. The authors explore IoT's role in enabling intelligent solutions for various issues such as smart energy, network monitoring, transportation, and waste management. They discuss the challenges related to data processing, storage, and resource management. Additionally, the chapter provides a brief overview of IoT technologies, their applications in different contexts, and an exploration of potential challenges and emerging trends.

CHAPTER 2: A REVIEW OF ARTIFICIAL INTELLIGENCE TECHNIQUES FOR IMPROVED CLOUD AND IoT SECURITY

Authored by Kassim Kalinaki, Wasswa Shafik, Magezi Masha, and Adam Alli from the Islamic University in Uganda, this chapter delves into the convergence of artificial intelligence (AI), cloud computing, and IoT security. The authors investigate how these state-of-the-art technologies can be leveraged to protect networks, data, and devices, presenting inventive solutions to address the evolving threat landscape. The chapter also sheds light on the challenges posed by AI-powered techniques and offers insights into future trends, making it a valuable resource for researchers, students, and cybersecurity professionals.

CHAPTER 3: DEEP LEARNING FOR IoT SECURITY APPLICATIONS AND CHALLENGES

Authored by Aized Amin Soofi and Haseeb Ahmad from the National Textile University in Faisalabad, Pakistan, this chapter explores the vital intersection of deep learning techniques and IoT security. The authors dissect the advanced phase of the internet, known as the Internet of Things (IoT), elucidating its architecture, applications, and security challenges. The chapter emphasizes the significance of deep learning in fortifying the security of IoT systems, transcending mere communication facilitation to enable the development of intelligent systems prioritizing security. The discussion encompasses the basic architecture of IoT, its applications, and the security challenges it poses. Various deep learning techniques are explored with a focus on their strengths and weaknesses in securing IoT devices.

CHAPTER 4: RECENT DEVELOPMENTS OF SEMANTIC WEB TECHNOLOGIES AND CHALLENGES

Kannadhasan Suriyan, Nagarajan R, K. Chandramohan, and R. Prabhu, affiliated with Study World College of Engineering and Gnanamani College of Technology in India, contribute a chapter that delves into the concept of the Semantic Web. This technology, proposed by Sir Tim Berners-Lee, shifts the focus from web content to data and facts. The authors explore technologies like SPARQL, RDF, OWL, and SKOS that enhance linked data, making large-scale integration and reasoning possible. While these technologies empower the semantic web, the chapter also highlights the challenges detailed in various publications.

CHAPTER 5: DEVELOPMENT OF ARTIFICIAL INTELLIGENCE OF THINGS AND CLOUD COMPUTING ENVIRONMENTS THROUGH SEMANTIC WEB CONTROL MODELS

In this chapter, authored by a collaborative team from various Indian institutions, the integration of Artificial Intelligence of Things (AIoT) with cloud computing environments is explored. The authors elucidate how Semantic Web control models can enhance the interoperability, intelligence, and efficiency of AIoT systems within cloud infrastructures. Beginning with foundational concepts, the chapter discusses challenges such as data heterogeneity and security concerns. Various Semantic Web control models are presented, including ontology-based reasoning and knowledge representation. Case studies and practical implementations demonstrate the benefits of employing Semantic Web control models in AIoT-cloud environments. Finally, the chapter outlines future research directions in this burgeoning field.

CHAPTER 6: PRIVACY-PRESERVING MACHINE LEARNING TECHNIQUES FOR IoT DATA IN CLOUD ENVIRONMENTS

Authored by Tarun Vashishth, Vikas Sharma, Kewal Sharma, Bhupendra Kumar, Sachin Chaudhary, and Manoj Gupta from IIMT University in Meerut, India, this chapter focuses on the privacy and security concerns arising from the proliferation of IoT devices. The authors provide an overview of privacy-preserving machine learning techniques, addressing key principles and methodologies. Considerations include data anonymization, secure transmission, and compliance with data protection regulations such as GDPR. Techniques like homomorphic encryption and secure multi-party computation are explored for secure computations on encrypted data, ensuring privacy while maintaining data utility.

CHAPTER 7: ChatGPT AND ENSEMBLE LEARNING FOR MOBILE TEXT MISINFORMATION IDENTIFICATION

This chapter, authored by researchers from the University of North Dakota, USA, tackles the problem of mobile text misinformation. With the prevalence of digital news consumption via mobile devices, misinformation spreads rapidly. The chapter proposes a method utilizing ensemble learning techniques, including ChatGPT and recurrent neural networks, to identify mobile misinformation. Experimental results demonstrate the efficacy of ensemble learning methods in achieving higher accuracy, though further refinements are deemed necessary.

CHAPTER 8: ANALYZING EFFICACY OF MACHINE LEARNING ALGORITHMS ON INTRUSION DETECTION SYSTEM

Hailing from Vellore Institute of Technology in Chennai, India, Bhuvaneswari Amma N G and Swanand Yamgar contribute a chapter that addresses the pressing issue of internet security. Focusing on Intrusion Detection Systems (IDSs), the authors explore classifiers such as Decision Trees, Support Vector Machines, Naive Bayes, Random Forests, and Logistic Regression to assess their efficacy. The study calculates accuracy, precision, recall, and false positives, with decision trees emerging with the highest accuracy. The chapter contributes to the understanding of machine learning algorithms' performance in enhancing intrusion detection.

CHAPTER 9: SECURE COMMUNICATION PROTOCOLS FOR CLOUD AND IoT: A COMPREHENSIVE REVIEW

In this chapter, Pawan Goel from Raj Kumar Goel Institute of Technology in Ghaziabad, India, delves into the crucial role of secure communication protocols in upholding the integrity, confidentiality, and availability of data within the interconnected realms of Cloud Computing and the Internet of Things (IoT). The comprehensive review commences with an exploration of the challenges posed by Cloud Computing and IoT to security, laying the groundwork for an in-depth discussion on communication protocols tailored for these environments. The analysis spans communication protocols for Cloud security, such as TLS/SSL and IPsec, unraveling their strengths, weaknesses, and practical use cases. The examination extends to IoT, evaluating protocols like MQTT and CoAP in various scenarios. The chapter also addresses integration challenges, incorporates real-world case studies, and explores emerging technologies like blockchain, enriching the discourse on secure communication protocols.

CHAPTER 10: LANDSCAPE OF SERVERLESS COMPUTING TECHNOLOGY AND IoT TOOLS IN THE IT SECTORS

Authored by a team from various Indian institutions, this chapter delves into the challenges of securing sensitive data and systems in the digital landscape. It discusses best practices for implementing security measures in serverless architectures and strategies for securing IoT ecosystems. Authentication protocols like multi-factor authentication and blockchain-based solutions are emphasized as crucial components of securing serverless computing and IoT environments.

CHAPTER 11: ENHANCING CLOUD AND IOT SECURITY: LEVERAGING IoT TECHNOLOGY FOR MULTI-FACTOR USER AUTHENTICATION

C.V. Suresh Babu, Abhinaba Pal, Vinith A, Venkatraman Muralirajan, and Sriram Gunasekaran, associated with Hindustan Institute of Technolgy and Science in India, contribute a chapter focusing on innovative approaches to user authentication within the broader context of "Security Frameworks for Cloud and IoT Systems." The chapter emphasizes the vulnerabilities of traditional single-factor authentication methods and advocates for enhanced security measures. The integration of bio-metric authentication, secure communication protocols, and the use of IoT devices for secure user authentication is discussed. The chapter also covers topics like behavioral analytics, user-friendly interfaces, and compliance with data privacy regulations, providing a comprehensive approach to enhancing security in cloud and IoT environments.

CHAPTER 12: SISA EN-DECRYPTION ALGORITHM FOR MULTILINGUAL DATA PRIVACY AND SECURITY IN IOT

Sivasakthi Kannan, Manju Thayammal, Sherly Alphonse, Priyanga P.T, and Abinaya S contribute a chapter proposing the SISA En-Decryption (SEDC) algorithm for multilingual data privacy and security in IoT. The authors highlight the global prevalence of multilingual databases and document transfers, emphasizing the need for data security against hackers. The SEDC method, capable of encrypting any language without size or language restrictions on the key, is presented as a secure alternative. The chapter explores the simplicity of the SEDC algorithm's design, making it adaptable to various computer languages. The proposed SEDC algorithm's potential fusion with technologies like cloud-based web applications, IoT, blockchain, and its applicability in multiple domains such as healthcare, smart agriculture, and mobile communication are also discussed, showcasing its effectiveness compared to existing algorithms.

As we bring this journey through the intricacies of securing the Cloud and IoT to a close, we reflect on the collective wisdom shared in the pages of *Emerging Technologies for Securing the Cloud and IoT*. In the evolving landscape of technological innovation and connectivity, cloud computing and the Internet of Things (IoT) have undeniably reshaped the fabric of our digital existence. The profound conveniences and connections these technologies bring forth are accompanied by unprecedented challenges, particularly in the realm of security.

This collaborative effort, orchestrated by Amina Ahmed Nacer from the University of Lorraine, France, and Mohammed Riyadh Abdmeziem from Ecole nationale Supérieure d'Informatique, Algeria, has resulted in a comprehensive reference book. Designed as a guiding beacon, this compilation serves as a valuable resource for researchers, students, professionals, and policymakers navigating the complex landscape of securing cloud-based IoT systems.

The chapters within this volume collectively span a wide spectrum, covering practical approaches, case studies, experimental evaluations, and theoretical frameworks. The exploration delves into multifaceted dimensions, addressing crucial aspects such as authentication and access control, data protection, privacy preservation, threat detection and prevention, secure communication protocols, risk assessment, and key management.

Contributors from academia and industry have shared their expertise and insights, fostering a rich exploration of best practices and emerging solutions. The thematic areas covered, including security frameworks, blockchain applications, artificial intelligence, machine learning, threat modeling, risk analysis, identity and access management, data protection, intrusion detection and prevention, secure communication protocols, forensics, incident response, and security standards, regulations, and compliance, offer a holistic view of the challenges and advancements in securing the Cloud and IoT.

This compilation is not just a testament to the collaborative efforts required to navigate the intricate challenges posed by the confluence of cloud computing and the Internet of Things; it is an invitation to further exploration and innovation in this dynamic field. We extend our heartfelt gratitude to the contributors who have shared their knowledge, making this reference book a cornerstone in understanding the advancements and challenges in securing the Cloud and IoT. May it serve as a catalyst for continuous exploration, collaboration, and innovation in the ever-evolving landscape of technology and security.

Editors:

Amina Ahmed Nacer
University of Lorraine, France

Mohammed Riyadh Abdmeziem
Ecole Nationale Supérieure d'Informatique, Algeria

Acknowledgement

We are highly grateful to all the authors who have shared their valuable research findings, which undoubtedly contribute to the advancement of the state of the art in their respective fields.

A special note of appreciation goes out to the reviewers for their dedication in carefully assessing the quality of the chapters that have been accepted for publication. Their time and expertise have been crucial in ensuring the quality and relevance of the content presented in this book.

We would also like to express our heartfelt gratitude to IGI Global for their unwavering support throughout the entire publication process. In particular, we extend our thanks to Kaylee for her assistance and guidance, which have been invaluable in bringing this project to fruition.

Chapter 1
Smart Applications Based on IoT:
Challenges and Emerging Trends Landscape

Elmustafa Sayed Ali Ahmed
https://orcid.org/0000-0003-4738-3216
Red Sea University, Sudan

Abdolsamed A. Bakhit
Red Sea University, Sudan

Rashid A. Saeed
https://orcid.org/0000-0002-9872-081X
Taif University, Saudi Arabia

ABSTRACT

The internet of things (IoT) has recently received a lot of attention, and it is an appealing technology that allows for the inclusion of intelligence in many applications by allowing communication between things, machines, and all things with people. It enables the exchange of environmental information with people via systems and software in a variety of human-related issues. IoT offers intelligent solutions to various issues such as smart energy, network monitoring, transportation, and waste management. The processes for processing enormous amounts of data, storage, and resource and energy management are the most significant problems. However, future IoT developments promise to provide many applications that are more complicated and intelligent than the usage of artificial intelligence approaches. In this chapter, we'll give a brief overview of IoT technologies, explore how they're used in different contexts, and explain why it's a good and promising technology. Additionally, we will examine a number of potential IoT applications while taking into account the difficulties they will encounter and upcoming trends.

DOI: 10.4018/979-8-3693-0766-3.ch001

INTRODUCTION

The Internet of Things (IoT) is a technology that enables all objects to communicate with the Internet by using standard computer and communication concepts. IoT components make it possible to incorporate gadgets like sensors, actuators, and other intelligent systems that can gather environmental data. For many applications in the Internet of Things, information can be handled, controlled, and processed (Ezechina et al., 2015). IoT makes it possible to manage resources efficiently to offer a variety of intelligent applications and enhances people's quality of life. These intelligent applications pertain to industrial, intelligent cities, healthcare, and home automation (Saranya et al., 2015). According to Sapandeep et al. (2016), in the Internet of Things, environmental sensor networks enable adaptive behaviour to adapt to changing environmental conditions and energy availability. These networks also use non-standard radio networks for communications, allowing wireless gateways to send sensor data to the Internet. Nodes in an IoT ecosystem allow for easy Internet access so that they can communicate data to other systems more confidently and easily.

In the near future, the development of IoT combined with artificial intelligence technology (AI) will allow for the management of several processes linked to testing and producing new goods (Ezechina et al., 2015; Misra et al., 2016). The IoT technology's ability to offer intelligent services that are spread across people and machines, as well as enable them to interact with their surroundings, is greatly influenced by artificial intelligence (AI). In order to develop decentralised resources capable of engaging with dynamic networks, AI-based IoT platforms can be coupled to sensors, M2M, and 6G communications (Jayavardhana et al., 2013). The IoT communication language is built on protocols that are used in a variety of platforms and situations and is dependent on intelligence algorithms.

IoT keeps an eye on a variety of environmental factors by placing quality and pollution sensors in urban areas and releasing the edited data to the general public. Since sensors have limited energy resources, the energy efficiency and network capacity of the IoT architecture should be carefully considered (Sapandeep et al., 2016). The frequency band being used and radio frequency communications will also have an impact on how well IoT networks function, which will be seen as one of the key IoT restrictions. In order to ensure adequate capacity in the event of expansion requirements as well as in the case of allocating additional radio spectrum when it becomes available, it is necessary to assess these limits and develop new solutions (Farheen et al., 2015). In light of the aforementioned, this chapter's contribution tries to analyse many significant IoT systems and applications. The chapter provides a quick overview of IoT communication systems and networks, along with information on the deployment obstacles and anticipated usage trends in the future.

The rest of the chapter is organized as follows; Section 2 provides a brief concept about IoT communications technologies. Section 3 provides some important IoT applications background. The vehicles and drones communications based IoT are discussed in Sections 4 and 5 respectively. The energy optimization for IoT based cloud computing is introduced in Section 6. Section 7 provides some of the most important IoT deployment challenges and solutions. The IoT related future technologies, trends and opportunities are discussed in Section 8 and 9 respectively. The chapter is concluded in Section 10.

IoT CONNECTIVITY: EMERGING TECHNOLOGIES

The Internet of Things (IoT) network made use of numerous well-known cellular, Wi-Fi, Bluetooth, ZigBee, and other communication technologies. In addition, new IoT technologies are being developed, including whitespace TV and an alternative for home automation applications (Amrita et al., 2016; N. Preethi et al., 2014). Due of the widespread use of IoT, these technologies are utilised in big cities. IoT network deployment requires selecting an appropriate communication technology or integrating between several technologies based on IoT application requirements, such as communication range, data processing, power utilisation, and security (Hele-Mai Haav, 2014). The influence of various IoT communication methods on the smart environment is shown in Table 1 (Gomez, 2019).

The technology known as Bluetooth makes it possible for numerous devices to connect to and be controlled by a network, and it has the potential to support more than 8 billion IoT devices. Bluetooth is now supported by a variety of devices, including smartphones, medical wearables, and even cars (Arko, 2016). With a communication range of more than 150 metres and a high data rate of approximately 1 Mbps, another version of the technology known as Bluetooth Low Energy (BLE) is available specifically for Internet of Things (IoT) smart applications (Ashraf et al., 2011; Nomusa, 2012). It offers efficient transportation that uses less energy (Nisha et al., 2015).

A technology that enables intelligent communications for industrial IoT is ZigBee. The 2.4GHz ZigBee standard, also known as the IEEE802.15.4 protocol, was used (Nisha et al., 2015). When sporadic data exchanges are needed in an Internet of Things (IoT) network with a low data rate across a short distance (less than 100 metres), such as in smart home applications, IEEE 802.15.4 ZigBee is utilised (Kondamudi et al., 2016). A mesh network based on ZigBee technology enables good communications, with low energy consumption, as well as effective management capabilities for machine-to-machine (M2M) and Internet of Things (IoT) connections (Nomusa, 2012). ZigBee offers a low-cost, low-power communication method for the Internet of Things (IoT).

By enabling IPv6 for numerous IoT applications, a new technology called as IPv6 Low-power wireless Personal Area Network (6LowPAN) makes it possible to deliver communications over ZigBee (Chen et al., 2015; Gupta et al., 2022). In order to transmit little data for various device features in mesh or star topology, 6LowPAN was developed by fusing IPv6 capabilities with low power ZigBee (Maryleen et al., 2015). The 6LowPAN standard, which supports communications for numerous systems supported by IPv6 as a key IoT idea, lacks a particular frequency range.

Other technologies, like Z-Wave, SIGFOX, LoRaWAN, and NB-IoT, are currently deployed in a variety of IoT applications (Kondamudi et al., 2016). Table 2 displays the features of these technologies. Data can be exchanged through low power communications in Z-Wave-based IoT networks, making them ideal for applications involving home automation. The implementation of a dependable network with low latency and a data throughput close to 100kbit/s is made possible by the usage of Z waves in IoT. Z-wave technology uses the sub-1GHz band and supports complete mesh networks. It facilitates simple device control and IoT network scalability (Sumithra A. et al., 2016).

According to Gupta et al. (2022) SigFox is a cellular-based communication system that enables low power and data rate communications for remote linked devices. With low cost and energy consumption, SigFox enables the connection of M2M

Table 1. Some of IoT communication technologies comparison

Technology	Bluetooth	Bluetooth 4.0 LE	ZigBee	Wi-Fi	6loWPAN
IEEE Spec.	IEEE 502.15.1	IEEE 502.15.4	EEE 502.15.4	EEE 502.11 a/b/g/n	IEEE 502.15.4 2006
Topology	Star	Star	Mesh, Star, Tree	Star	Mesh, Star
Bandwidth	1 Mbps	1 Mbps	250 Kbps	Up to 54Mbps	250 Kbps
Power Consumption	V.Low	V. Low	V. Low	Low	Very low
Max Data rate (Mbit/s)	0.72	5 to 10 m	0.25	54	sub GHz
Communication Range	< 30 m	5 to 10 m	10 to 300 m	4 to 20 m	800 m
Spectrum	2.4 GHz	2.4 GHz	2.4 GHz	2.4 - 5 GHz	2.4 GHz

and IoT applications in large area coverage to provide several applications services for remote monitoring, healthcare, transportation, and security purposes. To enable M2M networks to operate at low data rates and to conserve device energy, SigFox uses Ultra Narrow Band (UNB), with data rates that are limited to 1,000 bits per second (Shaikh F.K. et al., 2013).

LoRaWAN was created for battery-powered, wireless devices. According to Yinghui (2016), it supports IoT requirements including mobility and localization services. It makes it simple to interoperate IoT devices without requiring extensive network upgrades. With data speeds of up to 50 kbps, the LoRaWAN, which is optimised for low power communications with vast networks, can support a million devices (Gupta et al., 2022; Shaikh F.K. et al., 2013).

A variety of IoT networks are enabled with the new LPWAN technology known as NB-IoT. NB-IoT increases system capacity and spectrum efficiency while also reducing network energy usage. A broad network lifetime of more than 10 years is supported by NB-IoT. According to Li Zhenan et al. (2013), NB-IoT can coexist with cellular technologies ranging from 2G to 4G networks. Additionally, it operates in guard and IoT bands, works in LTE bands, and offers the majority of mobile network security and privacy capabilities (Wei et al., 2015).

STRATEGIC DEPLOYMENTS OF IoT

By strategically deploying the IoT, industries all over the world are being revolutionized and a new era of unprecedented connection and revolutionary opportunity is being ushered in. This paradigm shift involves the strategic alignment of IoT technologies to accomplish specific corporate objectives, improve operational efficiency, and develop novel solutions that tackle real-world difficulties. It goes beyond simple technology integration. The seamless integration of IoT into a variety of industries, including manufacturing, healthcare, logistics, agriculture, and more, is one of the most important components of strategic IoT deployment (Allioui and Mourdi. 2023) . To minimise downtime and increase overall productivity, IoT-enabled sensors

Table 2. Features of some IoT communication technologies

Technology	Data rates (kbps)	Topology	bands (MHz)	Communication Range
Z wave	40	Mesh	868	30 m
NB-IoT	26	Cell, star	700, 850,1700	25 Km
LoRaWAN	50	Star	868, 915	10 Km
SigFox	1	Star	868, 902	40 Km

and devices are strategically placed along production lines in the manufacturing industry to monitor equipment health, optimise operations, and facilitate predictive maintenance. In the healthcare industry, IoT devices are placed strategically to track patient health in real-time, allowing for remote patient monitoring, customised treatment regimens, and prompt interventions (Bibri et al, 2023).

Improving connectivity and communication between devices, systems, and stakeholders is the main goal of strategic IoT deployments. The smooth flow of data made possible by this interconnection promotes real-time decision-making and an operational environment that is more responsive and flexible. Strategic IoT deployment ensures a networked ecosystem that thrives on improved communication and collaboration, whether in smart cities where IoT sensors optimise traffic flow and resource management, or in agriculture where precision farming uses IoT for crop monitoring and irrigation control(Bibri et al, 2023). The creation and application of massive volumes of data are inextricably linked to the thoughtful implementation of IoT. Because it offers insights into user behaviour, operational patterns, and market trends, this data turns into a significant asset for enterprises. By utilising artificial intelligence and sophisticated analytics, businesses may remain ahead of the competition by making data-driven decisions that optimise workflows and forecast trends.

Strategic concerns for IoT implementations include strong security and privacy protocols. IoT solutions are strategically deployed by organisations with a focus on access control, secure communication routes, and data protection. In order to uphold regulatory obligations and foster trust among users and stakeholders, it is imperative to address these problems. Future-proofing and scalability are key design considerations for strategic IoT implementations. Businesses prepare for the incorporation of new ioT solutions because they recognise how quickly technology is developing (Tawalbeh et al, 2020). By taking a proactive stance, investments made now will be relevant and flexible enough to change with the times and eventually yield the highest possible return on investment. According to what was discussed, different applications for human life are made possible by the IoT to enable smart services. IoT makes it possible to create a wide range of intelligent applications for homes, cities, transportation, energy, and the environment (Ayyappadas, 2017). Some of these applications will be briefly covered in the sections that follow.

IoT-Powered Smart Environments

IoT offers a variety of smart environmental applications, including resource monitoring, management, and control (Ayyappadas, 2017). The quality of environmental resources, such as air and water, dangerous substances, radiation, or any other environmental resource quality indicators, can be monitored using specific environmental sensors (Nisha et al., 2015; Kondamudi et al., 2016). By installing sensors for each of the aforementioned resources for monitoring purposes and then making the right decisions regarding resource use, IoT technology offers effective ways to monitor the aforementioned resources (see figure 1). IoT can manage energy resources and control renewable resources like sunlight and wind to enable environmental applications (Aneeta, 2015). By utilising sensors that gather data and send it to smart cities, IoT technology aids in the monitoring of air quality. As is the case in China, where these technologies have been widely adopted, the IoT system provides complete coverage of a specific geographic area, it can manage traffic operations in major cities, and it can work to measure pollution levels in the air and water and take appropriate decisions.

The IoT is utilised in contemporary cities to manage garbage, which is related to the idea of a green environment free from the dangers to people, animals, and plants posed by the hazardous gases released by waste (Anjaiah, 2016). In order to enhance the environment, the IoT controls industrial pollution through integrated control and management systems with communication networks, decision-making, and forecasting systems (Shamisa et al., 2017). As they strive to monitor weather data with high precision and exchange data that is useful in various applications, such as traffic management and agriculture, IoT technologies have entered the field of weather forecasting and meteorology. Through wireless connections, which have lately been available in what is known as the internet of vehicle (IoV) Shamisa et al, 2017) (Qiulin et al, 2014), it is feasible to connect weather systems in vehicles, link vehicles to weather stations, and support meteorological data. These meteorological devices can also be mounted on structures, dispersed widely over numerous locations, and connected via the Internet of Things.

In recent years, numerous IoT-based environmental monitoring systems have been developed in accordance with various environmental requirements. A varying number of sensors and communication modules, such as ZigBee, LoRa, etc., are employed depending on the type of application. Smart metres and other portable smart gadgets are also available (Alaa et al., 2022). It was discovered that IoT plays a crucial role in facilitating communications and managing operations in the majority of these applications, which considerably improves the environment (Ali et al., 2021; Alqurashi et al., 2021).

Intelligent Cities: A Future Powered by IoT

Many large cities have adopted the idea of smart cities, as is the case in Seoul, Dubai, and Shanghai, all of which heavily rely on the IoT concept (Elmustafa et al., 2021). As it is the responsibility of governments and citizens to comprehend IoT applications and services, IoT implementation in smart cities is based on meticulous

Figure 1. Smart environment based internet of things (IoT)

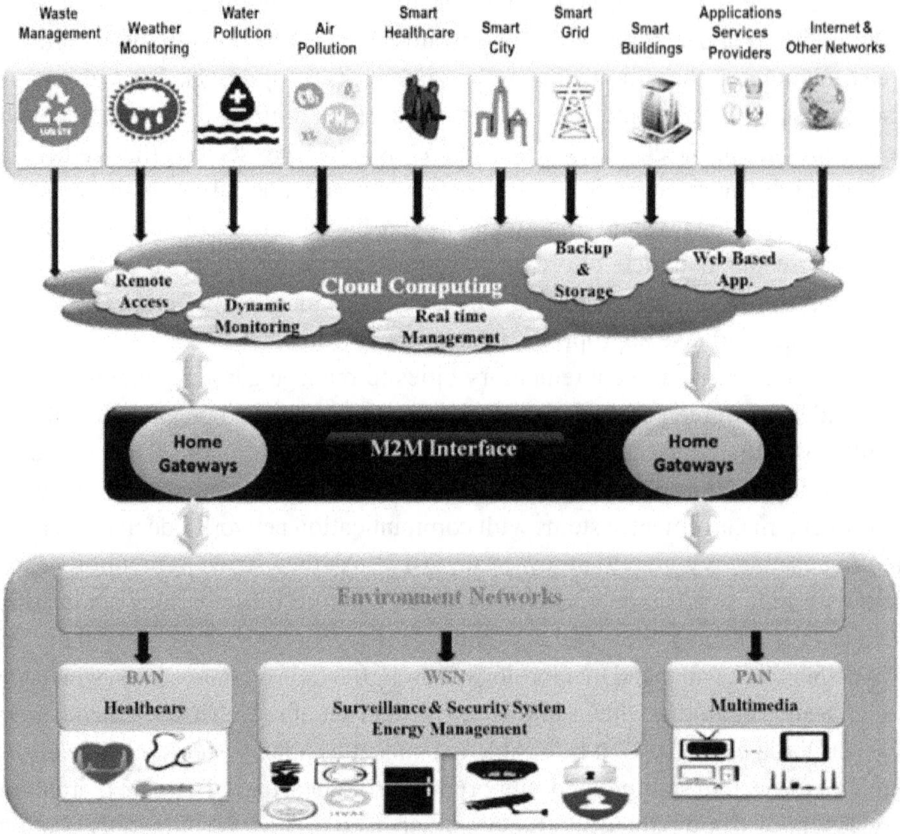

planning for each stage of constructing the systems and associated connections. The Internet of Things (IoT) enhances smart cities on a variety of infrastructure-related levels, including mass transit, traffic control, public safety, healthcare, and other neighbourhood services.

IoT technologies make it possible to connect all of the systems associated with the aforementioned infrastructures with one another, as well as with various monitoring procedures, and they help people access critical information via the Internet through a sizable database that gathers and stores data regarding airports, public transportation, and railroads (Hassan et al., 2021). Advanced artificial intelligence approaches and specialised protocols are used by all systems to interact with one another.

Among the most significant IoT-based applications in smart cities are road monitoring and transportation management. Intelligent sensing, traffic management, and other systems can all be developed using the IoT and AI methodologies (Elmustafa

Figure 2. Smart transportation application

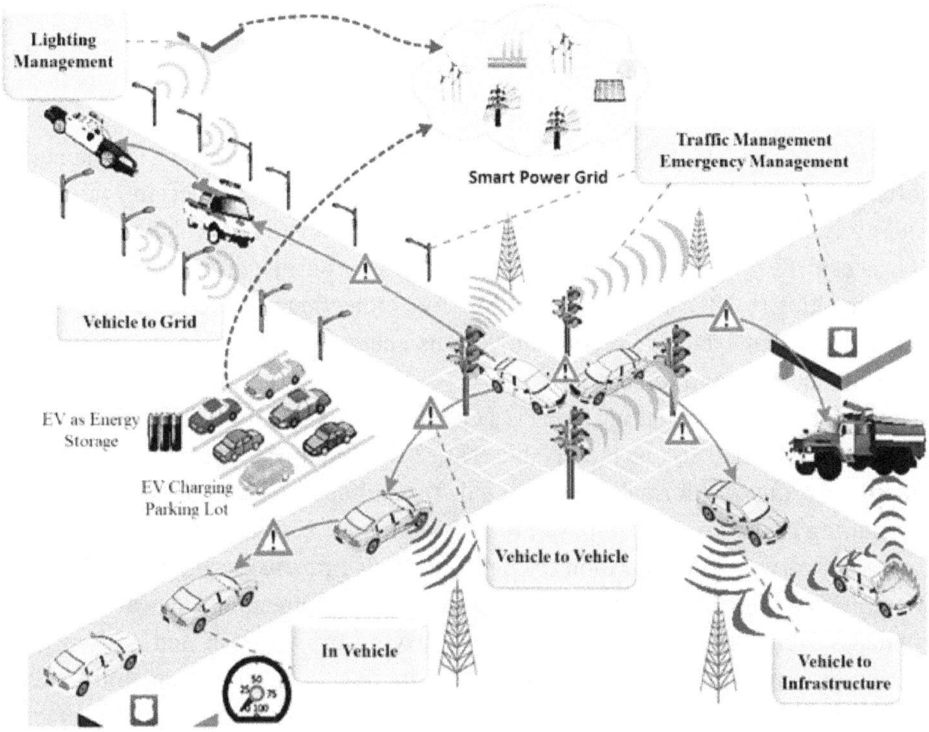

et al., 2021). It is beneficial for both drivers and transportation authorities to be aware of the current state of traffic congestion. As depicted in Figure 2, mobility in smart cities is tied to fundamental ideas about transportation analysis, control, and vehicle delivery. AI methods aid in streamlining the study and forecasting of traffic demand. Additionally, by connecting to IoT technologies, traffic management activities can be guided and speed managed for cars using a network vehicle architecture known as vehicles to every things (V2X) (Hassan et al., 2021). IoT are also incorporated into the design of electric vehicles and their charging systems because they save on fuel and have a smaller environmental impact.

Smart Energy Solutions Enabled by IoE

One of the most significant IoT technologies today is energy management, also referred to as the smart grid (Rania et al., 2020). In order to facilitate communication between energy suppliers and users, the power and electricity networks are interconnected with information and communication technologies. In order to properly manage and transmit electrical energy while ensuring its sustainability, the smart grid technology offers special solutions (Hassan et al., 2021). In addition to energy sensing technologies and monitoring systems, the smart energy grid also includes a variety of ICT-related components (see figure 3). Along with the capacity for consumption analysis and forecasting, its infrastructure also includes several devices including smart metres, control devices, automation, and processing.

The Internet of Things (IoT) provides a wide range of applications for managing different energies, both industrial and natural, which aids in merging numerous energy systems and advancing the integration of green and renewable technologies (Nada et al., 2021). As a recent advancement in smart grids, the idea of the Internet of Everything (IoE) offers a new paradigm for connecting numerous energy sources and devices that exchange reports on various energy networks, accept commands, perform analysis, and forecast.

The Internet of Everything (IoE) is a global network that links different electrical devices and smart grids together (Nahla et al., 2021; WadimStrielkowski et al., 2019). In order to convey information and signals throughout the network and modify the scheduling of energy consumption, IoE also provides new protocols that carry out smart network sensing and monitoring. In the IoE framework, Figure 4 illustrates a number of significant trends that support the development of renewable energy-related systems and applications that are driving a revolution and a significant transition in the field of electric energy and its management (Rania et al., 2020). These themes are concerned with the transformation of the electric power base through decentralisation, digitisation, and flexible electrification stages.

Figure 3. Smart grid architecture

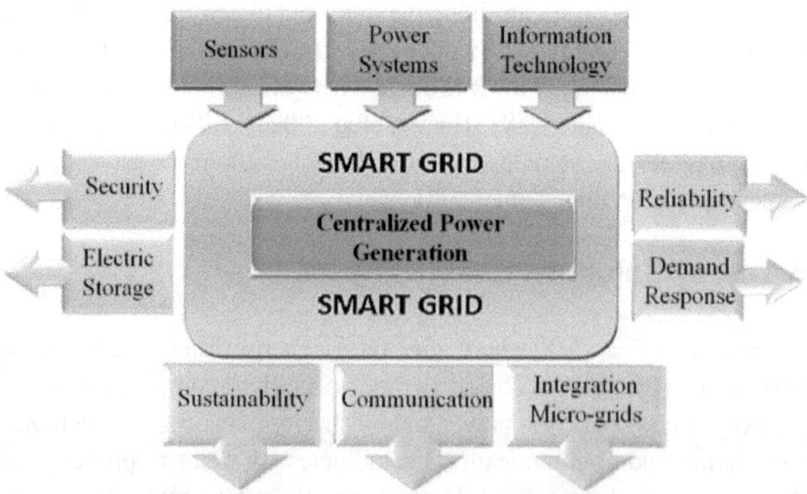

Figure 4. IoE framework innovation for high renewable energy sources

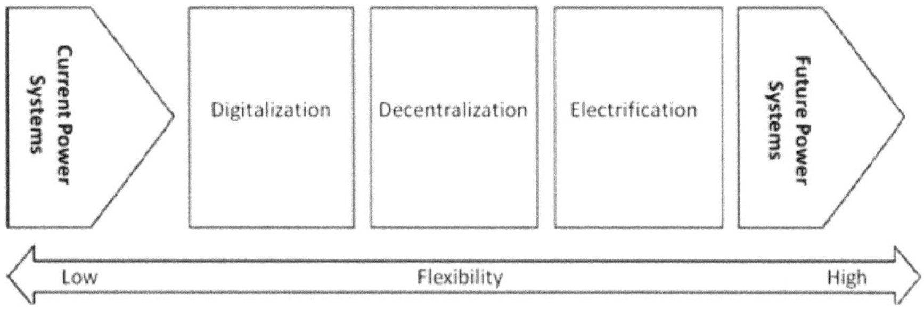

The Synergy of IoT and Industry 4.0

IoT technology has a significant impact on how industrial processes are developed. An enormous transformation known as Industry 4.0 was sparked by the rapid advancement of AI, machine learning, automation, and M2M communications techniques as well as their connection with the Internet (Agrawal et al., 2017). This technology is now often employed in the processes of product creation, production, and delivery. The integration of IoT into industrial processes has significantly improved workplace safety, decreased risks, and decreased the likelihood of accidents and disasters across numerous industries (Ghorpade et al., 2021). Additionally, when industrial machines are connected to machine learning technology, industrial Internet networks can offer special solutions for industrial decision-making.

The IoT is collaborating with new technologies like automation, robots, and autonomous mobility systems to create an intelligent manufacturing system. A smart factory's full potential is realised through internet-enabled M2M connections and industrial big data analysis (Ali et al., 2021). All of this design aids in enhancing industrial operations to decrease maintenance downtime, outages, and energy usage significantly.

The industrial revolution and industry have evolved into some of today's most cutting-edge technology, and it has taken several generations for this to happen. The first generation includes water and current strength in addition to mechanical devices (Butt et al., 2020). The mass production, assembly lines, and electricity that characterise the second generation of industry. The third generation of industries, which were in operation at the turn of the 20th century, were those controlled by automation and computers (Abbas et al., 2021; Rania et al., 2020).

Figure 5. The roadmap for smart industrial revolution

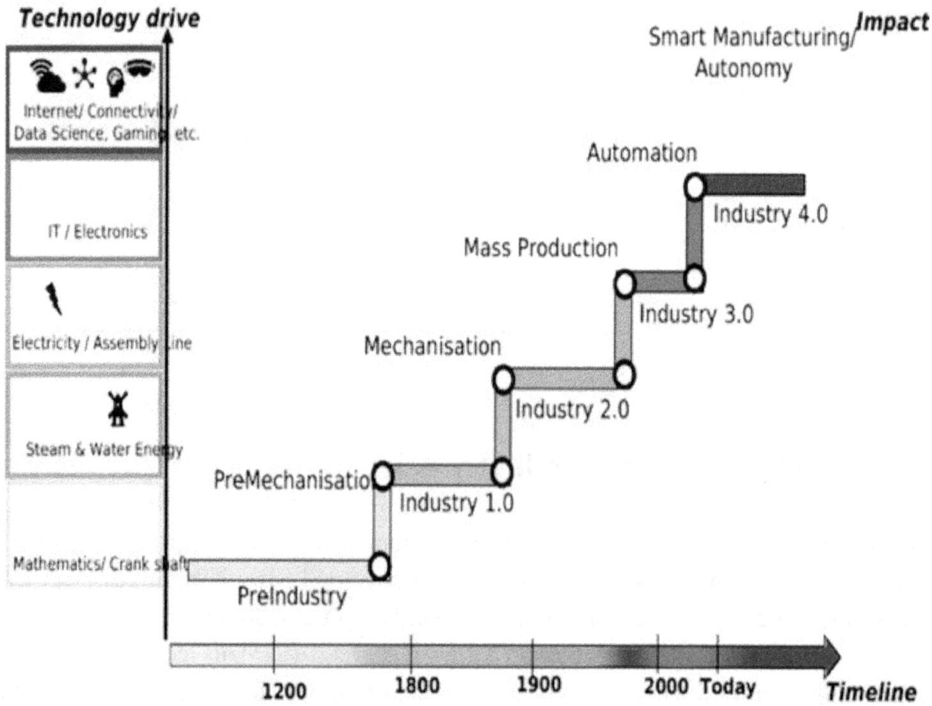

Physical systems that can link to the Internet are necessary for Industry 4.0. The idea that industry may meet high expectations for industries' solutions through IoT covers a variety of manufacturing-related topics (Zeinab et al., 2020). Figure 5 illustrates the progression of the industrial revolution through the use of machinery, automation, smart production, and intelligent industry. Global efforts in the future are anticipated to concentrate on research and innovation policies on projects that look to the future and deal with components of smart industries' scientific and technical advancements.

Connected Health: IoT Transforming Healthcare

IoT makes it possible to create intelligent healthcare systems and to provide numerous patients with medical care. The use of numerous health sensors that gather detailed physiological data has recently made it possible to continually monitor the patients' health state (Romany et al., 2021). To analyse, assess, and make medical judgements, these sensors are able to interface with monitoring systems, computing, and clouds over the internet.

The Internet of Health Things (IoHT) is a recently developed idea that offers a variety of applications, including telehealth, mobile healthcare, health analytics, and digitalized health systems. In order to analyse, diagnose, and make medical decisions pertaining to chronic diseases and epidemics, the IoHT is a contemporary framework that connects biosensing mechanisms, medical devices, and healthcare systems together (Ahmed et al., 2021; Romany et al., 2021). This was the case prior to and recently with the emergence of Covid 19 (Ahmed et al., 2021). The IoHT network enables the reduction of care expenses by lowering the cost of conventional care methods as well as data collecting and analysis, as well as the improvement of care quality through ongoing attention.

VEHICULAR IoT: DRIVING THE FUTURE OF CONNECTIVITY

Drivers anticipated that when using intelligent vehicular applications, the vehicles will be able to integrate other modern communication technologies and enable Internet access (Wesam et al., 2020). In addition to providing congestion control, intelligent vehicle systems (IVS) offer access to the internet for mobile data needs. Many businesses and academic institutions are working to create various IVS for effective cloud-based Internet of Vehicles (IoV) connections (Hao et al., 2018). There are various types of vehicle connectivity. The vehicles can communicate with roadside objects, sensors, other vehicles, and internet service providers.

In-Vehicle IoT Connectivity: Enabling Sensor Networks

The ability to assess pressure, coolant level, and other parameters thanks to vehicle to sensor communication offers various advantages. The driver's awareness of his situation is crucial, but improved sensors are also necessary for self- or autonomous control (Chin-Feng Lai et al., 2017; Daniel et al., 2020). Numerous cables are needed for the wired intra-vehicle connection to connect sensors to the electrical control unit (ECU). The sensors therefore communicate with the ECU by sending time-based information. It is possible to support the fundamental sensing inside vehicles by using a variety of low-power communication technologies, according to Khalid et al. (2013) and Mohd et al. (2015). Modern cellular communication and sensing technologies enable the connection between the ECUs of vehicles among themselves as well as with the various sensors in one network.

V2V Communication: Inter-Vehicle Connectivity

A variety of potential accident prevention applications are made possible by this kind of vehicle to vehicle (V2V) communication. Through this link, vehicles can exchange information about their whereabouts and speeds with one another over a specific network. Through single-hop systems or multi-hop systems, information can be effectively shared between the communication and control systems of the vehicles in vehicle-to-vehicle (V2V) connections. This kind of communication allows for the transmission of information from vehicle sensors to other vehicles, particularly in applications that require brief communications (Muhammad et al., 2019; Zhang et al., 2017). For V2V communication, there are numerous wireless access technologies available that can improve traffic efficiency and give drivers and passengers comfort. A select few of them are ccellular V2X, which offers communications for Device-to-Device (D2D) and Device-to-Network (D2N) in two 3GPP-supported modes of operation. A modification of the WLAN-based IEEE802.11p protocol called Dedicated Short-range Communications (DSRC) makes it possible to communicate with the physical layer (PHY) in accordance with the IEEE 802.11a standard. Additionally, 4G-LTE enables the majority of V2V communications applications' scalability and dependability.

Smart Roads and Vehicles: Exploring V2I Technology

Today's vehicles must be able to connect with their environment and the roadside communications infrastructure in order to enable the efficient administration of IT'S (Zhang et al., 2017). The vehicles-to-infrastructure (V2I) system architecture, based on access points with IEEE 802 11p network interfaces that are placed at predetermined locations along the highways, is used to provide communications between vehicles and infrastructure. The vehicle-to-infrastructure system can supply the information, notwithstanding the potential limitations of these sites (Zhang et al., 2017; Muhammad et al., 2019). The DSRC/WAVE technology makes it possible to build applications like traffic signal control by enabling communication between automobiles and ITS infrastructure. Other technology is a visible light communication (VLC) enable to transmit data from a road side units to a vehicles (Muhammad et al, 2019) (Azar et al, 2021).

Effective sensor networks are created by car communication networks with roadside access points, which can give vehicles information at lower prices. However, because they are battery-powered, the sensors attached to roadside access points have limitations in terms of processing power (Inés et al., 2018). The deployment of the WSN sensor network along the roadways can be used to communicate physical data, such as temperature, humidity, and light, or to detect and track movements and send them to the vehicles or vehicle management centre for traffic management.

IoT for Automotive: Connecting Vehicles to the Internet

Internet services can be delivered to vehicles with great reliability thanks to wireless Internet access technologies like 4G-LTE cellular networks. Vehicles can connect to the internet using roadside Wi-Fi access points as well (Koustabh et al., 2017; Juan et al., 2020). Vehicle Internet access over cellular network infrastructure is made possible by a number of options that fall into two categories. Connectivity offered: Provides people with the means to connect their smartphones to their cars. Additionally, embedded connectivity enables the integration of cellular communication service into the car's entertainment system. IoT is a term that has recently gained popularity and is now linked to infrastructure as a whole, home and automobile management systems, and smart phone systems. The Internet of Things has enabled a huge number of devices, including smart cars, to be connected (Zeinab et al, 2020). The concept of IoV has emerged as an integral part of the design of IoT infrastructure in smart cities.

The Internet of automobiles (IoV) network, which is made up of a variety of various hardware and software components, enables real-time data sharing between automobiles, pedestrians, and roadside units (RSU). The majority of the communication methods that were previously described play a role in the development of the vehicle's Internet infrastructure (Kanawaday et al., 2017). In general, the infrastructure is made up of the following sections: smart traffic lights, wearable technology for people, and vehicle gadgets like sensors and other walkie-talkies. Application software, object recognition software, and passenger apps. Additionally, there are several communication technologies, including 5G networks, V2V, V2I, and vehicle-to-human (V2H).

The idea of artificial intelligence (AI) and machine learning (ML) models has recently made an appearance in the provision of methods that aid in analysing the gathered data and determining the necessary action at any given instant in the internet systems of cars (Kanawaday et al, 2017). Additionally, deep learning (DL) techniques aid in controlling self-driving operations, classifying objects, and analysing massive data related to cloud computing systems.

IoT-ENABLED AERIAL COMMUNICATION FOR DRONES

Drones are one of the cutting-edge methods for data collecting in IoT networks. Unmanned aerial vehicles (UAV). Drones are autonomous robots that are employed in a wide range of industries, including data transfer, agriculture, security, emergency preparedness, and weather management. IoT networks for drone communication and data transmission are depicted in Figure 6 (Li et al., 2018; Lojka et al., 2016). The drone communication technologies have a number of difficulties that are related to several problems, such as scalability deterioration, implementation, coverage area, limited energy resources, and security. Drone internet technology requires the fundamental criteria, which are categorised in the sub-sections as communication requirements and security requirements (Langone et al., 2014). The next subsections go over these prerequisites.

The Art of Drone Communication

Most applications uses drones require ability to access many remote locations to providing monitoring and helping to preserve and protect the environment (Miranda et al, 2020)(Qingfei et al, 2019). Accordingly, it found that there are critical communication requirements to support such applications as following.

Figure 6. Internet of drone architecture

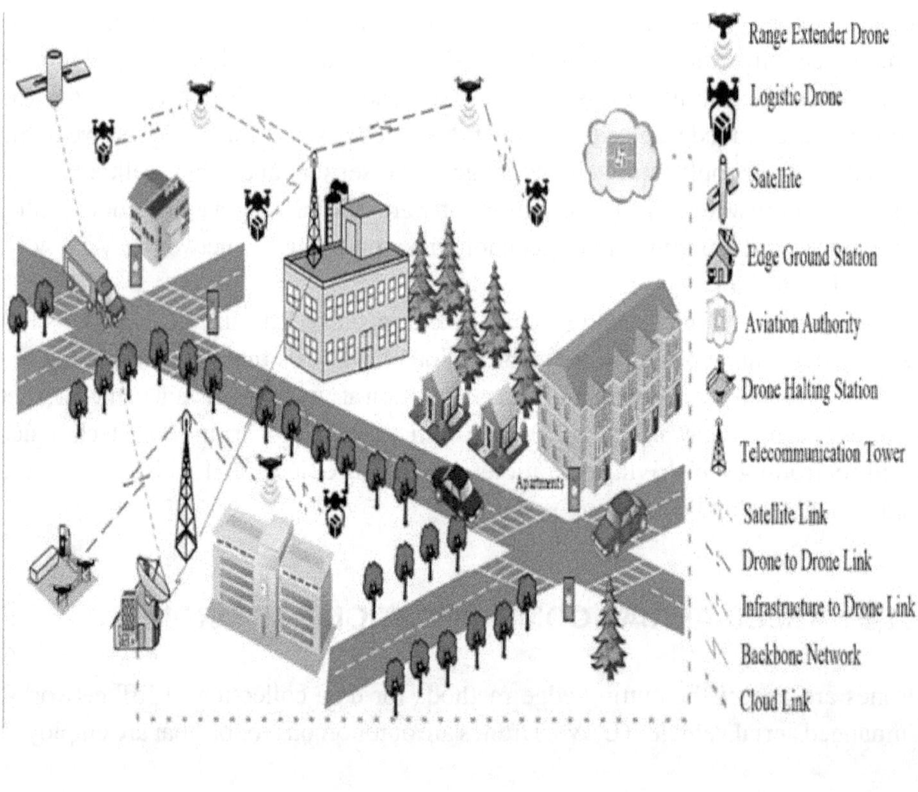

- Smooth coverage: The traditional network coverage that serves ground users is not useful for drone communications, so it was necessary to find seamless coverage of improved sky coverage to support drone users to fly in different regions.
- Real-time and remote communication: Real-time and remote control devices are mainly used for monitoring flight conditions, UAVs mission, in addition to emergency control. For those, latency and data rate are most meet the UAVs requirements.
- Identification and regulation of drones: Drones require identification and control by supporting drone registration, tracking, provisioning and coordination, and this can be done using mobile networks.
- High precision positioning: The requirements for GPS accuracy will increase with the development of UAV applications like agricultural land mapping that reach high accuracy of location at sub-meters.

Smart Security Solutions for IoD Ecosystems

For Internet of drones (IoD), authenticity, confidentiality, availability, and integrity re the main security and privacy requirements.

- Authenticity: Perfect forward secrecy, you need to use a secure key exchange using a method that produces session keys that are impossible to recover.
- Confidentiality: The confidentiality or privacy of the wireless communication channel protects against unauthorized disclosure of information. Another big barrier to implementing IoD is making data available and controlling access to that data (data confidentiality).
- Availability: Both the mechanism and the system must be able to recognize if a drone is available, engaged, or inoperative.
- Integrity: To ensure the credibility of the information, it must be of sufficient integrity, that is, it has not been changed during transmission, and that the source of the information is real.

Internet of Drones (IoD) is a new technology enables to let drones to communicates to the internet, which is related to different classification and IoT technology aspects including, architecture, middleware, data integration, data sharing, and security as shown in figure 7 (Pier et al, 2020). The architecture of IoD plays a vital role in controlling and managing drones to perform their operations efficiently. It can be classified into two main components.

- Components of architecture: The components of the IoD architecture interact and perform data management and communication operations in a stable manner. They also perform operations related to reporting and controlling drones, and ensure that data reaches the correct destination.
- Communication protocols: An IoD communication protocol must meet path planning requirements where data communication between source nodes to target nodes is critical. Therefore, the choice of IoD communication protocol must be carefully analysed.

The middleware layer plays an essential role in the environment of connected IoT devices, as it acts as an intermediary between different nodes and applications (Pinjia et al, 2020). In addition, in the middleware layer there is programming for the operating system and networking to work on the abstraction between the different IoD interfaces. There are two main middleware's are used in most IoD applications, a service-based and cloud-based middleware.

- Based on service: Service-based middleware makes it easy to provide network access, local message delivery, caching and name resolution to the IoD architecture.
- Cloud-based: Cloud-based middleware provides reliable communication between the terrestrial network and the drone.

For Data fusion and sharing, three different types of data integration and sharing for IoD can be used; they are distributed, centralized and cloud-based. The three types process and integrate many data sources to generate valid information for decision-making if several drones are connected to perform different operations simultaneously (Rateb et al, 2020)(Pinjia et al, 2020).

Decentralised data in a distributed system provides the IoD process with various advantages, including scalability, interoperability, and ease of redesign. These capabilities can be used to remove or reconfigure a specific drone that is not connected to or available in the IoD network (Ibrahim et al., 2021). Additionally, a dispersed environment can function as a collaborative partnership in an emergency and is better suited for independent decision-making (Azad et al., 2017). The early stages of deployment can be carried out more effectively and more quickly with the centralised system. Additionally, because to the difficulties of repositioning or manipulating the device, their efficiency declines over longer distances and in the latter stages of operations (Amal et al., 2016).

In order to avoid unauthorised access to or control of the drones, the security features in drones are crucial for the transfer of highly sensitive and secret information (Azad et al., 2017). To prevent unauthorised IoD authentication, the majority of

Figure 7. Internet of drones (IoDs) classifications

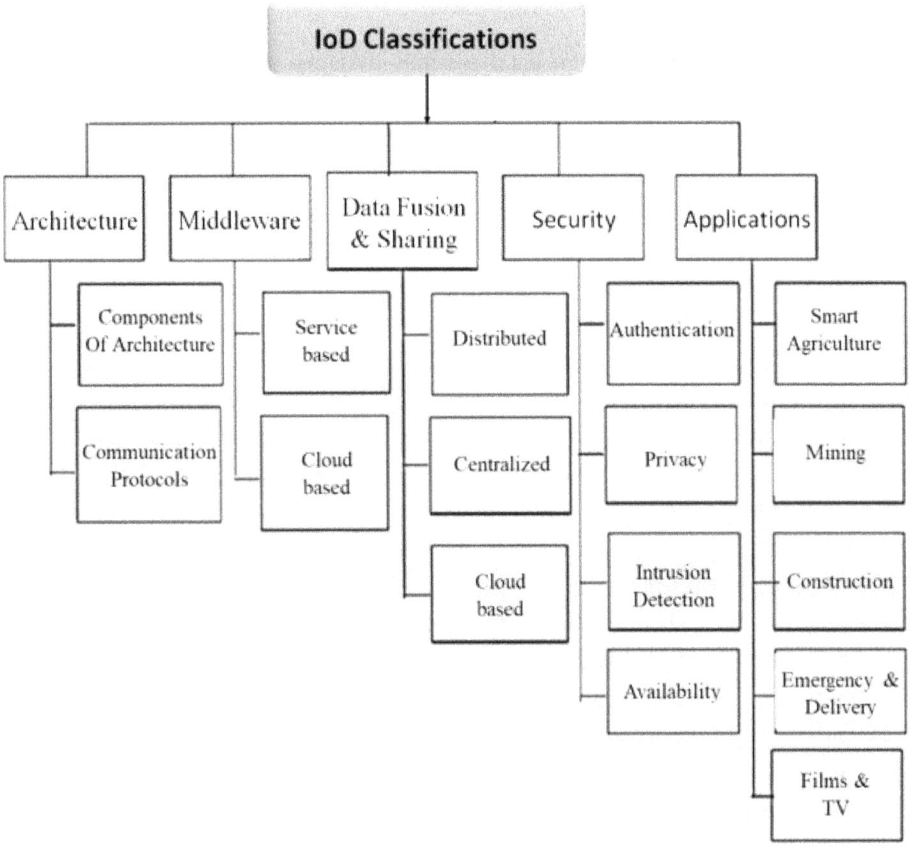

communication paths are secured using encryption methods. The potential harm to a person's or an organization's right to privacy could be increased by recent developments in the usage of drones by civic and commercial entities. According to Amal et al. (2016) and Xiantao et al. (2020), the intrusion detection system based on deep learning can effectively identify threats such overloads, flash crowds, worms, port scans, jamming attacks, etc. By utilising operations related to resource management, trajectory and path planning, energy management, and security, machine learning (ML) and deep learning (DL) algorithms will help to optimise various IoD classifications. They also promise to create a variety of intelligent applications, including smart agriculture, intelligent mining, as well as emergency services and delivery (Yang et al., 2014).

OPTIMIZING ENERGY CONSUMPTION IN IoT-ENABLED CLOUDS

By utilising objectives and functions that stand on decision parameters to reach the objective function value, energy optimisation is a technique used to identify the best solution for IoT difficulties (Yasir et al., 2018). In several domains, like the Internet of Vehicles (IoV) challenge and the Internet of Drones (IoD) communication, modern energy optimisation approaches are powerful in overcoming difficult obstacles. With minimal computing effort, energy optimisation strategies seek to identify the best answers to IoT-related problems (Tanwar et al., 2020; Yasir et al., 2018).

Processing time, storage space, and memory are three metrics for power optimisation technological endeavour. To discover the best option, the energy optimisation method can be used, typically with the use of intelligent processing. In order to address numerous problems with big data and real-time IoT applications, artificial intelligence (AI) technologies are used (Zolanvari et al., 2018). It also resolves complex energy optimisation problems despite having little computational power and subject expertise. Particle swarm optimisation (PSO), genetic algorithms (GA), ant colony optimisation (ACO), artificial bee colonies (ABC), and other swarm intelligence (SI) algorithms are regarded as the best approaches to energy optimisation problems. Table 3 (Ghorpade et al., 2021) displays the characteristics of SI algorithms according to various factors.

PSO has particles created from natural swarms by fusing individual and interpersonal communications with repeated calculations. A candidate outcome is available as a particle in the PSO technique (Mohd et al., 2015). It uses a collection of flying particles in a search area, existing and likely solutions, as well as the migration towards a promising area, to search out to a global optimum. ACO is enthused by the ants searching behavior. Researchers demoralized this characteristic of real ant colonies in ACO procedures to solve comprehensive Energy Optimization challenges. ACO has solid robustness as well as good discrete commutative mechanism (Pier et al, 2020). ACO can be joint easily with other techniques; it shows well performance in resolving the multifaceted energy Optimization challenge.

ABC was inspired by honeybee swarms' clever behaviour in seeking out a food supply. Three bee clusters make up the ABC method designs: scout bees randomly locate all food source sites based on dances; employed bees exploit a source of food that comes from scout bees; and spectator bees evaluate the quality of the food (Mohd et al., 2015; Ghorpade et al., 2021). It has been widely used in a variety of applications in many different domains, including the training of neural networks and ANNs and signal processing software. GA can be applied to problems with energy and search optimisation. According to GA, offspring that are better and

Table 3. General features of swarm intelligence techniques

Factors	PSO	ACO	ABC	GA
Methodology Base	Particle size	Number of ants	Number of employed bees	Population size
Search Initiation	Iterative	One iteration	Interactive	One generation
Fundamental Dependence	Based on particles flying group	Based on behavior of ant colonies	Based on interaction between the employed and un employed bees	Principle of survival of the fittest
Probabilistic Process	Based on particle positions and dynamics	Based on pheromone intensities	Based on nectar amount, onlookers bees	Based on crossover and mutation
Search Optimization	Physical movements of the individual particle	Search space by pheromone evaporation	Search space based on interaction between bees	Search space based on mutation operator
Setting Parameters	Inertia weight value Acceleration coefficients for cognitive and social	Initial pheromone value Global, and local pheromone decay rate	Ember of colony size Number of food sources	Single point crossover Crossover, and mutation probabilities

more optimised than their predecessors and have an improved fitness function are produced by combining remarkable traits from diverse ancestors (Alaa et al., 2022).

Energy management for many Internet of Things applications involves learning processes in a significant way. Neural networks are one of the most significant deep learning algorithms. This makes it possible to carry out learning or training methods, which are processes used to determine appropriate network parameters (Miranda et al., 2020). Finding a set of network parameters that minimises the cost function is the goal of learning a neural network, which may be seen as a nonlinear energy optimisation task. A subset of artificial intelligence is deep learning. It offers numerous benefits like robustness, generality, self-organization, self-learning, and self-adaptation. Recently, deep learning (DL) has made substantial advancements in a number of disciplines, including image classification, speech and face recognition, and face recognition (Miranda et al., 2020).

The technique was used in numerous IoT applications, including intelligent parking and traffic control, car theft identification, traffic incident detection, and traffic management system, because it also has powerful functions. By minimising or utilising one or more objectives, functions that stand on one or more decision parameters that achieve the objective function value, and algorithms like SI, ML, and DL, among others, enable energy optimisation, they address a variety of energy optimisation challenges in IoT applications. Many IoT services and applications for smart cities and vehicle communications are improved by these techniques.

COMPLEXITIES OF IoT: CHALLENGES AND SOLUTIONS

The outlined above IoT applications are very interesting because of smart technologies provided. However, many challenges can effect on the IoT networks and systems performances due to implementation cost and massive deployment (Hassan et al, 2021) (Ali et al, 2021).

IoT Challenges

The most important issues related to the IoT applications are considered, as main challenges in networking, operations, processing and security are describe as follows.

- IoT Network Scalability: In IoT, things are cooperated within an open environment. The communication and service discovery needed to be efficiently functioned in both small scale and large-scale environments.
- Self-Organizing: Smart things needed to move towards automation and self-organization by meet the computational and management issues to configure and adapt the things to particular situations.
- Data volumes: gathering big amount of data in some IoT applications require an efficient mechanism for storing, processing and management.
- Interoperability: IoT devices have different information, processing and communication capabilities with different energy availability and bandwidth, which needs a common standards for communications.
- Software complexity: Extensive software infrastructure are important in IoT network and to manage the smart objects and provide services to support them.
- Security and privacy: IoT security and protection are related to communications confidentiality, the authenticity and trustworthiness of communication partners, in addition to message integrity. There is a need to access certain services or prevent from communicating with other things in IoT in secure communications.
- Power supply: IoT devices, sensors and objects are moving and consume more power. Therefore, intelligent energy management mechanisms related to both hardware and system architecture are required to reduce the energy consumption.

Nowadays, IoT with machines and smart things becomes more real in our life and exceed the expectations of it expanding during last few years. The IoT technology now attacks many consumers around world and industrial companies a research groups to develop more IoT related technologies (Abbas et al, 2021). This Expansion of digitizing phenomenon through internet leads to more connected devices, things, machines those can interacting with people, so they possibly to cyber-attack. In next years, studies show that the technology of IoT will generates massive big data and being more attacked by different ways (Kanawaday et a;, 2017)(Lojka et al, 2016). Therefore, future researches will concentrated on taking attention to provide a smart security schemes for IoT data privacy. Although IoT applications provide enormous benefits to society by enabling interaction between many sectors of government services, they face a number of challenges and issues related to the following (Ezechina et al, 2015).

- Identification: The ability to characterize and identify a huge number of devices and objects by means of the Internet of Things to provide different services, which nccd to be uniquely identified across the network and managed.
- Processing: Effective methods of data conversion must be used for making the data compatible for further processing by IoT based Information.
- Interoperability: Incompatibilities can occur between IoT devices due to the lack of homogeneity of their work, which leads to poor services that they can provide. Therefore, standardization is important in order to manufacturing these devices and objects.
- Data Security: The encryption process generally helps to secure data, but the encryption process in the Internet of Things may face some problems related to encryption keys with a longer length that is not suitable for devices and very small objects.

There are some challenges facing IoT applications to monitor the environment, which are related to the design of monitoring IoT based systems (Gomez, 2019). These challenges are related to providing sensors that have the ability to conserve their energy as much as possible and work within the large scale IoT network in different environments. Another challenge relates to how to organize the exchange of data between the institutions that use environmental resources and the IoT control centres. To simplifying the data exchanges, various intelligent solutions such as ML and DL approaches are used for management and facilitating their analysis to make effective exchange decisions between smart city systems and institutions (Nomusa, 2012)(Alqurashi et al, 2021).

IoT Solutions

It makes sense to connect IoT devices via a cellular gateway for IoT network scalability. Despite using already-existing cellular towers, LTE-M and LTE-NB provide significantly larger coverage due to their low power and big area networks. In addition, thanks to LPWAN technologies with extensive coverage, such Sigfox and LoRaWAN, IoT devices can now operate within a few miles of network infrastructure. In the following years, satellite communication will likely become more commonly used. Global IoT solutions like emnify also solve this issue by entering into partnerships with carriers all around the world (Abbas et al., 2021). A single emnify SIM card enables your devices to connect to more than 540 networks across more than 195 nations.

For many IoT applications, including IoVs and IoDs, the self-organizing and Interoperability concerns, as well as various ML and DL techniques, enable intelligent interactions between the IoT systems and other terminals. Most IoT stack components may now be easily replaced with different technologies because to technological advancements (Koustabh et al., 2017). The goal of the industry trend is to increase the adaptability of IoT systems by simplifying integration.

Using unlicensed public bands like LoRaWAN helps tackle the big data volume problem that necessitates bandwidth availability. New IoT technologies are also exploring ways to utilise bandwidth more efficiently (Alqurashi et al., 2021). For instance, the guard bands, which are generally unoccupied spaces between networks, are included in the narrower bands used by narrowband IoT, a cellular network technology. Even while 5G isn't quite prepared for widespread IoT deployment, it will soon give businesses access to a far larger range of the RF spectrum (Rania et al., 2020). As a result, the spread of IoT devices over new frequencies will be made possible. When it comes to energy concerns, manufacturers can use their batteries more effectively using specific IoT routers and gateways. These components of the network architecture allow access to the applications and network entities that IoT devices must communicate with (Zeinab et al, 2020). The gateway or router can enable more advanced protocols and security measures like encryption and authentication to keep devices secure while using less power.

In order to solve security issues, low-power connectivity solutions use cutting-edge security technologies that authenticate devices through SIM cards. Security features like IMEI locks ensure that only the intended device may use a specific SIM card. Cellular networks also enable you to perform any necessary remote firmware updates while consuming very little power (Misra et al., 2016). And finally, with the help of their Virtual Private Network (VPN) capabilities, businesses like emnify can provide you more control over the connections between your devices while bridging security gaps.

TECHNOLOGICAL TRENDS IN THE FUTURE OF IoT

There are many new technologies that operate within the IoT technology, which enable the integration of communication and control mechanisms. These technologies link many sub-systems and different devices to the structure of the IoT networks, in addition to assisting in the control and management operations.

Innovations in Big Data: The IoT Connection

According to Raania et al. (2020), the Internet of Things (IoT) network is expanding exponentially, bringing with it a new era marked by an increase in sensors and gadgets across a range of businesses. Information networks, applications, and services are expected to proliferate as a result of this upsurge. An enormous amount of data from various industries, including smart homes, logistics, smart grids, transportation, automobiles, environmental monitoring, and healthcare, is about to flood the landscape with an estimated 20 billion nodes that have already been deployed and an additional 20 billion that are anticipated (Ashraf et al., 2011). The IoT glossary describes innovative technologies and solutions that are well-positioned to enable practical data integration into current data network schemes in the midst of this rush.

The expected increase in IoT node adoption signals an unprecedented amount of data being produced in a variety of industries. The use of sensors and gadgets is what is causing this development, opening up possibilities for use in the smart home, logistics, automotive, and healthcare industries. Notably, the huge amount of data produced—89% of which was created in the last two years alone—highlights how quickly data has been added to the Web and the Internet (Wesam et al., 2020). This data explosion is a sign of both technological progress and the revolutionary possibilities that lie ahead when this data is used for value-added services and real-time applications. After being processed and examined, sensor data from various incidents and events turns into a useful resource. According to Li et al. (2018), this transformational potential encompasses applications including smart product creation and services in industries like electricity consumption, traffic management, pollution monitoring, and healthcare. Integration of sensor data enables effective traffic control, measurement of pollution levels, and predictive modelling of electricity usage. Furthermore, advances in healthcare applications are being propelled by the management, processing, and tracking of medical data that is gathered via sensor nodes. New opportunities for developing intelligent services and applications with contextual and situational awareness are presented by this dynamic data landscape.

The IoT landscape is made even more complex and richer by the addition of user-generated data from social media platforms like Facebook, WhatsApp, Twitter, and YouTube, in addition to sensor data. Big Data, which is the term used to describe this deluge of data, allows IoT services and apps to integrate situation awareness and context into decision-making procedures. Combining data from various physical, social, cyber, and physical resources creates a rich environment for developing new, intelligent services and improving those that already exist (Li et al., 2018; Langone et al., 2014). However, there are inherent difficulties in automation, data analytics, and interoperability with the large influx of heterogeneous and scattered IoT data. In order to meet these problems, it becomes essential to have both machine-interpretable and readable data and platforms for mutual representation and data description. The need for creative platforms that can manage various data kinds while maintaining interoperability is a symptom of how IoT data management is developing. These platforms are essential for negotiating the challenges presented by the large volume and dispersed nature of Internet of Things data, providing opportunities for additional study and advancement.

IoT Security and Privacy

A strong security, trust, and privacy platform is essential given the wide range of applications that Internet of Things services can provide, including the capacity to link across different ownership domains and administration zones. Given the difficulties presented by privacy concerns, especially in cloud computing contexts, protecting user data becomes crucial (Saranya et al., 2015). Because of the multifaceted interactions between users and devices in trusted zones, a trust platform must be able to resist industry inspection and be free from vulnerabilities like invasions or denial-of-service attacks. Smart public key infrastructure (PKI), a crucial component of security management, is one example of the sophisticated and advanced methodologies required to establish such a trust platform (Misra et al., 2016). The integration of a smart keys management system becomes imperative to ensure secure encryption of data while adhering to the resource constraints inherent in IoT networks. Networks need high-quality metadata to fulfil their commitments regarding IoT data. A novel method for evaluating trust across users, data, and devices is to use a chain of trust policies to negotiate trust through dynamic negotiations (Farheen et al., 2015). It becomes imperative to define the least degree of trust necessary for information access services and to make sure that access control measures are implemented in compliance with legislation to prevent unauthorised access to data. As IoT networks become more and more important in determining the direction of the internet, the need for developing trust mechanisms becomes more and more important.

IoT is becoming more and more important, which has raised security and privacy issues. As a result, enhanced solutions are needed to prevent theft, attacks, and vulnerabilities like DDoS/DoS problems and compromised devices (Miranda et al., 2020). Large-scale IoT-based services and apps are becoming more vulnerable in this environment. To prevent assaults that could cause transportation, municipal infrastructures, and energy systems to become unstable or unusable, new security measures need to be put in place in a variety of fields. A variety of access restriction and privacy mechanisms are required by the diversity and flexibility of nodes/gateways in the IoT ecosystem in order to accommodate various permission and usage models (Saranya et al., 2015). Deep learning and AI must be integrated since almost all operating modes must be managed automatically without human intervention. These technologies become essential for directing networks of self-control in the Internet of Things. Additionally, cryptographic techniques like searchable and homomorphic encryptions become crucial for Internet of Things-based devices in order to guarantee the security of information/data processing, storage, and transfer. These cutting-edge cryptographic techniques provide an extra degree of security against the dangers of data contents being changed or transferred across networks.

A complex framework for security, trust, and privacy is necessary to address the issues of user data protection, access control, and potential vulnerabilities in the complex world of Internet of Things services. For IoT networks to remain secure and intact, cutting-edge technologies like smart PKI, smart key management systems, and cryptographic techniques must be included. The implementation of novel security protocols and the ongoing investigation of cutting-edge technologies will play a crucial role in strengthening the IoT domain against any risks and weaknesses as it develops, thus clearing the path for a reliable and safe IoT future.

Beyond the Cloud: Exploring Fog Computing

IoT and cloud both appear to be evolving quickly and independently. Although the two tracks are moving in different directions, their overall characteristics tend to complement one another, and cloud computing can be very helpful for IoT networks (Agrawal et al., 2017). IoT could benefit greatly from the resources and capabilities that cloud computing can provide. IoT requires large amounts of data flow, processing, storage, and accessibility. IoT systems can benefit from the excellent services that cloud computing can offer. Strong structure and platform are required for IoT composition, management, and application implementation for these systems to function well (Zeinab et al., 2020). On the other side, cloud computing providers can serve IoT by spreading its scope to cooperate with dynamic, distributed, and new services with huge number of devices with various and different types of data.

The cloud may in some cases act as an intermediary layer between servers and the Internet of Things. By eliminating all the functionalities and complexity involved in processing a large amount of data at a level, this is achieved (Agrawal et al., 2017). The complexity of collecting, transmitting, storing, and processing data will present many new issues and necessitate the development of several new solutions at all levels as IoT networks continue to grow and will do so very quickly in the near future. To support the IoT, a multi-cloud platform or fog computing specifically needs to be quick, inexpensive, and have an integrated end-to-end system (Zeinab et al., 2020; Koustabh et al., 2017).

In the context of cloud computing, fog computing and edge computing are connected. Fog computing is referred to as small, network-edge computational hardware in the context of the cloud. Location awareness, low latency, and wireless access are purportedly features of this platform (Koustabh et al., 2017). While edge computing and edge analytics may both refer to the accomplishment of analytics at nodes that are near or on the edge of the network, a fog computing platform would accomplish analytics on every node in the network, from the centre to the edge. IoT may be more probable to be reinforced by fog computing in which processing, storing, networking power and control may occur anywhere along the network, either in edge, data centers, cloud devices such as gateway or router, edge devices itself like machines or sensors.

IoT's Impact on Distributed Computing

Large-scale computations using computer networks are referred to as "distributed computing," according to (Farheen et al. 2015). This computational paradigm is the foundation of a dynamic technological landscape, sharing key properties with parallel and concurrent computing. The revolutionary idea of cloud computing has emerged as a result of the recent integration of numerous distributed computing approaches with application-oriented architecture, utility computing, cloud virtualization, and autonomous computing. But underneath the surface of technical progress, there is room for a closer look at the complexities and difficulties involved in this integration. In-depth examination of the commonalities between parallel and concurrent computing can reveal subtle relationships that lead to a deeper comprehension of the tensions and synergies present in these computer paradigms.

The fusion of distributed computing methods with application-oriented architecture, utility computing, autonomous computing, and infrastructure virtualization represents not only convergence but also a wider evolution of cloud computing. In spite of this, careful examination is required to explore the underlying structures, possible obstructions, and expandability of these combined technologies. In addition to pointing out the synergies, providing new perspectives requires carefully examining any trade-offs and difficulties that can arise as these technologies get more integrated (Farheen et al. 2015). Researchers can add to a more thorough understanding of the changing cloud computing market by delving into unknown territory and challenging preconceived notions. The future Internet, in which the digital and physical worlds coexist harmoniously, is embodied by the confluence of cloud computing and the IoT. Although this revolutionary potential has been acknowledged in prior conversations, a more critical examination calls for scholars to investigate the consequences of this interconnected future for privacy, ethics, and society. It is necessary to carefully consider the ethical implications of handling real-world objects in the digital sphere and to take preventative measures to reduce any hazards. By critically analysing the societal effects of IoT and cloud computing on the future Internet, experts may help ensure a balanced integration that respects user privacy and security.

One unique feature of this integration is the breaking down of conventional barriers between virtual and hardware entities. Hardware no longer acts as discrete things but rather as dynamic nodes that facilitate remote access and act as essential access points for Internet applications (Wesam et al., 2020). This transformation calls for a reassessment of user accessibility, data governance, and security measures within the framework of the dynamic interaction between virtual and physical entities. To identify potential weaknesses and guarantee that the integration of hardware into the digital ecosystem is not only smooth but also safe and robust, a critical examination of this change is essential.

IoT IN FUTURE: TRENDS AND ECONOMIC POSSIBILITIES

The market of IoT applications in smart environment are growth rapidly. The development in communications technologies, and artificial intelligence in the field of IoT adding more smart devices to the world communications (E.S Ali et al, 2021)(Lojka et al, 2016). There are a number of studies that predict the growth of the IoT market. Most of these studies provided an IoT analytics forecast and show that, the IoT market will growth to enable more than 75 billion devices to be fully IoT connected by the 2025. The expectations in this year 2022 show that the IoT segment and adoption of new IoT projects will exceeds the growth rate between 2015 and 2020. The global rise of sharing market revenue size expected to become 183 billion dollars by the end of 2024 as shown in figure 8.

The Americas make up most of IoT projects is 45%, followed by Europe with 35%, and Asia with 16%. Recently, IoT plays an important role in everyday life due to Covid-19 pandemic, since it becomes one of the most effective technology to handle different clinical situations by diffident medical devices connected to people (Lojka et al, 2016). In future, the technology of IoT will let humans more interacting with the environment, which will exceed the expectation, and make everything's under monitoring and control.

Figure 8. Analysis of different IoT projects revenues related to smart environment

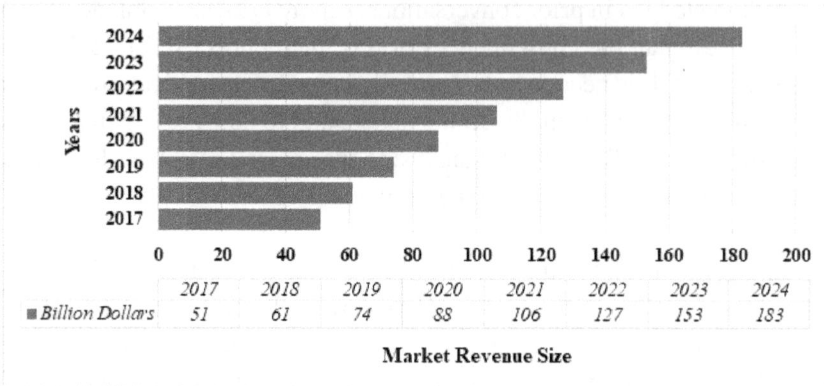

CONCLUSION

IoT is one of the big things recently has been innovated, which offers several services to link the utilities, things, and human to each other using Internet. Each thing in the network could be connected, identified in the Internet independently. All technologies and networks are utilized in structure the IoT concept such techniques are RFID, mobile computing, embedded systems, and wireless sensors networks, in addition to several protocols and approaches to have management processing, data storage, and cyber security matter. IoT needs consistent method for protocols identification approaches, architectures and all may occur in parallels. By the IoT several intelligent services are becoming tangible in our daily life, which allow peoples to contact and reach everything. In addition, amenities several vital features for human such as healthcare, homes automation, smart grid, artificial cities and environments monitoring and forecasting.

IoT may encounter couple of challenges to ensure continuous network admission. One of the vital issues is that nowadays there are various networks co-exist which need to be harmonized. Another problematic issue is the huge data amount that IoT will produce. In other hand, security, encryption and authentication would be a great venerable for these information and data. Automatic network administration, functions to transmit video and voice signals proficiently would perhaps be exaggerated in applying the concept of the IoT. However, with the fast growing of technology development these issues could be resolved easily.

The IoT potentials future new services when associated with big data, cloud computing, distributed computing, fog/edge computing and cyber security areas. Associating all these techniques with the IoT, smart services could be implemented and innovated. The chapter gave a detailed and extensive technical review of the major important services and applications that can be provided by IoT with special emphasis on what running nowadays in the related industry and the challenges that have been facing the industry for implementing the IoT, and the other related techniques associated with the IoT network.

REFERENCES

AbdelHafeez, K. (2013). Distributed Multichannel and Mobility-Aware Cluster-Based MAC Protocol for Vehicular Ad Hoc Networks. *IEEE Transactions on Vehicular Technology*, *62*(8), •••.

AgrawalA. (2017). A Comprehensive Survey of Mobile Sensing and Cloud Services. *Researchgate* 2017, doi:10.13140/RG.2.2.31698.56008

Ahmed, M. Z., Hashim, A. H. A., Khalifa, O. O., Saeed, R. A., Alsaqour, R. A., & Alkali, A. H. (2021). Connectivity Framework for Rendezvous and Mobile Producer Nodes Using NDN Interest Flooding. *2021 International Congress of Advanced Technology and Engineering (ICOTEN),* (pp. 1-5). IEEE. 10.1109/ICOTEN52080.2021.9493555

Alaa, M. Mukhtar et al (2022). Performance Evaluation of Downlink Coordinated Multipoint Joint Transmission under Heavy IoT Traffic Load. Wireless Communications and Mobile Computing. doi:10.1155/2022/6837780

Alatabani, L. E., Ali, E. S., & Saeed, R. A. (2021). Deep Learning Approaches for IoV Applications and Services. In N. Magaia, G. Mastorakis, C. Mavromoustakis, E. Pallis, & E. K. Markakis (Eds.), *Intelligent Technologies for Internet of Vehicles. Internet of Things (Technology, Communications, and Computing)*. Springer., doi:10.1007/978-3-030-76493-7_8

Ali, E. S., Hasan, M. K., Hassan, R., Saeed, R. A., Hassan, M. B., Islam, S., Nafi, N. S., & Bevinakoppa, S. (2021). Machine Learning Technologies for Secure Vehicular Communication in Internet of Vehicles: Recent Advances and Applications. *Wiley-Hindawi* [SCN]. *Security and Communication Networks*, *2021*, 1–23. Advance online publication. doi:10.1155/2021/8868355

Ali, E. S., Hassan, M. B., & Saeed, R. A. (2021). Machine Learning Technologies on Internet of Vehicles. In N. Magaia, G. Mastorakis, C. Mavromoustakis, E. Pallis, & E. K. Markakis (Eds.), *Intelligent Technologies for Internet of Vehicles. Internet of Things (Technology, Communications, and Computing)*. Springer., doi:10.1007/978-3-030-76493-7_7

Ali, E. S., Mohammed, Z. T., Hassan, M. B., & Saeed, R. A. (2021). Algorithms Optimization for Intelligent IoV Applications. In J. Zhao & V. Vinoth Kumar (Eds.), *Handbook of Research on Innovations and Applications of AI, IoT, and Cognitive Technologies* (pp. 1–25). IGI Global. doi:10.4018/978-1-7998-6870-5.ch001

Allioui, H., & Mourdi, Y. (2023). Exploring the Full Potentials of IoT for Better Financial Growth and Stability: A Comprehensive Survey. *Sensors (Basel)*, *23*(19), 8015. doi:10.3390/s23198015 PMID:37836845

Alnazir, A. (2021). Quality of Services Based on Intelligent IoT WLAN MAC Protocol Dynamic Real-Time Applications in Smart Cities. Computational Intelligence and Neuroscience. IEEE. doi:10.1155/2021/2287531

Alqurashi, F. (2021). Machine Learning Techniques in Internet of UAVs for Smart Cities Applications. *Journal of Intelligent & Fuzzy Systems,* 1-24. . doi:10.3233/JIFS-211009

Amrita Sajja, D. K. Kharde, Chandana Pandey (2016). A Survey on efficient way to Live: Smart Home - It's an Internet of Things. *ISAR - International Journal of Electronics and Communication Ethics*, *1*(1).

Ayyappadas, R. (2017, May). Design and Implementation of Weather Monitoring System using Wireless Communication. *International Journal of Advanced Information in Engineering Technology*, *4*(5), 1–7.

Azad, P., & Navimipour, N. J. (2017). An energy-aware task scheduling in the cloud computing using a hybrid cultural and ant colony optimization algorithm. *International Journal of Cloud Applications and Computing*, *7*(4), 20–40. doi:10.4018/IJCAC.2017100102

Azar, A., Koubaa, A., Ali Mohamed, N., Ibrahim, H. A., Ibrahim, Z. F., Kazim, M., Ammar, A., Benjdira, B., Khamis, A. M., Hameed, I. A., & Casalino, G. (2021). Drone Deep Reinforcement Learning: A Review. *Electronics (Basel)*, *10*(9), 999. doi:10.3390/electronics10090999

Bibri, S. E., & Jagatheesaperumal, S. K. (2023). Harnessing the Potential of the Metaverse and Artificial Intelligence for the Internet of City Things: Cost-Effective XReality and Synergistic AIoT Technologies. *Smart Cities*, *6*(5), 2397–2429. doi:10.3390/smartcities6050109

Chen, X. (2015). IoT-based air pollution monitoring and forecasting system; 2015 *International Conference on Computer and Computational Sciences*, (pp 257-260). IEEE. 10.1109/ICCACS.2015.7361361

Da Xu, L. (2018). Big data for cyber physical systems in industry 4.0: A survey. *Enterprise Information Systems*, *13*(1), 1–22.

Darwish, A., & Hassanien, A. E. (2011). Wearable and Implantable Wireless Sensor Network Solutions for Healthcare Monitoring. *Sensors (Basel)*, *11*(6), 5561–5595. doi:10.3390/s110605561 PMID:22163914

Djajadi, A. (2016). Ambient Environment quality monitoring Using IoT Sensor Network. *Interworking Indonesia Journal*, *8*(1), 41–47.

Dlodlo, N. (2012). Adopting the internet of things technologies in environmental management in South Africa, *2012 International Conference on Environment Science and Engineering*, Singapore 2012, pp 45-55.

Dolui, K. (2017). Comparison of Edge Computing Implementations: Fog Computing, Cloudlet and Mobile Edge Computing. *IEEE Access : Practical Innovations, Open Solutions*.

Elfatih, N. M. (2021). Internet of vehicle's resource management in 5G networks using AI technologies: Current status and trends. *IET Communications*, *2021*, 1–21.

Eltahir, A. A., Saeed, R. A., Mukherjee, A., & Hasan, M. K. (2016). Evaluation and Analysis of an Enhanced Hybrid Wireless Mesh Protocol for Vehicular Ad-hoc Network. *EURASIP Journal on Wireless Communications and Networking*, *2016*(1), 1–11. doi:10.1186/s13638-016-0666-5

Ezechina, A. (2015). The Internet of Things (Iot): A Scalable Approach to Connecting Everything. *The International Journal of Engineering and Science, 4*(1), 09-12.

Fatima, F. (2015, December). Internet of things: A Survey on Architecture, Applications, Security, Enabling Technologies, Advantages & Disadvantages. *International Journal of Advanced Research in Computer and Communication Engineering*, *4*(12).

Ferdin, J. J. J. (2019, April). IoT Based Weather Monitoring System for Effective Analytics. *International Journal of Engineering and Advanced Technology*, *8*(4), 311–315.

Ghorpade S. N et al (2021). Enhanced Differential Crossover and Quantum Particle Swarm Optimization for IoT Applications. *IEEE Access*. IEEE. . doi:10.1109/ACCESS.2021.3093113

Gomez, C., Chessa, S., Fleury, A., Roussos, G., & Preuveneers, D. (2019). Internet of Things for enabling smart environments: A technology-centric perspective. *Journal of Ambient Intelligence and Smart Environments*, *11*(1), 23–43. doi:10.3233/AIS-180509

Gubbia, J. (2013). Internet of Things (IoT): A vision, architectural elements, and future directions. *Future Generation Computer Systems*, *29*(7), 1645–1660. doi:10.1016/j.future.2013.01.010

Gupta, S., Tanwar, S., & Gupta, N. (2022). *A Systematic Review on Internet of Things (IoT): Applications & Challenges*. 2022 10th International Conference on Reliability, Infocom Technologies and Optimization (Trends and Future Directions) (ICRITO), Noida, India. 10.1109/ICRITO56286.2022.9964892

Guthi, A. (2016, July). Implementation of an Efficient Noise and Air Pollution Monitoring System Using Internet of Things (IoT). *International Journal of Advanced Research in Computer and Communication Engineering*, *5*(7), 237–242.

Haav, H.-M. (2014). Linked data connections with emerging information technologies: A survey. *International Journal of Computer Science and Applications*, *11*(3), 21–44.

Hassan, M. B., Alsharif, S., Alhumyani, H., Ali, E. S., Mokhtar, R. A., & Saeed, R. A. (2021). An Enhanced Cooperative Communication Scheme for Physical Uplink Shared Channel in NB-IoT. *Wireless Personal Communications*, *120*(3), 2367–2386. doi:10.1007/s11277-021-08067-1

Huang, Y. (2016). Remote Environmental Monitoring Embedded System Design Based on Wireless Sensor Networks. *Chemical Engineering Transactions*, *51*, 223–228. doi:10.3303/CET1651038

Ibrahim, S. E., Saeed, R. A., & Mukherjee, A. (2021). Resource Management in Vehicular Cloud Computing. *In Research Anthology on Architectures, Frameworks, and Integration Strategies for Distributed and Cloud Computing. edited by Management Association, Information Resources.* IGI Global.

Jiang, X., Ma, Z., Yu, F. R., Song, T., & Boukerche, A. (2020). Edge Computing for Video Analytics in the Internet of Vehicles with Blockchain. *In Proceedings of the 10th ACM Symposium on Design and Analysis of Intelligent Vehicular Networks and Applications (DIVANet '20)*. Association for Computing Machinery, New York, NY, USA, 1–7. 10.1145/3416014.3424582

Juan et al (2020). Machine learning applied in production planning and control: a state-of-the-art in the era of industry 4.0. *Journal of Intelligent Manufacturing*. Springer

Kanawaday. (2017). Machine learning for predictive maintenance of industrial machines using IoT sensor data. *2017 8th IEEE International Conference on Software Engineering and Service Science (ICSESS)*. IEEE. 10.1109/ICSESS.2017.8342870

Sapandeep, K. &, Ikvinderpal, S. (2016). A Survey Report on Internet of Things Applications. *International Journal of Computer Science Trends and Technology, 4*(2).

Khalifa, O. O., Omar, A. A., Ahmed, M. Z., Saeed, R. A., Hashim, A. H. A., & Esgiar, A. N. (2021). An Automatic Facial Age Progression Estimation System. *2021 International Congress of Advanced Technology and Engineering (ICOTEN)*. Research Gate.

Khan, M. F. (2019). *Moth Flame Clustering Algorithm for Internet of Vehicle (MFCA-IoV)*. IEEE., doi:10.1109/ACCESS.2018.2886420

Kondamudi, S. S. R. (2016, February). IoT based Data Logger System for weather monitoring using Wireless sensor networks. *International Journal of Engineering Trends and Technology, 32*(2), 71–75. doi:10.14445/22315381/IJETT-V32P213

Langone, R., Alzate, C., Bey-Temsamani, A., & Suykens, J. A. K. (2014). Alarm prediction in industrial machines using autoregressive LS-SVM models, *2014 IEEE Symposium on Computational Intelligence and Data Mining (CIDM)*. IEEE. 10.1109/CIDM.2014.7008690

Li, Z., Kai, W., & Bo, L. (2013, April). Sensor-Network based Intelligent Water Quality Monitoring and Control. *International Journal of Advanced Research in Computer Engineering and Technology, 2*(4), 1659–1662.

Lojka, T., Miškuf, M., & Zolotová, I. (2016). Industrial IoT Gateway with Machine Learning for Smart Manufacturing. In I. Nääs, (Eds.), *Advances in Production Management Systems. Initiatives for a Sustainable World. APMS. IFIP Advances in Information and Communication Technology* (Vol. 488). Springer. doi:10.1007/978-3-319-51133-7_89

Majeed Butt, O., Zulqarnain, M., & Majeed Butt, T. (2021, March). Butt. O. Majeed, M. Zulqarnain and T. Majeed Butt (2020). Recent advancement in smart grid technology: Future prospects in the electrical power network. *Ain Shams Engineering Journal, 12*(1), 687–695. doi:10.1016/j.asej.2020.05.004

McClellan, M., Cervelló-Pastor, C., & Sallent, S. (2020). Deep Learning at the Mobile Edge: Opportunities for5G Networks. *Applied Sciences (Basel, Switzerland), 10*(14), 4735. doi:10.3390/app10144735

Min, Q., Lu, Y., Liu, Z., Su, C., & Wang, B. (2019). Machine Learning based Digital Twin Framework for Production Optimization in Petrochemical Industry. *International Journal of Information Management*, *49*, 502–519. doi:10.1016/j.ijinfomgt.2019.05.020

Misra S. et al (2016). Security Challenges and Approaches in Internet of Things. *Springer Briefs in Electrical and Computer Engineering*, 2016.

Mohd, N. (2015). *A Comprehensive Review of Swarm Optimization Algorithms*. ResearchGate. doi:10.1371/journal.pone.0122827

Molina, D. (2020). Comprehensive Taxonomies of Nature- and Bio-inspired Optimization: Inspiration versus Algorithmic Behavior, *Critical Analysis and Recommendations*.

Ndubuaku, M., vid Okereafor (2015). Internet of Things for Africa: Challenges and Opportunities. *2015 International Conference on Cyberspace Governance – Cyber ABUJA*. IEEE.

Orrù, P. F., Zoccheddu, A., Sassu, L., Mattia, C., Cozza, R., & Arena, S. (2020). Machine Learning Approach Using MLP and SVM Algorithms for the Fault Prediction of a CentrifugalPump in the Oil and Gas Industry. *Sustainability (Basel)*, *12*(11), 4776. doi:10.3390/su12114776

Preethi, N. (2014). Performance Evaluation of IoT Result for Machine Learning. Transactions on Engineering and Sciences. 2(11).

Ravi, K. (2016). IoT based smart greenhouse. *IEEE Region 10 Humanitarian Technology Conference (R10-HTC)*. IEEE.

Romany, F. (2021). Mansour, Nada M. Alfar, Sayed Abdel-Khalek, Maha Abdelhaq, RA Saeed, Raed Alsaqour (2021). Optimal deep learning based fusion model for biomedical image classification. *Expert Systems: International Journal of Knowledge Engineering and Neural Networks*, (June). doi:10.1111/exsy.12764

Saranya, C. M., & Nitha, K. P. (2015, April). Analysis of Security methods in Internet of Things. *International Journal on Recent and Innovation Trends in Computing and Communication*, *3*(4).

Shaikh, F. K. (2013). Communication Technology That Suits IoT – A Critical Review. *WSN4DC 2013, CCIS 366. Springer-Verlag Berlin Heidelberg, 2013*, 14–25.

Strielkowski, W., Streimikiene, D., Fomina, A., & Semenova, E. (2019). Internet of Energy (IoE) and High-Renewables Electricity System Market Design. *MDPI. Energies*, *12*(24), 4790. doi:10.3390/en12244790

Sumithra, A. (2016, March). A Smart Environmental Monitoring System Using Internet of Things. *International Journal of Scientific Engineering and Applied Science*, *2*(3), 261–265.

Tan, Q., Zhang, Y., Zhang, X., Pei, X., Xiong, J., Xue, C., Liu, J., & Zhang, W. (2014, May 21). A Hazardous Chemical-Oriented Monitoring and Tracking System Based on Sensor Network. *International Journal of Distributed Sensor Networks*, *10*(5), 1–8. doi:10.1155/2014/410476

Tanwar, S., Bhatia, Q., Patel, P., Kumari, A., Singh, P. K., & Hong, W. (2020). Machine Learning Adoption in Blockchain-Based Smart Applications: The Challenges, and a Way Forward. *IEEE Access : Practical Innovations, Open Solutions*, *8*, 474–488. doi:10.1109/ACCESS.2019.2961372

Tawalbeh, L., Muheidat, F., Tawalbeh, M., & Quwaider, M. (2020). IoT Privacy and Security: Challenges and Solutions. *Applied Sciences (Basel, Switzerland)*, *10*(12), 4102. doi:10.3390/app10124102

Varghese, A. (2015, June). Weather Based Information System using IoT and Cloud Computing. *Journal of Computing Science and Engineering : JCSE*, *2*(6), 90–97.

Vimal, P. V. (2017). IOT Based Greenhouse Environment Monitoring and Controlling System using Arduino Platform. *2017 International Conference on Intelligent Computing, Instrumentation and Control Technologies (ICICICT)*, (pp. 1514- 1519). IEEE. 10.1109/ICICICT1.2017.8342795

Wei, Y. Y. (2015). A Survey of Wireless Sensor Network Based Air Pollution Monitoring Systems. *Sensors (Basel)*, *2015*(12), 31392–31427. doi:10.3390/s151229859 PMID:26703598

Zeinab, E. (2020). Ahmed, Hasan Kamrul, Rashid A Saeed, Sheroz Khan, Shayla Islam, Mohammad Akharuzzaman, Rania A. Mokhtar (2020). Optimizing Energy Consumption for Cloud Internet of Things. *Frontiers in Physics (Lausanne)*, *8*, 358. doi:10.3389/fphy.2020.00358

Zhang, Li, Q., Zhang, C., Liang, H., Li, P., Wang, T., Li, S., Zhu, Y., & Wu, C. (2017). Current trends in the development of intelligent unmanned autonomous systems. *Frontiers Inf Technol Electronic Eng*, *18*(1), 68–85. doi:10.1631/FITEE.1601650

Zolanvari, M., Teixeira, M. A., Gupta, L., Khan, K. M., & Jain, R. (2019, August). Machine Learning-Based Network Vulnerability Analysis of Industrial Internet of Things. *IEEE Internet of Things Journal*, *6*(4), 6822–6834. doi:10.1109/JIOT.2019.2912022

Chapter 2
A Review of Artificial Intelligence Techniques for Improved Cloud and IoT Security

Kassim Kalinaki
https://orcid.org/0000-0001-8630-9110
Islamic University in Uganda, Uganda

Wasswa Shafik
https://orcid.org/0000-0002-9320-3186
Dig Connectivity Research Laboratory, Uganda

Magezi Masha
Islamic University in Uganda, Uganda

Adam A. Alli
Islamic University in Uganda, Uganda

ABSTRACT

The current surge in interconnected devices, which includes the Internet of Things (IoT) devices and the continually expanding cloud infrastructure, marks a new era of digital transformation and convenience. This transformative wave is reshaping industries, ushering in the age of smart cities, autonomous vehicles, and effortless remote collaboration. Yet, the growing complexity and reach of these technologies bring an accompanying increase in potential vulnerabilities and security risks. Thus, this study delves into the convergence of artificial intelligence (AI), cloud computing, and IoT security. It investigates how these state-of-the-art technologies can be leveraged to protect networks, data, and devices, presenting inventive solutions to address the ever-evolving threat landscape. Additionally, it sheds light on the challenges posed by AI-powered techniques and offers insights into future trends, making it a valuable resource for researchers, students, and cybersecurity professionals.

DOI: 10.4018/979-8-3693-0766-3.ch002

INTRODUCTION

The prevailing proliferation of interconnected devices, encompassing both IoT devices and the ever-expanding cloud infrastructure, heralds an epoch of digital transformation and convenience, reshaping industries to enable smart cities, autonomous vehicles, and seamless remote collaboration (Kalinaki, Thilakarathne, et al., 2023; Shafik & Kalinaki, 2023). However, with these technologies' increasing scope and intricacy comes a corresponding amplification of potential vulnerabilities and security threats (Alli et al., 2021). In an era of exponential data generation, preserving cloud and IoT system integrity, confidentiality, and availability becomes paramount. In the early days of computing, data was primarily stored and processed on localized servers within an organization's premises (Sarker et al., 2023). This approach had limitations in terms of scalability and efficiency, as organizations needed to invest heavily in infrastructure to accommodate growing data volumes and computational demands.

The advent of cloud computing changed this landscape, allowing cloud service providers to establish massive data centers equipped with high-capacity storage, computing resources, and extensive networking capabilities (Tabrizchi & Kuchaki Rafsanjani, 2020). Organizations could now store and process their data on these remote servers, accessing them via the internet. This shift allowed organizations to reduce their reliance on on-premises hardware, reduce costs, and rapidly scale their operations as needed (Khoda Parast et al., 2022). Moreover, cloud computing revolutionizes data and application storage and management, making scalability, accessibility, and cost-efficiency more attainable than ever (Tabrizchi & Kuchaki Rafsanjani, 2020). However, the transition to cloud computing has introduced several security challenges. One of the most prominent challenges is data protection. Cloud service providers must ensure the confidentiality and integrity of customer data, and they employ various security measures to achieve this, including encryption, access controls, and security policies. However, the shared responsibility model in cloud security means that customers are responsible for securing their data and applications in the cloud (Alouffi et al., 2021). Additionally, access control is a fundamental aspect of data protection in the cloud. Customers control who can access their data and what actions can be performed. Access control lists, identity, access management, and role-based access control are commonly employed to manage user permissions and privileges (Alli et al., 2021).

IoT has presented a new age of connectivity, extending the internet's reach to an extensive array of devices (Kassab & Darabkh, 2020). IoT has transformed how we interact with and control our surroundings, from household appliances and wearable devices to industrial sensors and autonomous vehicles. However, this proliferation of interconnected devices, while promising significant efficiency and automation merits, has also brought various security challenges (HaddadPajouh et al., 2021). One of the foremost challenges in IoT security is IoT devices' vast and diverse landscape. Unlike traditional computing environments, IoT devices come in various shapes and sizes, operate on different operating systems, and use a multitude of communication protocols (Furstenau et al., 2023). This heterogeneity makes it challenging to implement standardized security measures, leaving many IoT devices vulnerable to exploitation (M. Ahmed & Haskell-Dowland, 2023). Traditional security approaches rely on standardization and consistent security measures, but uniformity is challenging in the IoT landscape. The absence of common security standards makes it difficult to apply one-size-fits-all security solutions, leaving gaps that malicious actors can exploit. These IoT devices communicate through various protocols, including Wi-Fi, Bluetooth, Zigbee, and cellular networks. These protocols have security considerations and vulnerabilities (Rasool et al., 2022). For instance, many IoT devices rely on Wi-Fi for connectivity, which can be vulnerable to common attacks such as eavesdropping and unauthorized access. Using multiple communication protocols further complicates security efforts, as different protocols require different security measures. Many IoT devices are constrained by limited computational resources, including processing power and memory (Wójcicki et al., 2022). These limitations often make implementing robust security measures on the devices themselves challenging. Traditional security practices that require significant computational resources may not be feasible in the IoT context.

Traditional security measures, once effective, are ill-suited to address the rapidly evolving threat landscape. Threat actors have grown increasingly sophisticated, leveraging advanced techniques to infiltrate systems, exfiltrate data, and disrupt critical infrastructure (Jangjou & Sohrabi, 2022). The rise of nation-state-sponsored cyberattacks, the prevalence of ransomware, and the menace of IoT botnets underscore the urgency for adopting more proactive and adaptive security strategies (Holt et al., 2023). Furthermore, the expanding attack surface and complexity of cloud and IoT environments compound the challenge of identifying vulnerabilities and responding promptly to threats (Pandey et al., 2023). Manual methodologies, once adequate, are rendered insufficient to keep pace with the evolving vectors of attack. Consequently, AI and machine learning (ML) / deep learning (DL), two formidable emerging technologies, are poised to address these continually evolving security challenges.

AI, a multidisciplinary field dedicated to imbuing machines with the capacity for intelligent behavior, represents an invaluable asset in security (Kamil Abed Angesh Anupam & Ali Kamil Abed, 2023; Mishra & Tyagi, 2022). These AI systems adeptly process vast data at speeds surpassing human capabilities, discerning patterns and anomalies and predicting potential threats. Moreover, these systems can assimilate historical data, adapt to emerging threats, and evolve synchronously with the perpetually shifting digital domain (Sarker et al., 2023). AI is pivotal in various security applications, encompassing intrusion detection, threat intelligence, behavioral analysis, and security automation. Furthermore, it facilitates proactive threat identification, allowing organizations to maintain a decisive advantage over cybercriminals (Jyoti et al., 2023). AI's real-time analytical capabilities are imperative for detecting and mitigating threats in the increasingly dynamic cloud and IoT landscapes (T. Mazhar et al., 2023). ML/DL, both subsets of AI, focus on formulating algorithms and models that learn from data, render predictions, and enhance their performance over time. In the security context, ML/DL proves indispensable for crafting predictive models capable of discerning patterns of malicious conduct, detecting anomalies, and making real-time decisions (Douiba et al., 2023). The beauty of ML/DL lies in their adaptability, allowing security systems to evolve in response to emerging data and threats, thus minimizing the necessity for manual rule updates. For example, ML-powered intrusion detection systems can self-train network traffic data, discern what constitutes normal behavior, and flag deviations indicative of a security breach (Oleiwi et al., 2022). This adaptability is particularly crucial within cloud and IoT environments, characterized by their ever-changing network configurations.

This chapter delves into the intersection of AI, cloud computing, and IoT security. It explores how these cutting-edge technologies can be harnessed to safeguard networks, data, and devices, offering innovative solutions to address the ever-evolving threat landscape. As we navigate this domain, it becomes evident that AI and ML are not merely supplemental tools for security but integral components that redefine protection, detection, and response mechanisms to threats in the cloud and IoT ecosystems. By the end of this chapter, readers will have a comprehensive understanding of how these emerging technologies are revolutionizing how we secure our interconnected digital world. The following are the contributions of this chapter;

Chapter Contributions

The main contributions of the chapter are highlighted.

- A comprehensive discussion of AI and its role in improving cloud and IoT security.
- A discussion of the shared security challenges and threat landscape in the cloud and IoT.
- A detailed discussion of AI-powered techniques for improved security of the cloud and IoT, encompassing supervised, semi-supervised, and unsupervised approaches.
- A highlight of the challenges of AI integration in cloud and IoT security.
- Finally, it discusses emerging trends in AI-powered approaches for improved cloud and IoT security.

Chapter Organization

Section 2 depicts the timeline of key developments in AI, cloud computing, and IoT security. Section 3 details the shared security challenges and emerging threat landscape in the cloud and IoT. Section 4 depicts a detailed discussion of AI-powered techniques for improved security of the cloud and IoT, encompassing supervised, semi-supervised, and unsupervised approaches. Section 5 contains the challenges of AI integration in cloud and IoT security. Section 6 depicts emerging trends and future cloud and IoT security directions. Finally, section 7 provides the conclusion.

TIMELINE OF KEY DEVELOPMENTS IN AI, CLOUD COMPUTING, AND IoT SECURITY

This section provides an infographic depicting the timeline of key developments in AI, cloud computing, and IoT security. As shown in Figure 1, the journey of AI, cloud computing, and the security landscape of the IoT has been marked by a series of transformative developments over the decades. From the conceptualization of AI in the 1950s to the contemporary fusion of AI with cloud computing and the imperative focus on securing the expanding realm of IoT devices, this timeline reflects the dynamic evolution of technologies that have redefined how we interact with information and machines.

SHARED SECURITY CHALLENGES AND EMERGING THREAT LANDSCAPE IN THE CLOUD AND IoT

In cloud computing and the IoT, shared security challenges converge with an evolving threat landscape. While diverse in their applications, these two distinct technological domains encounter several mutual security concerns (Raj et al., 2022). The cloud and IoT ecosystems are intricately involved in collecting, transmitting, and storing sensitive data, making privacy and adherence to stringent regulations such as the General Data Protection Regulation (GDPR) and the Health Insurance Portability and Accountability Act (HIPAA) of utmost importance. Unauthorized access, data breaches, and inadequate data encryption can unleash catastrophic consequences. Their scalability, enabling them to accommodate numerous users and devices, inadvertently opens the door to potential attackers, making the defense against formidable adversaries like distributed denial-of-service (DDoS) attacks a formidable task (Gankotiya et al., 2023; Nithiyanandam et al., 2022).

Figure 1. Timeline of Key Developments in AI, Cloud Computing, and IoT Security

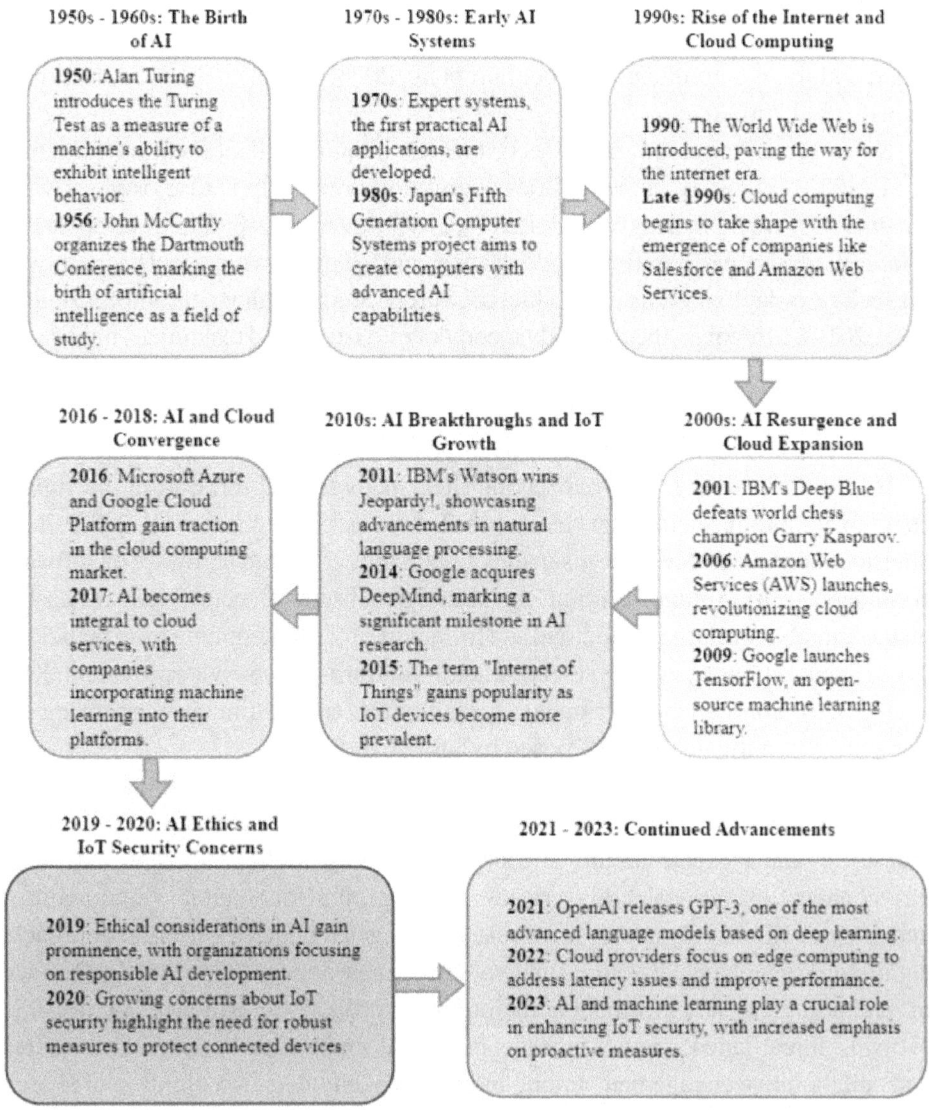

Furthermore, the extensive interconnectivity inherent in cloud and IoT systems enhances their functionality and exposes them to vulnerabilities (Huang et al., 2023). A compromised device or cloud service can be a perilous gateway for attackers to infiltrate the entire network. These ecosystems' intricacies make them challenging to secure; a single vulnerability in one component can trigger a cascading chain of consequences, underscoring the need for comprehensive vetting and securing each network element (Fazeldehkordi & Grønli, 2022). In various industries, including healthcare, finance, and government, stringent regulatory requirements govern data security and privacy, thereby adding a layer of complexity to security management in cloud and IoT environments (Alabdulatif et al., 2023; Fahim et al., 2023; Kalinaki, Fahadi, et al., 2023).

Several emerging cloud and IoT security threats require vigilant attention (Hadzovic et al., 2023). Zero-day vulnerabilities, signifying previously undisclosed software weaknesses, are increasingly exploited by cyber adversaries before developers can release necessary patches. Both cloud services and IoT devices represent prime targets for such zero-day exploits, offering lucrative prospects for malevolent actors (Stellios et al., 2019). Moreover, the rapid advancement of AI-powered techniques introduces a novel dimension to the security landscape. AI is harnessed by both attackers and defenders, enabling automated attacks and bolstered defense mechanisms, introducing a new layer of complexity into security strategies (Gürfidan et al., 2023).

In addition, attackers are redirecting their focus toward infiltrating the supply chain to compromise cloud services and IoT devices (Alsinglawi et al., 2022). This nefarious activity involves the insertion of malicious code into hardware or software components during manufacturing, constituting a substantial security hazard. Lastly, insider threats loom large in the cloud and IoT environments, stemming from malicious or negligent actions by employees, contractors, or third-party service providers (Kim et al., 2020). Consequently, stringent access controls and continuous monitoring are imperative to mitigate the risks posed by insider threats.

The confluence of shared security challenges and the dynamic threat landscape within cloud computing and the IoT underscores the imperative for robust security measures. The intricate nature of these ecosystems, along with their extensive interconnectivity and scalability, creates a fertile ground for potential vulnerabilities and attacks. Effectively addressing these challenges mandates a holistic approach, entailing comprehensive vetting and securing each network element. In the face of technological advancements, maintaining proactive resilience against the evolving threat landscape necessitates continual innovation in security measures and collaborative engagement among industry stakeholders. Recognition of shared security concerns and proactive adaptation to emerging threats empower organizations to enhance the safeguarding of their cloud and IoT environments, thereby mitigating potential risks to sensitive data.

AI-POWERED TECHNIQUES FOR IMPROVING CLOUD AND IoT SECURITY

The need for robust security measures intensifies as the digital landscape expands, driven by the proliferation of cloud computing and IoT. These technologies' complexity, scale, and interconnected nature create a fertile ground for potential security vulnerabilities and threats. AI-powered approaches have emerged as essential tools in bolstering the security of cloud and IoT systems. Accordingly, this section explores the myriad of AI-powered algorithms (supervised, semi-supervised, and unsupervised) for enhancing the safety of these interconnected environments, covering key areas such as anomaly detection, intrusion detection and prevention, malware analysis, data privacy, and access control.

Supervised Learning Techniques

These models are utilized in the realm of cloud and IoT security to anticipate the occurrence of security incidents by analyzing past data patterns. This enables the proactive identification of potential threats and facilitates the development of incident response plans.

Logistic Regression (LR)

Here, a classification method is employed to construct a model that estimates the probability of a binary result by considering input features. The system's functioning involves utilizing a trained model fed with datasets, including labeled security occurrences (de Azambuja et al., 2023). Through this process, the model acquires the ability to predict the probability of a security event occurring, relying on various features extracted from the data. LR is a valuable tool in cloud and IoT security as it predicts the probability of unauthorized access attempts, data breaches, or malicious activities (Sarker et al., 2023). This prediction is made by analyzing previous data, facilitating the implementation of proactive security measures.

Support Vector Machine (SVM)

Another classification technique that has strong performance in identifying the best hyperplane for segregating data points into distinct groups is. In IoT security, SVMs can effectively categorize network traffic or system events into normal and malicious classes. Detecting breaches and threats inside complex contexts is crucial in ensuring security (Li, 2023). Using SVM enables security teams to effectively delineate a distinct boundary between legal actions and those considered suspect.

This, in turn, facilitates prompt identification and response to deviations from the norm, enhancing the overall security stance.

Decision Trees (DT)

In addition to their conventional uses, decision trees possess significant value in the context of access control decisions about IoT and cloud-related technology security. Access control systems are crucial in determining the authorization of users or devices by evaluating their eligibility against predetermined qualities and criteria (Mahor et al., 2022). Through conditional decision-making, security measures are strengthened since they guarantee that only authorized entities are granted access to crucial resources, reducing the potential for illegal intrusion.

Naïve Bayes (NB)

A classification technique incorporating probabilistic principles, specifically Bayes' theorem, commonly assumes feature independence for simplification purposes. Naïve Bayes is a crucial email and message filtering tool in cloud and IoT security domains. Categorizing messages into spam or genuine categories counteract the potential risks posed by phishing and social engineering tactics, which can compromise the authenticity and reliability of communication channels (Hephzipah et al., 2023). The probabilistic basis of this technology contributes to the mitigation of false positives and negatives, hence augmenting the precision of email filtering and overall security measures.

Random Forest (RF)

Because cloud systems generate a vast amount of log data, RF can analyze log files to detect patterns associated with security incidents. This can help in the proactive identification and mitigation of security risks. Moreover, RF is essential for detecting malicious activities and intrusions in cloud and IoT environments. It can analyze various features related to network traffic, user behavior, and system logs to identify anomalies indicative of security threats (M. S. Mazhar et al., 2022).

Semi-Supervised Techniques

These approaches prove particularly valuable when the availability of labeled data is restricted, or the cost of acquiring such data is high. In cloud and IoT security, using semi-supervised learning techniques can be leveraged to enhance the efficiency of threat detection processes, as illustrated below.

Active Learning

A semi-supervised technique enables models to autonomously select the specific data points that want human annotation. A prudent approach involves directing attention toward identifying and categorizing the most pivotal data, alleviating the workload of security analysts, and expediting the training procedure. Active learning has significantly improved the effectiveness of threat detection in the cloud and IoT security (Jasim & Kurnaz, 2023). Identifying the most essential data samples for manual annotation enables security teams to enhance their limited resources' efficiency and the effectiveness of supervised models. Consequently, these outcomes are characterized by enhanced precision in forecasting, proactive identification of threats, and improved security results (Kunduru, 2023).

Reinforcement Learning

This approach is a semi-supervised strategy that integrates labeled data with feedback obtained from real-world scenarios. This particular technique plays a crucial role in developing adaptive security policies that can dynamically adapt to the ever-changing landscape of threats. Reinforcement learning exhibits significant potential within the realm of IoT and cloud security. This technology facilitates the ongoing acquisition of knowledge and adjustment of security responses by systems, drawing from past data and real-time environmental factors (Caviglione et al., 2023). By integrating input from actual security incidents, these models can gradually enhance their policies, increasing their resilience and adaptability toward future threats and weaknesses.

Un Supervised Techniques

These technologies facilitate identifying and mitigating irregularities, potential risks, and weaknesses inside the cloud and IoT infrastructures in computing.

K-Means

This unsupervised clustering technique partitions data points into K different groups, considering their similarities. The algorithm reduces the within-cluster variation, thereby assigning data points to clusters based on their proximity to the centroid of each cluster (Arunkumar, M., & Kumar, K. A., 2023). K-Means exhibits diverse practical applications, from marketing's consumer segmentation to computer vision's image reduction. For Cloud and IoT cybersecurity, the utilization of K-Means holds significant importance as it facilitates the examination of network traffic, hence enabling the identification of patterns that may signify irregularities and potential security risks (Aldhyani & Alkahtani, 2023). Network data clustering enables security teams to identify atypical data flows or connections, facilitating the timely discovery of potential threats.

Fuzzy C-Means

The Fuzzy C-Means method is a modified version of the K-Means algorithm that incorporates the principles of fuzzy logic. In contrast to the definitive assignments made by the K-Means algorithm, the Fuzzy C-Means algorithm assigns data points to clusters using membership values that express the extent to which a point belongs to each cluster (Hegde & Manvi, 2022). This methodology facilitates the implementation of more intricate clustering techniques, wherein data points can be assigned to several clusters with various degrees of membership. Fuzzy C-Means can be employed in security or IoT network traffic analysis (B. Ahmed et al., 2023). This enables the categorization of data flows based on their level of resemblance to established patterns. Using fuzzy logic in this context seems advantageous in identifying abnormalities that may display attributes associated with various threat categories.

Artificial Neural Network (ANN)

ANNs are computational models that draw inspiration from the structural and functional features of the human brain. ANNs consist of interconnected layers of artificial neurons that facilitate the processing and learning of data (Hua et al., 2023). This characteristic renders ANNs very adaptable and suitable for a diverse array of IoT and cloud applications. These technologies are extensively utilized in several domains, like IoT image identification and predictive modeling. Within the IoT and cloud security, ANNs detect intrusions (Hua et al., 2023). Moreover, ANNs can acquire knowledge of normal and harmful activity patterns through analyzing network traffic and system records. This attribute renders them highly effective instruments for detecting security risks and irregularities in cloud and IoT ecosystems.

Isolation Forest

The ensemble-based anomaly identification technique emphasizes isolating abnormalities rather than creating cloud or IoT normal data flow profiles. This is accomplished by employing a random partitioning technique to create isolation trees, wherein anomalies are identified and isolated more efficiently owing to their distinct attributes (Koblah et al., 2023). In practical applications, the Isolation Forest algorithm has demonstrated significant efficacy in detecting anomalies across several areas, encompassing the field of cybersecurity. When used in the cloud and IoT security context, this approach demonstrates exceptional proficiency in detecting network intrusions, atypical system behaviors, and instances of security breaches.

In isolating and identifying suspicious behavior within intricate cloud environments, IoTs facilitate the prompt identification of potential threats (Sagu et al., 2023). The sharing of knowledge and insights among industry through collaborative initiatives will play a crucial role in proactively addressing growing security threats. The increasing prevalence of cloud and IoT systems necessitates adaptability, learning, and responsiveness to safeguard the security and integrity of digital ecosystems (Shafik, 2023).

In summary, the amalgamation of AI-powered techniques with cloud and IoT security emerges as a formidable alliance against the evolving landscape of digital threats. The diverse array of supervised, semi-supervised, and unsupervised learning models showcased here reflects the versatility needed to fortify interconnected environments. As we navigate the intricate web of interconnected technologies, the collective efforts of human ingenuity and AI become the cornerstone of a secure and resilient digital future, as demonstrated in Table 1.

REAL-WORLD CASES OF AI INTEGRATION FOR IMPROVED CLOUD AND IoT SECURITY

To further illustrate, this section presents real-world cases, showcasing the power of AI in improving cloud and IoT security

Darktrace's AI-Powered Cyber Defense

Darktrace[1] is a cybersecurity startup well-known for its protection technologies driven by AI. Their solution uses AI and machine learning algorithms to quickly identify and neutralize cyber threats. The Enterprise Immune System, their flagship product, operates by identifying the "patterns of life" in a network. It establishes a baseline of typical system, user, and device behavior. Any departure from this standard is tagged as possibly malevolent, enabling prompt examination and handling of possible cyber hazards, such as insider threats, zero-day attacks, and other advanced types of cyberattacks. In an effort to keep ahead of changing cyber threats, Darktrace's AI is constantly learning and adapting to new dangers. This form of adaptive cybersecurity is essential in the current environment, where cyber threats are always changing, and traditional rule-based systems could find it difficult to keep up.

Table 1. Summary of AI-powered Techniques for Cloud and IoT Security

AI-powered techniques and algorithms		Application scenarios in cloud and IoT security	References
Supervised techniques	LR	Intrusion anomaly detection	(Mohamed & Ismael, 2023)
		Data breach prediction	(Sarker et al., 2023)
		Malware detection	(Waqas et al., 2022)
	SVM	Intrusion Detection	(Du et al., 2022)
		Malware detection	(Arunkumar & Kumar, 2023)
		Network Traffic Classification and QoS Management	(Qu et al., 2020)
	DT	Anomaly detection	(Douiba et al., 2023)
		Authentication and Authorization	(Zareen et al., 2024)
	NB	Email Filtering and Spam Detection in Cloud-Based Email Services	(Arya et al., 2023)
		Anomaly Detection in IoT Networks	(Manimurugan, 2021)
	RF	Network Traffic Analysis	(Chowdhury et al., 2023; M. S. Mazhar et al., 2022)
Semi-Supervised Techniques	Active learning	Threat detection	(Jasim & Kurnaz, 2023)
		Intrusion detection	(U. Ahmed et al., 2023)
	Reinforcement Learning	Resource Allocation and Optimization	(Nassar & Yilmaz, 2019)
Un Supervised Techniques	K-means	IoT device profiling	(Safi et al., 2022)
	ANN	Intrusion detection	(Hua et al., 2023)
	Isolation forest	Threat identification	

Though sophisticated and sometimes very successful, AI-powered defensive systems like Darktrace's are not infallible. Cybercriminals are constantly changing their strategies, so there's always a chance of sophisticated attacks that go undetected or false positives. As a result, even while these systems are a valuable addition to cybersecurity plans, a multi-layered strategy with human oversight is still essential. Darktrace utilizes unsupervised ML to create a baseline of normal behavior within IoT and cloud networks. The system continuously monitors network activity and identifies anomalies that deviate from the established baseline. Darktrace's approach is particularly effective in detecting novel and evolving threats that might go unnoticed by traditional rule-based systems. The platform employs ML algorithms to autonomously respond to detected threats in real-time, thereby fortifying the security posture of IoT and cloud environments (Sharma & Sharma, 2023).

Cylance's AI-Based Endpoint Security

Another cybersecurity firm well-known for its AI-powered endpoint protection products is Cylance[2]. Their strategy focuses on proactively preventing security breaches at the endpoint level (specific devices such as PCs, servers, or smartphones) by leveraging machine learning and artificial intelligence. Instead of depending on known signatures, Cylance's main product, CylancePROTECT, uses AI algorithms to evaluate files and determine if they are safe or harmful based on their traits and behavior. Real-time threat detection and blocking is the goal of this technique, even for zero-day or previously undisclosed threats.

CylancePROTECT's AI model is constantly learning and developing, which enhances its capacity to recognize and stop new malware strains and other online dangers. It tries to avoid cyber attackers who regularly alter or produce new malware to get around established security measures by concentrating on the behavior of files and apps rather than signatures.

Cylance's technology is a proactive protection mechanism, just like other AI-based security solutions. It's crucial to remember that no cybersecurity solution is perfect. There may be times when sophisticated and novel threats manage to avoid detection, or false positives happen. As a result, even while AI-based endpoint security is an effective weapon in the fight against cyberattacks, it usually works in tandem with other cybersecurity measures like human oversight and numerous levels of defense. Cylance also uses AI algorithms to analyze file characteristics and behaviors on endpoints. It employs ML models to predict and prevent known and unknown threats by identifying malicious patterns and behaviors. By focusing on predictive analysis rather than relying solely on known signatures, Cylance aims to provide advanced threat protection (BlackBerry, 2023). This approach is precious in countering new and evolving malware that might not yet have recognized signatures.

Cognitive Security with IBM QRadar

IBM QRadar[3] is an inclusive security intelligence platform with cognitive capabilities that improve an organization's ability to identify and address cybersecurity threats. The phrase "cognitive security" describes how artificial intelligence and machine learning methods enhance security operations through work automation, massive data analysis, and insight provision for security analysts. Through various AI technologies, such as machine learning, behavioral analytics, and threat intelligence, QRadar makes use of cognitive capabilities. It can process enormous volumes of data from various sources, including network traffic, logs, endpoints, and apps, to find possible security events and abnormalities. IBM QRadar integrates cognitive capabilities, including machine learning, to provide advanced security analytics. It applies ML algorithms for anomaly detection, threat prioritization, and incident response. IBM QRadar enhances security operations by automating the analysis of vast amounts of security data. ML helps identify patterns that may signify a security incident, enabling quicker response times and reducing the workload on security teams (Dheap, 2017).

Cloud Security with Microsoft Azure Sentinel

Microsoft Azure Sentinel[4] is a cloud-native security information and event management (SIEM) solution offering businesses intelligent security analytics. It is intended to gather, examine, and act upon security-related data throughout the whole hybrid enterprise of an enterprise, encompassing cloud, on-premises, and other platforms. Azure Sentinel combines AI-powered techniques and security orchestration to provide a holistic cloud security solution. It uses AI for threat intelligence, anomaly detection, and behavioral analysis. With Azure Sentinel, Microsoft aims to enable security teams to detect, investigate, and respond to security incidents across the cloud (Copeland, 2021; Ferrag et al., 2023; Peiris & Pillai, 2022). The integration of ML allows for identifying complex and evolving threats, improving overall cloud security posture.

Cisco's IoT Threat Defense

Cisco's IoT Threat Defense is A security solution created to handle the particular difficulties brought about by the growth of IoT devices inside business networks[5]. IoT devices provide unique security concerns because of their frequently constrained processing capacity, wide range of communication protocols, and potential vulnerabilities. These risks will only increase as the diversity and number of IoT devices increase. Cisco's IoT Threat Defense employs ML and behavioral analytics to monitor the activities of IoT devices. It focuses on understanding the typical behavior of devices and detecting anomalies. By applying ML to IoT security, Cisco helps organizations identify potentially malicious activities or compromised devices within their IoT ecosystems. This proactive approach is essential for securing the rapidly expanding landscape of interconnected devices (Reichert, 2017).

In summary, these cases collectively highlight the importance of leveraging AI and machine learning in addressing the evolving challenges of cybersecurity in both IoT and cloud environments. These technologies enable more proactive, adaptive, and effective security measures against a wide range of threats.

CHALLENGES OF AI INTEGRATION IN CLOUD AND IoT SECURITY

Integrating AI-driven solutions with existing security frameworks in cloud and IoT security offers significant advantages but is not devoid of challenges. These challenges, particularly relevant in cloud and IoT security, demand a closer examination to understand their implications fully. This section explores these challenges and provides illustrative examples that underscore their significance.

Complexity in Cloud and IoT Security

Integrating AI into security systems within cloud and IoT environments introduces a layer of complexity. These landscapes often comprise diverse devices, platforms, and communication protocols. Ensuring the seamless interaction of AI with this multifaceted ecosystem requires meticulous planning and engineering (Nagendran et al., 2023).

Data Privacy and Compliance in Cloud and IoT Security

AI systems, especially ML/DL models, frequently require access to substantial data volumes. In the context of cloud and IoT security, this data can encompass sensitive information from IoT devices. Adhering to data privacy regulations is imperative (Golightly et al., 2023). This includes obtaining consent from individuals where necessary and ensuring robust data protection measures.

Training and Expertise in Cloud and IoT Security

Integrating and managing AI systems within cloud and IoT security realms requires a profound understanding of security principles and AI technologies (Chemisto et al., 2023). Personnel involved must be proficient in navigating the unique security challenges of these environments while also mastering AI technologies. For instance, within a cloud-based healthcare IoT system, AI is employed for anomaly detection in patients' vital signs (Taghavirashidizadeh et al., 2022). In this setting, healthcare IT and security personnel undergo extensive training to comprehend the behavior of the AI model and its implications for patient data security. This rigorous training ensures they know how to configure the AI system correctly and respond adeptly to potential security issues (Koohang et al., 2022). Furthermore, they must adeptly manage the intricacies of securing patient data within a cloud-based IoT environment.

Adaptation in Cloud and IoT Security

Integrating AI-driven solutions into cloud and IoT security environments can necessitate adaptations to existing security measures and protocols. These adjustments may encompass revising access controls, refining incident response procedures, and realigning monitoring processes to harmonize with AI's capabilities and limitations (Meiryani et al., 2023; Neha et al., 2022). For example, in intelligent agriculture systems incorporating cloud-based AI for crop monitoring and IoT devices for soil moisture measurement, existing security measures may entail access controls to the cloud platform and established incident response plans designed for manual intervention. Adapting to the AI-driven system necessitates reconfiguring access controls to autonomously permit the AI model to respond to crop anomalies(Kalinaki, Shafik, et al., 2023). Simultaneously, the incident response procedures must be restructured to align seamlessly with the AI's capabilities, ensuring that human intervention is solicited only when essential.

Cost in Cloud and IoT Security

The deployment and maintenance of AI-driven security solutions within cloud and IoT environments can be financially demanding (Uddin & Bansal, 2022). Organizations must meticulously evaluate these costs in relation to the anticipated benefits, all while ensuring that the investment harmonizes with their overarching security objectives. In the context of a cloud-based IoT-enabled smart grid, AI is harnessed to predict and prevent power outages. The initiation of AI within this system encompasses considerable costs, encompassing the installation of advanced sensors, the establishment of cloud infrastructure for AI processing, and the procurement of AI software licenses (Alrasheed et al., 2022; Nair & Tyagi, 2023). Nevertheless, the investment is justifiable due to the subsequent reduction in maintenance expenses and the resultant enhancement in the reliability of the power grid, which, in turn, directly impacts customer satisfaction.

Ethical challenges in AI-Driven Cloud and IoT Security

The moral dimension of AI-driven security is multifaceted, encompassing concerns about transparency, fairness, accountability, and the potential misuse of these powerful technologies. Addressing these concerns is vital for maintaining trust in AI and ensuring that security measures are implemented responsibly and ethically. Organizations deploying these technologies must proactively work to ensure their security measures are effective and aligned with ethical principles. As the deployment of AI in security continues to expand, a focus on ethical considerations becomes increasingly critical to ensure the responsible and trustworthy use of these powerful technologies (Fares & Jammal, 2023; Rath et al., 2023). Organizations operating within cloud and IoT security domains must adopt a meticulously considered approach to navigate these integration challenges. A well-devised strategy is crucial for the successful integration of AI-driven security solutions. This approach maximizes the benefits and ensures the sustained effectiveness of existing security frameworks in the intricate and ever-changing cloud and IoT security domains.

EMERGING TRENDS AND FUTURE DIRECTIONS IN CLOUD AND IoT SECURITY

Cloud computing and IoT are evolving quickly. This evolution brings with it exciting opportunities but also new security challenges. As the landscape changes, keeping a close eye on emerging trends and future directions in cloud and IoT security is essential to stay ahead of potential threats.

Federated Learning for Distributed Security Intelligence

In the rapidly evolving landscape of cloud and IoT security, staying ahead of cyber threats has become an ever more challenging task. As the volume of data generated by IoT devices and the cloud continues to grow, traditional centralized security models are proving inadequate. This has led to the emergence of federated learning as a promising future trend in the field of distributed security intelligence (Sarhan et al., 2023).

Software-defined perimeter (SDP) for Zero Trust Security

The concept of Zero Trust Security is gaining traction as a fundamental approach to securing cloud and IoT environments. Zero Trust assumes that no entity, whether inside or outside the network, should be trusted by default. SDP is a technology that aligns with Zero Trust principles, creating a dynamic, identity-centric perimeter for securing resource access. This trend involves continuously adapting and verifying users and devices before granting access to applications and data (Tanimoto et al., 2023). In the context of IoT, where devices may vary widely in terms of trustworthiness, SDP can play a pivotal role in ensuring secure access.

Threat Intelligence Sharing and Collaboration

The sharing of threat intelligence across organizations and sectors is becoming increasingly essential for collective security. Collaborative security information-sharing platforms and frameworks are being developed to facilitate threat intelligence exchange (Sarhan et al., 2023). This trend is particularly relevant to cloud and IoT security, where threats can transcend organizational boundaries. Organizations can collectively bolster their security posture by sharing intelligence on emerging threats and vulnerabilities.

Security for Edge Devices and IoT Sensors

The proliferation of IoT devices, including sensors and edge devices, presents unique security challenges. These devices are often resource-constrained and may lack traditional security capabilities. Secure boot processes, embedded security chips, and lightweight encryption mechanisms are emerging trends to secure IoT endpoints. Moreover, edge computing security solutions are evolving to safeguard these devices and the data they generate at the edge (Sharmila et al., 2023; Walczak et al., 2023).

Security Automation and Orchestration

Security teams resort to automation and orchestration to respond rapidly and effectively as security threats become more sophisticated. Security automation uses AI-powered approaches to automate threat detection and incident response tasks (Admass et al., 2024). Security orchestration integrates and coordinates various security tools and processes to streamline and optimize security operations (Dimitrovski et al., 2023). These trends enable security teams to identify and respond to threats in real time, reducing manual intervention and response times.

Multi-Cloud and Hybrid Cloud Security

Many organizations adopt multi-cloud and hybrid cloud architectures to distribute workloads and reduce risk. Securing data and applications across multiple cloud providers and on-premises environments is complex. Emerging trends in multi-cloud and hybrid cloud security include cloud security posture management tools, container security solutions, and identity and access management (IAM) strategies that work seamlessly across cloud environments (Sohal et al., 2022; Zhang et al., 2024).

Self-Defending IoT Devices

IoT devices are increasingly being designed with self-defense mechanisms. These mechanisms include the ability to detect and respond to threats autonomously. For instance, a compromised IoT device may isolate itself from the network to prevent further attacks (Manikanta Narayana et al., 2023). Such self-defending devices reduce the burden on centralized security measures and enhance the overall security of IoT ecosystems.

Behavioral Biometrics for User Authentication

Traditional username and password combinations are often inadequate for securing cloud and IoT environments. Behavioral biometrics, which involves analyzing unique user behavior patterns such as typing speed, mouse movements, and device interaction, is gaining prominence as an additional layer of authentication. This trend helps ensure that the person accessing the system is the authorized user, enhancing security and reducing the risk of unauthorized access (Goyal & Srivastava, 2021).

Security Awareness Training for Employees

Human error remains a significant source of security vulnerabilities. Training employees and users on security best practices is an emerging trend. Regular security awareness training minimizes the risk of social engineering attacks and helps employees recognize and report security incidents promptly (Corallo et al., 2022; Tsouplaki, 2023).

Endpoint Detection and Response (EDR) for IoT

Endpoint Detection and Response (EDR) solutions, initially designed for traditional endpoints like laptops and desktops, are extending their reach to IoT devices. EDR solutions for IoT provide real-time monitoring, threat detection, and response capabilities for connected devices (Park et al., 2022). This trend is crucial in addressing the growing security concerns associated with the widespread deployment of IoT devices.

Container and Serverless Security

With the increasing adoption of containerization and serverless computing in cloud environments, the need for specialized security measures for these technologies is emerging. Container security tools, runtime protection, and serverless function security are becoming essential for protecting applications deployed in these environments (Cassel et al., 2022).

The cloud and IoT security landscape continuously evolves to address emerging threats and vulnerabilities. These trends reflect the industry's ongoing efforts to stay ahead of cyber threats, enhance data privacy, and ensure the security of cloud and IoT ecosystems. As organizations and security professionals adapt to these trends, they are better equipped to protect their data, devices, and digital assets in an ever-changing technological landscape.

CONCLUSION

This chapter has presented a comprehensive overview of the vital role that artificial intelligence plays in enhancing the security of both cloud and IoT environments. It began by delving into the fundamental concepts of AI and its relevance in addressing the ever-evolving security challenges these interconnected domains face. Our exploration of shared security challenges and the evolving threat landscape within the cloud and IoT ecosystems revealed the pressing need for innovative solutions. We underscored the imperative to adapt to the changing dynamics of cyber threats and vulnerabilities, emphasizing the significance of AI as a dynamic and adaptive tool. The chapter then embarked on an extensive discussion of AI-powered techniques, categorizing them into supervised, semi-supervised, and unsupervised approaches. When judiciously applied, these techniques demonstrated remarkable potential in enhancing security measures, enabling proactive threat detection and mitigation. Moreover, the challenges of integrating AI into cloud and IoT security were meticulously addressed. Understanding the obstacles discussed is essential for successfully leveraging AI in this context. Lastly, we discussed promising and emerging trends in AI-powered cloud and IoT security approaches. These trends paint a dynamic future for cloud and IoT security. Innovation in AI will continue to shape and transform the security paradigms of cloud and IoT domains. As we reflect on the contents of this chapter, it becomes clear that AI has emerged as a formidable ally in the relentless battle to secure the cloud and IoT. In embracing this technological synergy, the potential for safer, more resilient, and more efficient cloud and IoT ecosystems becomes tangible. Future research and practical implementations will further solidify the role of AI as a cornerstone of security in these vital domains. With its dynamic capabilities, AI holds the key to staying one step ahead of the ever-adapting threat landscape, ensuring the integrity and availability of digital infrastructure for years to come.

REFERENCES

Admass, W. S., Munaye, Y. Y., & Diro, A. A. (2024). Cyber security: State of the art, challenges and future directions. *Cyber Security and Applications*, *2*, 100031. doi:10.1016/j.csa.2023.100031

Ahmed, B., Shuja, M., Mishra, H. M., Qtaishat, A., & Kumar, M. (2023). IoT Based Smart Systems using Artificial Intelligence and Machine Learning: Accessible and Intelligent Solutions. *2023 6th International Conference on Information Systems and Computer Networks (ISCON)*, (pp. 1–6). IEEE. 10.1109/ISCON57294.2023.10112093

Ahmed, M., & Haskell-Dowland, P. (2023). *Cybersecurity for Smart Cities* (M. Ahmed & P. Haskell-Dowland, Eds.). Springer International Publishing. doi:10.1007/978-3-031-24946-4

Ahmed, U., Lin, J. C. W., Srivastava, G., Yun, U., & Singh, A. K. (2023). Deep Active Learning Intrusion Detection and Load Balancing in Software-Defined Vehicular Networks. *IEEE Transactions on Intelligent Transportation Systems*, *24*(1), 953–961. doi:10.1109/TITS.2022.3166864

Alabdulatif, A., Thilakarathne, N. N., & Kalinaki, K. (2023). A Novel Cloud Enabled Access Control Model for Preserving the Security and Privacy of Medical Big Data. *Electronics (Basel)*, *12*(12), 2646. doi:10.3390/electronics12122646

Aldhyani, T. H. H., & Alkahtani, H. (2023). Cyber Security for Detecting Distributed Denial of Service Attacks in Agriculture 4.0: Deep Learning Model. *Mathematics*, *11*(1), 233. doi:10.3390/math11010233

Alli, A. A., Kassim, K., Mutwalibi, N., Hamid, H., & Ibrahim, L. (2021). Secure Fog-Cloud of Things: Architectures, Opportunities and Challenges. In M. Ahmed & P. Haskell-Dowland (Eds.), *Secure Edge Computing* (1st ed., pp. 3–20). CRC Press. doi:10.1201/9781003028635-2

Alouffi, B., Hasnain, M., Alharbi, A., Alosaimi, W., Alyami, H., & Ayaz, M. (2021). A Systematic Literature Review on Cloud Computing Security: Threats and Mitigation Strategies. *IEEE Access : Practical Innovations, Open Solutions*, *9*, 57792–57807. doi:10.1109/ACCESS.2021.3073203

Alrasheed, S. H., Aied Alhariri, M., Adubaykhi, S. A., & El Khediri, S. (2022). Cloud Computing Security and Challenges: Issues, Threats, and Solutions. *5th Conference on Cloud and Internet of Things, CIoT 2022*, (pp. 166–172). IEEE. 10.1109/CIoT53061.2022.9766571

Alsinglawi, B., Zheng, L., Kabir, M. A., Islam, M. Z., Swain, D., & Swain, W. (2022). Internet of Things and Microservices in Supply Chain: Cybersecurity Challenges, and Research Opportunities. *Lecture Notes in Networks and Systems, 451 LNNS*, (pp. 556–566). Springer. doi:10.1007/978-3-030-99619-2_52

Arunkumar, M., & Kumar, K. A. (2023). GOSVM: Gannet optimization based support vector machine for malicious attack detection in cloud environment. *International Journal of Information Technology : an Official Journal of Bharati Vidyapeeth's Institute of Computer Applications and Management*, *15*(3), 1653–1660. doi:10.1007/s41870-023-01192-z

Arya, V., Almomani, A. A. D., Mishra, A., Peraković, D., & Rafsanjani, M. K. (2023). *Email Spam Detection Using Naive Bayes and Random Forest Classifiers*., doi:10.1007/978-3-031-22018-0_31

BlackBerry. (2023). *CylanceENDPOINT – Endpoint Protection Powered by Cybersecurity AI*. BlackBerry. https://www.blackberry.com/us/en/products/cylance-endpoint-security/cylance-endpoint

Cassel, G. A. S., Rodrigues, V. F., da Rosa Righi, R., Bez, M. R., Nepomuceno, A. C., & André da Costa, C. (2022). Serverless computing for Internet of Things: A systematic literature review. *Future Generation Computer Systems*, *128*, 299–316. doi:10.1016/j.future.2021.10.020

Caviglione, L., Comito, C., Guarascio, M., & Manco, G. (2023). Emerging challenges and perspectives in Deep Learning model security: A brief survey. *Systems and Soft Computing*, *5*, 200050. doi:10.1016/j.sasc.2023.200050

Chemisto, M., Gutu, T. J., Kalinaki, K., Mwebesa Bosco, D., Egau, P., Fred, K., Tim Oloya, I., & Rashid, K. (2023). Artificial Intelligence for Improved Maternal Healthcare: A Systematic Literature Review. *2023 IEEE AFRICON*, (pp. 1–6). IEEE. doi:10.1109/AFRICON55910.2023.10293674

Chowdhury, R. R., Idris, A. C., & Abas, P. E. (2023). Identifying SH-IoT devices from network traffic characteristics using random forest classifier. *Wireless Networks*. Advance online publication. doi:10.1007/s11276-023-03478-3

Copeland, M. (2021). Azure Sentinel Overview. *Cloud Defense Strategies with Azure Sentinel*, 3–38. doi:10.1007/978-1-4842-7132-2_1

Corallo, A., Lazoi, M., Lezzi, M., & Luperto, A. (2022). Cybersecurity awareness in the context of the Industrial Internet of Things: A systematic literature review. *Computers in Industry*, *137*, 103614. doi:10.1016/j.compind.2022.103614 de Azambuja, A. J. G., Plesker, C., Schützer, K., Anderl, R., Schleich, B., & Almeida, V. R. (2023). Artificial Intelligence-Based Cyber Security in the Context of Industry 4.0—A Survey. *Electronics, 12*(8), 1920. doi:10.3390/electronics12081920

Dheap, V. (2017). *IBM QRadar Advisor with Watson: Revolutionizing the Way Security Analysts Work*. IBM. https://securityintelligence.com/ibm-qradar-advisor-with-watson-revolutionizing-the-way-security-analysts-work/

Dimitrovski, T., Bergman, T., & Zuraniewski, P. (2023). IaC cloud testbed for secure ML based management of IoT services. *Proceedings - 2023 6th Conference on Cloud and Internet of Things, CIoT 2023*, (pp. 239–246). IEEE. 10.1109/CIoT57267.2023.10084903

Douiba, M., Benkirane, S., Guezzaz, A., & Azrour, M. (2023). An improved anomaly detection model for IoT security using decision tree and gradient boosting. *The Journal of Supercomputing*, *79*(3), 3392–3411. doi:10.1007/s11227-022-04783-y

Du, R., Li, Y., Liang, X., & Tian, J. (2022). Support Vector Machine Intrusion Detection Scheme Based on Cloud-Fog Collaboration. *Mobile Networks and Applications*, *27*(1), 431–440. doi:10.1007/s11036-021-01838-x

Fahim, K. E., Kalinaki, K., & Shafik, W. (2023). Electronic Devices in the Artificial Intelligence of the Internet of Medical Things (AIoMT). In Handbook of Security and Privacy of AI-Enabled Healthcare Systems and Internet of Medical Things (1st Edition, pp. 41–62). CRC Press. https://doi.org/ doi:10.1201/9781003370321-3

Fares, N. Y., & Jammal, M. (2023). AI-Driven IoT Systems and Corresponding Ethical Issues. *AI & Society*, 233–248. doi:10.1201/9781003261247-17

Fazeldehkordi, E., & Grønli, T. M. (2022). A Survey of Security Architectures for Edge Computing-Based IoT. *IoT, 3*(3), 332–365. doi:10.3390/iot3030019

Ferrag, A., Maglaras, L., Janicke, H., Tuyishime, E., Balan, T. C., Cotfas, P. A., Cotfas, D. T., & Rekeraho, A. (2023). Enhancing Cloud Security—Proactive Threat Monitoring and Detection Using a SIEM-Based Approach. *Applied Sciences 2023, Vol. 13, Page 12359, 13*(22), 12359. doi:10.3390/app132212359

Furstenau, L. B., Rodrigues, Y. P. R., Sott, M. K., Leivas, P., Dohan, M. S., López-Robles, J. R., Cobo, M. J., Bragazzi, N. L., & Choo, K. K. R. (2023). Internet of things: Conceptual network structure, main challenges and future directions. *Digital Communications and Networks*, *9*(3), 677–687. doi:10.1016/j.dcan.2022.04.027

Gankotiya, A., Agarwal, S. K., Prasad, D., & Kumar, S. (2023). Cloud Computing and IoT Integration: Issues, Challenges and Opportunities. *2023 International Conference on Power, Instrumentation, Control and Computing, PICC 2023*. 10.1109/PICC57976.2023.10142839

Golightly, L., Modesti, P., Garcia, R., & Chang, V. (2023). Securing distributed systems: A survey on access control techniques for cloud, blockchain, IoT and SDN. *Cyber Security and Applications*, *1*, 100015. doi:10.1016/j.csa.2023.100015

Goyal, M., & Srivastava, D. (2021). A Behaviour-Based Authentication to Internet of Things Using Machine Learning. *Design and Development of Efficient Energy Systems*, 245–263. doi:10.1002/9781119761785.ch14

Gürfidan, R., Ersoy, M., & Kilim, O. (2023). *AI-Powered Cyber Attacks Threats and Measures*. (pp. 434–444). Springer. doi:10.1007/978-3-031-31956-3_37

Hadzovic, S., Mrdovic, S., & Radonjic, M. (2023). A Path Towards an Internet of Things and Artificial Intelligence Regulatory Framework. *IEEE Communications Magazine*, *61*(7), 90–96. doi:10.1109/MCOM.002.2200373

Hegde, N., & Manvi, S. S. (2022). Approaches for Detecting and Predicting Attacks Based on Deep and Reinforcement Learning to Improve Information Security. In *Convergence of Deep Learning and Internet of Things* (pp. 113–130). Computing and Technology. doi:10.4018/978-1-6684-6275-1.ch006

Hephzipah, J. J., Vallem, R. R., Sheela, M. S., & Dhanalakshmi, G. (2023). An efficient cyber security system based on flow-based anomaly detection using Artificial neural network. *Mesopotamian Journal of Cyber Security*, 48–56. doi:10.58496/MJCS/2023/009

Holt, T. J., Griffith, M., Turner, N., Greene-Colozzi, E., Chermak, S., & Freilich, J. D. (2023). Assessing nation-state-sponsored cyberattacks using aspects of Situational Crime Prevention. *Criminology & Public Policy*, *22*(4), 825–848. doi:10.1111/1745-9133.12646

Hua, H., Li, Y., Wang, T., Dong, N., Li, W., & Cao, J. (2023). Edge Computing with Artificial Intelligence: A Machine Learning Perspective. *ACM Computing Surveys*, *55*(9), 1–35. doi:10.1145/3555802

Huang, W., Xie, X., Wang, Z., Feng, J. Y., Han, G., & Zhang, W. (2023). ZT-Access: A combining zero trust access control with attribute-based encryption scheme against compromised devices in power IoT environments. *Ad Hoc Networks*, *145*, 103161. doi:10.1016/j.adhoc.2023.103161

Jangjou, M., & Sohrabi, M. K. (2022). A Comprehensive Survey on Security Challenges in Different Network Layers in Cloud Computing. *Archives of Computational Methods in Engineering*, *29*(6), 3587–3608. doi:10.1007/s11831-022-09708-9

Jasim, A. F. J., & Kurnaz, S. (2023). New automatic (IDS) in IoTs with artificial intelligence technique. *Optik (Stuttgart)*, *273*, 170417. doi:10.1016/j.ijleo.2022.170417

Jyoti, K. S., & Chhabra, A. (2023). Machine Learning-Based Threat Identification Systems: Machine Learning-Based IDS Using Decision Tree. In Handbook of Research on Machine Learning-Enabled IoT for Smart Applications Across Industries (pp. 127–151). IGI Global. doi:10.4018/978-1-6684-8785-3.ch007

Kalinaki, K., Fahadi, M., Alli, A. A., Shafik, W., Yasin, M., & Mutwalibi, N. (2023). Artificial Intelligence of Internet of Medical Things (AIoMT) in Smart Cities: A Review of Cybersecurity for Smart Healthcare. In Handbook of Security and Privacy of AI-Enabled Healthcare Systems and Internet of Medical Things (1st Edition, pp. 271–292). CRC Press. https://doi.org/ doi:10.1201/9781003370321-11

Kalinaki, K., Shafik, W., Gutu, T. J. L., & Malik, O. A. (2023). Computer Vision and Machine Learning for Smart Farming and Agriculture Practices. In *Artificial Intelligence Tools and Technologies for Smart Farming and Agriculture Practices* (pp. 79–100). IGI Global. doi:10.4018/978-1-6684-8516-3.ch005

Kalinaki, K., Thilakarathne, N. N., Mubarak, H. R., Malik, O. A., & Abdullatif, M. (2023). Cybersafe Capabilities and Utilities for Smart Cities. In *Cybersecurity for Smart Cities* (pp. 71–86). Springer. doi:10.1007/978-3-031-24946-4_6

Kamil Abed Angesh Anupam, A., & Ali Kamil Abed, C. (2023). Review of security issues in Internet of Things and artificial intelligence-driven solutions. *Security and Privacy*, *6*(3), e285. doi:10.1002/spy2.285

Kassab, W., & Darabkh, K. A. (2020). A–Z survey of Internet of Things: Architectures, protocols, applications, recent advances, future directions and recommendations. *Journal of Network and Computer Applications*, *163*, 102663. doi:10.1016/j.jnca.2020.102663

Khoda Parast, F., Sindhav, C., Nikam, S., Izadi Yekta, H., Kent, K. B., & Hakak, S. (2022). Cloud computing security: A survey of service-based models. *Computers & Security*, *114*, 102580. doi:10.1016/j.cose.2021.102580

Kim, A., Oh, J., Ryu, J., & Lee, K. (2020). A review of insider threat detection approaches with IoT perspective. *IEEE Access : Practical Innovations, Open Solutions*, *8*, 78847–78867. doi:10.1109/ACCESS.2020.2990195

Koblah, D., Acharya, R., Capecci, D., Dizon-Paradis, O., Tajik, S., Ganji, F., Woodard, D., & Forte, D. (2023). A Survey and Perspective on Artificial Intelligence for Security-Aware Electronic Design Automation. *ACM Transactions on Design Automation of Electronic Systems*, *28*(2), 1–57. doi:10.1145/3563391

Koohang, A., Sargent, C. S., Nord, J. H., & Paliszkiewicz, J. (2022). Internet of Things (IoT): From awareness to continued use. *International Journal of Information Management*, *62*, 102442. doi:10.1016/j.ijinfomgt.2021.102442

Kunduru, A. R. (2023). ARTIFICIAL INTELLIGENCE USAGE IN CLOUD APPLICATION PERFORMANCE IMPROVEMENT. *CENTRAL ASIAN JOURNAL OF MATHEMATICAL THEORY AND COMPUTER SCIENCES, 4*(8), 42–47. https://cajmtcs.centralasianstudies.org/index.php/CAJMTCS/article/view/491

Li, J. (2023). IOT security analysis of BDT-SVM multi-classification algorithm. *International Journal of Computers and Applications*, *45*(2), 170–179. doi:10.1080/1206212X.2020.1734313

Mahor, V., Bijrothiya, S., Rawat, R., Kumar, A., Garg, B., & Pachlasiya, K. (2022). IoT and Artificial Intelligence Techniques for Public Safety and Security. *Smart Urban Computing Applications*, 111–126. doi:10.1201/9781003373247-5

Manikanta Narayana, D. S., Bharadwaj Nookala, S., Chopra, S., & Shanmugam, U. (2023). An Adaptive Threat Defence Mechanism Through Self Defending Network to Prevent Hijacking in WiFi Network. *IEEE International Conference on Advances in Electronics, Communication, Computing and Intelligent Information Systems, ICAECIS 2023 - Proceedings*, (pp. 133–138). IEEE. 10.1109/ICAECIS58353.2023.10170470

Manimurugan, S. (2021). IoT-Fog-Cloud model for anomaly detection using improved Naïve Bayes and principal component analysis. *Journal of Ambient Intelligence and Humanized Computing*, *1*, 1–10. doi:10.1007/s12652-020-02723-3

Mazhar, M. S., Saleem, Y., Almogren, A., Arshad, J., Jaffery, M. H., Rehman, A. U., Shafiq, M., & Hamam, H. (2022). Forensic Analysis on Internet of Things (IoT) Device Using Machine-to-Machine (M2M) Framework. *Electronics, 11*(7), 1126. doi:10.3390/electronics11071126

Meiryani, J. Fahlevi, M., & Purnomo, A. (2023). The Integration of Internet of Things (IoT) And Cloud Computing in Finance and Accounting: Systematic Literature Review. *2023 8th International Conference on Business and Industrial Research, ICBIR 2023 - Proceedings*, (pp. 525–529). IEEE. 10.1109/ICBIR57571.2023.10147688

Mishra, S., & Tyagi, A. K. (2022). The Role of Machine Learning Techniques in Internet of Things-Based Cloud Applications. *Internet of Things : Engineering Cyber Physical Human Systems*, 105–135. doi:10.1007/978-3-030-87059-1_4

Mohamed, D., & Ismael, O. (2023). Enhancement of an IoT hybrid intrusion detection system based on fog-to-cloud computing. *Journal of Cloud Computing (Heidelberg, Germany)*, *12*(1), 1–13. doi:10.1186/s13677-023-00420-y

Nagendran, G. A., Raj, R. J. S., Priya, C. S. R., & Singh, H. (2023). IoT Cloud Systems: A Survey. *Proceedings - 5th International Conference on Smart Systems and Inventive Technology, ICSSIT 2023*, (pp. 415–418). IEEE. 10.1109/ICSSIT55814.2023.10060983

Nair, M. M., & Tyagi, A. K. (2023). AI, IoT, blockchain, and cloud computing: The necessity of the future. *Distributed Computing to Blockchain: Architecture, Technology, and Applications*, (pp. 189–206). IEEE. doi:10.1016/B978-0-323-96146-2.00001-2

Nassar, A., & Yilmaz, Y. (2019). Reinforcement learning for adaptive resource allocation in fog RAN for IoT with heterogeneous latency requirements. *IEEE Access : Practical Innovations, Open Solutions*, *7*, 128014–128025. doi:10.1109/ACCESS.2019.2939735

Neha, G., Gupta, P., & Alam, M. A. (2022). Challenges in the Adaptation of IoT Technology. *Intelligent Systems Reference Library*, *210*, 347–369. doi:10.1007/978-3-030-76653-5_19

Nithiyanandam, N., Rajesh, M., Sitharthan, R., Shanmuga Sundar, D., Vengatesan, K., & Madurakavi, K. (2022). Optimization of Performance and Scalability Measures across Cloud Based IoT Applications with Efficient Scheduling Approach. *International Journal of Wireless Information Networks*, *29*(4), 442–453. doi:10.1007/s10776-022-00568-5

Oleiwi, H. W., Mhawi, D. N., & Al-Raweshidy, H. (2022). MLTs-ADCNs: Machine Learning Techniques for Anomaly Detection in Communication Networks. *IEEE Access : Practical Innovations, Open Solutions*, *10*, 91006–91017. doi:10.1109/ACCESS.2022.3201869

Pandey, N. K., Kumar, K., Saini, G., & Mishra, A. K. (2023). Security issues and challenges in cloud of things-based applications for industrial automation. *Annals of Operations Research*. Advance online publication. doi:10.1007/s10479-023-05285-7 PMID:37361100

Park, S. H., Yun, S. W., Jeon, S. E., Park, N. E., Shim, H. Y., Lee, Y. R., Lee, S. J., Park, T. R., Shin, N. Y., Kang, M. J., & Lee, I. G. (2022). Performance Evaluation of Open-Source Endpoint Detection and Response Combining Google Rapid Response and Osquery for Threat Detection. *IEEE Access : Practical Innovations, Open Solutions*, *10*, 20259–20269. doi:10.1109/ACCESS.2022.3152574

Peiris, C., & Pillai, B. (2022). Microsoft Azure Cloud Threat Prevention Framework. In hreat Hunting in the Cloud: Defending AWS, Azure and Other Cloud Platforms Against Cyberattacks (pp. 101–182). Wiley.

Qu, H., Jiang, J., Zhao, J., Zhang, Y., & Yang, J. (2020). A novel method for network traffic classification based on robust support vector machine. *Transactions on Emerging Telecommunications Technologies*, *31*(11), e4092. doi:10.1002/ett.4092

Raj, H., Kumar, M., Kumar, P., Singh, A., & Verma, O. P. (2022). Issues and Challenges Related to Privacy and Security in Healthcare Using IoT, Fog, and Cloud Computing. *Advanced Healthcare Systems: Empowering Physicians with IoT-Enabled Technologies*, 21–32. doi:10.1002/9781119769293.ch2

Rasool, R. U., Ahmad, H. F., Rafique, W., Qayyum, A., & Qadir, J. (2022). Security and privacy of internet of medical things: A contemporary review in the age of surveillance, botnets, and adversarial ML. *Journal of Network and Computer Applications*, *201*, 103332. doi:10.1016/j.jnca.2022.103332

Rath, M., Tripathy, N., Tripathy, S. S., Sharma, V., & Garanayak, M. K. (2023). Development in IoT and Cloud Computing Using Artificial Intelligence. *Integration of Cloud Computing with Emerging Technologies*, 118–129. doi:10.1201/9781003341437-12

Reichert, C. (2017). *Cisco launches IoT Threat Defense*. ZDNET. https://www.zdnet.com/article/cisco-launches-iot-threat-defense/#google_vignette

Safi, M., Dadkhah, S., Shoeleh, F., Mahdikhani, H., Molyneaux, H., & Ghorbani, A. A. (2022). A Survey on IoT Profiling, Fingerprinting, and Identification. *ACM Transactions on Internet of Things*, *3*(4), 1–39. doi:10.1145/3539736

Sagu, A., Gill, N. S., Gulia, P., Singh, P. K., & Hong, W. C. (2023). Design of Metaheuristic Optimization Algorithms for Deep Learning Model for Secure IoT Environment. *Sustainability, 15*(3), 2204. doi:10.3390/su15032204

Sarhan, M., Layeghy, S., Moustafa, N., & Portmann, M. (2023). Cyber Threat Intelligence Sharing Scheme Based on Federated Learning for Network Intrusion Detection. *Journal of Network and Systems Management*, *31*(1), 1–23. doi:10.1007/s10922-022-09691-3

Sarker, I. H., Khan, A. I., Abushark, Y. B., & Alsolami, F. (2023). Internet of Things (IoT) Security Intelligence: A Comprehensive Overview, Machine Learning Solutions and Research Directions. *Mobile Networks and Applications*, *28*(1), 296–312. doi:10.1007/s11036-022-01937-3

Shafik, W. (2023). A Comprehensive Cybersecurity Framework for Present and Future Global Information Technology Organizations. In Effective Cybersecurity Operations for Enterprise-Wide Systems (pp. 56–79). Springer. doi:10.4018/978-1-6684-9018-1.ch002

Shafik, W., & Kalinaki, K. (2023). Smart City Ecosystem: An Exploration of Requirements, Architecture, Applications, Security, and Emerging Motivations. In Handbook of Research on Network-Enabled IoT Applications for Smart City Services (pp. 75–98). IGI Global. doi:10.4018/979-8-3693-0744-1.ch005

Sharma, T., & Sharma, P. (2023). AI-Based Cybersecurity Threat Detection and Prevention. In *Perspectives on Artificial Intelligence in Times of Turbulence* (pp. 81–98). Theoretical Background to Applications. doi:10.4018/978-1-6684-9814-9.ch006

Sharmila, K., Kumar, P., Bhushan, S., Kumar, M., & Alazab, M. (2023). Secure Key Management and Mutual Authentication Protocol for Wireless Sensor Network by Linking Edge Devices using Hybrid Approach. *Wireless Personal Communications*, *130*(4), 2935–2957. doi:10.1007/s11277-023-10410-7

Sohal, M., Bharany, S., Sharma, S., Maashi, M. S., & Aljebreen, M. (2022). A Hybrid Multi-Cloud Framework Using the IBBE Key Management System for Securing Data Storage. *Sustainability, 14*(20), 13561. doi:10.3390/su142013561

Stellios, I., Kotzanikolaou, P., & Psarakis, M. (2019). Advanced persistent threats and zero-day exploits in industrial internet of things. *Advanced Sciences and Technologies for Security Applications*, (pp. 47–68). Springer. doi:10.1007/978-3-030-12330-7_3

Tabrizchi, H., & Kuchaki Rafsanjani, M. (2020). A survey on security challenges in cloud computing: Issues, threats, and solutions. *The Journal of Supercomputing*, *76*(12), 9493–9532. doi:10.1007/s11227-020-03213-1

Taghavirashidizadeh, A., Zavvar, M., Moghadaspour, M., Jafari, M., Garoosi, H., & Zavvar, M. H. (2022). Anomaly Detection In IoT Networks Using Hybrid Method Based On PCA-XGBoost. *Proceedings - 2022 8th International Iranian Conference on Signal Processing and Intelligent Systems, ICSPIS 2022*. IEEE. 10.1109/ICSPIS56952.2022.10043986

Tanimoto, S., Hori, S., Sato, H., & Kanai, A. (2023). Operation Management Method of Software Defined Perimeter for Promoting Zero-Trust Model. *Proceedings - 2023 IEEE/ACIS 21st International Conference on Software Engineering Research, Management and Applications, SERA 2023*, (pp. 440–445). IEEE. 10.1109/SERA57763.2023.10197716

Tsouplaki, A. (2023). Internet of Cloud (IoC): The Need of Raising Privacy and Security Awareness. *Lecture Notes in Business Information Processing*. Springer. doi:10.1007/978-3-031-33080-3_36

Uddin, M. S., & Bansal, J. C. (Eds.). (2022). *Computer Vision and Machine Learning in Agriculture* (Vol. 2)., doi:10.1007/978-981-16-9991-7

Walczak, R., Koszewski, K., Olszewski, R., Ejsmont, K., & Kálmán, A. (2023). Acceptance of IoT Edge-Computing-Based Sensors in Smart Cities for Universal Design Purposes. *Energies, 16*(3), 1024. doi:10.3390/en16031024

Waqas, M., Kumar, K., Laghari, A. A., Saeed, U., Rind, M. M., Shaikh, A. A., Hussain, F., Rai, A., & Qazi, A. Q. (2022). Botnet attack detection in Internet of Things devices over cloud environment via machine learning. *Concurrency and Computation, 34*(4), e6662. doi:10.1002/cpe.6662

Wójcicki, K., Biegańska, M., Paliwoda, B., & Górna, J. (2022). Internet of Things in Industry: Research Profiling, Application, Challenges and Opportunities—A Review. *Energies, 15*(5), 1806. doi:10.3390/en15051806

Zareen, M. S., Tahir, S., & Aslam, B. (2024). Authentication and Authorization of IoT Edge Devices Using Artificial Intelligence. *IFIP International Internet of Things Conference*, 442–453. 10.1007/978-3-031-45878-1_32

Zhang, H., Wang, J., Zhang, H., & Bu, C. (2024). Security computing resource allocation based on deep reinforcement learning in serverless multi-cloud edge computing. *Future Generation Computer Systems, 151*, 152–161. doi:10.1016/j.future.2023.09.016

ENDNOTES

1 https://www.darktrace.com/
2 http://www.blackberry.com/
3 https://www.ibm.com/qradar
4 https://azure.microsoft.com/
5 https://www.tenable.com/

Chapter 3
Deep Learning for IoT Security: Applications and Challenges

Aized Amin Soofi
National Textile University, Faisalabad, Pakistan

Haseeb Ahmad
National Textile University, Faisalabad, Pakistan

ABSTRACT

The term internet of things (IoT) denotes the advanced phase of the internet, wherein a worldwide communication infrastructure is established between individuals and machines. The IoT is now being developed as a worldwide infrastructure that has the potential to significantly transform various aspects of human life. Nevertheless, the interconnected nature of IoT systems and the involvement of other disciplines in their implementation have presented novel security obstacles. However, the utilization of deep learning techniques holds significant importance in enhancing the security of IoT systems. This transformation goes beyond the facilitation of secure communication between devices, as it enables the development of intelligent systems that prioritize security. In this chapter, the basic architecture of IoT has been discussed with its applications and security challenges. Different deep-learning techniques for securing IoT devices with their strengths and weaknesses have also been explored.

IoT OVERVIEW

The Internet of Things (IoT) is a concept that involves interconnected devices that can communicate, collect data from their surroundings, analyze that data, and share it to accomplish specified objectives. Currently, the IoT has played a pivotal role in

DOI: 10.4018/979-8-3693-0766-3.ch003

facilitating automation across all facets of our daily existence. This encompasses the incorporation of intelligent home technologies such as air conditioning, security systems, lighting, and several other services and gadgets (Aldahmani et al., 2023). Furthermore, it has significantly influenced multiple facets of human existence, resulting in the development of intelligent education systems, advanced healthcare solutions, innovative agricultural practices, and sophisticated industrial processes, among others. The IoT sector is anticipated to experience significant expansion, with an estimated 22 billion intelligent gadgets projected by the end of 2025 (Yunana et al., 2021). Figure 1 illustrates the concept of IoT, where people and things can be connected through various paths/networks and services, regardless of time or location.

The concept of the IoT encompasses the interrelationships of many objects, such as industrial systems, intelligent sensors, autonomous vehicles, mechanisms, terminals, and mechanical systems (Sharma et al., 2020; Zhang et al., 2023). IoT devices possess the capability to store a wide range of crucial information, including but not limited to sound data, light intensity, temperature readings, electricity consumption, mechanical motions, chemical reactions, impact measurements, biological changes, and geo-location data (Gaurav et al., 2023). IoT devices are utilized to facilitate machine-to-machine communication, machine-to-human engagement, and human-to-human activity.

IoT systems are intricate and consist of integrated configurations. Hence, it is resilient to uphold the security need in the extensive attack surface of the IoT system. To meet the security requirement, solutions must incorporate comprehensive considerations (Sarker et al., 2023). Nevertheless, IoT devices primarily operate in an unsupervised setting. As a result, an unauthorized individual may gain physical access to these devices. IoT devices typically connect over wireless networks, which might be vulnerable to eavesdropping, allowing unauthorized individuals to intercept private information transmitted across the communication channel (Salman & Arslan, 2023). The dissemination of information will occur within the public domains, specifically the network layer and application layer (Yazdinejad et al., 2023). If there is a lack of an efficient mechanism for safeguarding information, it may be susceptible to theft, hence posing a risk to privacy. Consequently, ensuring security and privacy are important considerations for IoT-enabled devices.

Security breaches have become a significant concern in the ever-changing realm of the IoT, highlighting the susceptibility of networked devices and systems (Siwakoti et al., 2023). Prominent examples involve extensive Distributed Denial of Service (DDoS) attacks that use compromised IoT devices to inundate networks with excessive traffic, resulting in massive outages of services (de Oliveira et al., 2023). Furthermore, illicit entry into IoT devices has resulted in data breaches, which have exposed confidential data and jeopardized user privacy (P. Kumar et al., 2023). Malicious actors exploit vulnerabilities in inadequately secured devices to perform

Figure 1. IoT definition

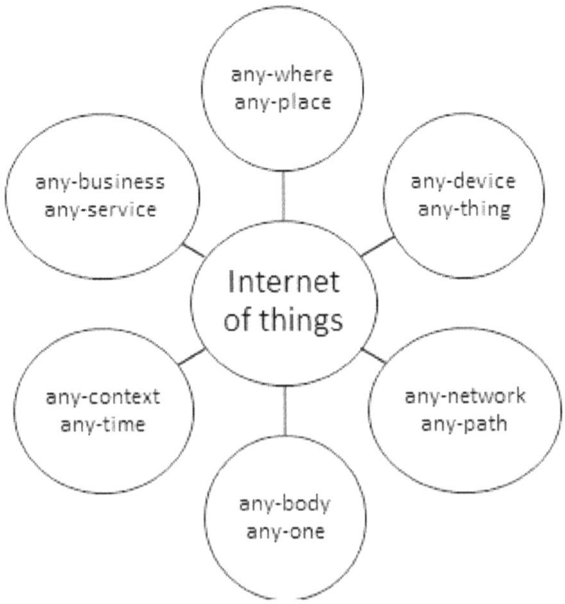

code injections, allowing them to change functionalities or obtain unauthorized control (Kandhro et al., 2023). These breaches have the ability to attack whole networks, compromising essential infrastructure and services. Given the ongoing growth of the IoT ecosystem, it is crucial to comprehend and tackle these security risks in order to safeguard the reliability, privacy, and accessibility of IoT implementations (Sarker et al., 2023). To effectively counteract potential dangers in the IoT, it is necessary to adopt a proactive strategy that incorporates strong encryption, frequent software upgrades, and strict access controls (Shiraly et al., 2024). This approach will strengthen the interconnected network of the IoT and protect it from emerging risks. However, implementing these measures is challenging due to the diverse range of IoT devices. Hence, it is important to ascertain a resolution for ensuring the security of IoT gadgets.

IoT ARCHITECTURE

The structure of the IoT can be generically classified into three layers: the application layer, the network layer, and the perception layer (Subashini et al., 2024). Several IoT solutions incorporate various support technologies for networks, including network processing, third-party middleware, and distributed technology, which serve as a processing layer. The layers of the IoT structure were further elucidated in an examination of potential threats and needs for ensuring the security of IoT architecture (Bathla & Kaur, 2024). The three layers of IoT architecture have been presented in Figure 2. The three tier IoT architecture with three levels of IoT security threats has been shown in figure 3.

Application Layer

This layer is the top-level layer of IoT architecture, and it is directly accessible to the end user. The application layer's objective is to globally manage and supply applications based on information acquired by the perception layer, which is then processed by the information processing unit (Kaur et al., 2023). It enables end users

Figure 2. IoT three-layer architecture

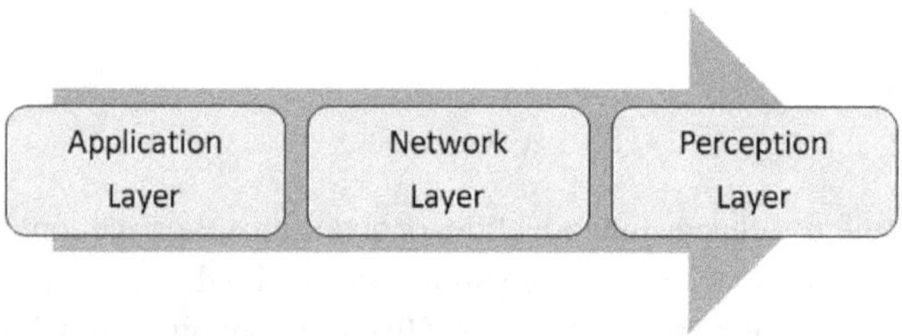

Figure 3. IoT three-tier architecture with security threats

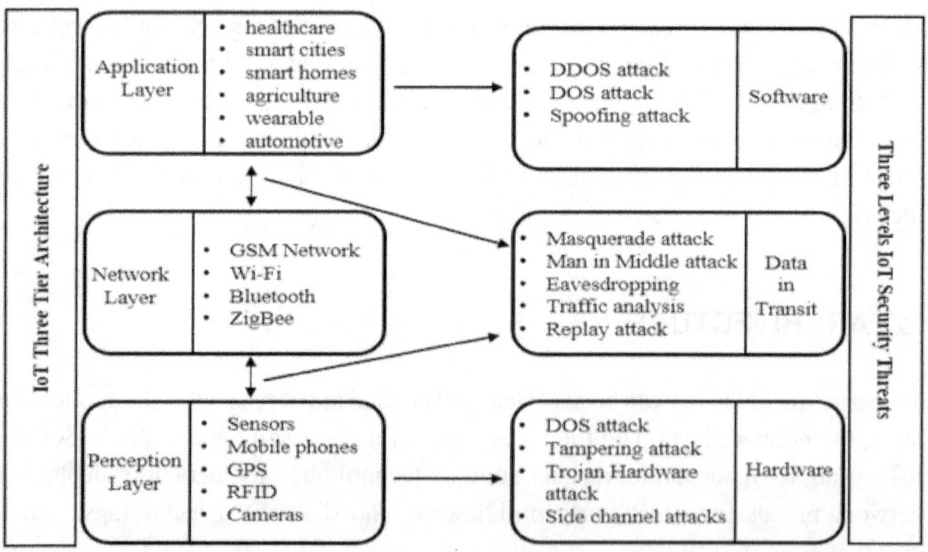

to access personalized services across the network using different handheld devices and terminal equipment, based on their specific requirements.

Network Layer

The network layer is a crucial component of an IoT system. The network layer, also known as the transmission layer, facilitates the transfer and routing of data from sensor devices to the IoT system (Saied et al., 2024). The network layer is responsible for facilitating communication between multiple physical devices in an IoT system. It manages the network and ensures the flow of information by utilizing various communication protocols.

Perception Layer

The perception layer is accountable for the detection and acquisition of data via sensor nodes and other hardware components (Štuikys & Burbaitė, 2024). The sensors are responsible for gathering, detecting, and analyzing various types of data, including position, vibration, humidity, wind speed, and airborne dust particles, from the surrounding environment. Subsequently, they transfer this gathered information to the network layer.

IoT APPLICATIONS

The applications of IoT have not only revolutionized our interactions with the environment but also accelerated significant transformations in diverse sectors, including healthcare, agriculture, transportation, and smart cities. As we begin to explore IoT applications, it becomes clear that this technology is changing our world, providing several opportunities and problems, and has the ability to alter how we connect and make decisions based on data. The typical application of IoT has been depicted in Figure 4.

Smart Healthcare

In the dynamic field of healthcare, the IoT has emerged as a powerful catalyst, reshaping our approach to patient care and medical services. The utilization of IoT technology in healthcare provides numerous advantages that surpass the limitations of conventional healthcare systems. The utilization of IoT devices and sensors holds the capability to augment patient monitoring, boost treatment outcomes, optimize operational operations, and maybe aid in disease prevention.

Figure 4. Typical application of IoT

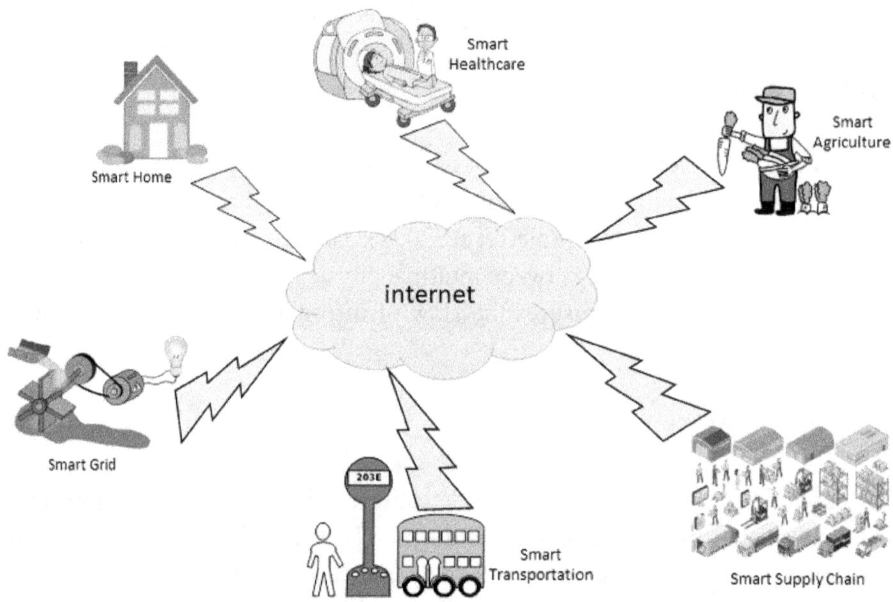

The extensive use of technology in healthcare not only enhances the standard of patient care but also alleviates the strain on healthcare systems, making it a crucial component in tackling the difficulties posed by an aging population and the continuously growing need for healthcare services. In recent years, there has been a surge in the use of IoT devices within the realm of health applications. The IoT system is increasingly emerging as a pivotal tool in the field of healthcare (Hammad et al., 2022; Qahtan et al., 2022).

A significant application of IoT in the healthcare sector is remote patient monitoring (Sangeethalakshmi et al., 2023). This involves the use of wearable devices such as smartwatches and health-monitoring patches to gather real-time data. This enables healthcare personnel to remotely monitor patients' vital signs and health parameters (Al-Nbhany et al., 2024). Intelligent medical devices, such as interconnected insulin pumps and pacemakers, provide the immediate transmission of data to enhance patient care and monitoring (Ratnakar et al., 2024). The IoT enables telehealth and telemedicine, allowing for remote consultations and diagnostics, hence decreasing the necessity for in-person visits. In addition, the IoT facilitates medication adherence by utilizing intelligent pill dispensers that transmit reminders and notifications to healthcare practitioners or family members in the event of missed doses (Sahu et al., 2023).

IoT also plays a crucial role in the hospital environment by facilitating asset management, improving resource allocation, and ensuring the availability of essential equipment (Rejeb et al., 2023). Smart hospitals utilize integrated systems to facilitate patient tracking, automate workflows, and enhance energy economy. Smart IoT sensors can find problems and help emergency responders in homes or care facilities better in cases of falls and caring for the elders (Mohan et al., 2024). Health and wellness applications, like as fitness trackers and smart scales, help to the promotion of overall well-being (Bathla & Kaur, 2024). The huge amount of data that IoT devices produce makes analytics and predictive maintenance possible. This helps find health problems early and makes sure that medical equipment works well. The implementation of IoT technology in healthcare facilities improves environmental monitoring by addressing aspects such as temperature, humidity, and air quality to ensure patient comfort and safety (Chataut et al., 2023). However, the integration of IoT in healthcare necessitates meticulous consideration of security, privacy, and interoperability standards to protect sensitive patient data and guarantee smooth communication between devices and systems.

Smart Grid

The IoT has become a prominent factor in the smart grid due to increasing energy needs and the need to shift towards sustainable, efficient, and resilient power systems. The smart grid, an upgraded and technologically sophisticated power distribution network, depends on the IoT as a crucial element to transform the energy industry (Alavikia & Shabro, 2022). The utilization of IoT technologies provides utilities, grid operators, and customers with immediate data, connectivity, and automation, thereby allowing for a more prompt and intelligent electrical infrastructure. This connectivity not only improves energy efficiency and grid dependability, but also allows for the integration of renewable energy sources, electric vehicles, and demand-side control.

The electrical grid transforms into a dynamic and responsive network by implementing IoT devices like sensors and smart meters (Rao et al., 2024). The real-time monitoring of power flow, consumption patterns, and the prompt discovery of defects or outages improve grid management and ensure its reliability (Mazhar et al., 2023). Smart meters, which are connected with IoT capabilities, allow utilities and consumers to obtain up-to-date data on energy usage. This promotes the ability to make well-informed decisions and adopt energy-efficient practices (Oprea & Bâra, 2023). IoT-enabled demand response systems permit intelligent gadgets and appliances to autonomously regulate their energy usage during periods of high demand, thereby aiding in the balancing of electrical loads. IoT sensors installed on grid components provide predictive maintenance, which allows for the timely detection of possible problems, optimizing maintenance schedules and reducing downtime (Qays et al., 2023).

The incorporation of renewable energy sources is made easier by the IoT, which enables the continuous monitoring and fine-tuning of the power grid to meet the fluctuations in sources like solar and wind power (Jahangir et al., 2023). Energy storage devices, controlled via the IoT, have a vital function in maintaining the stability of the power grid. They store surplus energy when demand is low and release it when demand is high (Renugadevi et al., 2023). In addition, the IoT improves grid security through the surveillance of network traffic, identification of irregularities, and provision of timely alerts regarding potential cyber risks. The IoT facilitates effective data sharing across grid components, such as smart meters, substations, and control centers, over communication networks (Ghiasi et al., 2023). Moreover, the IoT plays a significant role in overseeing the electric vehicle charging infrastructure by efficiently scheduling charging sessions according to the grid's power requirements and the availability of renewable energy sources. Grid analytics, utilizing data generated by the IoT, provide significant insights into the performance, demand patterns, and efficiency enhancements of utility systems (Dimitriadou et al., 2023). This supports the use of data-driven decision-making by utilities and regulatory authorities. IoT implementation in smart grids not only updates the grid infrastructure but also promotes a more sustainable, robust, and adaptable energy ecology.

Smart Homes

The utilization of IoT components is employed in the implementation of intelligent residential dwellings. The ability to remotely monitor and operate household IoT devices and systems, such as refrigerators, televisions, doors, air conditioners, and heating systems, has become readily accessible (Babangida et al., 2022). A smart home system possesses the capability to comprehend and react to alterations in its environment, shown by its ability to autonomously activate air conditioning units following weather forecasts and unlock doors with facial recognition technology. The utilization of IoT in smart homes not only improves convenience but also promotes energy conservation, security, and a more streamlined and interconnected living environment. With the ongoing advancement of technology, the potential for developing highly intelligent and customized homes is practically boundless.

IoT-enabled gadgets such as smart thermostats, lighting systems, and locks enable homeowners to automate and remotely control many parts of their living spaces in a smart home environment (Orfanos et al., 2023). Smart lighting systems enable users to customize brightness and hue, resulting in improved energy efficiency and unique lighting experiences (Huang et al., 2023). Smart thermostats utilize machine learning algorithms to optimize heating and cooling based on customer preferences, and also provide the convenience of remote control via smartphones (Malik et al., 2023). The use of IoT devices, such as smart cameras and motion sensors, greatly enhances home security by providing real-time monitoring and the ability to control the system remotely (Vasilescu et al., 2023). The IoT enables consumers to remotely control and monitor domestic equipment such as refrigerators and ovens. Health and wellness monitoring is also included into smart homes, where wearable devices are integrated into the IoT system to monitor vital signs and exercise habits (Shafi & Mallinson, 2023). Automated window coverings, water leak detection systems, and pet care gadgets enhance the overall usefulness of smart houses. Centralized smart home hubs, frequently paired with voice assistants, simplify the management of diverse IoT devices, enabling operations to be effortlessly executed using voice commands (Rane et al., 2023). Essentially, the IoT turns traditional houses into smart, networked spaces where people have more control, efficiency, and safety than ever before provided by a wide variety of interoperable devices and systems.

Smart Transportation

The advent of IoT technology has made it possible to achieve the implementation of intelligent transport systems. The primary goal of smart transportation is to effectively regulate urban traffic by utilizing data collected from interconnected sensors situated in various locations (Liu & Ke, 2023). The utilization of data analytics in the context of smart transport has the potential to effectively optimize cargo schedules, enhance road safety, and optimize delivery time. Connected vehicles, equipped with IoT capabilities, form a network via which they may connect with one other and with infrastructure (Whig et al., 2024). This allows them to exchange real-time data regarding traffic conditions and road hazards.

IoT-enabled car telematics collect and transmit vital information about a vehicle's whereabouts, velocity, and fuel usage, enabling streamlined fleet management and maintenance scheduling (Gupta et al., 2023). IoT sensors integrated into urban roadways and infrastructure aid in efficient traffic management by gathering data on traffic movement, congestion, and parking availability. IoT-powered smart parking solutions offer up-to-date data on parking space availability via mobile applications, resulting in reduced search durations and mitigated traffic congestion. Intelligent Transportation Systems (ITS), utilizing the IoT, combine several technologies to enhance the efficiency of traffic signals, electronic toll collection, and the distribution of real-time information (Dui et al., 2024). The utilization of IoT sensors on vehicles enables predictive maintenance, which improves reliability by facilitating timely repairs and reducing the likelihood of breakdowns. The IoT enhances public transportation networks by providing up-to-the-minute data on timetables, delays, and passenger capacity, hence enhancing overall operational efficiency and dependability (Y. Wang et al., 2024).

Interconnected infrastructure components, such as traffic lights and road signs outfitted with IoT sensors, improve safety by delivering up-to-date information to drivers regarding road conditions and possible dangers (Mohandass et al., 2023). Within the domain of self-driving vehicles, the IoT plays a crucial role by enabling communication between vehicles and their environment (Bautista & Mester, 2023). The implementation of IoT in smart transportation enhances the effectiveness and security of transportation systems, while also aiding in the reduction of traffic congestion, minimizing emissions, and fostering a sustainable and interconnected mobility ecosystem (Oladimeji et al., 2023). The continuous advancement of technology presents great potential for the IoT to revolutionize the transportation sector. This will ultimately result in the development of smarter, more efficient, and environmentally friendly transportation systems.

Smart Agriculture

The utilization of the IoT in smart agriculture, commonly known as "precision agriculture" or "agriculture 4.0," is fundamentally transforming the methods employed in crop cultivation and livestock rearing. The utilization of IoT technology has various advantages, such as enhanced agricultural productivity, optimized utilization of resources, and the promotion of sustainable practices. The application of IoT technologies has the potential to enhance the agricultural sector. The implementation of IoT sensors has the potential to facilitate real-time monitoring within the agriculture industry (Rastegari et al., 2023). These sensors can gather valuable data about humidity levels, temperature levels, weather conditions, and moisture levels. IoT-enabled smart irrigation systems autonomously monitor soil moisture and meteorological conditions, facilitating accurate and sustainable water management in agricultural settings (Gupta & Nahar, 2023). The utilization of intelligent collars or tags improves livestock monitoring by offering immediate observations on the well-being and conduct of animals, hence enhancing overall farm administration.

Unmanned Aerial Vehicles (UAVs) integrated with IoT sensors and cameras enable aerial agricultural monitoring, providing precise data on crop condition, growth trends, and any problems (Sun et al., 2023). Automated machinery and robotics, powered by IoT technology, optimize diverse operations such as planting and harvesting, enhancing efficiency and accuracy while diminishing the need for human labor. IoT-enabled tracking is used to optimize the supply chain, guaranteeing the freshness and quality of agricultural products throughout the whole production and distribution process (AlZubi & Galyna, 2023). The utilization of IoT devices allows farmers to access up-to-date weather and climatic data, enabling them to predict alterations and organize their actions accordingly. Smart greenhouses utilize IoT technology to observe and regulate environmental factors, hence enhancing the cultivation of crops in controlled environments (Zaguia, 2023). Utilizing remote sensing and IoT-connected cameras, crop health imaging facilitates the early identification of illnesses and nutrient deficits, allowing for precise treatments.

Smart Supply Chain

One significant utilization of IoT technology in practical contexts involves the advancement of commercial procedures that are more streamlined and adaptable compared to previous methods. The advancement of IoT-embedded sensors, such as Radio Frequency Identification (RFID) and Near Field Communication (NFC), facilitates the communication between IoT sensors integrated within products and company administrators (Pal, 2023).

Furthermore, the implementation of IoT applications in smart supply chain management enables organizations to function with greater efficiency, save expenses, and improve customer satisfaction. The advancement of IoT technology is leading to supply chain operations that rely increasingly on data and are able to adapt quickly to changes in the business environment, resulting in increased agility and resilience.

IoT Security Challenges

Different industries have implemented various IoT applications, each with its own set of industry standards and specifications. However, there is currently a lack of a uniform standard for IoT security. Several organizations, including IEEE and the European Telecommunications Standards Institute (ETSI), endeavor to establish standards for security in the IoT. The literature has documented the progress made in establishing security standards for the IoT (Schiller et al., 2022). At now, IoT-based frameworks primarily operate independently inside small networks, with a limited number of frameworks designed for large-scale networks. As the IoT continues to advance, smaller networks progressively merge to form a larger interconnected network. The establishment of robust security measures is crucial for ensuring the protection of a vast IoT network (Douiba et al., 2023). Addressing the security problems associated with IoT development is imperative for ensuring its long-term sustainability. Some of the major security challenges are shown in Figure 5. When establishing an effective strategy for IoT security, it is important to consider the following main security properties.

Figure 5. IoT security challenges

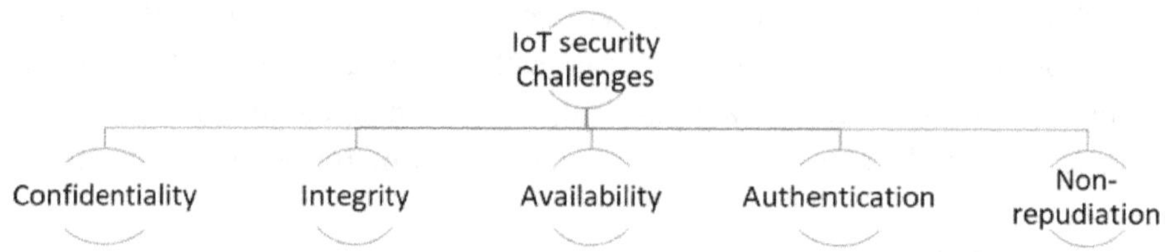

Confidentiality

The preservation of confidentiality is an essential security attribute of IoT systems. The IoT devices can store and transmit confidential data that must remain undisclosed to unauthorized individuals. Various techniques and protocols have been suggested within the realm of the IoT to offer secure and confidential services for sensitive IoT data (Picoto et al., 2023). Ensuring confidentiality can be achieved through the implementation of good practices such as data encryption, authentication, and authorization processes.

Integrity

The preservation of data integrity is a crucial security measure in IoT systems, as the exchange of sensitive information across networked devices is susceptible to unauthorized modification or substitution by malicious actors. The data integrity service is responsible for verifying the authenticity and integrity of information sent between devices, ensuring that it has not been falsified or altered by unauthorized individuals (Juma et al., 2023). The implementation of read and write protection mechanisms can potentially serve as an effective solution for addressing these difficulties. Checksum and Cyclic Redundancy Check (CRC) are fundamental error detection methods utilized to verify the integrity and precision of a data segment.

Availability

The provision of services by IoT systems necessitates the consistent availability of those services exclusively to authorized organizations. The presence of availability is a crucial aspect in ensuring the effective implementation of IoT systems. Nevertheless, IoT systems and devices remain susceptible to many threats, including Denial of Service (DoS) attacks and active jamming, which can result in their unavailability (Sarker et al., 2022).

Authentication

It is imperative to confirm the identity of entities thoroughly before undertaking any subsequent processes. However, the authentication needs of IoT systems vary depending on the specific system. In an IoT system, authentication mechanisms must exhibit a high level of robustness (Adeel et al., 2022). This is particularly crucial when a service inside the system aims to provide robust security as opposed to prioritizing flexibility.

Non-Repudiation

The purpose of the non-repudiation feature is to generate access logs that can be used as conclusive evidence in instances when users or objects are unable to deny their involvement in an action (Divya et al., 2022). In the context of IoT systems, non-repudiation is typically not seen as a fundamental security attribute. However, non-repudiation is a significant security attribute in certain situations, such as payment systems, where neither party can deny a payment transaction.

DEEP LEARNING (DL) METHODS FOR IoT SECURITY

DL is a sub-field of machine learning (ML) that employs multiple layers of non-linear processing for discriminative or generative feature abstraction and transformation to analyze patterns. DL methods are commonly referred to as hierarchical learning methods due to their ability to capture hierarchical representations inside a deep architecture. The integration of DL applications into IoT frameworks has emerged as a significant area of research in recent times. When comparing DL to traditional ML, one notable advantage of DL is its superior performance in handling large-scale datasets (Khan et al., 2022). Given the vast amount of data generated by various IoT frameworks, DL algorithms are well-suited for analyzing and processing this data.

DL provides a wide range of applications that enhance the security and resilience of IoT ecosystems, making it a formidable asset in the domain of IoT security (Nadhan & Jacob, 2024). An important use of DL algorithms is in anomaly detection, where they analyze network traffic and device activity in real-time to quickly identify and prevent potential intrusions or cyber threats (Liao et al., 2024). Furthermore, these models demonstrate exceptional performance in identifying and analyzing code patterns and network connections, hence enhancing the security of IoT devices against harmful software. DL's expertise encompasses authentication and access control, bolstering security measures using biometric authentication and behavioral analysis to strengthen protection against illegal access (R. Kumar et al., 2023). DL techniques are employed to enhance the security of communication between IoT devices by employing encryption and decryption methods. This ensures that the sent data remains confidential and maintains its integrity.

DL-based video analytics enhances physical security by enabling surveillance and detecting potential threats (Berroukham et al., 2023). Additionally, firmware and software vulnerabilities are proactively mitigated by discovering security gaps through code analysis. DL plays a role in safeguarding privacy by employing federated learning, which enables model training without revealing raw data (Khan et al., 2023). Behavior analysis is crucial in identifying trends that indicate malicious behaviors in DL. Additionally, supply chain security is strengthened by continuously checking the integrity of components throughout the whole lifespan of the device (Hosseinnia Shavaki & Ebrahimi Ghahnavieh, 2023). DL models utilize extensive volumes of threat intelligence data to predict and mitigate potential risks, providing a proactive approach to defense. It is important to recognize that although DL is a powerful tool, a comprehensive security approach that includes encryption, secure protocols, regular upgrades, and user education is necessary to fully safeguard against the ever-changing dangers in the IoT environment (Pham et al., 2024). DL algorithms have the potential to facilitate the establishment of deep connections inside the IoT ecosystem (Sharma et al., 2024). Deep linking is a standardized protocol that enables seamless communication between IoT devices and their corresponding applications, facilitating automatic interaction without the need for human intervention. Table 1 summarize the DL techniques with their advantages, disadvantages and security applications in IoT environment. Some of the potential DL techniques for IoT security have been discussed below.

Convolution Neural Networks (CNN)

CNNs were initially developed to reduce the number of data parameters utilized in a conventional Artificial Neural Network (ANN). A CNN is composed of two distinct types of layers includes; convolutional layers and pooling layers (Gong et al., 2024). The convolutional layers perform convolution operations on data parameters using several filters that are of the same size (Bhatt et al., 2021). The pooling layers are responsible for down-sampling the subsequent layers by utilizing either max pooling or average pooling techniques to reduce their sizes (Kattenborn et al., 2021).

CNNs can undergo training processes that enable them to effectively identify and discern patterns within the data that is generated by IoT sensors. Through the process of acquiring knowledge about the typical functioning of these devices, CNNs possess the ability to identify abnormalities or departures from the established regular patterns (Xu et al., 2021). This capability aids in the detection of unauthorized access, malicious activity, or anomalous behaviors that may be indicative of a security breach.

CNNs can undergo training using diverse datasets about various categories of malware, hence facilitating their ability to identify and discern bad code or behavioral patterns. When included in IoT security systems, these CNNs can detect and prevent malicious activities associated with malware.

Recurrent Neural Networks (RNNs)

RNNs are considered to be a crucial category of DL techniques. RNNs were initially introduced as a solution for processing sequential input. In numerous applications, the prediction of the present output relies on the examination of the correlations derived from multiple preceding samples. The output of the neural network is contingent upon both the current and previous inputs (Almiani et al., 2020).

The investigation of RNNs and their various adaptations holds great importance in enhancing the security of IoT systems, particularly in addressing threats that are based on time series data. IoT devices provide substantial volumes of sequential data from multiple origins, including network traffic flows. This characteristic is crucial for identifying various potential network assaults (Ullah & Mahmoud, 2022).

RNNs have the potential to aid in the development of behavioral biometric profiles for authorized users of IoT devices (Narayana et al., 2023). RNNs have the potential to enhance multi-factor authentication systems through the examination of user interaction patterns over some time (Ackerson et al., 2021). Furthermore, RNNs possess the capability to examine network data and discern patterns that are indicative of harmful actions or illegal access, in addition to their application in intrusion detection. This measure can effectively mitigate the occurrence of data breaches and unauthorized access.

Deep Autoencoders (AEs)

A deep AE refers to a type of neural network that operates on unsupervised learning principles, intending to replicate its input as accurately as possible in its output. An AE consists of a hidden layer, denoted as, h, which serves the purpose of encoding the input data into a code representation (He et al., 2021).

Deep AE has the potential to contribute to data privacy by converting sensitive IoT data into a latent space representation. The aforementioned representation can be disseminated or archived without compromising the confidentiality of the underlying data. Subsequently, parties with proper authorization possess the capability to recreate the initial data from the latent space as and when required (Shoukat et al., 2022). Deep AE can be employed for the analysis of firmware binaries associated with IoT devices. The autoencoder can boost the security of IoT devices by effectively identifying deviations or malicious code inside the firmware through its training on a substantial dataset of valid firmware.

Restricted Boltzmann Machines (RBMs)

The RBM is a type of model that is entirely undirected, meaning that there are no connections or links between any two nodes within the same layer. RBMs are composed of two distinct types of layers, namely visible and hidden layers. The visible layer contains the input that is known, while the hidden layer comprises numerous layers that encompass the latent variables (Melko et al., 2019).

RBMs can effectively analyze and acquire knowledge from the sensor data that is produced by IoT devices. This enables RBMs to identify and recognize any deviations or anomalies that may occur concerning the anticipated behaviors (Elsaeidy et al., 2019). RBM can generate synthetic data that accurately replicates the patterns observed in real IoT data. The utilization of synthetic data in the evaluation and instruction of security systems allows for the avoidance of potential risks associated with the exposure of genuine sensitive data.

Deep Belief Networks (DBNs)

A DBN is composed of a series of RBMs that undergo a greedy layer-wise training process, which enables the network to achieve resilient performance in an unsupervised setting. In a Deep DBN, the training process is conducted in a layered manner, where each layer is trained sequentially as an RBM on top of the previously trained layer (Mohamed et al., 2011). During the pre-training phase, the initial features are trained greedily using a layer-wise unsupervised technique. Subsequently, in the fine-tuning phase, a softmax layer is employed on the top layer to refine the features based on the labeled samples (Zhang et al., 2018).

The implementation of DBNs for IoT security necessitates the execution of several key steps, including data preprocessing, training, and the meticulous tuning of hyperparameters. The computational resources required for training and inference of DBNs may be greater in comparison to simpler models, owing to their inherent complexity. One potential avenue for effectively addressing specific difficulties in IoT security is the exploration of hybrid systems that integrate DBNs with other machine learning techniques.

Generative Adversarial Networks (GANs)

GANs offer a promising approach to improving different aspects of IoT security. Within the domain of anomaly detection, GANs function by training a generator to accurately reproduce common data patterns, while a discriminator acquires the ability to differentiate between authentic and synthesized data (Guo et al., 2023). This mechanism enables the detection of anomalies or deviations in IoT networks, efficiently indicating potential security concerns or anomalous behaviors. Creating synthetic datasets for security model training with GANs enhances the training process and strengthens security algorithms. Utilizing GANs to generate authentic deception mechanisms, like honeypots, in an IoT network provides a distinct benefit by accurately imitating the actions of genuine devices.

GANs are useful in behavioral analysis for intrusion detection because they can learn typical patterns of device behavior (Boppana & Bagade, 2023). This allows them to detect any variations that may indicate potential security breaches or anomalous behaviors. GANs can be utilized to generate secure firmware for IoT devices, effectively mitigating typical vulnerabilities and enhancing the overall security and integrity of IoT ecosystems. When using advanced technology like GANs to enhance IoT security, it is important to carefully develop and apply them to reduce potential dangers and ensure their efficiency.

Long Short-Term Memory (LSTM)

LSTM is a specific type of RNN that has become a powerful tool in the field of IoT security. Within the realm of anomaly detection, LSTMs are highly important as they create models of the typical behavior exhibited by devices and their communication patterns (Shanmuganathan & Suresh, 2023). This allows for the detection of any variations that could potentially indicate security concerns or malicious activity. In IoT networks, it is very important to have advanced monitoring systems in place to detect any illegal access or odd behavior due to the interconnected nature of devices. LSTMs play a crucial role in intrusion detection systems by constantly observing and acquiring knowledge about network traffic patterns (Hanafi et al., 2023). This enables them to detect abnormal behavior, such as both familiar attack patterns and new types of threats.

The utilization of LSTM models in analyzing the behavior of IoT devices offers advantages in capturing temporal patterns. This enables the real-time detection of potentially malicious activities, hence improving the effectiveness of adaptive security measures. Predictive security analytics utilize LSTM models to anticipate possible vulnerabilities, providing a proactive strategy for identifying and reducing threats before they become more severe (Tayfour et al., 2023). LSTMs also plays a crucial role in communication security by creating models that predict normal communication patterns and identify any unusual behavior. This helps protect the privacy and integrity of data flows in IoT contexts.

Neural Turing Machines (NTM)

NTMs, an advanced neural network architecture, show great potential in the field of IoT security. NTMs combine neural networks with an external memory matrix, making them more advanced and useful for jobs that involve storing and retrieving information. This adds another level of security to the IoT that was not possible before (Malekmohamadi Faradonbe et al., 2020). Contributing to the field of key management and encryption, NTMs learn cryptographic keys and store them in their external memory, strengthening the security of communication channels and protecting data transfers across IoT devices.

Another use case for NTMs is adaptive access control, which involves the real-time modification of access rights in response to learnt patterns and contextual data. In addition, NTMs have exceptional proficiency in acquiring and retaining dynamic security protocols, guaranteeing flexibility in response to the shifting security environment of IoT networks. Their function also includes intrusion detection and response, where NTMs keep their external memory up-to-date with new threat information, allowing for the quick detection and mitigation of security issues. For firmware upgrades, NTMs also examine cryptographic signatures and integrity checks to make sure only approved updates are implemented, protecting against vulnerabilities.

Feedforward Neural Networks (FNN)

FNNs are essential in the field of neural network architectures and are highly helpful for enhancing the security of the IoT. FNNs are very good at working with sequential data, and they can be used in intrusion detection to learn historical data trends and spot changes that could mean there are security threats or unauthorized access in IoT networks (Ezhilarasi et al., 2023). In addition, FNNs play a vital role in detecting anomalies by acquiring knowledge of and identifying the typical behavior of IoT devices, thereby proactively indicating probable security breaches or hacked devices (Prashanthi & Reddy, 2023).

FNNs provide secure communication protocols by learning and adapting to predicted communication patterns, ensuring IoT device data integrity and secrecy. Their utilization in predictive security analytics allows FNNs to anticipate potential vulnerabilities and new attacks, providing a proactive method for tackling security risks in IoT ecosystems. Finally, in the context of malware detection, FNNs examine patterns linked to recognized malware, aiding in the detection and prevention of harmful software in IoT settings (Singh et al., 2023).

Deep Reinforcement Learning (DRL)

The field of Reinforcement Learning (RL) has evolved into a highly efficient approach that enables a learning agent to adapt its policy and attain an ideal solution through iterative experimentation, ultimately achieving the optimal long-term objective without the need for any pre-existing knowledge about the environment (Li, 2023).

The utilization of DRL has the potential to greatly enhance the security of the IoT by enabling the acquisition of optimal actions in contexts that are both dynamic and uncertain. Within the realm of IoT security, DRL has the potential to be effectively utilized in various domains, including but not limited to adaptive intrusion detection, dynamic resource allocation, and network defense (Liu & Li, 2022). DRL agents can autonomously adjust their security methods in response to changing threat landscapes by leveraging insights gained from interactions within the IoT ecosystem. For example, DRL has the potential to facilitate the development of adaptive intrusion detection systems. These systems can acquire the ability to distinguish between legal and malicious activity by continuously analyzing network traffic patterns and learning from them over an extended period. Additionally, DRL can enhance the allocation of resources among IoT devices, thereby achieving a harmonious equilibrium between security protocols and energy conservation. Through the utilization of trial and error as a learning method, DRL possesses the capability to generate intelligent security mechanisms that are capable of self-learning. These mechanisms are specifically designed to address the distinct difficulties and dynamics that are inherent to the IoT environment.

CONCLUSION

This chapter provides a thorough analysis of the IoT, including its basic overview, architectural components, practical applications, and inherent security problems. The discussion explores the increasing difficulty of ensuring the security of IoT devices, which is made worse by the need to protect various technologies like physical devices, wireless transmission, mobile architectures, and cloud architectures, while also seamlessly integrating them with other technological frameworks. Furthermore, a comprehensive investigation into the existing deep-learning methods for tackling IoT security issues has been carried out. Significant progress in deep learning has resulted in strong analytical methods, demonstrating their ability to strengthen the security infrastructure of the IoT ecosystem. The combination of these observations highlights the changing nature of IoT security, underlining the need for flexible and advanced strategies to guarantee the reliability and durability of interconnected devices and systems.

Table 1. Summary of DL Techniques with their pros, cons, and security applications in IoT environment

DL Technique	Pros	Cons	IoT security applications
CNN	automatically learns and extracts IoT features without feature engineering (Alabsi et al., 2023).	may not apply to new IoT security scenarios, especially if data distribution differs from training data. (Anand et al., 2021).	man-in-the-middle attacks, malware detection, DOS attack and intrusion detection
RNN	can handle variable-length and size inputs, which is useful in IoT when data is noisy and unpredictable. (Ullah & Mahmoud, 2022)	computationally expensive, especially with huge datasets, limiting its use in some IoT applications (Syed et al., 2023)	prediction and prevention, malware detection and intrusion detection
AE	provide accurate anomaly detection by learning how the gadget normally acts (Yoon et al., 2023)	limited labeled training data for fine-tuning may influence performance.	anomaly and intrusion detection
RBM	efficiently model complicated IoT links for anomaly detection and feature learning (Saied et al., 2024)	computationally intensive for high-dimensional data in IoT environment (Ntizikira et al., 2024)	intrusion detection, traffic analysis and filtering, and secure firmware verification
DBN	efficiently model IoT data hierarchies (Biju & Franklin, 2024)	limited use in time-sensitive IoT security scenarios	predictive security analytics, privacy-preserving data processing
GAN	making security analytics and anomaly detection better (X. Wang et al., 2024)	a lack of interpretability and training stability (Alwahedi et al., 2024)	honeypots and deception
LSTM	Capable of capturing time-series data with long-term dependencies (Liao et al., 2024)	A lot of labeled data is often needed for training to work well (J. Wang et al., 2024).	anomaly and intrusion detection
NTM	Well suited for secure protocol learning in IoT environment (Chen et al., 2023)	Learned representations could be difficult to understand.	secure protocol learning and anomaly detection in device behavior
FNN	Useful for capturing IoT data with complex connections (Telidevara & Kothandaraman, 2023)	lacks the ability to handle sequential data and capture temporal relationships.	traffic classification and filtering
DRL	Good for adaptive access control in IoT security (Z. Wang et al., 2024)	Training DRL models can be resource-intensive (Cai et al., 2024)	adaptive access control and secure firmware updates

REFERENCES

Ackerson, J. M., Dave, R., & Seliya, N. (2021). Applications of recurrent neural network for biometric authentication & anomaly detection. *Information (Basel)*, *12*(7), 272. doi:10.3390/info12070272

Adeel, A., Ali, M., Khan, A. N., Khalid, T., Rehman, F., Jararweh, Y., & Shuja, J. (2022). A multi-attack resilient lightweight IoT authentication scheme. *Transactions on Emerging Telecommunications Technologies*, *33*(3), e3676. doi:10.1002/ett.3676

Al-Nbhany, W. A., Zahary, A. T., & Al-Shargabi, A. A. (2024). Blockchain-IoT Healthcare Applications and Trends: A Review. *IEEE Access : Practical Innovations, Open Solutions*, *12*, 4178–4212. doi:10.1109/ACCESS.2023.3349187

Alabsi, B. A., Anbar, M., & Rihan, S. D. A. (2023). CNN-CNN: Dual Convolutional Neural Network Approach for Feature Selection and Attack Detection on Internet of Things Networks. *Sensors (Basel)*, *23*(14), 6507. doi:10.3390/s23146507 PMID:37514801

Alavikia, Z., & Shabro, M. (2022). A comprehensive layered approach for implementing internet of things-enabled smart grid: A survey. *Digital Communications and Networks*, *8*(3), 388–410. doi:10.1016/j.dcan.2022.01.002

Aldahmani, A., Ouni, B., Lestable, T., & Debbah, M. (2023). Cyber-security of embedded IoTs in smart homes: Challenges, requirements, countermeasures, and trends. *IEEE Open Journal of Vehicular Technology*, *4*, 281–292. doi:10.1109/OJVT.2023.3234069

Almiani, M., AbuGhazleh, A., Al-Rahayfeh, A., Atiewi, S., & Razaque, A. (2020). Deep recurrent neural network for IoT intrusion detection system. *Simulation Modelling Practice and Theory*, *101*, 102031. doi:10.1016/j.simpat.2019.102031

Alwahedi, F., Aldhaheri, A., Ferrag, M. A., Battah, A., & Tihanyi, N. (2024). Machine learning techniques for IoT security: Current research and future vision with generative AI and large language models. *Internet of Things and Cyber-Physical Systems*.

AlZubi, A. A., & Galyna, K. (2023). Artificial Intelligence and Internet of Things for Sustainable Farming and Smart Agriculture. *IEEE Access : Practical Innovations, Open Solutions*, *11*, 78686–78692. doi:10.1109/ACCESS.2023.3298215

Anand, A., Rani, S., Anand, D., Aljahdali, H. M., & Kerr, D. (2021). An efficient CNN-based deep learning model to detect malware attacks (CNN-DMA) in 5G-IoT healthcare applications. *Sensors (Basel)*, *21*(19), 6346. doi:10.3390/s21196346 PMID:34640666

Babangida, L., Perumal, T., Mustapha, N., & Yaakob, R. (2022). Internet of things (IoT) based activity recognition strategies in smart homes: A review. *IEEE Sensors Journal*, *22*(9), 8327–8336. doi:10.1109/JSEN.2022.3161797

Bathla, N., & Kaur, A. (2024). Security challenges of IoT with its applications and architecture. In *Artificial Intelligence, Blockchain* [CRC Press.]. *Computers & Security*, *2*, 170–179.

Bautista, C., & Mester, G. (2023). Internet of Things in Self-driving Cars Environment. *Interdisciplinary Description of Complex Systems: INDECS*, *21*(2), 188–198. doi:10.7906/indecs.21.2.8

Berroukham, A., Housni, K., Lahraichi, M., & Boulfrifi, I. (2023). Deep learning-based methods for anomaly detection in video surveillance: A review. *Bulletin of Electrical Engineering and Informatics*, *12*(1), 314–327. doi:10.11591/eei.v12i1.3944

Bhatt, D., Patel, C., Talsania, H., Patel, J., Vaghela, R., Pandya, S., Modi, K., & Ghayvat, H. (2021). CNN variants for computer vision: History, architecture, application, challenges and future scope. *Electronics (Basel)*, *10*(20), 2470. doi:10.3390/electronics10202470

Biju, A., & Franklin, S. W. (2024). Evaluated bird swarm optimization based on deep belief network (EBSO-DBN) classification technique for IOT network intrusion detection. *Automatika (Zagreb)*, *65*(1), 108–116. doi:10.1080/00051144.2023.2269646

Boppana, T. K., & Bagade, P. (2023). GAN-AE: An unsupervised intrusion detection system for MQTT networks. *Engineering Applications of Artificial Intelligence*, *119*, 105805. doi:10.1016/j.engappai.2022.105805

Cai, H., Bian, Y., & Liu, L. (2024). Deep reinforcement learning for solving resource constrained project scheduling problems with resource disruptions. *Robotics and Computer-integrated Manufacturing*, *85*, 102628. doi:10.1016/j.rcim.2023.102628

Chataut, R., Phoummalayvane, A., & Akl, R. (2023). Unleashing the power of IoT: A comprehensive review of IoT applications and future prospects in healthcare, agriculture, smart homes, smart cities, and industry 4.0. *Sensors (Basel)*, *23*(16), 7194. doi:10.3390/s23167194 PMID:37631731

Chen, Y., Zhang, Y., Wang, H., Feng, N., Yang, L., & Huang, Z. (2023). Differentiable-Decision-Tree-Based Neural Turing Machine Model Integrated Into FDTD for Implementing EM Problems. *IEEE Transactions on Electromagnetic Compatibility*, *65*(6), 1579–1586. doi:10.1109/TEMC.2023.3273724

de Oliveira, G. W., Nogueira, M., dos Santos, A. L., & Batista, D. M. (2023). Intelligent VNF Placement to Mitigate DDoS Attacks on Industrial IoT. *IEEE Transactions on Network and Service Management*, *20*(2), 1319–1331. doi:10.1109/TNSM.2023.3274364

Dimitriadou, K., Rigogiannis, N., Fountoukidis, S., Kotarela, F., Kyritsis, A., & Papanikolaou, N. (2023). Current Trends in Electric Vehicle Charging Infrastructure; Opportunities and Challenges in Wireless Charging Integration. *Energies*, *16*(4), 2057. doi:10.3390/en16042057

Divya, K., Roopashree, H., & Yogeesh, A. (2022). Non-repudiation-based network security system using multiparty computation. *International Journal of Advanced Computer Science and Applications*, *13*(3).

Douiba, M., Benkirane, S., Guezzaz, A., & Azrour, M. (2023). An improved anomaly detection model for IoT security using decision tree and gradient boosting. *The Journal of Supercomputing*, *79*(3), 3392–3411. doi:10.1007/s11227-022-04783-y

Dui, H., Zhang, S., Liu, M., Dong, X., & Bai, G. (2024). IoT-Enabled Real-Time Traffic Monitoring and Control Management for Intelligent Transportation Systems. *IEEE Internet of Things Journal*, 1. doi:10.1109/JIOT.2024.3351908

Elsaeidy, A., Munasinghe, K. S., Sharma, D., & Jamalipour, A. (2019). Intrusion detection in smart cities using Restricted Boltzmann Machines. *Journal of Network and Computer Applications*, *135*, 76–83. doi:10.1016/j.jnca.2019.02.026

Ezhilarasi, M., Gnanaprasanambikai, L., Kousalya, A., & Shanmugapriya, M. (2023). A novel implementation of routing attack detection scheme by using fuzzy and feed-forward neural networks. *Soft Computing*, *27*(7), 4157–4168. doi:10.1007/s00500-022-06915-1

Gaurav, A., Gupta, B. B., & Panigrahi, P. K. (2023). A comprehensive survey on machine learning approaches for malware detection in IoT-based enterprise information system. *Enterprise Information Systems*, *17*(3), 2023764. doi:10.1080/17517575.2021.2023764

Ghiasi, M., Niknam, T., Wang, Z., Mehrandezh, M., Dehghani, M., & Ghadimi, N. (2023). A comprehensive review of cyber-attacks and defense mechanisms for improving security in smart grid energy systems: Past, present and future. *Electric Power Systems Research*, *215*, 108975. doi:10.1016/j.epsr.2022.108975

Gong, L.-H., Pei, J.-J., Zhang, T.-F., & Zhou, N.-R. (2024). Quantum convolutional neural network based on variational quantum circuits. *Optics Communications*, *550*, 129993. doi:10.1016/j.optcom.2023.129993

Guo, D., Liu, Z., & Li, R. (2023). RegraphGAN: A graph generative adversarial network model for dynamic network anomaly detection. *Neural Networks*, *166*, 273–285. doi:10.1016/j.neunet.2023.07.026 PMID:37531727

Gupta, A., & Nahar, P. (2023). Classification and yield prediction in smart agriculture system using IoT. *Journal of Ambient Intelligence and Humanized Computing*, *14*(8), 10235–10244. doi:10.1007/s12652-021-03685-w

Gupta, P., Gupta, H., Ushasukhanya, S., & Vijayaragavan, E. (2023). Telemetry Simulation & Analysis. 2023 International Conference on Networking and Communications (ICNWC), Hammad, M., Abd El-Latif, A. A., Hussain, A., Abd El-Samie, F. E., Gupta, B. B., Ugail, H., & Sedik, A. (2022). Deep learning models for arrhythmia detection in IoT healthcare applications. *Computers & Electrical Engineering*, *100*, 108011.

Hanafi, A. V., Ghaffari, A., Rezaei, H., Valipour, A., & arasteh, B. (2023). Intrusion detection in Internet of things using improved binary golden jackal optimization algorithm and LSTM. *Cluster Computing*, •••, 1–18. doi:10.1007/s10586-023-04102-x

He, X., He, Q., & Chen, J.-S. (2021). Deep autoencoders for physics-constrained data-driven nonlinear materials modeling. *Computer Methods in Applied Mechanics and Engineering*, *385*, 114034. doi:10.1016/j.cma.2021.114034

Hosseinnia Shavaki, F., & Ebrahimi Ghahnavieh, A. (2023). Applications of deep learning into supply chain management: A systematic literature review and a framework for future research. *Artificial Intelligence Review*, *56*(5), 4447–4489. doi:10.1007/s10462-022-10289-z PMID:36212799

Huang, B., Chaki, D., Bouguettaya, A., & Lam, K.-Y. (2023). A survey on conflict detection in iot-based smart homes. *ACM Computing Surveys*, *56*(5), 1–40. doi:10.1145/3570326

Jahangir, H., Lakshminarayana, S., Maple, C., & Epiphaniou, G. (2023). A Deep Learning-Based Solution for Securing the Power Grid against Load Altering Threats by IoT-Enabled Devices. *IEEE Internet of Things Journal*, *10*(12), 10687–10697. doi:10.1109/JIOT.2023.3240289

Juma, M., Alattar, F., & Touqan, B. (2023). Securing Big Data Integrity for Industrial IoT in Smart Manufacturing Based on the Trusted Consortium Blockchain (TCB). *IoT*, *4*(1), 27–55. doi:10.3390/iot4010002

Kandhro, I. A., Alanazi, S. M., Ali, F., Kehar, A., Fatima, K., Uddin, M., & Karuppayah, S. (2023). Detection of Real-Time Malicious Intrusions and Attacks in IoT Empowered Cybersecurity Infrastructures. *IEEE Access : Practical Innovations, Open Solutions*, *11*, 9136–9148. doi:10.1109/ACCESS.2023.3238664

Kattenborn, T., Leitloff, J., Schiefer, F., & Hinz, S. (2021). Review on Convolutional Neural Networks (CNN) in vegetation remote sensing. *ISPRS Journal of Photogrammetry and Remote Sensing*, *173*, 24–49. doi:10.1016/j.isprsjprs.2020.12.010

Kaur, B., Dadkhah, S., Shoeleh, F., Neto, E. C. P., Xiong, P., Iqbal, S., Lamontagne, P., Ray, S., & Ghorbani, A. A. (2023). Internet of things (IoT) security dataset evolution: Challenges and future directions. *Internet of Things : Engineering Cyber Physical Human Systems*, *22*, 100780. doi:10.1016/j.iot.2023.100780

Khan, A. R., Kashif, M., Jhaveri, R. H., Raut, R., Saba, T., & Bahaj, S. A. (2022). Deep learning for intrusion detection and security of Internet of things (IoT): Current analysis, challenges, and possible solutions. *Security and Communication Networks*, *2022*, 2022. doi:10.1155/2022/4016073

Khan, M., Glavin, F. G., & Nickles, M. (2023). Federated learning as a privacy solution-an overview. *Procedia Computer Science*, *217*, 316–325. doi:10.1016/j.procs.2022.12.227

Kumar, P., Kumar, R., Gupta, G. P., Tripathi, R., Jolfaei, A., & Islam, A. N. (2023). A blockchain-orchestrated deep learning approach for secure data transmission in IoT-enabled healthcare system. *Journal of Parallel and Distributed Computing*, *172*, 69–83. doi:10.1016/j.jpdc.2022.10.002

Kumar, R., Joshi, G., Chauhan, A. K. S., Singh, A. K., & Rao, A. K. (2023). A Deep Learning and Channel Sounding Based Data Authentication and QoS Enhancement Mechanism for Massive IoT Networks. *Wireless Personal Communications*, *130*(4), 2495–2514. doi:10.1007/s11277-023-10389-1

Li, S. E. (2023). Deep reinforcement learning. In *Reinforcement Learning for Sequential Decision and Optimal Control* (pp. 365–402). Springer. doi:10.1007/978-981-19-7784-8_10

Liao, H., Murah, M. Z., Hasan, M. K., Aman, A. H. M., Fang, J., Hu, X., & Khan, A. U. R. (2024). A Survey of Deep Learning Technologies for Intrusion Detection in Internet of Things. *IEEE Access : Practical Innovations, Open Solutions*, *12*, 4745–4761. doi:10.1109/ACCESS.2023.3349287

Liu, C., & Ke, L. (2023). Cloud assisted Internet of things intelligent transportation system and the traffic control system in the smart city. *Journal of Control and Decision*, *10*(2), 174–187. doi:10.1080/23307706.2021.2024460

Liu, L., & Li, Z. (2022). Permissioned blockchain and deep reinforcement learning enabled security and energy efficient Healthcare Internet of Things. *IEEE Access : Practical Innovations, Open Solutions*, *10*, 53640–53651. doi:10.1109/ACCESS.2022.3176444

Malekmohamadi Faradonbe, S., Safi-Esfahani, F., & Karimian-Kelishadrokhi, M. (2020). A review on neural turing machine (NTM). *SN Computer Science*, *1*(6), 333. doi:10.1007/s42979-020-00341-6

Malik, I., Bhardwaj, A., Bhardwaj, H., & Sakalle, A. (2023). IoT-Enabled Smart Homes: Architecture, Challenges, and Issues. *Revolutionizing Industrial Automation Through the Convergence of Artificial Intelligence and the Internet of Things*, 160-176.

Melko, R. G., Carleo, G., Carrasquilla, J., & Cirac, J. I. (2019). Restricted Boltzmann machines in quantum physics. *Nature Physics*, *15*(9), 887–892. doi:10.1038/s41567-019-0545-1

Mohamed, A., Dahl, G. E., & Hinton, G. (2011). Acoustic modeling using deep belief networks. *IEEE Transactions on Audio, Speech, and Language Processing*, *20*(1), 14–22. doi:10.1109/TASL.2011.2109382

Mohan, D., Al-Hamid, D. Z., Chong, P. H. J., Sudheera, K. L. K., Gutierrez, J., Chan, H. C., & Li, H. (2024). Artificial Intelligence and IoT in Elderly Fall Prevention: A Review. *IEEE Sensors Journal*, *24*(4), 4181–4198. doi:10.1109/JSEN.2023.3344605

Mohandass, M., Kaliraj, I., Maareeswari, R., & Vimalraj, R. (2023). IoT Based Traffic Management System for Emergency Vehicles. 2023 9th International Conference on Advanced Computing and Communication Systems (ICACCS), Nadhan, A. S., & Jacob, I. J. (2024). Enhancing healthcare security in the digital era: Safeguarding medical images with lightweight cryptographic techniques in IoT healthcare applications. *Biomedical Signal Processing and Control*, *88*, 105511.

Oladimeji, D., Gupta, K., Kose, N. A., Gundogan, K., Ge, L., & Liang, F. (2023). Smart transportation: An overview of technologies and applications. *Sensors (Basel)*, *23*(8), 3880. doi:10.3390/s23083880 PMID:37112221

Oprea, S.-V., & Bâra, A. (2023). An Edge-Fog-Cloud computing architecture for IoT and smart metering data. *Peer-to-Peer Networking and Applications*, *16*(2), 1–28. doi:10.1007/s12083-022-01436-y

Orfanos, V. A., Kaminaris, S. D., Papageorgas, P., Piromalis, D., & Kandris, D. (2023). A Comprehensive Review of IoT Networking Technologies for Smart Home Automation Applications. *Journal of Sensor and Actuator Networks*, *12*(2), 30. doi:10.3390/jsan12020030

Pal, K., & Yasar, A.-U.-H. (2023). Internet of Things Impact on Supply Chain Management. *Procedia Computer Science*, *220*, 478–485. doi:10.1016/j.procs.2023.03.061

Pham, C.-H., Huynh-The, T., Sedgh-Gooya, E., El-Bouz, M., & Alfalou, A. (2024). Extension of physical activity recognition with 3D CNN using encrypted multiple sensory data to federated learning based on multi-key homomorphic encryption. *Computer Methods and Programs in Biomedicine*, *243*, 107854. doi:10.1016/j.cmpb.2023.107854 PMID:37865060

Picoto, W. N., Abreu, J. C., & Martins, P. (2023). Integrating the Internet of Things Into E-Commerce: The Role of Trust, Privacy, and Data Confidentiality Concerns in Consumer Adoption. [IJEBR]. *International Journal of E-Business Research*, *19*(1), 1–18. doi:10.4018/IJEBR.321647

Qays, M. O., Ahmad, I., Abu-Siada, A., Hossain, M. L., & Yasmin, F. (2023). Key communication technologies, applications, protocols and future guides for IoT-assisted smart grid systems: A review. *Energy Reports*, *9*, 2440–2452. doi:10.1016/j.egyr.2023.01.085

Rao, C. K., Sahoo, S. K., & Yanine, F. F. (2024). Demand side energy management algorithms integrated with the IoT framework in the PV smart grid system. In *Advanced Frequency Regulation Strategies in Renewable-Dominated Power Systems* (pp. 255-277). Elsevier. 10.1007/978-981-99-0838-7_14

Rastegari, H., Nadi, F., Lam, S. S., Abdullah, M. I., Kasan, N. A., Rahmat, R. F., & Mahari, W. A. W. (2023). Internet of Things in aquaculture: A review of the challenges and potential solutions based on current and future trends. *Smart Agricultural Technology*, *4*, 100187. doi:10.1016/j.atech.2023.100187

Ratnakar, N. C., Prajapati, B. R., Prajapati, B. G., & Prajapati, J. B. (2024). Smart Innovative Medical Devices Based on Artificial Intelligence. In *Handbook on Augmenting Telehealth Services* (pp. 150–172). CRC Press.

Rejeb, A., Rejeb, K., Treiblmaier, H., Appolloni, A., Alghamdi, S., Alhasawi, Y., & Iranmanesh, M. (2023). The Internet of Things (IoT) in healthcare: Taking stock and moving forward. *Internet of Things : Engineering Cyber Physical Human Systems*, *22*, 100721. doi:10.1016/j.iot.2023.100721

Renugadevi, N., Saravanan, S., & Sudha, C. N. (2023). IoT based smart energy grid for sustainable cites. *Materials Today: Proceedings*, *81*, 98–104. doi:10.1016/j.matpr.2021.02.270

Sahu, D. K., Pradhan, B. K., Wilczynski, S., Anis, A., & Pal, K. (2023). Development of an internet of things (IoT)-based pill monitoring device for geriatric patients. In *Advanced Methods in Biomedical Signal Processing and Analysis* (pp. 129–158). Elsevier. doi:10.1016/B978-0-323-85955-4.00012-0

Saied, M., Guirguis, S., & Madbouly, M. (2024). Review of artificial intelligence for enhancing intrusion detection in the internet of things. *Engineering Applications of Artificial Intelligence*, *127*, 107231. doi:10.1016/j.engappai.2023.107231

Salman, H., & Arslan, H. (2023). PLS-IoT Enhancement against Eavesdropping via Spatially Distributed Constellation Obfuscation. *IEEE Wireless Communications Letters*, *12*(9), 1508–1512. doi:10.1109/LWC.2023.3279989

Sangeethalakshmi, K., Preethi, U., & Pavithra, S. (2023). Patient health monitoring system using IoT. *Materials Today: Proceedings*, *80*, 2228–2231. doi:10.1016/j.matpr.2021.06.188

Sarker, I. H., Khan, A. I., Abushark, Y. B., & Alsolami, F. (2022). Internet of things (iot) security intelligence: A comprehensive overview, machine learning solutions and research directions. *Mobile Networks and Applications*, 1–17.

Sarker, I. H., Khan, A. I., Abushark, Y. B., & Alsolami, F. (2023). Internet of things (iot) security intelligence: A comprehensive overview, machine learning solutions and research directions. *Mobile Networks and Applications*, *28*(1), 296–312. doi:10.1007/s11036-022-01937-3

Schiller, E., Aidoo, A., Fuhrer, J., Stahl, J., Ziörjen, M., & Stiller, B. (2022). Landscape of IoT security. *Computer Science Review*, *44*, 100467. doi:10.1016/j.cosrev.2022.100467

Shafi, S., & Mallinson, D. J. (2023). The potential of smart home technology for improving healthcare: A scoping review and reflexive thematic analysis. *Housing and Society*, *50*(1), 90–112. doi:10.1080/08882746.2021.1989857

Shanmuganathan, V., & Suresh, A. (2023). LSTM-Markov based efficient anomaly detection algorithm for IoT environment. *Applied Soft Computing*, *136*, 110054. doi:10.1016/j.asoc.2023.110054

Sharma, A., Singh, P. K., & Kumar, Y. (2020). An integrated fire detection system using IoT and image processing technique for smart cities. *Sustainable Cities and Society*, *61*, 102332. doi:10.1016/j.scs.2020.102332

Sharma, B., Sharma, L., Lal, C., & Roy, S. (2024). Explainable artificial intelligence for intrusion detection in IoT networks: A deep learning based approach. *Expert Systems with Applications, 238*, 121751. doi:10.1016/j.eswa.2023.121751

Shiraly, D., Eslami, Z., & Pakniat, N. (2024). Certificate-based authenticated encryption with keyword search: Enhanced security model and a concrete construction for Internet of Things. *Journal of Information Security and Applications, 80*, 103683. doi:10.1016/j.jisa.2023.103683

Shoukat, A., Hassan, M. A., Rizwan, M., Imad, M., Ali, S. H., & Ullah, S. (2022). Design a framework for IoT-Identification, Authentication and Anomaly detection using Deep Learning: A Review. *EAI Endorsed Transactions on Smart Cities, 7*(1).

Singh, P., Borgohain, S. K., Sarkar, A. K., Kumar, J., & Sharma, L. D. (2023). Feed-forward deep neural network (FFDNN)-based deep features for static malware detection. *International Journal of Intelligent Systems, 2023*, 2023. doi:10.1155/2023/9544481

Siwakoti, Y. R., Bhurtel, M., Rawat, D. B., Oest, A., & Johnson, R. (2023). Advances in IoT Security: Vulnerabilities, Enabled Criminal Services, Attacks and Countermeasures. *IEEE Internet of Things Journal, 10*(13), 11224–11239. doi:10.1109/JIOT.2023.3252594

Štuikys, V., & Burbaitė, R. (2024). Methodological Aspects of Educational Internet of Things. In *Evolution of STEM-Driven Computer Science Education: The Perspective of Big Concepts* (pp. 167–189). Springer. doi:10.1007/978-3-031-48235-9_6

Subashini, S., Kamalam, G., & Vanitha, P. (2024). A Survey of IoT in Healthcare: Technologies, Applications, and Challenges. *Artificial Intelligence and Machine Learning*, 136-144.

Sun, G., Zheng, X., Li, J., Kang, H., & Liang, S. (2023). Collaborative WSN-UAV Data Collection in Smart Agriculture: A Bi-objective Optimization Scheme. *ACM Transactions on Sensor Networks*, 3597025. doi:10.1145/3597025

Syed, N. F., Ge, M., & Baig, Z. (2023). Fog-cloud based intrusion detection system using Recurrent Neural Networks and feature selection for IoT networks. *Computer Networks, 225*, 109662. doi:10.1016/j.comnet.2023.109662

Tayfour, O. E., Mubarakali, A., Tayfour, A. E., Marsono, M. N., Hassan, E., & Abdelrahman, A. M. (2023). Adapting deep learning-LSTM method using optimized dataset in SDN controller for secure IoT. *Soft Computing*, 1–9. doi:10.1007/s00500-023-08348-w

Wang, X., Wan, Z., Hekmati, A., Zong, M., Alam, S., Zhang, M., & Krishnamachari, B. (2024). IoT in the Era of Generative AI: Vision and Challenges. *arXiv preprint arXiv:2401.01923*.

Wang, Y., Cui, Y., Kong, Z., Liao, X., & Wang, W. (2024). Design of Public Transportation System Scheduling and Optimization in the Internet of Things (IoT) Environment. *Advances in Engineering Technology Research*, *9*(1), 89–89. doi:10.56028/aetr.9.1.89.2024

Wang, Z., Goudarzi, M., Gong, M., & Buyya, R. (2024). Deep Reinforcement Learning-based scheduling for optimizing system load and response time in edge and fog computing environments. *Future Generation Computer Systems*, *152*, 55–69. doi:10.1016/j.future.2023.10.012

Whig, P., Velu, A., Nadikattu, R. R., & Alkali, Y. J. (2024). Role of AI and IoT in Intelligent Transportation. In *Artificial Intelligence for Future Intelligent Transportation* (pp. 199–220). Apple Academic Press.

Xu, L., Zhou, X., Tao, Y., Liu, L., Yu, X., & Kumar, N. (2021). Intelligent security performance prediction for IoT-enabled healthcare networks using an improved CNN. *IEEE Transactions on Industrial Informatics*, *18*(3), 2063–2074. doi:10.1109/TII.2021.3082907

Yazdinejad, A., Dehghantanha, A., Parizi, R. M., Srivastava, G., & Karimipour, H. (2023). Secure intelligent fuzzy blockchain framework: Effective threat detection in iot networks. *Computers in Industry*, *144*, 103801. doi:10.1016/j.compind.2022.103801

Yoon, S., Song, J., Seo, G., Han, S., & Hwang, E. (2023). A Content-assisted Dynamic PUF Key Generation Scheme Using Compressive Autoencoder for Internet-of-Things. *IEEE Sensors Journal*, *23*(15), 17572–17584. doi:10.1109/JSEN.2023.3285784

Yunana, K., Alfa, A. A., Misra, S., Damasevicius, R., Maskeliunas, R., & Oluranti, J. (2021). Internet of things: applications, adoptions and components-a conceptual overview. *Hybrid Intelligent Systems: 20th International Conference on Hybrid Intelligent Systems (HIS 2020)*. Springer. 10.1007/978-3-030-73050-5_50

Zaguia, A. (2023). Smart greenhouse management system with cloud-based platform and IoT sensors. *Spatial Information Research*, 1-13.

Zhang, D.-S., Song, W.-Z., Wu, L.-X., Li, C.-L., Chen, T., Sun, D.-J., Zhang, M., Zhang, T.-T., Zhang, J., Ramakrishna, S., & Long, Y.-Z. (2023). The influence of in-plane electrodes on TENG's output and its application in the field of IoT intelligent sensing. *Nano Energy*, *110*, 108313. doi:10.1016/j.nanoen.2023.108313

Zhang, Q., Yang, L. T., Chen, Z., & Li, P. (2018). A survey on deep learning for big data. *Information Fusion*, *42*, 146–157. doi:10.1016/j.inffus.2017.10.006

Chapter 4
Recent Developments of Semantic Web:
Technologies and Challenges

Kannadhasan Suriyan
https://orcid.org/0000-0001-6443-9993
Study World College of Engineering, India

R. Nagarajan
https://orcid.org/0000-0002-4990-5869
Gnanamani College of Technology, India

K. Chandramohan
Gnanamani College of Technology, India

R. Prabhu
Gnanamani College of Technology, India

ABSTRACT

Sharing data and facts rather than the content of a website is what the semantic web is all about. Sir Tim Berners-Lee proposed the semantic web concept in 2001. The semantic web assists in the development of a technological stack that supports a "web of data" rather of a "web of documents." The ultimate goal of the web of data is to provide computers the ability to do more meaningful jobs and to create systems that can enable trustworthy network connections. Different data interchange formats (e.g. Turtle, RDF/XML, N3, NTriples), query languages (SPARQL, DL query), ontologies, and notations (e.g. RDF Schema and Web Ontology Language (OWL)) are all used in semantic web technologies (SWTs) to provide a formal description of entities and correspondences within a given knowledge domain. These technologies are useful in accomplishing the semantic web's ultimate goal. Linked data is at the core of the semantic web since it allows for large-scale data integration and reasoning. SPARQL, RDF, OWL, and SKOS are among the technologies that have made linked data more powerful; however, there are many difficulties that have been detailed in different publications.

DOI: 10.4018/979-8-3693-0766-3.ch004

INTRODUCTION

Ontologies are the foundation for organising linked data, and they play a critical role in establishing connections between datasets and across datasets. They provide users with the ability to search a schematic representation of all data included in the apps. We can integrate deep domain knowledge with raw data and connect datasets across domains by utilising ontology. Ontologies are attempts to more accurately categorise portions of data and to allow communication between data in different forms. Web ontology language is the global standard for exchanging ontologies and data on the Semantic Web. In the domain of the semantic web benchmarks, the database is not publicly appropriate since it is built in the direction of a relational data model. The set theory, which is a component of the Cartesian product, is the mathematical concept underlying the relational data model. On the other hand, the web ontology language data model offers a great deal of flexibility.

The concept of graph theory underpins the resource description framework (RDF). In addition, web ontology language is built on description logic, which contains DL expressions and axioms or restrictions. The semantic web would not be complete without a knowledge graph. Google created the term "Information Graph" in 2012 to describe any graph-based knowledge. Many other kinds of knowledge graphs exist, including DBpedia, Freebase, Open- Cyc, Wikidata, YAGO, and so on. In the end, extensive knowledge bases such as DBPEDIA and WIKIDATA are critical in addressing the issue of information overload. The idea of introducing semantics to web search is not apparent in an exclusive way. Other significant difficulties for the semantic web, which offers paths for researchers, include scalability, content availability, visualisation, ontology creation and evolution, multilingualism, and stability of semantic web languages.

Understanding Web queries and Web resources annotated with background information specified by ontologies and looking into the structured large datasets and knowledge bases of the semantic web as an alternative or a supplement to the current web are the two most common behaviours of semantic web technology. Semantic web technologies' wide range of applications enable them to help various areas such as sensor networks, big data, cloud computing, the Internet of Things, and so on. The learning scenario in e-Learning is completely different from traditional learning, in which the instructor serves as an intermediary between the learner and the learning material: instructors no longer control the delivery of material, and learners have the ability to combine learning material in courses on their own. In addition, learning processes must be quick and precise. Not only does speed need appropriate learning material content, but it also requires a strong method for organising that information (Yang, 2020) (Pereiro, 2020). E-learning should also be a personalised online solution based on user profiles and company needs. The above-mentioned criteria are not met by current web-based solutions. Information overload, a lack of reliable data, and material that is not machine-understandable are all potential problems.

The Semantic Web, the next generation of the internet, seems to be a viable technology for e-learning implementation. The major industrial firms, as well as academic and research institutions, have begun to seriously consider the use and applications of Semantic Web technology, in which machine-processable information can coexist and complement the current web, allowing computers and people to work together more effectively. The Semantic Web is a semantically based ecosystem in which human and machine agents may interact. Items may simply be grouped into personalised learning courses (quick and just-in-time) and provided to users on demand, based on their profile and company requirements. This article discusses e-Learning, including its advantages and needs, as well as the prospective applications of semantic web technologies in e-Learning. In the educational process, technology has always played a significant role. Radio, and subsequently television, were utilised as tools for distant education around the turn of the twentieth century.

Today's main technology for improving learning is the Internet and computers. With the growth of the World Wide Web in 1996, the first online web-based educational systems appeared, and they began to profit from the fast development of web technology. The bulk of today's learning systems are web-based, with an emphasis on either individual students or teamwork, and are designed for both blended and online learning. Curriculum management, courseware creation, student registration and administration, reporting, and event management are some of the basic features of such a system. Traditional educational systems rely on instructors or subject experts to create closed corpus instructional materials. External content cannot be provided by such systems. The World Wide Web creates an open corpus environment in which knowledge may be found relatively quickly. Because this massive quantity of data must be machine-processable in order to be linked to educational systems, it poses a challenge for exploration. The semantic web movement, which offers a standard foundation that enables data to be shared and reused across application, business, and community borders, is one potential answer to this issue. It allows for the creation of learning ontologies and the semantic tagging of learning resources (Jin T., 2021) (P. Markellou, 2005).

Apart from open corpus syndrome, there has been a demand for a more customised approach to education in the past century, particularly in the last few decades as computer technology has advanced. Various levels of previous knowledge and skills among people, sociocultural and demographic variations, different abilities or impairments, and student emotional states such as dissatisfaction, motivation, and confidence are all causes for content adaptation. Some researchers are attempting to overcome this by using semantic web technologies into the adaption process.

Over the past decade, the World Wide Web has changed dramatically. Initially, the internet was mainly made up of static HTML pages with little or no dynamic interaction. Scripting languages were created throughout time with the goal of creating dynamic web pages, thus improving the web's interaction and general quality. As a result, the second generation of the web, known as Web 2.0, was born. Despite its potential, Web 2.0 is restricted by the fact that it is intended for human interaction rather than machine interaction. The goal of Web 3.0 is to create a web that allows machines to analyse and comprehend the content on it as well as communicate with one another. The semantic web, headed by the World Wide Web Consortium (W3C), is a collaborative effort that aims to achieve this goal. The semantic web is a vision of data that can be understood by computers, allowing robots to do the job of locating and integrating data on the internet. The phrase "semantic web" was invented by Tim Barnes Lee. He is widely regarded as the web's inventor, and as the director of the W3C, he is one of the key figures in the development of the new semantic web. In practise, the semantic web should be capable of rapidly completing activities like arranging trip reservations. Users should be able to enter their desired trip destination and time, and a virtual agent should be able to provide them with the best travel arrangements by pulling data from relevant websites. That is only feasible if all relevant machines interpret information in the same way. The semantic web faces many challenges due to the rapid development of the World Wide Web. Finding, sorting, and presenting relevant data has become considerably more challenging as more data and multimedia material has been accessible (Baoyao, 2006) (Gizem, 2010). Its practical practicality has been questioned, but supporters say that applications in industry, biology, and human sciences research have already proved the concept's validity.

SEMANTIC WEB TECHNOLOGIES

The semantic web is built on ontologies. "Ontology is a formal statement of a shared conceptualization," says the most frequent definition. Ontologies attempt to explain things as well as how they may be linked and organised into hierarchies. Because earlier ontology languages, such as RDF and RDF schema, were faulty, the semantic web necessitated the development of a better ontology language. Various research organisations collaborated to create DAML+OIL, a collaborative effort that generated the new Web Ontology Language (OWL). Every ontology language must have well-defined syntax, semantics, and reasoning support, as well as adequate expressive power for entity description, and OWL meets all of these requirements. OWL full, OWL DL, and OWL light are the three OWL languages that have been specified. RDF and RDF schema are fully compatible with OWL full, and the two may be used together. To improve computer performance, OWL DL was created by limiting the usage of some OWL complete constructors. The incompatibility of OWL DL with RDF is its fault. Further OWL restrictions resulted in the development of OWL light, which is the most straightforward to apply and comprehend.

The Semantic Web is a web of data that can be imagined. It is typically constructed on syntaxes that utilise URIs to describe data, usually in triples-based structures, or interchanged over the web using RDF (Resource Description Framework) syntaxes, which were created specifically for the purpose. RDF is the building block for publishing and connecting data. Semantic web also uses OWL to create vocabularies, or "ontologies," and SKOS to create knowledge organisation that enriches data with extra meaning and improves online search by instructing the search engine to seek for compact and more relevant information on the web. Query languages and databases go hand in hand.

The query language for the Semantic Web is SPARQL. Cloud computing, on the other hand, refers to computation done via the Internet, such as allowing users to access database resources over the Internet without having to maintain them, enabling the use of dynamic and scalable databases. Cloud computing allows users to access shared resources and infrastructure on demand via the internet, allowing them to conduct activities that suit changing business requirements. The end user is usually unaware of the location of the physical resources and devices being used. It also allows customers to create, deploy, and administer their applications 'on the cloud,' which involves resource virtualization that maintains and controls itself.

Mobile technology offers users the ability to access information from any device at any time. Because mobile phones provide portability, maneuverability, transportability, and high performance, their usage as an information retrieval platform may open up a large industry. Incorporating the former two technologies, namely the SEMANTIC WEB & CLOUD on a mobile platform, may be able to meet the need for fast, semantic access to cloud data. According to recent estimates, there will be 7.2 billion mobile subscribers by 2012. According to a recent study from Juniper Research, the number of users accessing the internet on their mobile phones is expected to almost triple from 577 million now to more than 1.7 billion by 2013. With the advent of 3G, 4G, and mobile Internet, IT support systems that offer large amounts of storage space and rapid processing power are in high demand is shown in Figure 1.

Because of the rapid adoption of mobile technology, the digital world is concentrating all of its efforts on the creation of and for mobile platforms. The decoupling of data storage, processing, and administration from mobile hardware will improve performance, scalability, and agility, despite the fact that hardware costs are dropping. The cloud is the mobile's future. The reliance on hardware can be greatly reduced by transferring data and processing to the cloud, which provides

Figure 1. Semantic web technologies

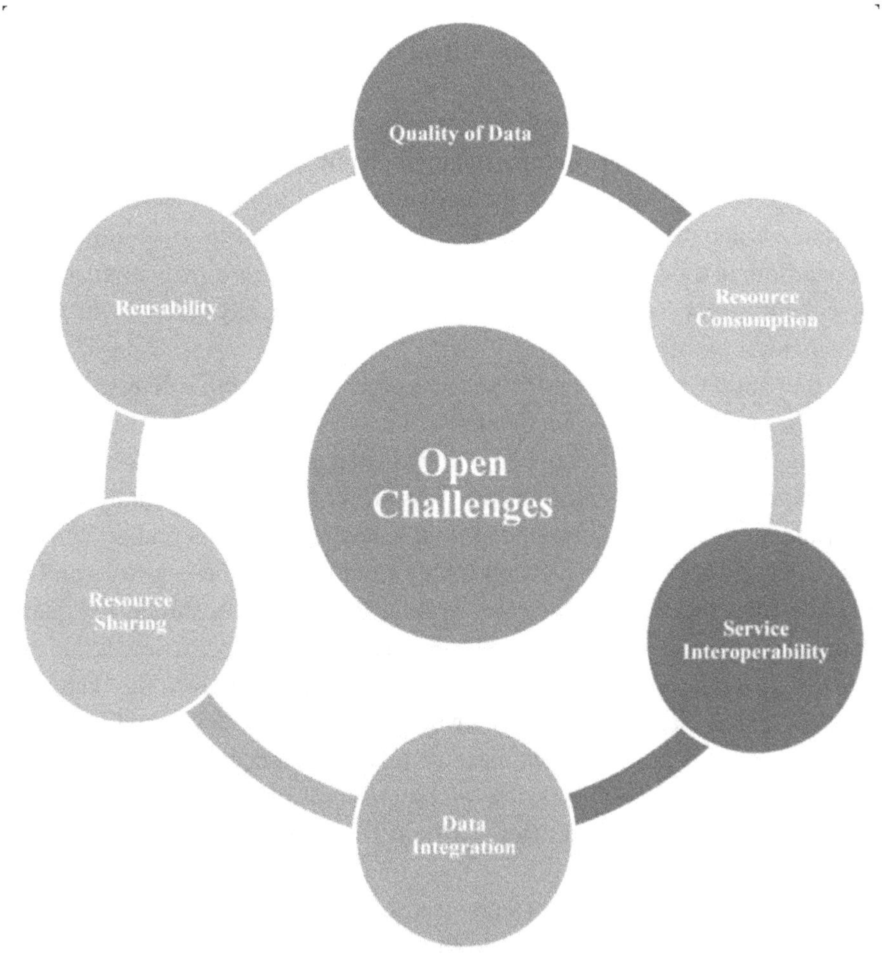

high performance, low cost, and high scalability features, as well as processing management and storage capability for large amounts of data, without the hassle of having to worry about mobile hardware configuration. Hosting in the cloud also eliminates the danger of losing critical data due to system failure, hardware failure, malware attack, and other factors.

Although the Semantic Web and DWs have taken distinct research paths in the context of BI applications over the past several years, certain recent findings indicate that convergence is not only inevitable but also advantageous for both sides. As a result, academics researching DW development are paying attention to the investigation and application of Semantic Web technologies. The idea of a web of connected data has recently emerged as a method for making all data accessible through the HTTP protocol, similar to how HTML pages work. Because it enables data integration on the web, linked open data (LOD) has been proposed as a viable paradigm for opening up data. LOD may be created to allow advanced data analysis, similar to data warehousing methods. Because data integration is one of the most challenging aspects of DWs, some academics suggest using data interchange standards such as RDF to store structured information and publish DW material as linked data. There is still a gap between conceptual methods for modelling architectures for linked data, systems, and data models, as well as their implementation, operationalization, and execution, in the business and enterprise sector. Furthermore, companies must resolve the inherent conflict between the value they typically place on private data and the benefit of transparency.

The Semantic Web and data storage ideas originate from quite diverse places. As a result, the studies that have been published have taken a variety of approaches to integrating these issues. The number of published papers and findings has grown as the advancement of these fields has progressed. As a result, it is rapidly becoming essential to summarise and provide a broad analysis of the integration of various subjects. As a consequence, it's impossible to tell where these ideas stand right now. In essence, the effect of these research investigations, as well as the maturity level of their findings, remains unknown. For academics, categorising the scientific contributions made on this subject, for example, is helpful since the themes that address the Semantic Web and DWs have not always been developed in the same manner. Each subject does, in fact, have its own conferences and publications. As a result, providing a broad overview of progress in merging these two domains is helpful in summarising and categorising research as well as identifying future research problems.

The systematic mapping (MP) study is a secondary research technique that has lately gained a lot of interest, owing to the fact that it provides a unique means of systematically evaluating the literature on a given subject. The types of research reports that have been completed, as well as the classification of their published findings, are organised in a systematic map. It typically provides a visual representation of their findings, such as a map. A thorough literature map has been suggested primarily for study areas where there are few relevant primary studies, such as the reported usage of Semantic Web technologies in DW development. In recent years, the number of publications on DWs and the Semantic Web that include methodological ideas and methods, among other things, has increased. This is due to the fact that these studies come from a wide range of academic fields, including Databases, Artificial Intelligence, and Natural Language Processing, as well as the fact that the connection between the Semantic Web and DWs is a hot topic right now. Given the enormous quantity of existing data (i.e., Big Data) and its usage on the web, it's important to figure out what kind of research is being done on how Semantic Web technologies are being used to DW development. A systematic map provides for the classification of the findings as well as the visual presentation of a summary.

Despite the fact that the data management community has historically concentrated on problems such as performance, scalability, and query expressiveness, there has been significant evidence of a growing interest in incorporating semantic information into various data management procedures. The University of Pennsylvania Workshop on Information Integration, for example, has identified the need to modify techniques for query responding, matching, and mapping to accommodate ontologies. Schema mapping techniques may benefit from the usage of ontologies. Various methods for storing and querying various types of metadata, such as data quality characteristics, provenance, overlay information, or annotations, have also been created, while relevant values have been utilised to improve database querying. Because of the complexity of data and the difficulty of fully comprehending its semantics, methods comparable to those used in the Semantic Web have been developed. For example, work on keyword searching in relational databases has previously been done.

Furthermore, query processing in the emerging field of dataspaces anticipates that users would often engage in exploratory behaviour with the system, posing imprecise questions, defining mappings on a pay-as-you-go basis, and expecting extremely diverse and frequently probabilistic query responses. Even the data model often employed in dataspaces is triple-based, as in RDF, and the query method is based on the concept of entities, which is the backbone of Semantic Web data, rather than structures like tuples, columns, components, or values. Based on the above, it's clear that the Semantic Web presents new data engineering research problems and possibilities. First, we may enhance the already available capabilities by integrating ontologies and other semantic models and reasoners into existing query and integration engines. Second, the RDF paradigm opens up new research avenues for storing and querying large amounts of RDF data. One of our objectives is to increase awareness of all of these possibilities and to encourage academics to pursue these (and other) research avenues. It's worth noting that the narrative of RDF's evolution is similar to that of XML. It was also presented by another community, but it turned out to be a popular study subject that continues to this day.

While it is obvious that one of our objectives is to encourage database researchers to work on Semantic Web issues, a higher-level goal is to bring the Data Management and Semantic Web groups together. So far, the two groups have pursued research in mostly separate directions (by publishing to different venues). The first is primarily concerned with scalability and performance, whereas the second is concerned with semantic interoperability of data on the Internet. We think that both contribute significantly to the success of contemporary Web apps. As a result, we anticipate having great chances to bring academics and practitioners from both fields together. The opening and invited presentation at PODS 2009 (on a Web of Concepts) demonstrated that the database community has begun to pay attention to the Semantic Web community's ideas and problems. For the last two years, ICDE has hosted a Workshop on the confluence of the Semantic Web and Databases: Data Engineering Meets the Semantic Web (DESWeb). Semantic Data Management (SemData) was held at VLDB 2010 and Semantic Web Information Management (SWIM) was held at SIGMOD 2011. The fact that one of the PODS 2011 lectures was on "Querying Semantic Web data using SPARQL" and that the best paper prize at VLDB 2007 was on storing RDF are further signs of a rising interest. The Semantic Web is an emerging extension of the World Wide Web in which the semantics of online-based information and services are specified, allowing the web to comprehend and respond to requests from humans and machines to utilise web content.

SEMANTIC WEB ANALYTICS

The Semantic Web is a set of metadata-based infrastructures enabling web-based reasoning. It complements rather than replaces the existing Web. The majority of the information on the Internet nowadays is appropriate for human consumption. People now utilise the Web to search for and consume information, as well as to find and communicate with other humans. Only search engines exist as software tools to assist these tasks, which are not especially well developed. These tools' technology is essentially the same, and Web content outgrows technical advancements. The retrieval of information is not adequately supported. The main issue is that the meaning of Web material is now inaccessible to machines, in the sense that computers are unable to understand words, phrases, and the connections between them. The W3C (World Wide Web Consortium) has been working on the development of open standards to enable the construction of the semantic Web.

These standards are necessary for defining information on the Web in such a manner that computers may utilise it not only for display, but also for interoperability and integration across systems and applications, thus addressing heterogeneity issues. Bioinformatics as a subject has evolved mainly from the molecular biology labs where it began. In general, each lab focused on a specific area of biology, and there are only a few laboratories focusing on a single issue globally. Many of these laboratories have made their own data publicly accessible. This material is often unstructured or semi-structured. Although most of the data is made up of DNA or protein sequences, it is usually accompanied by huge amounts of text. The Semantic Web's ultimate goal is to provide meaning to the present Web by retrieving the meaning of data, object characteristics, and complex connections between them using a set of formal rules that make information accessible to computers.

Machine accessibility should be regarded as encoding data in such a manner that queries may be made based on the data's meaning. The Semantic Web is a growing body of information designed to enable anybody with access to the Internet to contribute their knowledge and discover answers to their queries. Rather of being in natural language text, information on the Semantic Web is kept in a structured format that is relatively simple to deal with for both computers and humans. The study of the relationships between the system of signs and their meanings is known as semantics. Three types of semantics have been proposed.

Personalized recommendation systems have become critical tools for determining user preferences as the amount of information available on the internet has grown rapidly. Spotify, Hulu, Netflix, Pandora, Amazon, and Sigchi are the most popular recommendations all around the globe. Amazon and Netflix provide product and movie recommendations based on a user's profile, past purchase history, and online activity. According on user characteristics and behaviour, Facebook and Google News suggest news items. Companies use recommender systems to increase sales and attract consumers with a customised offer as a consequence of more positive feedback from customers. Recommendations usually speed up searches and make it simpler for people to access their own material alone, as well as surprising them with offers they would not have looked for. Personalization is increasingly extensively utilised in e-commerce as a powerful tool for tailoring buy suggestions. Personalization is a need for every website or app that offers a dependable user experience. It keeps consumers from spending time looking for what they want and promotes quick searches. When browsing the internet, a number of variables contribute to determining the user's preferences. Today's search technologies, on the other hand, provide irrelevant information for many queries. As a result, the most pressing requirement now is to anticipate user demands in order to enhance a website's usability and user retention. Because semantic web can create languages for expressing information in a machine-readable manner, it is the best platform for implementing Personalization.

The semantic web is an expansion of the existing web in which information has a defined meaning, allowing computers and humans to work together. Machines will also be able to process and "understand" the information. The Semantic Web's backbone is ontology. A acknowledged and clear definition of a common conception is an ontology. It is made up of domain-related notions such as entities, characteristics, and properties. Re Movender is a content-based and collaborative movie recommendation system that uses a hybrid approach. To compare the different users' interests with movie content information, a collaborative missing data prediction method is employed. Users are asked to evaluate movies on a scale of one to five using the ReMovender recommendation system. Collaborate Filtering anticipates missing ratings data as well as similarities between evaluations from various users.

The movies are correlated using a collection of movie information and suggestions are given to the viewers using a content-based approach.

A hybrid system that utilises both collaborative filtering and content-based methods to personalise videos for viewers. It produces more powerful outcomes by combining various techniques rather than utilising pure methods alone. The Adsorption algorithm is enhanced by the Content-based method in this thesis to provide improved recommendations. Aside from rating archives, video and movie content information is also utilised to propose new products, assisting in the reinforcement of suggestions. When the data is not sparse, the system performs better. That is why the findings from MovieLens data are superior than those from YouTube. HRSWM (Human Resource Semantic Web Management System) is a system that helps companies accomplish their objectives by converting diverse, fragmented data into useful information that can answer important questions. This research describes a system that combines the advantages of the Resource Descriptive Framework (RDF) with the high performance of database management systems, resulting in improved real-time retrieval performance.

CONCLUSION

SemAware is a generic framework that incorporates semantic data into online use mining. Semantic data may be used into pattern finding. In the fixed sequential pattern mining method, a semantic distance matrix is utilised to reduce the search area and partly relieve the algorithm from support counting. The mining method is based on a 1st-order Markov model that has been supplemented with semantic data. Framework that works as an intelligent agent, providing users with dynamically suggested websites. PagePrompter is a kind of programme that learns from online use statistics and user behaviour. An agent, like a guide, assists a user in exploring the website. PagePrompter may also be used to analyse user behaviour, website design, system performance analysis, website designer for website improvement, and adaptable website generation. The suggestions are generated across various domains using a system based on temporal ontologies and a trust network. In the form of a trust update procedure, similarity metrics are taken into account. Intuitionistic Fuzzy Sets (IFS) are utilised in this Personalization system to reflect the uncertainty that is inherent in the suggestion process. The tourism domain, which includes subdomains such as air travel, geography, cuisine, entertainment, and sports, is considered a major research. The case study currently utilises two domains: destination and travel, which may easily be expanded to include additional domains. The suggestions in this suggested model are derived only from trustworthy agents, and the data as well as the techniques used to create the recommendations are kept by the agents, making the recommendation process visible to the users.

REFERENCES

Aquilani, B., Piccarozzi, M., Abbate, T., & Codini, A. (2020). The Role of Open Innovation and Value Co-creation in the Challenging Transition from Industry 4.0 to Society 5.0: Toward a Theoretical Framework. *Sustainability (Basel)*, *2020*(13), 2682. doi:10.3390/su12218943

Jin, T., Li, J., Yang, J., Li, J., Hong, F., Long, H., Deng, Q., Qin, Y., Jiang, J., Zhou, X., Song, Q., Pan, C., & Luo, P. (2021). SARS-Cov-2 presented in the air of an intensive car unit (ICU). *Sustainable Cities and Society*, *2021*(65), 102446. doi:10.1016/j.scs.2020.102446 PMID:32837871

Karaman, H. (2010). *A Content Based Movie Recommendation System Empowered By Collaborative Missing Data Prediction*. [Master Thesis, The Graduate School Of Natural And Applied Sciences Of Middle East Technical University].

Li, J. (2016). Industrial Big Data: Intelligent Transformation and Value Innovation in the Age of Industry 4.0. *CommonWealth Magazine Group*, 90–93.

Liris, C. O., Lahoud, I., El Khoury, H., & Liris, P.-A. C. (2018). Ontology-based Recommender System in Higher Education. *IW3C2 (International World Wide Web Conference Committee)*. ACM. ISBN 978-1-4503-5640-4/18/04.

Ozturk, G. (2010). A *Hybrid Video Recommendation System Based On A Graph-Based Algorithm*. [Master thesis, Computer Engineering Department, Middle East Technical University].

Pereira, A. G., Lima, T. M., & Charrua-Santos, F. (2020). Industry 4.0 and Society 5.0. *Opportunities and Threats. Int. J. Recent Technol. Eng.*, *2020*(8), 3305–3308.

Popitsch, N., & Haslhofer, B. (2011). DSNotify – A solution for event detection and link maintenance in dynamic datasets. *Journal of Web Semantics*, *9*(3), 266–283. doi:10.1016/j.websem.2011.05.002

YangG.PangZ.DeenJ.DongM.ZhangY.-T (2020).;Lovell, N., & Rahmani, A. M. (2020). Homecare Robotic Systems for Healthcare 4.0: Visions and Enabling Technologies. *IEEE Journal of Biomedical and Health Informatics*, *24*(9), 2535–2549. doi:10.1109/JBHI.2020.2990529 PMID:32340971

Chapter 5
Development of Artificial Intelligence of Things and Cloud Computing Environments Through Semantic Web Control Models

B. Revathi
Department of Artificial Intelligence and Data Science, Jaishriram Engineering College, Tirupur, India

S. Hamsa
Department of Electronics and Communication Engineering, Jyothy Institute of Technology, India

Nazeer Shaik
https://orcid.org/0009-0008-1361-258X
Department of Computer Science and Engineering, Srinivasa Ramanujan Institute of Technology (SRIT), India

Susanta Kumar Satpathy
Department of Computer Science and Engineering, Vignan Foundation of Science, Technology, and Research, Guntur, India

Hari
https://orcid.org/0000-0002-4778-3802
Department of Mechanical Engineering, Kongu Engineering College, Erode, India

Sureshkumar Myilsamy
Bannari Amman Institute of Technology, Erode, India

ABSTRACT

This chapter delves into the integration of artificial intelligence of things (AIoT) with cloud computing environments, facilitated by semantic web control models. It explores how leveraging semantic technologies can enhance the interoperability, intelligence, and efficiency of AIoT systems within cloud infrastructures. The chapter begins by elucidating the foundational concepts of AIoT, cloud computing, and the

DOI: 10.4018/979-8-3693-0766-3.ch005

Semantic Web. It then discusses the challenges associated with integrating AIoT devices and cloud platforms, such as data heterogeneity, interoperability issues, and security concerns. Next, it presents various semantic web control models and their applicability in AIoT-cloud integration, including ontology-based reasoning, knowledge representation, and semantic interoperability standards. Furthermore, the chapter analyzes case studies and practical implementations showcasing the benefits of employing Semantic Web control models in AIoT-cloud environments. Lastly, it outlines future research directions and potential advancements in this burgeoning field.

INTRODUCTION

The integration of Artificial Intelligence of Things (AIoT) and cloud computing has led to a new era of interconnectedness and intelligence in digital ecosystems. The proliferation of smart devices and the growing amount of data generated by these devices have prompted innovative approaches to harness this information. The Semantic Web is at the core of this convergence, enhancing interoperability, intelligence, and control in AIoT and cloud computing environments. AIoT applications are transforming various domains, from smart homes and wearable devices to industrial automation and smart cities, revolutionizing how we interact with and harness the capabilities of connected devices (Sadeeq et al., 2021).

Cloud computing has become a crucial tool for scalability, flexibility, and accessibility of digital services and applications. It allows organizations to access advanced analytics, machine learning, and AI-driven capabilities. However, integrating AIoT devices with cloud computing environments presents challenges due to the heterogeneity of data generated by IoT devices, which often differs in format, structure, and semantics, preventing interoperability and hindering the seamless exchange of information between devices and cloud platforms. The security and privacy of data transmitted between AIoT devices and cloud servers is crucial due to increasing cyber threats and data breaches (Mukhopadhyay et al., 2021). Robust security measures are needed to protect sensitive information and maintain user trust in AIoT systems. Scalability and resource management challenges in cloud computing environments pose logistical challenges, potentially leading to performance bottlenecks and degraded user experiences.

Researchers and practitioners are increasingly using Semantic Web control models to enhance AIoT and cloud computing. These models imbue digital data with well-defined meaning and context, allowing machines to understand and interpret information intelligently. They use ontologies, semantic reasoning, and knowledge representation techniques to facilitate enhanced data interoperability, semantic integration, and context-aware decision-making in AIoT and cloud computing environments (Hansen & Bøgh, 2021). This enables seamless data exchange and interoperability across heterogeneous systems. This chapter explores the application of Semantic Web control models in AIoT-cloud integration, focusing on their foundational concepts, practical implementations, and future trends. Through case studies, practical implementations, and a forward-looking analysis, the chapter aims to highlight the transformative potential of these models in shaping AIoT and cloud computing landscapes (Chang et al., 2021).

AIoT is the integration of AI technologies with IoT infrastructure, enabling intelligent, interconnected systems to perceive, reason, and act autonomously. It extends traditional IoT devices' capabilities by integrating AI algorithms, allowing real-time data analysis, actionable insights, and adapting behavior based on changing environmental conditions. The advancements in AIoT are primarily driven by several significant technological advancements (Zhang & Tao, 2020). Recent AI research advancements, including machine learning, deep learning, and natural language processing, have enabled advanced AIoT applications. These algorithms enable devices to learn from experience, recognize patterns, and make intelligent decisions without explicit programming. Edge computing architectures have democratized AIoT deployment by bringing computational resources closer to data sources, reducing latency, bandwidth usage, and enhancing privacy and security (L. Sun et al., 2020).

Sensor technologies, miniaturization, and cost reduction have led to the rise of connected devices in various sectors, including smart homes, wearables, industrial machinery, and autonomous vehicles. These sensors provide real-time data, enabling AIoT systems to monitor and control environments with unprecedented granularity. Standardization efforts, such as interoperability protocols and communication standards, have facilitated seamless integration and interoperability between different manufacturers and ecosystems (Balas et al., 2020).

Evolution of Cloud Computing Environments

Since its inception, cloud computing has transformed the way organizations provision, deploy, and manage IT resources. Initially designed for on-demand internet delivery, it has evolved into a multifaceted ecosystem with a wide range of services and deployment models, spanning several important stages. Cloud computing initially focused on providing infrastructure components like virtual machines, storage, and networking resources on a pay-per-use basis. IaaS offered dynamic IT infrastructure scaling without significant upfront capital investment. PaaS introduced higher-level abstractions and services like development frameworks, databases, and middleware, abstracting underlying infrastructure complexities. PaaS platforms enabled developers to build, deploy, and manage applications more efficiently, accelerating innovation and software delivery (Sunyaev & Sunyaev, 2020).

Software as a Service (SaaS) has revolutionized software delivery by offering on-demand access to fully managed applications and services over the internet. SaaS solutions include productivity tools, CRM software, and ERP systems, providing organizations with greater flexibility in adopting and scaling software solutions. As cloud adoption matures, organizations are increasingly adopting hybrid and multi-cloud deployment strategies to leverage the strengths of different providers and deployment models. Hybrid cloud environments enable seamless integration between on-premises infrastructure and public cloud services, while multi-cloud architectures mitigate vendor lock-in and enhance resilience (Shamshirband et al., 2020). Edge and fog computing paradigms extend cloud computing by bringing computational resources closer to the data source, enabling real-time processing and analysis at the network edge. The evolution of cloud computing has shifted towards higher-level abstractions, automation, and scalability, driven by innovations in AI, edge computing, and hybrid architectures, necessitating organizations to adapt their IT strategies to fully harness its potential in an interconnected world (Shafiq et al., 2022).

i. The Semantic Web facilitates interoperability between AIoT devices and cloud computing platforms by providing a common semantic framework for data representation and exchange. This enhances communication, collaboration, and data sharing, allowing AIoT devices to effectively utilize cloud-based resources.
ii. Semantic technologies enable AIoT systems to intelligently interpret and contextualize data by inferring context and semantics. This context-aware approach enhances data processing accuracy and relevance, leading to more nuanced insights and decision-making capabilities, resulting in more intelligent and adaptive AIoT applications.
iii. Semantic Web technologies enable AIoT devices to search for and retrieve relevant information from cloud-based data sources. Ontology-based query languages like SPARQL enable complex queries across multiple repositories, improving data retrieval efficiency. This semantic querying capability allows AIoT systems to access and leverage vast cloud-stored information, enabling data-driven decision-making and analytics.
iv. Semantic Web technologies enable dynamic service composition and orchestration in AIoT-cloud environments. They use ontologies to represent services, capabilities, and constraints, allowing AIoT devices to discover and compose composite services from available cloud resources, enabling autonomous orchestration of complex workflows and interactions.

v. Semantic Web technologies enable AIoT devices to model and reason about domain-specific knowledge and relationships. Ontologies serve as a formal framework for capturing domain knowledge and encoding semantic relationships. This knowledge-driven approach enhances the intelligence and autonomy of AIoT systems, allowing them to make informed decisions based on contextual understanding and domain knowledge.

CHALLENGES IN AIOT-CLOUD INTEGRATION

Data Heterogeneity and Interoperability Issues

The integration of AIoT with cloud computing environments faces significant challenges due to data heterogeneity and interoperability issues. The diverse data generated by IoT devices, varying in format, structure, semantics, and context, poses significant obstacles to seamless integration and interoperability between AIoT devices and cloud platforms (Houssein et al., 2021). The figure 1 depicts data heterogeneity and interoperability issues related to AIOT-Cloud integration.

- **Data Format and Structure Variability:** IoT devices produce data in various formats, including text, images, videos, sensor readings, and telemetry data. Moreover, different devices may use proprietary data formats or protocols, further exacerbating the complexity of data integration. Standardizing data formats and establishing interoperability protocols are essential steps to address this challenge (Pramila et al., 2023; Rahamathunnisa et al., 2023; Ramudu et al., 2023).
- **Semantic Misinterpretation:** IoT data often lack explicit semantics, making it challenging to interpret and infer the meaning or context of the data. For example, sensor readings may lack metadata or annotations describing the units of measurement, timestamps, or the physical context in which the data was collected. As a result, interpreting IoT data accurately and deriving meaningful insights becomes a daunting task. Semantic technologies, such as ontologies and metadata standards, can help address this challenge by providing a formal framework for representing and enriching IoT data with contextual information.
- **Integration with Legacy Systems:** Many AIoT deployments coexist with legacy systems and infrastructure, which may use outdated protocols or lack support for modern data interchange standards. Integrating legacy systems with cloud-based AIoT platforms requires careful planning and retrofitting to ensure compatibility and interoperability. Legacy system modernization

Figure 1. Data heterogeneity and interoperability issues for AIOT-cloud integration

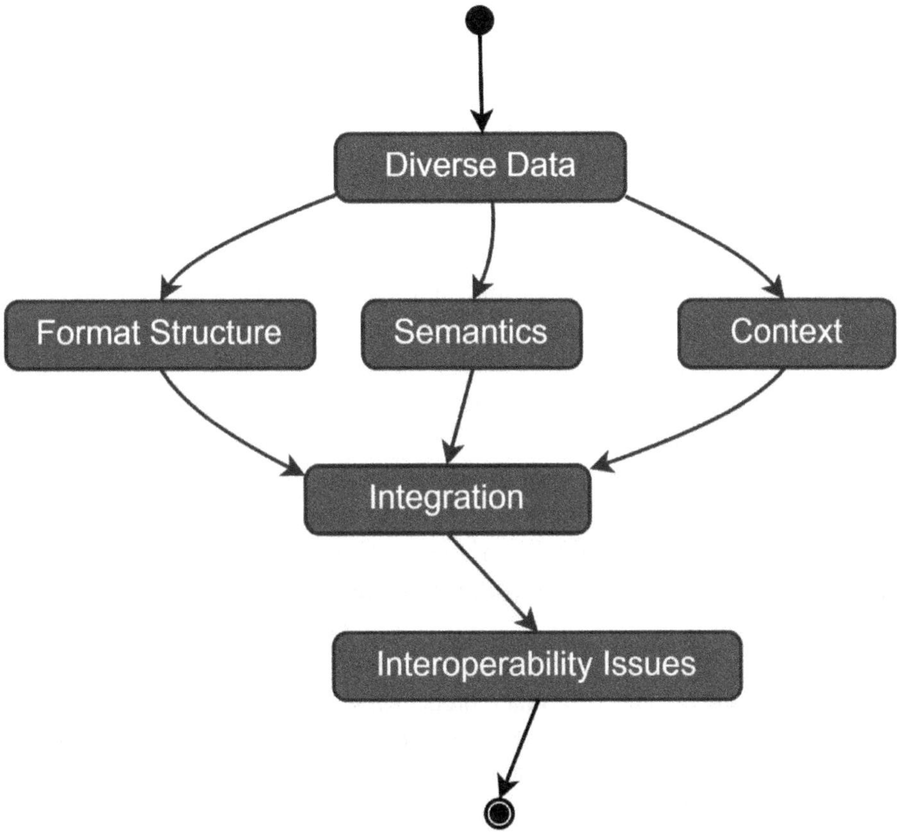

initiatives, such as protocol translation gateways and middleware layers, can help bridge the gap between legacy systems and cloud environments (Hussain et al., 2023; M. Kumar et al., 2023).

- **Scalability and Performance:** As the number of IoT devices and data streams continues to proliferate, scalability and performance become critical concerns in AIoT-cloud integration. Traditional cloud architectures may struggle to handle the massive influx of data and processing demands imposed by AIoT workloads. Scalable and distributed data processing frameworks, such as Apache Kafka and Apache Spark, can alleviate scalability bottlenecks and enhance the performance of AIoT applications in cloud environments.
- **Security and Privacy:** The integration of AIoT devices with cloud computing introduces new security and privacy challenges, including data breaches, unauthorized access, and data leakage. Securing data transmission

channels, implementing encryption mechanisms, and enforcing access control policies are essential measures to mitigate security risks in AIoT-cloud integration (Nanda et al., 2024a; Rahamathunnisa et al., 2023; Sonia et al., 2024). Additionally, ensuring compliance with data privacy regulations, such as GDPR and CCPA, is paramount to safeguarding user privacy and maintaining trust in AIoT systems.

To effectively integrate AIoT and cloud computing, organizations must address data heterogeneity and interoperability challenges through a comprehensive approach that includes standardization, semantic enrichment, legacy system integration, scalable infrastructure solutions, and robust security measures.

Security and Privacy Concerns

The integration of AIoT devices with cloud computing presents security and privacy challenges, as AIoT systems often involve the collection, transmission, and processing of sensitive data, necessitating the confidentiality, integrity, and availability of this data to prevent unauthorized access or manipulation (Heidari & Jafari Navimipour, 2022; Houssein et al., 2021).

AIoT devices are vulnerable to security threats like malware, ransomware, and DDoS attacks, which can lead to data breaches, service disruptions, and financial losses. To protect data, robust authentication mechanisms, encryption protocols, and intrusion detection systems are needed. Privacy concerns arise from the ubiquitous nature of AIoT devices, which can capture sensitive information about individuals' behaviors (Revathi et al., 2024). As AIoT systems expand, stakeholders must implement privacy-preserving technologies like differential privacy and data anonymization to uphold user privacy rights and regulatory compliance.

Scalability and Resource Management Challenges

Cloud computing environments face scalability and resource management challenges for AIoT integration due to the exponential growth of AIoT devices and data streams. Inadequate scalability can lead to performance bottlenecks, increased latency, and degraded user experiences, especially during peak usage periods (Houssein et al., 2021; Shamshirband et al., 2020).

In multi-tenant cloud environments, AIoT applications can face resource contention and allocation inefficiencies due to limited computational resources, storage capacity, and network bandwidth. Without effective resource management strategies like workload balancing, auto-scaling, and reservation mechanisms, AIoT applications may experience resource starvation or underutilization, hindering scalability and performance. The heterogeneous nature of AIoT devices also presents challenges for resource provisioning and management. Optimizing resource allocation requires adaptive algorithms and intelligent scheduling policies considering device constraints, application requirements, and environmental conditions (Boopathi et al., 2021; Haribalaji et al., 2021; Naveeenkumar et al., 2024). A comprehensive approach combining cloud-native technologies like containerization and serverless computing with AI-driven optimization techniques like machine learning can effectively address scalability and resource management issues, enabling organizations to efficiently scale AIoT deployments.

SEMANTIC WEB CONTROL MODELS

Semantic Web control models are crucial for improving interoperability, intelligence, and efficiency in various domains like AIoT and cloud computing. They offer a formal framework for representing, reasoning, and exchanging semantic information, allowing machines to interpret data more meaningfully. This section delves into the foundational components of semantic web control models, including ontology-based reasoning, knowledge representation techniques, and semantic interoperability standards (Rhayem et al., 2020). The figure 2 depicts semantic web control models.

Figure 2. Semantic web control models

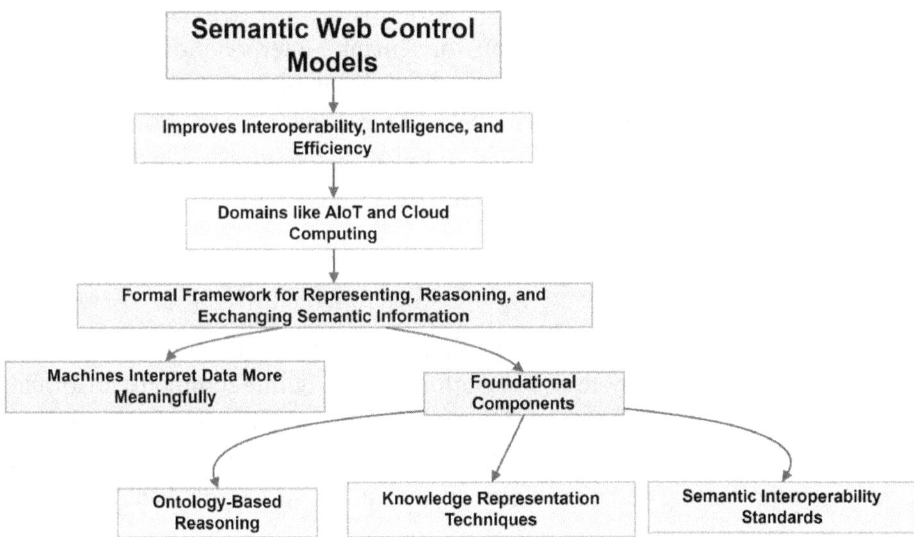

Ontology-Based Reasoning

Ontology-based reasoning lies at the heart of semantic web control models, enabling machines to infer implicit knowledge and make intelligent decisions based on explicit domain knowledge. Ontologies are formal representations of domain concepts, relationships, and axioms, encoded using ontology languages such as OWL (Web Ontology Language) or RDF (Resource Description Framework). These ontologies provide a shared vocabulary and semantics for describing and reasoning about domain-specific entities and their interrelationships(Yahya et al., 2021).

Ontology-based reasoning encompasses various inferential mechanisms, including classification, deduction, and consistency checking, that enable machines to derive new knowledge from existing ontological axioms and data instances. For example, through ontology-based reasoning, an AIoT device can infer the type and capabilities of a discovered sensor based on its ontological classification, enabling more accurate interpretation and utilization of sensor data. Ontologies enable semantic querying and retrieval, allowing machines to formulate complex queries across multiple data sources and ontological hierarchies. AIoT devices and cloud platforms can perform semantic search and discovery tasks, improving knowledge retrieval and decision-making in diverse environments.

Knowledge Representation Techniques

Knowledge representation techniques are essential in semantic web control models for formalizing domain knowledge. They enable the representation of complex knowledge structures in a machine-readable format. Formalisms like Description Logics and Semantic Web Rule Language are used to encode domain knowledge and specify inferential rules and constraints for semantic interpretation and reasoning (D. M. Sharma et al., 2024). Graph-based representations like RDF graphs and property graphs are widely used to model and represent semantic information in a distributed and interconnected manner, enabling the integration and fusion of diverse data sources and ontologies (Patel & Jain, 2021).

Semantic Interoperability Standards

Semantic interoperability standards facilitate seamless communication and data exchange between diverse systems and platforms. They define common data formats, vocabularies, and communication protocols. The Resource Description Framework (RDF) is a significant standard in semantic interoperability, providing a standardized format for representing and exchanging metadata and structured data on the web.

RDF enables the creation of linked data structures, facilitating data integration from diverse sources and domains (Dadkhah et al., 2020).

Ontology languages like OWL and RDFS provide standardized vocabularies and semantics for defining ontologies and domain models, enhancing interoperability and semantic understanding across heterogeneous systems. Semantic web services standards like SAWSDL and WSDL allow for the annotation of web services with semantic metadata, facilitating automated service discovery, composition, and invocation based on semantic descriptions. Semantic web control models, based on ontology-based reasoning, knowledge representation techniques, and semantic interoperability standards, enable machines to understand, interpret, and exchange semantic information meaningfully (Rhayem et al., 2020). These foundational components can enhance interoperability, intelligence, and efficiency in AIoT and cloud computing systems, paving the way for more intelligent digital ecosystems.

INTEGRATION APPROACHES FOR AIOT AND CLOUD COMPUTING

Semantic interoperability frameworks are crucial for integrating AIoT devices with cloud computing environments, ensuring seamless communication, data exchange, and interoperability between heterogeneous systems. This section explores integration approaches for AIoT and cloud computing, focusing on semantic interoperability frameworks (Rong et al., 2021). The figure 3 depicts various integration approaches for AIOT and cloud computing.

Semantic Data Integration Strategies

The integration of AIoT with cloud computing environments requires effective strategies for seamlessly combining data from heterogeneous sources while preserving semantic coherence and context. Semantic data integration approaches play a crucial role in achieving this objective by leveraging semantic technologies to harmonize, reconcile, and interlink data from diverse AIoT devices and cloud platforms. In this section, we will explore semantic data integration strategies and their applicability in the context of AIoT-cloud integration (Xiong & Chen, 2020).

Ontology Mapping and Alignment: Ontology mapping and alignment techniques facilitate the integration of ontological schemas and data models from heterogeneous sources, enabling semantic interoperability and data exchange. These techniques involve identifying correspondences and mappings between concepts, properties, and relationships in different ontologies and aligning them to establish semantic correspondences. Through ontology mapping and alignment, AIoT devices and cloud

Figure 3. Integration Approaches for AIOT and Cloud Computing

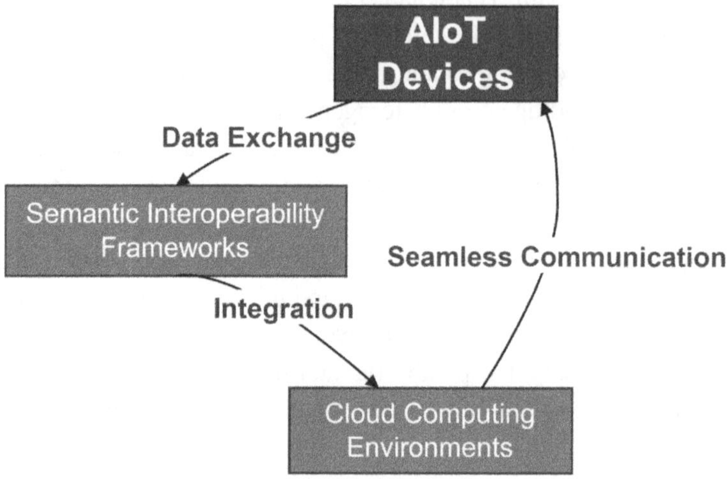

platforms can reconcile differences in terminology, semantics, and schema structures, enabling seamless data integration and interpretation across heterogeneous systems (Agrawal et al., 2023; Hema et al., 2023, 2023). For example, mappings between sensor ontologies and domain-specific ontologies can enable the integration of sensor data with contextual information, such as environmental conditions or user preferences, enhancing the richness and relevance of AIoT applications.

Semantic Data Mediation: Semantic data mediation involves the transformation and mediation of data between different semantic representations and formats, enabling interoperability and data exchange across heterogeneous systems. Semantic mediators act as intermediaries that translate data between source and target ontologies, resolving semantic heterogeneity and ensuring semantic coherence during data integration processes (Boopathi, 2024a; Pachiappan et al., 2024a; Venkateswaran et al., 2023). By employing semantic data mediation techniques, AIoT devices and cloud platforms can accommodate differences in data models, vocabularies, and semantics, enabling seamless communication and collaboration. For instance, semantic mediators can translate sensor data from proprietary formats to standardized ontologies, facilitating interoperability and data sharing with external systems and applications.

Semantic Interoperability Standards: Semantic interoperability standards define common vocabularies, ontologies, and communication protocols that facilitate the integration and exchange of semantic data across heterogeneous systems and platforms. These standards enable AIoT devices and cloud environments to communicate and collaborate effectively by providing shared semantic frameworks and vocabularies. Standards such as the Resource Description Framework (RDF),

Web Ontology Language (OWL), and Semantic Web Rule Language (SWRL) provide formalisms for representing, exchanging, and reasoning about semantic data and knowledge. By adhering to these standards, AIoT devices and cloud platforms can ensure semantic coherence and interoperability, enabling seamless data integration and interpretation.

Semantic Data Annotation and Enrichment: Semantic data annotation and enrichment involve augmenting raw data with semantic metadata and annotations, enhancing its interpretability, and contextual relevance. Through semantic annotation, AIoT devices can enrich sensor data with additional contextual information, such as location, time, and provenance, facilitating more comprehensive and meaningful data interpretation. Furthermore, semantic enrichment techniques enable the integration of external knowledge sources, such as domain-specific ontologies, taxonomies, and linked data repositories, to augment AIoT data with additional semantics and domain-specific insights. By leveraging semantic enrichment, AIoT devices and cloud platforms can enhance the intelligence and relevance of data-driven applications and services.

Semantic data integration strategies are essential for seamless data interpretation in AIoT devices and cloud computing environments. They enable ontology mapping, semantic data mediation, interoperability standards, and data annotation techniques, achieving semantic coherence, interoperability, and contextual relevance, thereby unlocking the full potential of AIoT-cloud integration in various domains.

Semantic Interoperability Frameworks

Semantic interoperability frameworks enable the seamless integration of AIoT devices with cloud computing platforms by establishing common vocabularies, ontologies, and communication protocols, thereby facilitating consistent and context-aware data interpretation, thus fostering an intelligent digital ecosystem (Jiyi et al., 2021).

- **Ontology-Based Integration:** Ontology-based integration approaches leverage domain-specific ontologies to mediate data exchange and interoperability between AIoT devices and cloud platforms. These ontologies provide a shared conceptual framework for representing domain knowledge, enabling semantic alignment and integration of heterogeneous data sources. By mapping data instances to ontological concepts and relationships, AIoT devices and cloud platforms can achieve semantic interoperability, facilitating seamless data exchange and integration.
- **Semantic Mediation and Transformation:** Semantic mediation and transformation techniques enable the harmonization of data semantics across heterogeneous systems by translating between different ontologies

and data formats. These techniques leverage ontology mapping and alignment algorithms to reconcile semantic discrepancies and enable interoperability between AIoT devices and cloud platforms. By transforming data representations into a common semantic model, semantic mediation facilitates seamless integration and interoperability, enabling AIoT devices to communicate and collaborate with cloud-based services and applications.

- **Semantic Querying and Discovery:** Semantic querying and discovery mechanisms enable AIoT devices to formulate complex queries and discover relevant resources and services in cloud environments based on semantic descriptions. By leveraging ontology-based query languages, such as SPARQL (SPARQL Protocol and RDF Query Language), AIoT devices can perform semantic search and discovery tasks, enabling them to locate and access relevant data sources, services, and resources in the cloud. Semantic querying and discovery facilitate dynamic service composition and orchestration, enabling AIoT applications to adapt to changing requirements and environmental conditions.
- **Semantic Web Services:** Semantic web services standards, such as Semantic Annotations for WSDL and XML Schema (SAWSDL), enable the annotation of web services with semantic metadata, facilitating automated service discovery, composition, and invocation based on semantic descriptions. By annotating web services with semantic metadata, AIoT devices can discover and invoke cloud-based services and resources dynamically, based on their semantic capabilities and constraints. Semantic web services standards enhance the interoperability and agility of AIoT applications, enabling them to leverage cloud-based resources and services effectively.

Semantic interoperability frameworks are essential for integrating AIoT devices with cloud computing platforms. They establish common vocabularies, ontologies, and communication protocols, facilitating seamless data exchange. By utilizing ontology-based integration, semantic mediation, querying, and web services standards, AIoT devices can effectively access and utilize cloud-based resources.

Ontology Mapping and Alignment Techniques

Integration between AIoT and cloud computing environments is essential for leveraging the combined capabilities of intelligent devices and cloud-based resources. Various integration approaches have been developed to facilitate seamless communication, data exchange, and interoperability between AIoT devices and cloud platforms. One of the important approaches involves ontology mapping and alignment techniques, which enable the integration of heterogeneous ontologies and data schemas across AIoT and cloud environments (Rhayem et al., 2020; Yahya et al., 2021).

Ontology Mapping and Alignment Techniques

Ontology mapping and alignment techniques are essential for reconciling semantic heterogeneity between AIoT devices and cloud computing platforms, identifying correspondences and relationships between concepts, properties, and instances, thereby facilitating interoperability and semantic integration across different systems (Rong et al., 2021).

- **Lexical Matching:** Lexical matching techniques leverage linguistic similarities between ontology terms to establish correspondences based on lexical similarity metrics such as edit distance or string similarity. By comparing labels, synonyms, and textual descriptions of ontology entities, lexical matching techniques identify potential mappings between concepts and properties in different ontologies. However, lexical matching may be prone to ambiguity and inconsistency due to variations in language usage and semantics.
- **Structure-Based Matching:** Structure-based matching techniques focus on identifying structural similarities and alignments between ontology entities based on their hierarchical relationships and property mappings. These techniques analyze the hierarchical structure, subsumption relationships, and property hierarchies of ontologies to identify correspondences and mappings between concept hierarchies and properties. Structure-based matching enables more precise and context-aware ontology alignment by considering the semantics and relationships between ontology entities (Boopathi, 2024d; Boopathi et al., 2022).
- **Instance-Based Matching:** Instance-based matching techniques involve comparing instances and data instances across different ontologies to identify semantic correspondences and mappings. By analyzing instance data and metadata, instance-based matching techniques identify commonalities and overlaps between data instances and entities in different ontologies, enabling the alignment of heterogeneous data sources and ontologies. Instance-based matching facilitates semantic data integration and interoperability by leveraging real-world data instances to guide ontology alignment and mapping.
- **Semantic Similarity Measures:** Semantic similarity measures quantify the similarity between ontology entities based on their semantic properties and relationships. These measures assess the semantic relatedness and similarity

between concepts, properties, and instances in different ontologies, enabling more nuanced and context-aware ontology mapping and alignment. Semantic similarity measures leverage ontological semantics, axioms, and relationships to compute similarity scores and alignments between ontology entities, facilitating more accurate and meaningful ontology integration.

Ontology mapping and alignment techniques enable AIoT systems to integrate with cloud computing environments, promoting interoperability, data exchange, and semantic integration. This facilitates communication, collaboration, and data sharing between AIoT devices and cloud platforms, enhancing decision-making, analytics, and intelligence. These techniques also create shared conceptual frameworks, bridging the semantic gap between AIoT devices and cloud platforms, fostering more interconnected and intelligent digital ecosystems.

PRACTICAL IMPLEMENTATIONS

Semantic Web Control Models in Industrial IoT Applications

The application of Semantic Web control models in Industrial Internet of Things (IIoT) settings represents a transformative approach to enhancing interoperability, intelligence, and efficiency in industrial operations. By leveraging semantic technologies, such as ontologies, knowledge representation techniques, and semantic interoperability standards, industrial organizations can realize significant benefits in areas such as asset management, predictive maintenance, and supply chain optimization. In this section, we explore practical implementations of Semantic Web control models in various industrial IoT applications. The figure 4 depicts the use of semantic web control models in industrial IoT applications (Rong et al., 2021; Xiong & Chen, 2020).

Asset Management and Inventory Control: Semantic Web control models help organizations create unified, semantically enriched representations of their assets, equipment, and inventory across various systems and data sources. These models capture domain-specific knowledge about assets, their properties, and relationships, enabling more effective asset management, tracking, and utilization. For instance, in manufacturing, these models can create digital twins of production equipment, incorporating detailed metadata about equipment specifications, maintenance history, and operational parameters, enabling real-time monitoring, predictive maintenance, and optimization of production processes.

Predictive Maintenance and Condition Monitoring: Semantic Web control models enable organizations to implement proactive maintenance strategies by

Figure 4. Semantic web control models in industrial IoT applications

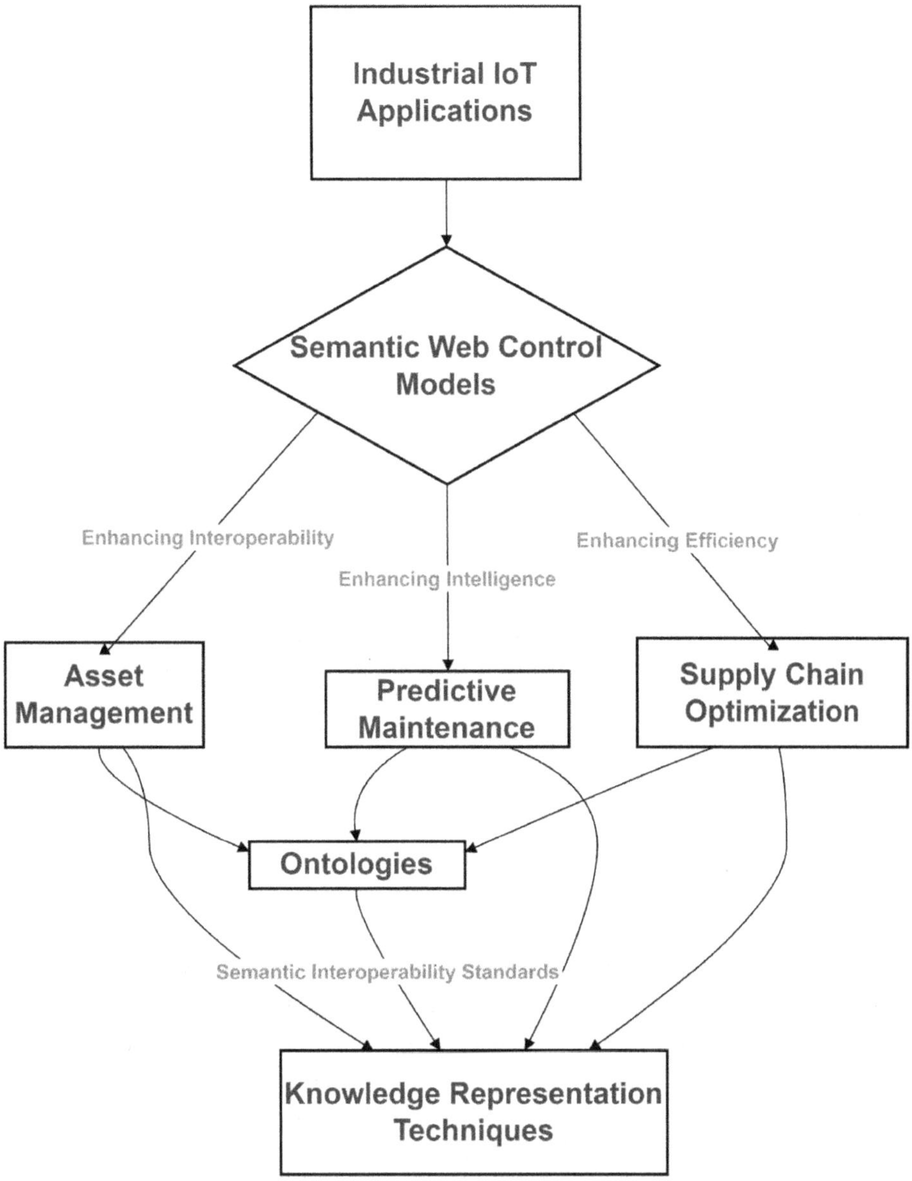

integrating sensor data, equipment telemetry, and maintenance records within a semantic framework. These models develop ontologies representing domain-specific knowledge about equipment health, failure modes, and maintenance procedures, enabling predictive maintenance algorithms to identify and mitigate potential equipment failures (M. Sharma et al., 2024a). For example, in energy infrastructure, these models can analyze real-time data from power generation assets, transmission lines, and distribution networks, optimizing maintenance schedules, reducing downtime, and extending asset lifespan.

Supply Chain Optimization and Logistics: Semantic Web control models enable the integration and interoperability of various supply chain data sources, enhancing visibility, traceability, and efficiency (Mohanty et al., 2023; Verma et al., 2024). They can be used in logistics and transportation to create semantic representations of shipment data, enabling intelligent supply chain management systems to optimize routing decisions, reduce delivery delays, and streamline inventory processes. Implementing these models in Industrial IoT applications can enhance asset management, predictive maintenance, and supply chain optimization, unlocking actionable insights, optimizing operational efficiency, and driving competitive advantage in the Industry 4.0 era.

Semantic-Driven Decision Making in Smart Cities

Smart cities use AIoT and cloud computing to improve urban infrastructure, services, and sustainability. Semantic-driven decision making is crucial for analyzing and interpreting vast data from IoT sensors and urban systems. This section explores practical implementations of semantic-driven decision making in smart cities, highlighting its impact on urban governance, resource management, and citizen services (Hansen & Bøgh, 2021; Sadeeq et al., 2021).

- **Intelligent Urban Mobility:** Semantic-driven decision making enables smart cities to optimize urban mobility systems, including transportation networks, public transit, and traffic management. By integrating data from diverse sources, such as GPS sensors, traffic cameras, and weather forecasts, AIoT systems can analyze real-time traffic patterns, predict congestion hotspots, and dynamically adjust traffic signals and routing algorithms to alleviate congestion and improve traffic flow. Semantic technologies facilitate the integration and fusion of heterogeneous data streams, enabling urban planners and transportation authorities to make informed decisions and implement adaptive traffic management strategies that enhance efficiency, safety, and sustainability (Boopathi, 2024b).
- **Environmental Monitoring and Sustainability:** Semantic-driven decision making enables smart cities to monitor and manage environmental quality, including air and water pollution, noise levels, and climate change impacts. By integrating data from IoT sensors, weather stations, and environmental monitoring networks, AIoT systems can analyze environmental indicators,

identify pollution sources, and assess the effectiveness of environmental policies and interventions. Semantic technologies facilitate the integration of disparate environmental data sources, enabling policymakers and environmental agencies to make data-driven decisions and implement targeted interventions that mitigate environmental risks and promote sustainability (Boopathi, 2022b, 2022a).

- **Citizen Engagement and Participatory Governance:** Semantic-driven decision making fosters citizen engagement and participatory governance by empowering residents to contribute data, insights, and feedback to urban decision-making processes. By providing access to open data platforms and participatory sensing applications, smart cities enable citizens to collect, share, and analyze data related to urban issues, such as public safety, infrastructure maintenance, and community development. Semantic technologies facilitate the integration and aggregation of citizen-generated data, enabling policymakers and city officials to incorporate citizen perspectives and priorities into urban planning and decision-making processes.
- **Emergency Response and Crisis Management:** Semantic-driven decision making enhances emergency response and crisis management capabilities in smart cities by enabling real-time situational awareness, resource allocation, and coordination among emergency responders. By integrating data from IoT sensors, social media feeds, and emergency service databases, AIoT systems can analyze emergency incidents, identify response priorities, and allocate resources based on evolving needs and priorities. Semantic technologies facilitate the integration of heterogeneous emergency response data sources, enabling emergency managers and first responders to make timely and informed decisions that enhance public safety and resilience (Revathi et al., 2024; M. Sharma et al., 2024a).
- **Infrastructure Planning and Asset Management:** Semantic-driven decision making supports infrastructure planning and asset management in smart cities by enabling proactive maintenance, optimization, and utilization of urban infrastructure assets. By integrating data from IoT sensors, building management systems, and infrastructure databases, AIoT systems can monitor asset health, predict maintenance needs, and optimize resource allocation for infrastructure maintenance and upgrades. Semantic technologies facilitate the integration of diverse infrastructure data sources, enabling city planners and infrastructure managers to make data-driven decisions that improve asset performance, longevity, and cost-effectiveness.

Semantic-driven decision making in smart cities uses AIoT and cloud computing to analyze and act on vast data, improving urban governance, resource management, and citizen services. This integration fosters innovation, sustainability, and inclusivity, creating more livable, resilient, and equitable urban environments for residents and stakeholders.

Healthcare Applications of AIoT-Cloud Integration

The integration of AIoT with cloud computing in healthcare is revolutionizing patient care, clinical workflows, and healthcare delivery. By utilizing AIoT devices and cloud-based resources, healthcare organizations can improve patient monitoring, diagnosis, treatment, and management, leading to better outcomes and efficiencies in the healthcare ecosystem (Malathi et al., 2024a).

- **Remote Patient Monitoring:** AIoT devices, such as wearable sensors, smartwatches, and implantable devices, enable remote monitoring of patients' vital signs, activities, and health parameters in real-time. By collecting and transmitting data to cloud-based platforms, these devices facilitate continuous monitoring of patients' health status and adherence to treatment regimens, enabling early detection of health issues and timely interventions. Cloud-based analytics and machine learning algorithms analyze streaming sensor data to detect anomalies, predict adverse events, and provide personalized recommendations to patients and healthcare providers. Practical implementations of remote patient monitoring include wearable ECG monitors for cardiac patients, smart insulin pumps for diabetes management, and remote monitoring systems for elderly patients living independently at home (Boopathi, 2023a; Malathi et al., 2024b).
- **Telemedicine and Telehealth Services:** Cloud-based telemedicine platforms enable virtual consultations, remote diagnosis, and telemonitoring of patients, expanding access to healthcare services and reducing geographical barriers. AIoT devices integrated with telemedicine platforms enable synchronous and asynchronous communication between patients and healthcare providers, facilitating remote consultations, medication management, and post-discharge monitoring. Cloud-based AI algorithms analyze patient data, medical images, and diagnostic tests to support clinical decision-making, triage patients, and prioritize care delivery. Practical implementations of telemedicine and telehealth services include remote consultations for chronic disease management, virtual urgent care visits, and telepsychiatry services for mental health support (Anitha et al., 2023; Pramila et al., 2023; Rebecca et al., 2024; Subha et al., 2023).
- **Predictive Analytics and Disease Management:** AIoT devices combined with cloud-based predictive analytics enable proactive management of

chronic diseases and population health. By analyzing longitudinal patient data, genetic information, and environmental factors, predictive models identify individuals at risk of developing chronic conditions, such as diabetes, hypertension, and heart disease. Cloud-based population health management platforms aggregate and analyze data from disparate sources, including electronic health records (EHRs), wearable devices, and public health databases, to identify trends, patterns, and risk factors at the population level. Practical implementations of predictive analytics and disease management include remote monitoring programs for patients with chronic conditions, personalized health coaching interventions, and targeted preventive screenings based on predictive risk scores (Malathi et al., 2024b; Ramudu et al., 2023; Veeranjaneyulu et al., 2023).

- **Smart Hospital Infrastructure:** AIoT devices integrated with cloud-based smart hospital infrastructure solutions optimize clinical workflows, resource utilization, and patient experiences within healthcare facilities. Smart sensors, IoT-enabled medical devices, and RFID tracking systems monitor the location, status, and utilization of hospital assets, equipment, and personnel in real-time. Cloud-based analytics platforms analyze streaming data from AIoT devices to optimize patient flow, reduce wait times, and enhance operational efficiency. Practical implementations of smart hospital infrastructure include real-time location systems (RTLS) for asset tracking, smart patient rooms equipped with IoT sensors for remote monitoring, and AI-powered predictive maintenance systems for medical equipment (Boopathi & Khang, 2023; Rebecca et al., 2024).

AIoT-cloud integration in healthcare is being implemented in various applications such as remote patient monitoring, telemedicine services, predictive analytics, and smart hospital infrastructure. These technologies enhance patient care, clinical workflows, and healthcare delivery, leading to improved health outcomes and efficiencies.

FUTURE DIRECTIONS AND RESEARCH OPPORTUNITIES

Emerging Trends in Semantic AIoT and Cloud Computing

The integration of AIoT and cloud computing is set to undergo significant evolution due to emerging trends and research opportunities in semantic technologies. As the demand for interconnected, intelligent systems increases, researchers and practitioners are exploring innovative ways to utilize AIoT and cloud computing for transformative applications (Boopathi, 2024c; Nanda et al., 2024b; M. Sharma et al., 2024b). The figure 5 reveals the emergence of new trends in semantic AI and cloud computing.

- **Semantic-Driven Edge Computing:** The proliferation of edge computing architectures and AIoT devices at the network edge presents opportunities to integrate semantic technologies into edge computing environments. Semantic-driven edge computing enables AIoT devices to perform context-aware data processing, inference, and decision-making at the edge, reducing latency, bandwidth usage, and reliance on centralized cloud resources. Future research will focus on developing lightweight semantic reasoning mechanisms tailored to edge devices' resource-constrained environments, enabling more intelligent and autonomous edge computing applications (P. R. Kumar et al., 2023; D. M. Sharma et al., 2024).
- **Knowledge Graphs for AIoT Analytics:** Knowledge graphs represent a promising approach to integrating heterogeneous data sources, ontologies, and AI models in AIoT and cloud computing environments. By constructing knowledge graphs from diverse data streams, including sensor data, electronic

Figure 5. Emerging trends in semantic AIoT and cloud computing

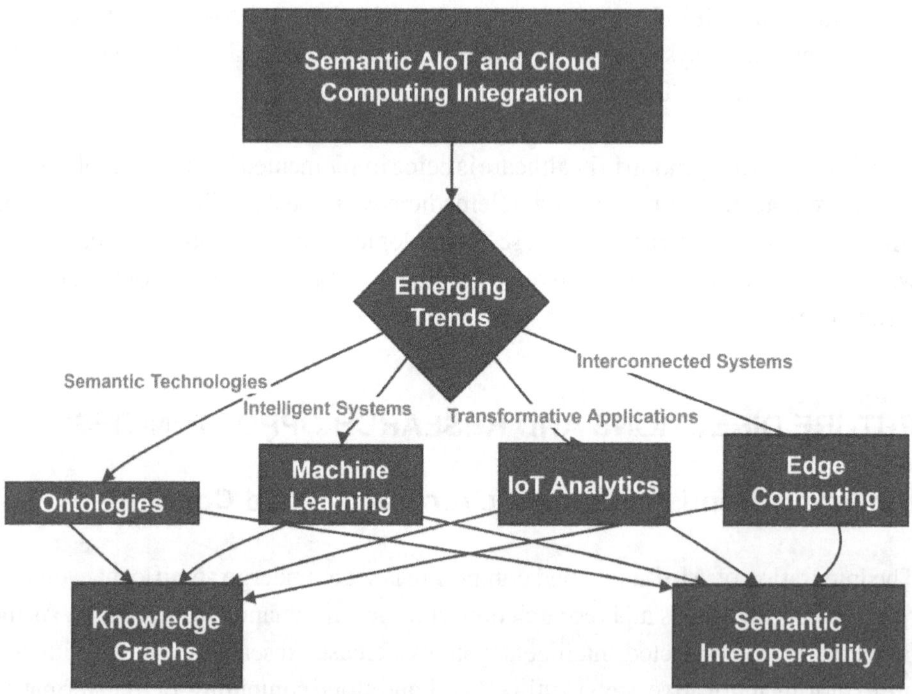

health records, and IoT metadata, researchers can enable semantic querying, analytics, and inference over interconnected data sources (Das et al., 2024; Maguluri et al., 2023). Future research will explore knowledge graph construction techniques, ontology alignment algorithms, and graph-based analytics methods tailored to AIoT and cloud environments, facilitating more comprehensive and context-aware data analysis.

- **Semantic-Driven IoT Platforms:** The development of semantic-driven IoT platforms and middleware solutions will enable seamless integration and interoperability of AIoT devices with cloud computing infrastructures. Semantic-driven IoT platforms provide abstraction layers and semantic interoperability standards that enable AIoT devices to communicate, collaborate, and share data effectively across heterogeneous systems. Future research will focus on developing standardized APIs, ontological frameworks, and semantic middleware solutions that streamline AIoT-cloud integration, facilitating rapid development and deployment of intelligent IoT applications.
- **Privacy-Preserving Semantic AIoT:** Addressing privacy and security concerns in semantic AIoT and cloud computing is critical to fostering user trust and regulatory compliance. Future research will explore privacy-preserving semantic AIoT techniques, such as federated learning, homomorphic encryption, and differential privacy, that enable AIoT devices to perform semantic reasoning and analytics while preserving data privacy and confidentiality. Additionally, research will focus on developing robust access control mechanisms, data anonymization techniques, and privacy-enhancing technologies tailored to semantic AIoT and cloud computing environments.

Future research in semantic AIoT and cloud computing will focus on edge computing, knowledge graph analytics, IoT platform development, and privacy-preserving techniques to unlock the full potential of interconnected, intelligent systems in diverse application domains.

Addressing Remaining Challenges and Limitations

Future research in AIoT and cloud computing should focus on addressing the remaining challenges and limitations to realize the full potential of integrated systems. This includes advancing security and privacy mechanisms to protect sensitive healthcare data transmitted between AIoT devices and cloud platforms. Additionally, efforts should be made to enhance scalability and resource management algorithms to accommodate the growing influx of AIoT devices and data streams in cloud environments. Furthermore, research is needed to develop standardized interoperability frameworks and semantic integration techniques to facilitate seamless communication and data exchange across heterogeneous systems. By addressing these challenges, researchers can lay the groundwork for more robust and resilient AIoT-cloud integration solutions (Boopathi, 2024e; Malathi et al., 2024a; Pachiappan et al., 2024b; Rahamathunnisa et al., 2024).

Novel Applications and Use Cases

The future of AIoT and cloud computing holds promise for novel applications and use cases across various domains. In healthcare, researchers can explore the integration of AIoT devices with cloud-based genomic analysis platforms to enable personalized medicine and precision healthcare interventions (Boopathi, 2023b; Ramudu et al., 2023). Moreover, AIoT-cloud integration can revolutionize environmental monitoring and sustainability efforts by leveraging sensor networks and cloud-based analytics to monitor air quality, water pollution, and climate change in real-time. In the industrial sector, researchers can investigate the use of AIoT devices and cloud-based predictive maintenance systems to optimize equipment reliability and minimize downtime in manufacturing plants (Bronner et al., 2021; Nahr et al., 2021; Z. Sun et al., 2021; Zhu et al., 2022). Additionally, AIoT-cloud integration can enhance smart city initiatives by enabling intelligent transportation systems, energy management solutions, and urban planning strategies that leverage real-time data and analytics. By exploring these novel applications and use cases, researchers can unlock new opportunities for innovation and societal impact in the era of interconnected and intelligent systems.

CONCLUSION

The study explores the integration of AIoT with cloud computing using Semantic Web control models. It reveals important findings on foundational components, integration approaches, and practical implementations of AIoT-cloud integration. Semantic Web control models provide a robust framework for seamless communication, data exchange, and interoperability between AIoT devices and cloud platforms. AIoT-cloud integration has shown transformative potential in healthcare, improving patient care, clinical workflows, and optimizing healthcare delivery through remote monitoring, telemedicine services, predictive analytics, and smart hospital infrastructure.

AIoT-cloud integration has significant implications for various industries, including healthcare, manufacturing, transportation, energy, and smart cities. It enhances operational efficiency, cost savings, and innovation opportunities. Academia plays a crucial role in advancing research and development, addressing challenges and unlocking new opportunities. Collaborative initiatives between industry and academia can foster interdisciplinary research, knowledge sharing, and technology transfer, driving advancements in AIoT, cloud computing, and Semantic Web technologies.

The convergence of AIoT and cloud computing is a significant shift in digital technologies, enabling innovative solutions and addressing complex challenges. Semantic Web control models can unlock new opportunities for interconnected systems, improving decision-making, resource utilization, and quality of life. Collaboration, innovation, and ethical use of technology are crucial for a future where AIoT-enabled solutions empower individuals, organizations, and societies to thrive.

ABBREVIATIONS

AI: Artificial Intelligence
AIOT: Artificial Intelligence of Things
API: Application Programming Interface
CRM: Customer Relationship Management
DD: Data Heterogeneity and Interoperability Issues (based on the context provided)
ECG: Electrocardiogram
EHR: Electronic Health Record
ERP: Enterprise Resource Planning
GPS: Global Positioning System
II: Industrial IoT (Internet of Things)
IT: Information Technology
OWL: Web Ontology Language
RDF: Resource Description Framework
RDFS: RDF Schema
RFID: Radio-Frequency Identification
RTLS: Real-Time Location System
SAWSDL: Semantic Annotations for WSDL
SPARQL: SPARQL Protocol and RDF Query Language
SWRL: Semantic Web Rule Language
WSDL: Web Services Description Language
XML: Extensible Markup Language

REFERENCES

Agrawal, A. V., Magulur, L. P., Priya, S. G., Kaur, A., Singh, G., & Boopathi, S. (2023). Smart Precision Agriculture Using IoT and WSN. In *Handbook of Research on Data Science and Cybersecurity Innovations in Industry 4.0 Technologies* (pp. 524–541). IGI Global. doi:10.4018/978-1-6684-8145-5.ch026

Anitha, C., Komala, C., Vivekanand, C. V., Lalitha, S., & Boopathi, S. (2023). Artificial Intelligence driven security model for Internet of Medical Things (IoMT). *IEEE Explore*, (pp. 1–7). IEEE.

Balas, V. E., Kumar, R., Srivastava, R., & ... (2020). *Recent trends and advances in artificial intelligence and internet of things*. Springer. doi:10.1007/978-3-030-32644-9

Boopathi, S. (2022a). An investigation on gas emission concentration and relative emission rate of the near-dry wire-cut electrical discharge machining process. *Environmental Science and Pollution Research International*, *29*(57), 86237–86246. doi:10.1007/s11356-021-17658-1 PMID:34837614

Boopathi, S. (2022b). Cryogenically treated and untreated stainless steel grade 317 in sustainable wire electrical discharge machining process: A comparative study. *Springer :Environmental Science and Pollution Research*, (pp. 1–10). Springer.

Boopathi, S. (2023a). Internet of Things-Integrated Remote Patient Monitoring System: Healthcare Application. In *Dynamics of Swarm Intelligence Health Analysis for the Next Generation* (pp. 137–161). IGI Global. doi:10.4018/978-1-6684-6894-4.ch008

Boopathi, S. (2023b). Securing Healthcare Systems Integrated With IoT: Fundamentals, Applications, and Future Trends. In Dynamics of Swarm Intelligence Health Analysis for the Next Generation (pp. 186–209). IGI Global.

Boopathi, S. (2024a). Advancements in Machine Learning and AI for Intelligent Systems in Drone Applications for Smart City Developments. In *Futuristic e-Governance Security With Deep Learning Applications* (pp. 15–45). IGI Global. doi:10.4018/978-1-6684-9596-4.ch002

Boopathi, S. (2024b). Advancements in Machine Learning and AI for Intelligent Systems in Drone Applications for Smart City Developments. In *Futuristic e-Governance Security With Deep Learning Applications* (pp. 15–45). IGI Global. doi:10.4018/978-1-6684-9596-4.ch002

Boopathi, S. (2024c). Balancing Innovation and Security in the Cloud: Navigating the Risks and Rewards of the Digital Age. In Improving Security, Privacy, and Trust in Cloud Computing (pp. 164–193). IGI Global.

Boopathi, S. (2024d). Energy Cascade Conversion System and Energy-Efficient Infrastructure. In Sustainable Development in AI, Blockchain, and E-Governance Applications (pp. 47–71). IGI Global.

Boopathi, S. (2024e). Sustainable Development Using IoT and AI Techniques for Water Utilization in Agriculture. In Sustainable Development in AI, Blockchain, and E-Governance Applications (pp. 204–228). IGI Global.

Boopathi, S., & Khang, A. (2023). AI-Integrated Technology for a Secure and Ethical Healthcare Ecosystem. In *AI and IoT-Based Technologies for Precision Medicine* (pp. 36–59). IGI Global. doi:10.4018/979-8-3693-0876-9.ch003

Boopathi, S., Myilsamy, S., & Sukkasamy, S. (2021). *Experimental Investigation and Multi-Objective Optimization of Cryogenically Cooled Near-Dry Wire-Cut EDM Using TOPSIS Technique*. IJAMT PREPRINT.

Boopathi, S., Thillaivanan, A., Mohammed, A. A., Shanmugam, P., & VR, P. (2022). Experimental investigation on Abrasive Water Jet Machining of Neem Wood Plastic Composite. *IOP: Functional Composites and Structures, 4*, 025001.

Bronner, W., Gebauer, H., Lamprecht, C., & Wortmann, F. (2021). Sustainable AIoT: how artificial intelligence and the internet of things affect profit, people, and planet. *Connected Business: Create Value in a Networked Economy*, 137–154. Research Gate.

Chang, Z., Liu, S., Xiong, X., Cai, Z., & Tu, G. (2021). A survey of recent advances in edge-computing-powered artificial intelligence of things. *IEEE Internet of Things Journal*, *8*(18), 13849–13875. doi:10.1109/JIOT.2021.3088875

Dadkhah, M., Araban, S., & Paydar, S. (2020). A systematic literature review on semantic web enabled software testing. *Journal of Systems and Software*, *162*, 110485. doi:10.1016/j.jss.2019.110485

Das, S., Lekhya, G., Shreya, K., Shekinah, K. L., Babu, K. K., & Boopathi, S. (2024). Fostering Sustainability Education Through Cross-Disciplinary Collaborations and Research Partnerships: Interdisciplinary Synergy. In Facilitating Global Collaboration and Knowledge Sharing in Higher Education With Generative AI (pp. 60–88). IGI Global.

Hansen, E. B., & Bøgh, S. (2021). Artificial intelligence and internet of things in small and medium-sized enterprises: A survey. *Journal of Manufacturing Systems*, *58*, 362–372. doi:10.1016/j.jmsy.2020.08.009

Haribalaji, V., Boopathi, S., & Asif, M. M. (2021). Optimization of friction stir welding process to join dissimilar AA2014 and AA7075 aluminum alloys. *Materials Today: Proceedings*, *50*, 2227–2234. doi:10.1016/j.matpr.2021.09.499

Heidari, A., & Jafari Navimipour, N. (2022). Service discovery mechanisms in cloud computing: A comprehensive and systematic literature review. *Kybernetes*, *51*(3), 952–981. doi:10.1108/K-12-2020-0909

Hema, N., Krishnamoorthy, N., Chavan, S. M., Kumar, N., Sabarimuthu, M., & Boopathi, S. (2023). A Study on an Internet of Things (IoT)-Enabled Smart Solar Grid System. In *Handbook of Research on Deep Learning Techniques for Cloud-Based Industrial IoT* (pp. 290–308). IGI Global. doi:10.4018/978-1-6684-8098-4.ch017

Houssein, E. H., Gad, A. G., Wazery, Y. M., & Suganthan, P. N. (2021). Task scheduling in cloud computing based on meta-heuristics: Review, taxonomy, open challenges, and future trends. *Swarm and Evolutionary Computation*, *62*, 100841. doi:10.1016/j.swevo.2021.100841

Hussain, Z., Babe, M., Saravanan, S., Srimathy, G., Roopa, H., & Boopathi, S. (2023). Optimizing Biomass-to-Biofuel Conversion: IoT and AI Integration for Enhanced Efficiency and Sustainability. In Circular Economy Implementation for Sustainability in the Built Environment (pp. 191–214). IGI Global.

Jiyi, W., Wenjuan, L., Jian, C., Shiyou, Q., Qifei, Z., & Rajkumar, B. (2021). AIoT: a taxonomy, review and future directions. *Telecommunications Science, 37*(8).

Kumar, M., Kumar, K., Sasikala, P., Sampath, B., Gopi, B., & Sundaram, S. (2023). Sustainable Green Energy Generation From Waste Water: IoT and ML Integration. In Sustainable Science and Intelligent Technologies for Societal Development (pp. 440–463). IGI Global.

Kumar, P. R., Meenakshi, S., Shalini, S., Devi, S. R., & Boopathi, S. (2023). Soil Quality Prediction in Context Learning Approaches Using Deep Learning and Blockchain for Smart Agriculture. In Effective AI, Blockchain, and E-Governance Applications for Knowledge Discovery and Management (pp. 1–26). IGI Global. doi:10.4018/978-1-6684-9151-5.ch001

Maguluri, L. P., Arularasan, A., & Boopathi, S. (2023). Assessing Security Concerns for AI-Based Drones in Smart Cities. In Effective AI, Blockchain, and E-Governance Applications for Knowledge Discovery and Management (pp. 27–47). IGI Global. doi:10.4018/978-1-6684-9151-5.ch002

Malathi, J., Kusha, K., Isaac, S., Ramesh, A., Rajendiran, M., & Boopathi, S. (2024a). IoT-Enabled Remote Patient Monitoring for Chronic Disease Management and Cost Savings: Transforming Healthcare. In Advances in Explainable AI Applications for Smart Cities (pp. 371–388). IGI Global.

Malathi, J., Kusha, K., Isaac, S., Ramesh, A., Rajendiran, M., & Boopathi, S. (2024b). IoT-Enabled Remote Patient Monitoring for Chronic Disease Management and Cost Savings: Transforming Healthcare. In Advances in Explainable AI Applications for Smart Cities (pp. 371–388). IGI Global.

Mohanty, A., Venkateswaran, N., Ranjit, P., Tripathi, M. A., & Boopathi, S. (2023). Innovative Strategy for Profitable Automobile Industries: Working Capital Management. In Handbook of Research on Designing Sustainable Supply Chains to Achieve a Circular Economy (pp. 412–428). IGI Global.

Mukhopadhyay, S. C., Tyagi, S. K. S., Suryadevara, N. K., Piuri, V., Scotti, F., & Zeadally, S. (2021). Artificial intelligence-based sensors for next generation IoT applications: A review. *IEEE Sensors Journal*, *21*(22), 24920–24932. doi:10.1109/JSEN.2021.3055618

Nahr, J. G., Nozari, H., & Sadeghi, M. E. (2021). Green supply chain based on artificial intelligence of things (AIoT). *International Journal of Innovation in Management. Economics and Social Sciences*, *1*(2), 56–63.

Nanda, A. K., Sharma, A., Augustine, P. J., Cyril, B. R., Kiran, V., & Sampath, B. (2024a). Securing Cloud Infrastructure in IaaS and PaaS Environments. In Improving Security, Privacy, and Trust in Cloud Computing (pp. 1–33). IGI Global. doi:10.4018/979-8-3693-1431-9.ch001

Nanda, A. K., Sharma, A., Augustine, P. J., Cyril, B. R., Kiran, V., & Sampath, B. (2024b). Securing Cloud Infrastructure in IaaS and PaaS Environments. In Improving Security, Privacy, and Trust in Cloud Computing (pp. 1–33). IGI Global. doi:10.4018/979-8-3693-1431-9.ch001

Naveeenkumar, N., Rallapalli, S., Sasikala, K., Priya, P. V., Husain, J., & Boopathi, S. (2024). Enhancing Consumer Behavior and Experience Through AI-Driven Insights Optimization. In *AI Impacts in Digital Consumer Behavior* (pp. 1–35). IGI Global. doi:10.4018/979-8-3693-1918-5.ch001

Pachiappan, K., Anitha, K., Pitchai, R., Sangeetha, S., Satyanarayana, T., & Boopathi, S. (2024a). Intelligent Machines, IoT, and AI in Revolutionizing Agriculture for Water Processing. In *Handbook of Research on AI and ML for Intelligent Machines and Systems* (pp. 374–399). IGI Global.

Pachiappan, K., Anitha, K., Pitchai, R., Sangeetha, S., Satyanarayana, T., & Boopathi, S. (2024b). Intelligent Machines, IoT, and AI in Revolutionizing Agriculture for Water Processing. In *Handbook of Research on AI and ML for Intelligent Machines and Systems* (pp. 374–399). IGI Global.

Patel, A., & Jain, S. (2021). Present and future of semantic web technologies: A research statement. *International Journal of Computers and Applications*, *43*(5), 413–422. doi:10.1080/1206212X.2019.1570666

Pramila, P., Amudha, S., Saravanan, T., Sankar, S. R., Poongothai, E., & Boopathi, S. (2023). Design and Development of Robots for Medical Assistance: An Architectural Approach. In Contemporary Applications of Data Fusion for Advanced Healthcare Informatics (pp. 260–282). IGI Global.

Rahamathunnisa, U., Subhashini, P., Aancy, H. M., Meenakshi, S., Boopathi, S., & ... (2023). Solutions for Software Requirement Risks Using Artificial Intelligence Techniques. In *Handbook of Research on Data Science and Cybersecurity Innovations in Industry 4.0 Technologies* (pp. 45–64). IGI Global.

Rahamathunnisa, U., Sudhakar, K., Padhi, S., Bhattacharya, S., Shashibhushan, G., & Boopathi, S. (2024). Sustainable Energy Generation From Waste Water: IoT Integrated Technologies. In Adoption and Use of Technology Tools and Services by Economically Disadvantaged Communities: Implications for Growth and Sustainability (pp. 225–256). IGI Global.

Ramudu, K., Mohan, V. M., Jyothirmai, D., Prasad, D., Agrawal, R., & Boopathi, S. (2023). Machine Learning and Artificial Intelligence in Disease Prediction: Applications, Challenges, Limitations, Case Studies, and Future Directions. In Contemporary Applications of Data Fusion for Advanced Healthcare Informatics (pp. 297–318). IGI Global.

Rebecca, B., Kumar, K. P. M., Padmini, S., Srivastava, B. K., Halder, S., & Boopathi, S. (2024). Convergence of Data Science-AI-Green Chemistry-Affordable Medicine: Transforming Drug Discovery. In *Handbook of Research on AI and ML for Intelligent Machines and Systems* (pp. 348–373). IGI Global.

Revathi, S., Babu, M., Rajkumar, N., Meti, V. K. V., Kandavalli, S. R., & Boopathi, S. (2024). Unleashing the Future Potential of 4D Printing: Exploring Applications in Wearable Technology, Robotics, Energy, Transportation, and Fashion. In Human-Centered Approaches in Industry 5.0: Human-Machine Interaction, Virtual Reality Training, and Customer Sentiment Analysis (pp. 131–153). IGI Global.

Rhayem, A., Mhiri, M. B. A., & Gargouri, F. (2020). Semantic web technologies for the internet of things: Systematic literature review. *Internet of Things : Engineering Cyber Physical Human Systems*, *11*, 100206. doi:10.1016/j.iot.2020.100206

Rong, G., Xu, Y., Tong, X., & Fan, H. (2021). An edge-cloud collaborative computing platform for building AIoT applications efficiently. *Journal of Cloud Computing (Heidelberg, Germany)*, *10*(1), 1–14. doi:10.1186/s13677-021-00250-w

Sadeeq, M. M., Abdulkareem, N. M., Zeebaree, S. R., Ahmed, D. M., Sami, A. S., & Zebari, R. R. (2021). IoT and Cloud computing issues, challenges and opportunities: A review. *Qubahan Academic Journal*, *1*(2), 1–7. doi:10.48161/qaj.v1n2a36

Shafiq, D. A., Jhanjhi, N., & Abdullah, A. (2022). Load balancing techniques in cloud computing environment: A review. *Journal of King Saud University. Computer and Information Sciences*, *34*(7), 3910–3933. doi:10.1016/j.jksuci.2021.02.007

Shamshirband, S., Fathi, M., Chronopoulos, A. T., Montieri, A., Palumbo, F., & Pescapè, A. (2020). Computational intelligence intrusion detection techniques in mobile cloud computing environments: Review, taxonomy, and open research issues. *Journal of Information Security and Applications*, *55*, 102582. doi:10.1016/j.jisa.2020.102582

Sharma, D. M., Ramana, K. V., Jothilakshmi, R., Verma, R., Maheswari, B. U., & Boopathi, S. (2024). Integrating Generative AI Into K-12 Curriculums and Pedagogies in India: Opportunities and Challenges. *Facilitating Global Collaboration and Knowledge Sharing in Higher Education With Generative AI*, 133–161.

Sharma, M., Sharma, M., Sharma, N., & Boopathi, S. (2024a). Building Sustainable Smart Cities Through Cloud and Intelligent Parking System. In *Handbook of Research on AI and ML for Intelligent Machines and Systems* (pp. 195–222). IGI Global.

Sharma, M., Sharma, M., Sharma, N., & Boopathi, S. (2024b). Building Sustainable Smart Cities Through Cloud and Intelligent Parking System. In *Handbook of Research on AI and ML for Intelligent Machines and Systems* (pp. 195–222). IGI Global.

Sonia, R., Gupta, N., Manikandan, K., Hemalatha, R., Kumar, M. J., & Boopathi, S. (2024). Strengthening Security, Privacy, and Trust in Artificial Intelligence Drones for Smart Cities. In *Analyzing and Mitigating Security Risks in Cloud Computing* (pp. 214–242). IGI Global. doi:10.4018/979-8-3693-3249-8.ch011

Subha, S., Inbamalar, T., Komala, C., Suresh, L. R., Boopathi, S., & Alaskar, K. (2023). A Remote Health Care Monitoring system using internet of medical things (IoMT). *IEEE Explore*, (pp. 1–6). IEEE.

Sun, L., Jiang, X., Ren, H., & Guo, Y. (2020). Edge-cloud computing and artificial intelligence in internet of medical things: Architecture, technology and application. *IEEE Access : Practical Innovations, Open Solutions*, *8*, 101079–101092. doi:10.1109/ACCESS.2020.2997831

Sun, Z., Zhu, M., Zhang, Z., Chen, Z., Shi, Q., Shan, X., Yeow, R. C. H., & Lee, C. (2021). Artificial Intelligence of Things (AIoT) enabled virtual shop applications using self-powered sensor enhanced soft robotic manipulator. *Advancement of Science*, *8*(14), 2100230. doi:10.1002/advs.202100230 PMID:34037331

Sunyaev, A., & Sunyaev, A. (2020). Cloud computing. *Internet Computing: Principles of Distributed Systems and Emerging Internet-Based Technologies*, 195–236.

Veeranjaneyulu, R., Boopathi, S., Narasimharao, J., Gupta, K. K., Reddy, R. V. K., & Ambika, R. (2023). Identification of Heart Diseases using Novel Machine Learning Method. *IEEE- Explore*, 1–6.

Venkateswaran, N., Vidhya, R., Naik, D. A., Raj, T. M., Munjal, N., & Boopathi, S. (2023). Study on Sentence and Question Formation Using Deep Learning Techniques. In *Digital Natives as a Disruptive Force in Asian Businesses and Societies* (pp. 252–273). IGI Global. doi:10.4018/978-1-6684-6782-4.ch015

Verma, R., Christiana, M. B. V., Maheswari, M., Srinivasan, V., Patro, P., Dari, S. S., & Boopathi, S. (2024). Intelligent Physarum Solver for Profit Maximization in Oligopolistic Supply Chain Networks. In *AI and Machine Learning Impacts in Intelligent Supply Chain* (pp. 156–179). IGI Global. doi:10.4018/979-8-3693-1347-3.ch011

Xiong, J., & Chen, H. (2020). Challenges for building a cloud native scalable and trustable multi-tenant AIoT platform. *Proceedings of the 39th International Conference on Computer-Aided Design*, (pp. 1–8). ACM. 10.1145/3400302.3415756

Yahya, M., Breslin, J. G., & Ali, M. I. (2021). Semantic web and knowledge graphs for industry 4.0. *Applied Sciences (Basel, Switzerland)*, *11*(11), 5110. doi:10.3390/app11115110

Zhang, J., & Tao, D. (2020). Empowering things with intelligence: A survey of the progress, challenges, and opportunities in artificial intelligence of things. *IEEE Internet of Things Journal*, *8*(10), 7789–7817. doi:10.1109/JIOT.2020.3039359

Zhu, S., Ota, K., & Dong, M. (2022). Energy-efficient artificial intelligence of things with intelligent edge. *IEEE Internet of Things Journal*, *9*(10), 7525–7532. doi:10.1109/JIOT.2022.3143722

Chapter 6
Privacy-Preserving Machine Learning Techniques for IoT Data in Cloud Environments

Tarun Kumar Vashishth
https://orcid.org/0000-0001-9916-9575
IIMT University, India

Bhupendra Kumar
https://orcid.org/0000-0001-9281-3655
IIMT University, India

Vikas Sharma
https://orcid.org/0000-0001-8173-4548
IIMT University, India

Sachin Chaudhary
https://orcid.org/0000-0002-8415-0043
IIMT University, India

Kewal Krishan Sharma
https://orcid.org/0009-0001-2504-9607
IIMT University, India

Manoj Gupta
IIMT University, India

ABSTRACT

The proliferation of internet of things (IoT) devices has resulted in an unprecedented influx of data, leading to heightened concerns regarding the privacy and security of sensitive information in cloud environments. Privacy-preserving machine learning techniques have emerged as essential tools for ensuring the confidentiality of IoT data while facilitating meaningful analysis. This chapter provides an overview of the key principles and methodologies employed in privacy-preserving machine learning for IoT data in cloud environments. Key considerations encompass data anonymization, secure transmission, and adherence to stringent data protection regulations such as the General Data Protection Regulation (GDPR). Robust encryption and access control mechanisms are implemented to safeguard data integrity while allowing for effective analysis. Techniques like homomorphic encryption and secure multi-party computation enable secure computations on encrypted data, ensuring privacy while maintaining the utility of the data.

DOI: 10.4018/979-8-3693-0766-3.ch006

INTRODUCTION

The rapid proliferation of Internet of Things (IoT) devices has ushered in a transformative era of data-driven insights and connectivity across industries. IoT promises increased efficiency, enhanced decision-making and improved quality of life. However, this abundance of IoT data, particularly when processed in cloud environments, has brought forth an array of profound privacy and security concerns. The amalgamation of IoT data with cloud computing capabilities is undeniably powerful. Cloud environments offer scalability, on-demand resources, and the computational muscle required to process vast volumes of data efficiently. Simultaneously, machine learning has emerged as a vital tool for extracting valuable insights from this deluge of information.

Yet, as we embark on this data-driven journey, we must navigate a delicate balance between harnessing the potential of IoT data and safeguarding the privacy of individuals, enterprises, and entities. The information collected by IoT devices, including personal and sensitive data, necessitates robust protection against unauthorized access, data breaches, and privacy violations.

This chapter, "Privacy-Preserving Machine Learning Techniques for IoT Data in Cloud Environments," embarks on a comprehensive exploration of the critical techniques and strategies that ensure the secure and responsible processing of IoT data within the cloud, without compromising the confidentiality and privacy of the data and its owners. In this introduction, we set the stage for the journey ahead. We elucidate the significance of privacy in an era defined by data, emphasize the challenges posed by IoT data in cloud environments, and outline the objectives of this book. We recognize the delicate dance between harnessing data's power and preserving the individual's right to privacy. In a world where IoT devices are omnipresent and data flows ceaselessly, this book is an essential guide for researchers, professionals, and policymakers seeking to harness the full potential of IoT data while upholding the principles of privacy and security. It is a journey through the evolving landscape of data, technology, and ethics, culminating in a harmonious coexistence of innovation and privacy protection.

Background and Context

The background and context of privacy-preserving machine learning techniques for IoT data in cloud environments are rooted in the convergence of several transformative technological trends. The Internet of Things (IoT) has brought about an unprecedented surge in data generation, with countless interconnected devices collecting and transmitting vast amounts of information. Simultaneously, cloud computing has revolutionized data processing and storage by offering scalable

Figure 1. Privacy-Preserving machine learning techniques for IoT data in cloud environments

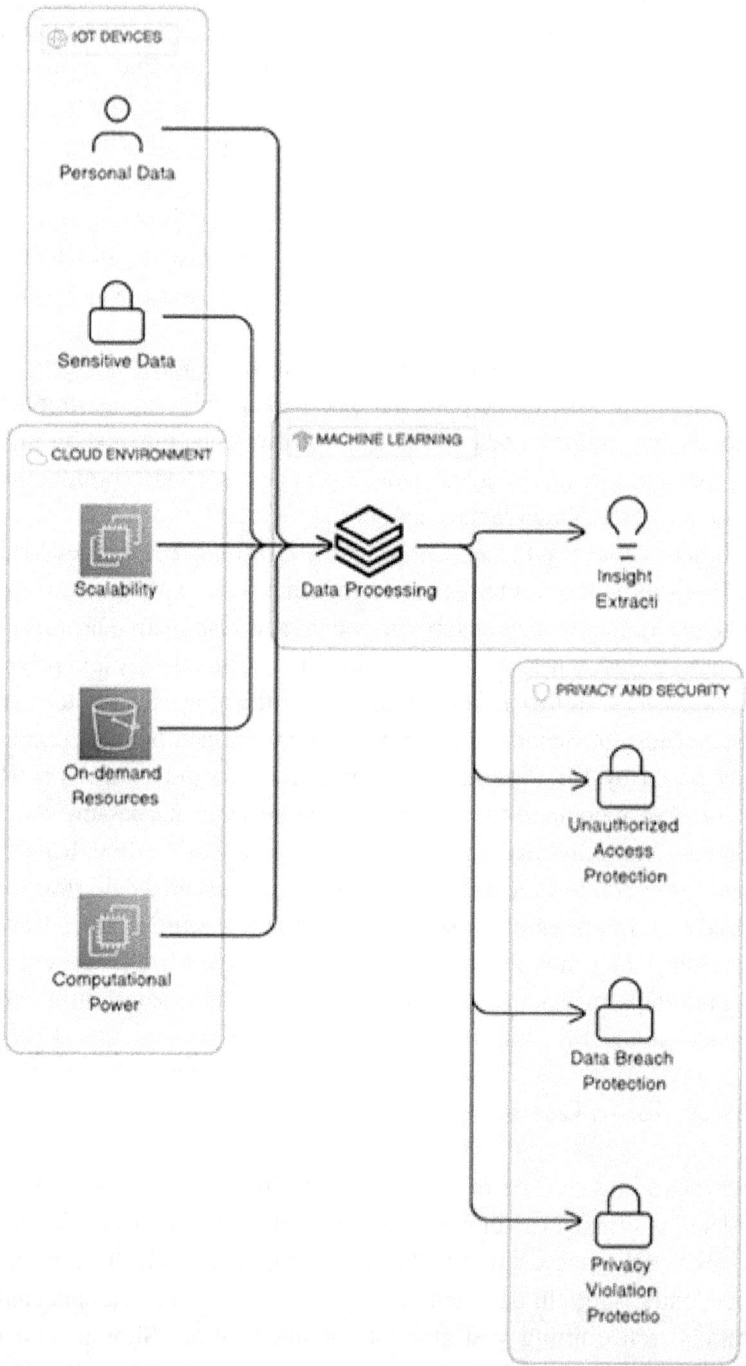

and cost-effective solutions. However, the amalgamation of IoT data with cloud environments has raised significant privacy and security concerns, as this data often contains sensitive, personal, or proprietary information. This amalgamation has necessitated the development of advanced privacy-preserving techniques that enable meaningful analysis while ensuring data confidentiality. To address these challenges, this research explores innovative methods such as homomorphic encryption, secure multi-party computation, differential privacy, and blockchain integration, all aimed at balancing the need for data-driven insights with the imperative of safeguarding privacy. Understanding this background and context is essential to navigate the intricacies of preserving privacy in the age of IoT and cloud computing.

Objectives and Scope

Objectives

Comprehensive Exploration: To provide an in-depth exploration of the challenges and opportunities related to the secure and responsible processing of IoT data within cloud environments, emphasizing the critical role of privacy preservation.

Technical Understanding: To offer a technical understanding of the fundamental principles and techniques that underpin privacy-preserving machine learning, encompassing encryption, access control, secure computation, and more.

Real-World Relevance: To bridge the gap between theoretical knowledge and practical implementation by presenting real-world case studies and successful applications of privacy-preserving methods in IoT and cloud settings.

Regulatory Compliance: To delve into the regulatory landscape, including key data protection regulations like the GDPR, and provide guidance on implementing compliance measures within IoT and cloud environments.

Future Outlook: To forecast emerging technologies, trends, and challenges in the domain of IoT data privacy, offering insights into the evolving landscape.

Scope

Data Anonymization and Pseudonymization: Techniques for concealing the identity of individuals and entities in IoT data.

Data Encryption and Access Control: Mechanisms to ensure data confidentiality and regulate access to sensitive information.

Secure Transmission and Storage: Methods for protecting data during transit and while at rest in cloud environments.

Authentication and Authorization Mechanisms: Strategies to authenticate users and devices and grant appropriate data access permissions.

Figure 2. Objectives of data processing in cloud environments

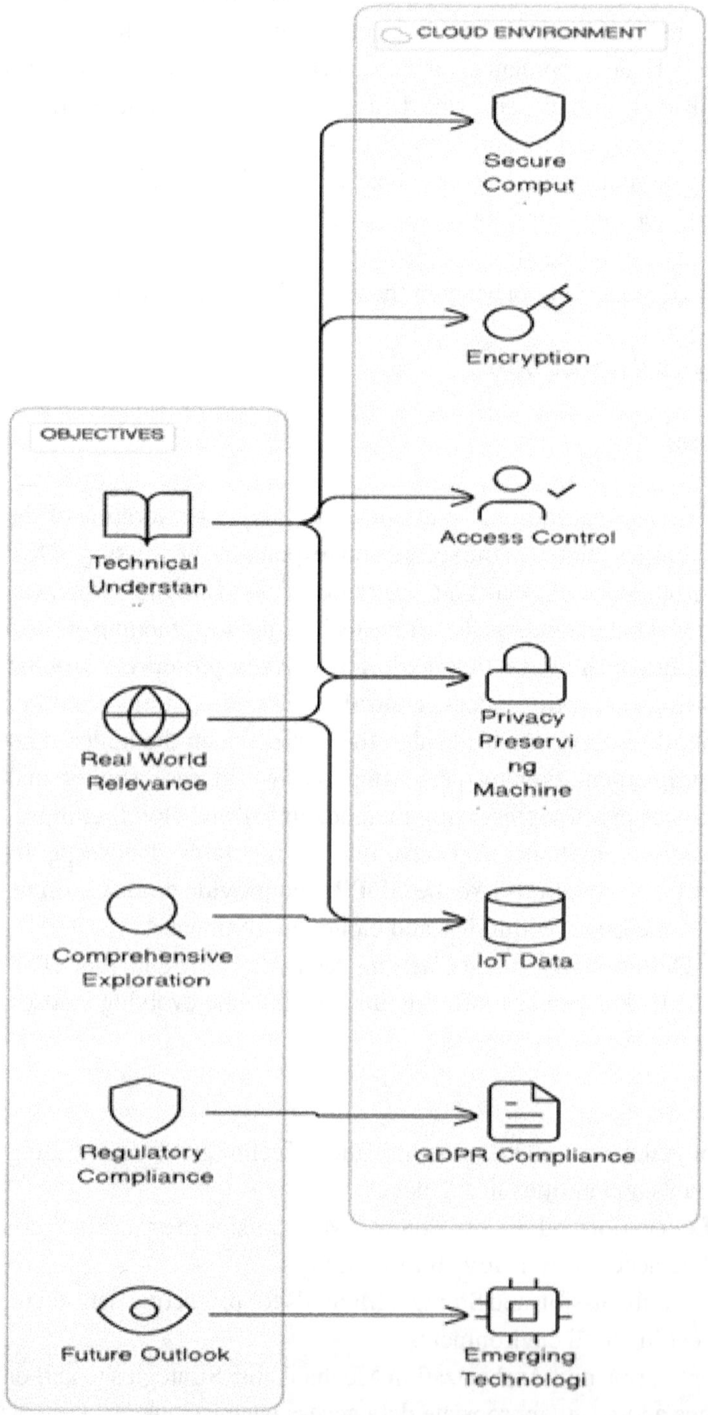

Privacy-Preserving Machine Learning Techniques: In-depth exploration of advanced techniques like homomorphic encryption, secure multi-party computation, differential privacy, and blockchain integration.

Risk Assessment and Threat Modeling: Identifying potential threats and vulnerabilities, evaluating risks, and developing mitigation strategies to protect IoT data.

Regulatory Compliance: Analyzing data protection regulations, such as GDPR, and guidelines for adhering to these regulations.

Secure Cloud-Based Data Processing: Design principles for secure cloud architectures, incident response procedures, and configuration hardening guidelines.

Case Studies: Real-world implementations, lessons learned, and best practices derived from successful deployments.

Future Trends and Research Directions: Anticipated advancements in cloud security, regulatory changes, and prospective developments in privacy-enhancing mechanisms.

1.3 Significance of Privacy-Preserving Techniques in IoT and Cloud

The significance of privacy-preserving techniques in the realms of IoT (Internet of Things) and cloud computing is paramount in our data-centric era. IoT devices are prolific data generators, often collecting personal and sensitive information. Cloud computing provides the computational power for processing and storing this data. Privacy-preserving techniques are indispensable for protecting this data against unauthorized access, breaches, and misuse. They uphold the principles of data protection regulations, such as GDPR, ensuring compliance and shielding organizations from substantial fines. Moreover, these techniques foster trust among users, encouraging them to consent to data collection, and they enable secure data sharing among stakeholders, essential for collaborative IoT applications. By safeguarding data and adhering to ethical data usage, privacy-preserving techniques underpin the responsible and secure evolution of IoT and cloud technologies, bolstering user trust, data quality, and the long-term sustainability of data-driven solutions.

LITERATURE REVIEW

Al-Qarafi et al. (2022) propose an optimal machine learning-based privacy-preserving blockchain for IoT in smart cities, their approach lacks a comprehensive evaluation of potential security vulnerabilities. Briggs, Fan, and Andras (2021) provide a review of privacy-preserving federated learning for IoT, however, their work lacks a detailed discussion on the practical implementation challenges and potential solutions. Bugshan et al.'s (2022) work on a trustworthy and privacy-preserving federated deep learning service framework for industrial IoT, while promising, does not sufficiently address the scalability issues that may arise in large-scale industrial applications. Can and Ersoy's (2021) study on privacy-preserving federated deep learning for wearable IoT-based biomedical monitoring offers a novel approach, but it lacks a thorough analysis of the potential impact of data heterogeneity on model performance.

Gheisari, Wang, and Chen's (2020) edge computing-enhanced IoT framework for privacy preservation in smart cities, while innovative, does not adequately address the potential latency issues that may arise in real-time applications. Gupta et al.'s (2020) machine learning and probabilistic analysis model for preserving security and privacy in cloud environments, while theoretically sound, lacks empirical evidence to support its effectiveness in diverse and complex real-world scenarios. Gupta et al.'s (2022) IoT-centric data protection method for preserving security and privacy in the cloud, while innovative, does not sufficiently address the potential challenges related to data integrity and recovery in case of breaches. Kant et al.'s (2023) proposal of a blockchain deployment mechanism for IoT-based security, while promising, lacks a comprehensive analysis of the potential impact on system performance and resource consumption. Lakshmanna et al.'s (2022) deep learning-based privacy-preserving data transmission scheme for clustered IIoT environments, while theoretically sound, lacks a robust evaluation against a diverse set of potential cyber threats. Lee et al.'s (2023) exploration of privacy-preserving techniques in Cloud/Fog and IoT, while comprehensive, does not sufficiently address the trade-off between privacy preservation and system performance.

Li et al.'s (2020) work on secure and privacy-preserving distributed deep learning in fog-cloud computing, while innovative, does not adequately address the potential challenges related to data synchronization and consistency across the distributed nodes. Ma et al.'s (2022) privacy-preserving content-based image retrieval method based on deep learning in cloud computing, while promising, lacks a comprehensive evaluation of its performance under varying network conditions and data loads. Park, Kim, and Lim's (2020) study on privacy-preserving reinforcement learning using homomorphic encryption in cloud computing infrastructures, while innovative, does not sufficiently address the computational overhead associated with homomorphic encryption.

Ren et al.'s (2021) approach to privacy preservation using homomorphic encryption in Mobile IoT systems, while theoretically sound, does not adequately address the potential impact on system latency and energy consumption, particularly critical in mobile environments.

Sharma and Kumar (2023) discuss the role of Artificial Intelligence in enhancing the security and privacy of data in smart cities. While the topic is promising, the paper lacks a critical analysis of potential limitations and ethical considerations associated with AI implementation in urban environments. Will (2022) presents a privacy-preserving data aggregation scheme for IoT applications using a trusted execution environment, but fails to provide a comprehensive evaluation of the scheme's practical feasibility and scalability in real-world fog/cloud environments. Xu, Baracaldo, and Joshi (2021) provides a comprehensive overview of privacy-preserving machine learning, but lacks specific practical solutions or case studies, which would enhance its utility for practitioners seeking to implement privacy-preserving techniques in real-world applications. Zhou et al. (2021) introduces a secure machine learning model sharing scheme for IoT, but lacks a detailed analysis of potential vulnerabilities and attacks that could compromise the privacy and security of the system, leaving practical concerns unaddressed. Zhu et al. (2021) discusses privacy-preserving machine learning training in IoT aggregation scenarios but lacks a rigorous exploration of potential performance and communication overhead challenges that may arise when deploying privacy-preserving techniques in resource-constrained IoT environments

FUNDAMENTALS OF IoT DATA PRIVACY

IoT Architecture and Data Flow

IoT architecture and data flow constitute the backbone of the Internet of Things (IoT), a dynamic ecosystem of interconnected devices, sensors, and systems that collect, transmit, and process data to enable a wide range of applications. Understanding the intricacies of IoT architecture and data flow is essential for harnessing the full potential of this transformative technology. IoT architecture typically consists of three main components: edge devices, edge computing, and cloud-based platforms. Edge devices are the frontline data collectors, ranging from smart sensors in industrial machinery to wearable devices tracking personal health data. These devices collect a wealth of information, including temperature readings, location data, or user preferences. The data collected by edge devices is then transmitted to edge computing systems, which may be gateways, routers, or local servers. Edge computing processes data closer to the source, offering low latency and reduced bandwidth usage. This local analysis can filter and preprocess data, ensuring that only relevant information is forwarded to the cloud, which is particularly important in scenarios with limited network capacity or when real-time decisions are crucial. The final destination for IoT data is the cloud-based platforms, which serve as central hubs for data aggregation, storage, and analysis. These platforms are scalable and can accommodate vast amounts of data from numerous devices. Cloud computing enables advanced analytics, machine learning, and long-term data storage, facilitating the extraction of valuable insights and the development of innovative IoT applications. Data flow in IoT can follow various paths, depending on the specific use case. It can proceed from edge devices directly to the cloud, from edge to edge (local processing), or involve complex, multi-step data flow through intermediate edge layers. Understanding these data flow patterns is pivotal for optimizing data processing, ensuring timely decision-making, and mitigating potential privacy and security risks.

IoT architecture and data flow are foundational elements of the IoT ecosystem, enabling the seamless collection, transmission, and analysis of data from countless devices. Mastery of these concepts is essential for designing efficient, secure, and privacy-conscious IoT applications that harness the wealth of data generated by IoT devices to drive innovation and efficiency in various domains, from smart cities and industrial automation to healthcare and environmental monitoring.

Privacy Challenges in IoT

Privacy challenges in the Internet of Things (IoT) are a complex and multifaceted issue that arises due to the massive volume and variety of data collected by IoT devices. These challenges encompass a wide array of concerns, underscoring the need for robust privacy-preserving measures in the IoT ecosystem. One of the foremost challenges is data security. IoT devices are prone to cyberattacks, making it crucial to protect the data they collect from unauthorized access, breaches, and tampering. With many devices lacking sophisticated security features, data vulnerabilities are pervasive, making privacy protection an urgent priority. Ownership and control

Figure 3. IOT architecture and data flow

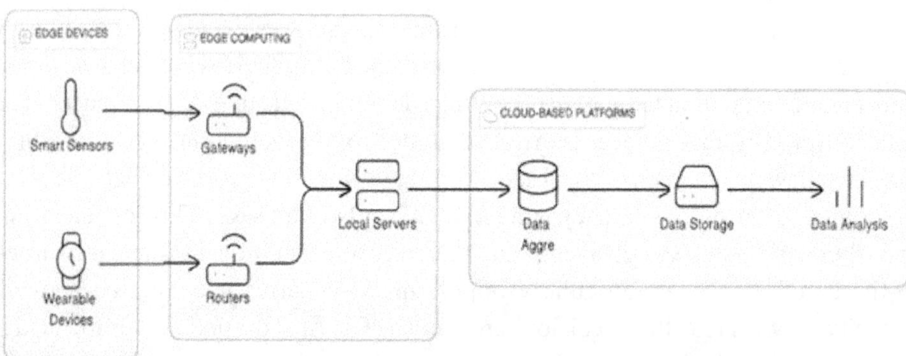

of data are also significant challenges. Determining who owns the data generated by IoT devices and how users can exercise control over their information is often ambiguous. This lack of clarity can lead to disputes and privacy violations, highlighting the importance of establishing clear data ownership and governance frameworks.

Consent and transparency issues are central to privacy in IoT. Users must be fully informed about what data is being collected, how it will be used, and must provide informed consent for data collection. Additionally, users should be able to modify their consent settings and have control over their data, including the right to be forgotten. Data minimization is another challenge. Collecting only the data necessary for a specific purpose is essential for reducing privacy risks. Yet, many IoT devices gather extensive data, which, if not appropriately protected, can lead to unwarranted privacy intrusions. Cross-border data flow and compliance with various data protection laws pose additional challenges. As IoT devices and data often transcend international borders, adhering to differing regulations such as the General Data Protection Regulation (GDPR) can be intricate and necessitates robust legal and technical frameworks. Data retention practices are a common privacy challenge in IoT. Defining data retention policies and ensuring that data is not stored longer than necessary is essential to prevent the accumulation of excessive, potentially risky data.

The privacy challenges in IoT are multifaceted and substantial. To address them, a multifaceted approach is required, involving robust security measures, clear data ownership and consent mechanisms, and strict adherence to data protection regulations. By proactively addressing these challenges, IoT can continue to thrive as a transformative technology while respecting individual and organizational privacy rights.

MACHINE LEARNING FOR IOT DATA PROCESSING

IoT Data Analytics

IoT data analytics stands at the forefront of harnessing the wealth of information generated by the Internet of Things (IoT). In the IoT ecosystem, a myriad of interconnected devices continuously collect a vast array of data, spanning from environmental sensor readings and health monitoring data to industrial machinery metrics. However, the true value of this data emerges through the process of analytics, which involves systematic examination and interpretation of the information to extract valuable insights, detect patterns, and make data-driven decisions.

One of the primary challenges in IoT data analytics is the sheer volume, velocity, and variety of the data. Traditional data analysis techniques often fall short when applied to IoT data, which is characterized by its dynamic nature and a combination of structured and unstructured data. IoT data analytics encompasses various key elements:

Data Preprocessing: This crucial step involves cleaning and preparing the raw data. It includes handling missing values, outliers, and noise, ensuring that the data is in a suitable form for analysis.

Real-time Analytics: In many IoT applications, especially those in domains like industrial IoT and smart cities, real-time analytics are essential. This approach involves analyzing streaming data as it is generated, enabling immediate actions and decision-making, such as predictive maintenance to prevent equipment failures.

Predictive Analytics: Using historical IoT data to build predictive models that forecast future events. This is instrumental in optimizing operations, preventing failures, and improving overall efficiency.

Anomaly Detection: Identifying unusual patterns or anomalies in IoT data that may indicate faults, security breaches, or other irregularities. Anomaly detection is pivotal for ensuring the reliability and security of IoT systems.

Descriptive Analytics: Summarizing and visualizing data to gain insights into historical trends and patterns. It provides a foundation for understanding the past and identifying areas for improvement.

Prescriptive Analytics: Moving beyond insights to recommend actions or interventions based on IoT data analysis. It plays a crucial role in optimizing processes, mitigating risks, and achieving specific goals.

IoT data analytics is a cornerstone of deriving meaningful insights from the vast and complex data generated by IoT devices. It empowers organizations and individuals to make informed decisions, optimize processes, enhance efficiency, and uncover hidden opportunities. As IoT continues to grow and influence various domains, the role of data analytics becomes increasingly critical, driving innovation and transformation in industries ranging from healthcare and smart cities to manufacturing and environmental monitoring.

Machine Learning Algorithms for IoT

Machine learning algorithms play a pivotal role in the context of the Internet of Things (IoT), enabling the extraction of valuable insights and predictive capabilities from the deluge of data generated by IoT devices. Several types of machine learning algorithms are commonly applied in IoT applications, each serving distinct purposes and catering to specific data analysis requirements. Some key machine learning algorithms for IoT include:

Supervised Learning Algorithms: These algorithms learn from labeled training data to make predictions. In the context of IoT, supervised learning is often used

Figure 4. IoT data analytics architecture

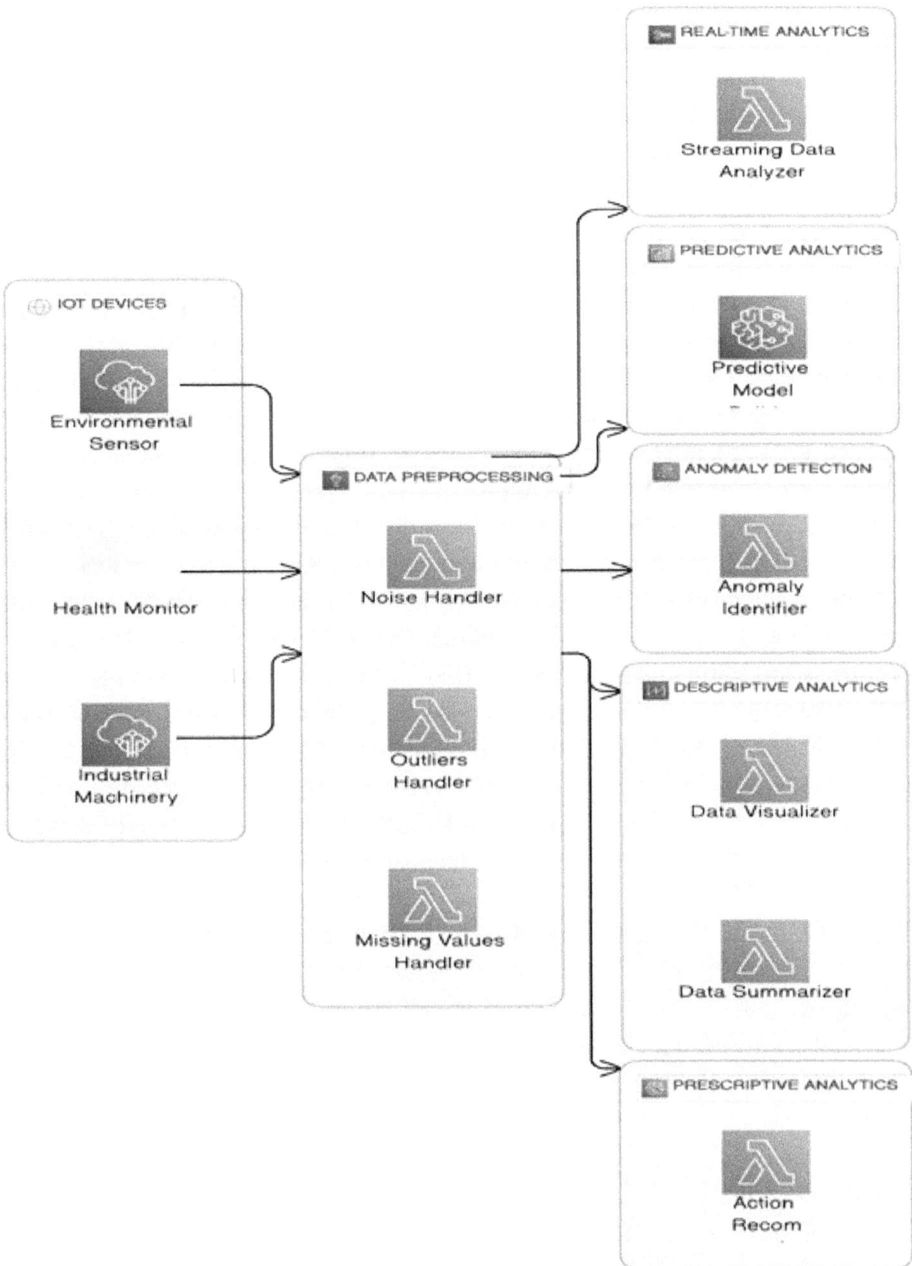

for tasks such as predictive maintenance, anomaly detection, and classification of data into predefined categories.

Unsupervised Learning Algorithms: Unsupervised learning is used for finding patterns and structures in data that do not have labeled outcomes. Clustering algorithms, such as k-means, hierarchical clustering, and DBSCAN, are commonly employed to group similar IoT devices or data points based on their characteristics.

Reinforcement Learning Algorithms: Reinforcement learning enables IoT systems to learn by trial and error through interactions with the environment. This approach is valuable for applications where the IoT system needs to make sequential decisions to achieve specific goals, such as optimizing energy consumption in smart buildings or managing autonomous robotic systems.

Deep Learning Algorithms: Deep learning, a subset of machine learning, involves the use of neural networks with multiple layers to learn complex patterns and representations from data. Convolutional neural networks (CNNs) are employed for tasks like image and video analysis in IoT, while recurrent neural networks (RNNs) are used for sequential data analysis, such as time series forecasting or natural language processing in IoT applications.

Time Series Analysis Algorithms: Time series analysis techniques are particularly crucial for handling temporal data commonly generated by IoT devices. These algorithms include autoregressive integrated moving average (ARIMA), exponential smoothing methods, and long short-term memory (LSTM) networks, which are used for forecasting, anomaly detection, and trend analysis in IoT data streams.

By leveraging these diverse machine learning algorithms, IoT applications can effectively process, analyze, and derive actionable insights from the vast and varied data produced by interconnected devices, contributing to improved decision-making, operational efficiency, and innovative advancements in a wide range of domains, including smart cities, healthcare, manufacturing, and environmental monitoring.

Role of Cloud Computing in IoT Data Processing

The role of cloud computing in IoT data processing is pivotal, serving as the linchpin that enables the efficient, secure, and scalable management of the massive volumes of data generated by Internet of Things (IoT) devices. Cloud computing brings a multitude of benefits to IoT data processing:

First and foremost, cloud computing provides scalability. IoT devices produce a continuous stream of data, and their numbers continue to grow. Cloud platforms offer the elasticity needed to handle this surge in data volume. As the IoT ecosystem expands, cloud resources can be dynamically scaled to accommodate the increasing workload, ensuring that data processing remains smooth and uninterrupted. Data storage is another key function of the cloud in IoT. Cloud services offer cost-effective, secure, and scalable data storage solutions. IoT-generated data is centralized in the cloud, where it can be readily accessed and protected. This centralized storage facilitates data management, retrieval, and historical analysis, making it an essential component for applications that require compliance, auditing, and data management. In addition to data storage, cloud computing provides the computational power required for advanced data processing. IoT data can be analyzed, transformed, and aggregated in the cloud to extract meaningful insights. Cloud-based machine learning and analytics tools facilitate real-time data analysis and decision-making, allowing organizations to respond promptly to events, automate actions, and ensure the reliability of real-time systems.

The cost efficiency of cloud computing is a significant advantage for IoT applications. Organizations pay for cloud resources on a usage basis, eliminating the need for extensive on-premises infrastructure. This cost-effective model is particularly beneficial for startups, small and medium-sized businesses, and enterprises alike, allowing them to harness the power of IoT data analytics without significant upfront investments. Data security is paramount in IoT, and cloud providers implement robust security measures to protect IoT data. Encryption, access controls, and compliance with data protection regulations help safeguard sensitive information and reduce the risks of unauthorized access or data breaches.

Cloud computing is the cornerstone of IoT data processing, enabling organizations to efficiently and securely manage the deluge of data generated by IoT devices. Its role in scalability, data storage, processing, cost efficiency, security, and integration fosters the extraction of valuable insights and the optimization of processes in various IoT domains, from smart cities and industrial automation to healthcare and environmental monitoring.

SAFEGUARDING PRIVACY IN THE IOT ERA: TECHNIQUES AND CHALLENGES IN CLOUD ENVIRONMENTS

Privacy-preserving machine learning techniques for IoT data in cloud environments address a critical need in the era of the Internet of Things (IoT). As IoT devices proliferate, they generate vast amounts of data, including sensitive and personal information, which necessitates robust privacy protection measures. This discussion explores the significance, challenges, and techniques associated with preserving privacy while harnessing the potential of IoT data in cloud environments.

Significance of Privacy-Preserving Techniques in IoT and Cloud:

The significance of privacy-preserving techniques in IoT and cloud environments cannot be overstated. IoT devices collect data from various sources, including personal wearables, smart home devices, industrial sensors, and healthcare equipment. This data often contains sensitive information, such as location, health metrics, and user behavior. In a cloud-based IoT ecosystem, data is transmitted and stored, making it susceptible to privacy breaches and unauthorized access. The consequences of inadequate privacy protection range from individual privacy violations to regulatory non-compliance and compromised security.

Moreover, privacy preservation fosters trust among users, encouraging them to participate in data collection and share information. This trust is vital for the success of IoT applications, as users are more likely to engage with systems they perceive as secure and respectful of their privacy. Additionally, privacy-preserving techniques enable secure data sharing among stakeholders, which is crucial for collaborative IoT applications in sectors like healthcare, smart cities, and industrial automation.

Challenges in Privacy-Preserving IoT Data Processing:

Privacy-preserving techniques in IoT data processing confront several challenges:

Data Security: Protecting data in transit and at rest is a core challenge, as IoT data is transmitted from devices to cloud environments. Encryption and access controls are essential to mitigate security risks.

Data Ownership and Consent: Determining data ownership and managing user consent for data collection are complex issues, especially in shared IoT environments. Clear guidelines are needed to address these challenges.

Data Minimization: IoT devices often collect more data than necessary for specific applications. Implementing data minimization practices is a challenge, as it requires distinguishing between valuable and extraneous information.

Compliance with Regulations: Adhering to data protection regulations, such as the GDPR, while processing IoT data in cloud environments is intricate, necessitating privacy-by-design approaches and robust governance.

Data Interoperability: Ensuring data privacy in multi-vendor, multi-device IoT environments is challenging. Privacy standards and data protection measures must be interoperable across systems and platforms.

Privacy-Preserving Techniques:

Various techniques can help address these challenges:

Data Encryption: Encrypting data at rest and in transit to protect it from unauthorized access.

Differential Privacy: Adding noise to query results to protect individual data while still allowing aggregate analysis.

Homomorphic Encryption: Performing computations on encrypted data without decrypting it, preserving privacy during data analysis.

Secure Multi-Party Computation (SMPC): Allowing multiple parties to jointly compute results on their data while keeping it private from each other.

Data Anonymization and Pseudonymization: Replacing sensitive data with anonymous identifiers to protect individual identities.

Privacy-Preserving Machine Learning: Employing techniques like federated learning to train machine learning models on decentralized, privacy-sensitive data.

In conclusion, the fusion of IoT and cloud computing holds immense potential, but it must be balanced with robust privacy protection. Privacy-preserving techniques are instrumental in preserving individual rights, building user trust, and ensuring regulatory compliance. As IoT continues to evolve and expand into various domains, the development and implementation of effective privacy measures will be crucial for its long-term success and societal benefits.

METHODOLOGY FOR IMPLEMENTING PRIVACY-PRESERVING MACHINE LEARNING TECHNIQUES

The methodology for implementing privacy-preserving machine learning techniques for IoT data in cloud environments involves a systematic approach that addresses the complexities and challenges associated with preserving data privacy while leveraging the power of machine learning for data analysis. This methodology emphasizes the adoption of robust techniques and frameworks that ensure data security, user privacy, and regulatory compliance. The following steps outline an effective methodology for implementing privacy-preserving machine learning techniques for IoT data in cloud environments:

Threat and Risk Assessment: Conduct a comprehensive assessment to identify potential threats and risks associated with the processing of IoT data in cloud environments. Evaluate the vulnerabilities in data transmission, storage, and processing that could compromise data privacy and security. Understand the potential impact of data breaches and privacy violations on stakeholders and the overall IoT ecosystem.

Privacy Impact Assessment (PIA): Perform a thorough PIA to evaluate the potential privacy implications of processing IoT data in cloud environments. Assess the data collection practices, data storage mechanisms, and data processing workflows to identify potential privacy risks and compliance gaps. Consider the implications of data sharing, data retention, and third-party data access on individual privacy rights and regulatory requirements.

Privacy-Preserving Framework Selection: Choose appropriate privacy-preserving frameworks and methodologies that align with the specific requirements of IoT data processing in cloud environments. Consider techniques such as differential privacy, homomorphic encryption, federated learning, and secure multi-party computation (SMPC) to ensure data privacy during various stages of data processing, including data collection, storage, and analysis.

Data Encryption and Anonymization: Implement robust data encryption and anonymization techniques to protect sensitive information and personal identifiers in IoT datasets. Apply encryption protocols for data at rest and in transit, and adopt anonymization techniques such as data masking, data perturbation, and pseudonymization to prevent the identification of individual data subjects.

Privacy-Preserving Machine Learning Model Development: Develop machine learning models using privacy-preserving techniques such as federated learning and secure enclaves that enable collaborative model training without exposing raw data. Leverage techniques like encrypted model training and inference to ensure that sensitive IoT data remains protected during the model development process.

Regulatory Compliance Integration: Integrate regulatory compliance measures into the privacy-preserving machine learning framework to ensure adherence to data protection regulations such as the General Data Protection Regulation (GDPR) and other regional privacy laws. Implement data access controls, data subject rights management, and data governance mechanisms to facilitate compliance with regulatory requirements.

Security Testing and Validation: Conduct rigorous security testing and validation of the implemented privacy-preserving machine learning framework. Perform vulnerability assessments, penetration testing, and data integrity checks to identify and mitigate potential security loopholes and data privacy vulnerabilities. Validate the effectiveness of the privacy-preserving techniques in safeguarding IoT data from unauthorized access and privacy breaches.

Continuous Monitoring and Evaluation: Establish a continuous monitoring and evaluation process to track the performance and effectiveness of the privacy-preserving machine learning techniques. Implement data auditing, anomaly detection, and incident response mechanisms to detect and address any deviations from the established privacy and security protocols. Regularly update the framework to

Figure 5. Privacy-Preserving machine learning techniques for IoT data in cloud environments

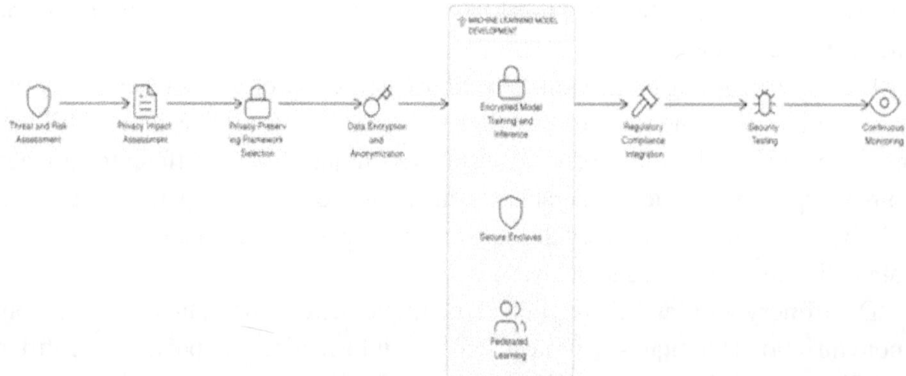

incorporate emerging privacy technologies and address evolving privacy challenges in IoT data processing.

By following this comprehensive methodology, organizations can effectively implement privacy-preserving machine learning techniques for IoT data in cloud environments, ensuring the protection of sensitive information, maintaining user privacy, and fostering regulatory compliance. This methodology serves as a structured framework for organizations to build robust privacy-preserving machine learning solutions that support responsible data processing practices in the IoT ecosystem.

MACHINE LEARNING TECHNIQUES FOR PRIVACY-PRESERVING

Homomorphic Encryption and Secure Multi-Party Computation

Homomorphic encryption and secure multi-party computation (SMPC) are two fundamental privacy-preserving machine learning techniques that play a crucial role in safeguarding sensitive data in IoT applications processed in cloud environments. These techniques enable data analysis while preserving data privacy and confidentiality. Let's delve into each of them:

Homomorphic Encryption:

Homomorphic encryption is a revolutionary cryptographic technique that allows computations to be performed on encrypted data without the need to decrypt it. This means that sensitive data remains encrypted at all times, even during processing. It is particularly valuable for IoT data in cloud environments because it ensures that data privacy is maintained during machine learning and analytics operations. Here's how homomorphic encryption works:

- Data Encryption: IoT data is encrypted before it is transmitted or stored in the cloud. This encryption ensures that the data remains confidential and secure.
- Computation on Encrypted Data: With homomorphic encryption, mathematical operations can be performed on the encrypted data. This allows for machine learning models and analytics to process the data without ever exposing its underlying content.
- Result Decryption: The final output of the computations remains encrypted, and only the authorized party with the corresponding decryption key can reveal the results. This means that data remains private, and the results are only accessible to those with the appropriate privileges.

Homomorphic encryption ensures that the privacy of IoT data is upheld while enabling useful analysis, making it an excellent choice for scenarios where data confidentiality is paramount, such as healthcare or financial data processing.

Secure Multi-Party Computation (SMPC):

Secure multi-party computation is another privacy-preserving technique that enables multiple parties to jointly compute a function over their inputs while keeping those inputs private. This technique is invaluable in situations where different stakeholders need to collaborate on machine learning tasks without sharing their sensitive data. Here's how SMPC works:

- Data Splitting: IoT data is divided among multiple parties, each holding a portion of the data. Each party's data remains private, and no single party has access to the complete dataset.
- Collaborative Computation: Using secure protocols, the parties collectively compute machine learning models or analytics without revealing their private data to each other.
- Result Aggregation: The final results are aggregated from the computations, ensuring that no party gains access to the inputs of others.

SMPC is ideal for scenarios where data privacy is a significant concern, and parties need to collaborate while maintaining the confidentiality of their data. It is

Figure 6. Secure multi-party computation architecture

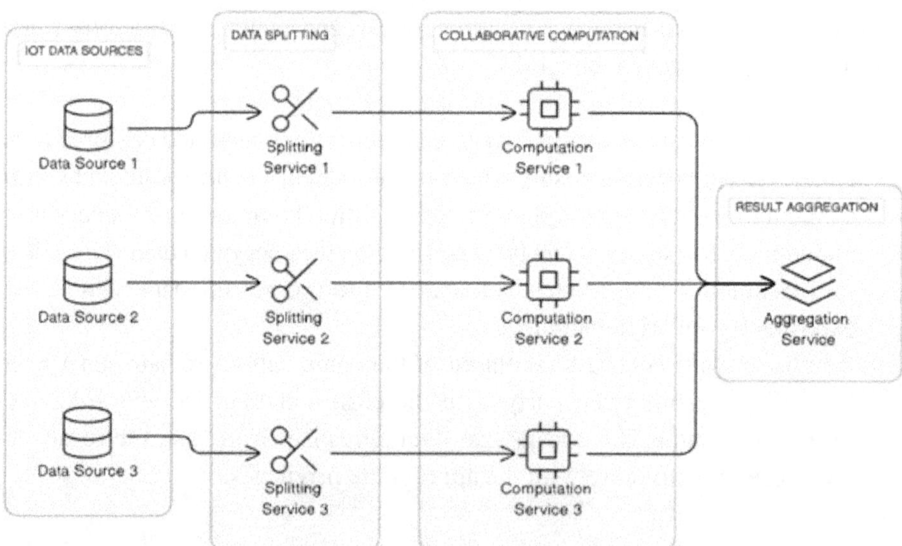

often used in situations involving sensitive industrial data or cross-organizational data analysis.

In conclusion, both homomorphic encryption and secure multi-party computation are powerful techniques for ensuring the privacy of IoT data during machine learning and analytics in cloud environments. These techniques allow organizations to reap the benefits of data analysis without compromising data security, making them essential components of responsible and secure IoT data processing.

Navigating the landscape of privacy-preserving machine learning techniques tailored for IoT data in cloud environments, the comprehensive exploration encompasses an insightful examination of emerging technologies, notably quantum computing, and its profound implications for data privacy. Quantum computing, with its revolutionary computational paradigm, introduces a transformative dimension to the discourse on safeguarding sensitive information. This inclusion acknowledges the dynamic nature of the technological landscape, recognizing that traditional cryptographic methods may face challenges posed by the computational capabilities of quantum systems. Recent studies focusing on quantum-resistant cryptographic approaches and the potential vulnerabilities that quantum computing may exploit in existing privacy-preserving techniques are integral to understanding the evolving threat landscape. By delving into quantum computing impact on data privacy, the chapter embraces a forward-looking perspective, acknowledging the need for adaptive privacy-preserving methodologies in the face of rapidly advancing technologies. This nuanced exploration ensures that the discourse remains at the forefront of contemporary challenges and opportunities, providing readers with a holistic understanding of how quantum computing shapes the landscape of privacy in the era of IoT and cloud computing. The incorporation of quantum computing in this narrative underscores the importance of anticipating and addressing the implications of cutting-edge technologies for the future of privacy-preserving techniques.

Differential Privacy Techniques

Differential privacy techniques are a fundamental component of privacy-preserving machine learning, particularly in the context of IoT data in cloud environments. Differential privacy is a mathematical framework that focuses on adding controlled noise to data or query responses to protect individual privacy while still allowing meaningful analysis. Here's an exploration of differential privacy and its role in safeguarding IoT data privacy:

Differential Privacy Principles:

Differential privacy is founded on the following key principles:

Privacy Budget: It introduces the concept of a privacy budget, which determines the amount of noise that can be added to data or responses without compromising individual privacy. The budget ensures a balance between data utility and privacy.

Randomized Responses: Differential privacy often involves introducing randomness into data to obscure individual details. This randomization can occur during data collection, query responses, or data sharing.

Role of Differential Privacy in IoT Data Processing:

Differential privacy techniques are highly relevant in IoT data processing for several reasons:

Privacy-Preserving Data Collection: IoT devices often collect sensitive data, such as location information, health records, and user behavior. Differential privacy can be applied at the device level to protect individual data while still allowing aggregate data collection for analysis.

Secure Data Sharing: In IoT ecosystems involving multiple stakeholders or organizations, secure data sharing is crucial. Differential privacy enables data sharing while preserving the privacy of individual data subjects. This is essential in collaborative IoT applications like healthcare, smart cities, and supply chain management.

Privacy-Preserving Analytics: IoT analytics often require data to be analyzed without revealing individual-specific details. By applying differential privacy to analytics and machine learning models, it's possible to protect individual data subjects while still extracting valuable insights.

Compliance with Data Protection Regulations: In scenarios where IoT data processing must adhere to data protection regulations like the General Data Protection Regulation (GDPR), differential privacy techniques can help ensure compliance by safeguarding data privacy.

Differential Privacy Techniques:

Differential privacy employs a variety of techniques to protect data privacy:

Laplace Mechanism: This technique adds Laplace-distributed noise to query responses, making it a fundamental method for differential privacy. The scale of the noise is determined by the privacy budget.

Exponential Mechanism: The exponential mechanism provides a way to select items or responses with differential privacy. It introduces randomness into the selection process, ensuring that the selection is privacy-preserving.

Local Differential Privacy: Local differential privacy adds noise directly at the data source (e.g., IoT device) before data is transmitted. This preserves privacy even before data leaves the device.

Global Differential Privacy: Global differential privacy introduces noise at the aggregation or analysis stage, allowing multiple data sources to collaborate while preserving the privacy of their individual data.

Figure 7. Role of differential privacy in IoT data processing

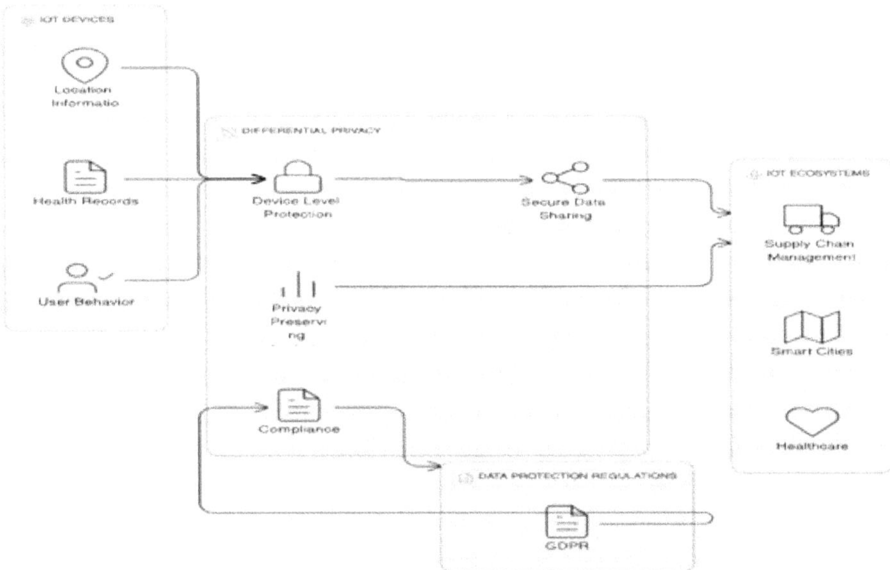

Differential privacy techniques are highly adaptable and can be tailored to the specific requirements and constraints of IoT data processing scenarios. By implementing differential privacy, organizations can harness the insights and benefits of IoT data analytics while respecting the privacy and security of individuals' data, which is of utmost importance in today's data-driven world.

Blockchain Integration for Data Integrity

The integration of blockchain technology in the context of privacy-preserving machine learning techniques for IoT data in cloud environments serves a dual purpose – ensuring data integrity and preserving privacy. This technique leverages the inherent characteristics of blockchain, such as immutability, transparency, and decentralization, to create a secure and privacy-conscious environment for IoT data processing. Here's an exploration of blockchain integration for data integrity in this context:

Blockchain for Data Integrity:

Blockchain technology is renowned for its ability to provide data integrity and security. By design, blockchain is a distributed ledger where data is stored in a tamper-evident and tamper-resistant manner. Each block in the chain contains a cryptographic hash of the previous block, creating a linked and irreversible record of transactions or data entries. This design ensures the following benefits for data integrity:

Immutability: Once data is recorded on the blockchain, it cannot be altered or deleted. This property guarantees the historical integrity of data, making it suitable for applications where data audit trails and provenances are crucial.

Transparency: Blockchain transactions are transparent and visible to all authorized parties. This transparency allows for data verification and accountability, reducing the risk of fraudulent or unauthorized changes to data.

Decentralization: Blockchain networks are typically decentralized, meaning that no single entity has full control. This decentralization enhances data resilience and reliability, as there is no central point of failure.

Role of Blockchain Integration in IoT Data Processing:

Integrating blockchain with privacy-preserving machine learning techniques in IoT data processing provides a secure and privacy-conscious framework for the following aspects:

Data Integrity: Blockchain ensures that IoT data remains unchanged and trustworthy throughout its lifecycle. Data collected from IoT devices can be securely timestamped and stored on the blockchain, providing an immutable record of the data's history.

Auditing and Compliance: For IoT applications subject to regulatory compliance, such as healthcare or supply chain management, blockchain integration helps maintain compliance by offering transparent and traceable data records.

Privacy-Preserving Smart Contracts: Smart contracts on blockchain platforms can execute privacy-preserving algorithms and analytics while keeping individual data confidential. This allows secure and automated data processing.

Data Sharing and Collaboration: Blockchain enables secure data sharing and collaboration in multi-stakeholder IoT environments. Data is shared only with authorized parties, preserving data privacy and integrity.

Challenges and Considerations:

While blockchain integration offers significant advantages, it also poses certain challenges, such as scalability issues, energy consumption, and complexity. Therefore, selecting the appropriate blockchain platform and consensus mechanism is crucial. Additionally, addressing data privacy concerns is essential, as the transparency of the blockchain may conflict with data protection regulations.

The integration of blockchain technology in IoT data processing in cloud environments enhances data integrity, transparency, and security. This, combined with privacy-preserving machine learning techniques, establishes a robust framework for responsible IoT data analysis and collaborative applications, ensuring that sensitive data remains protected and reliable throughout its journey in the cloud.

Figure 8. Role of differential privacy in iot data processing

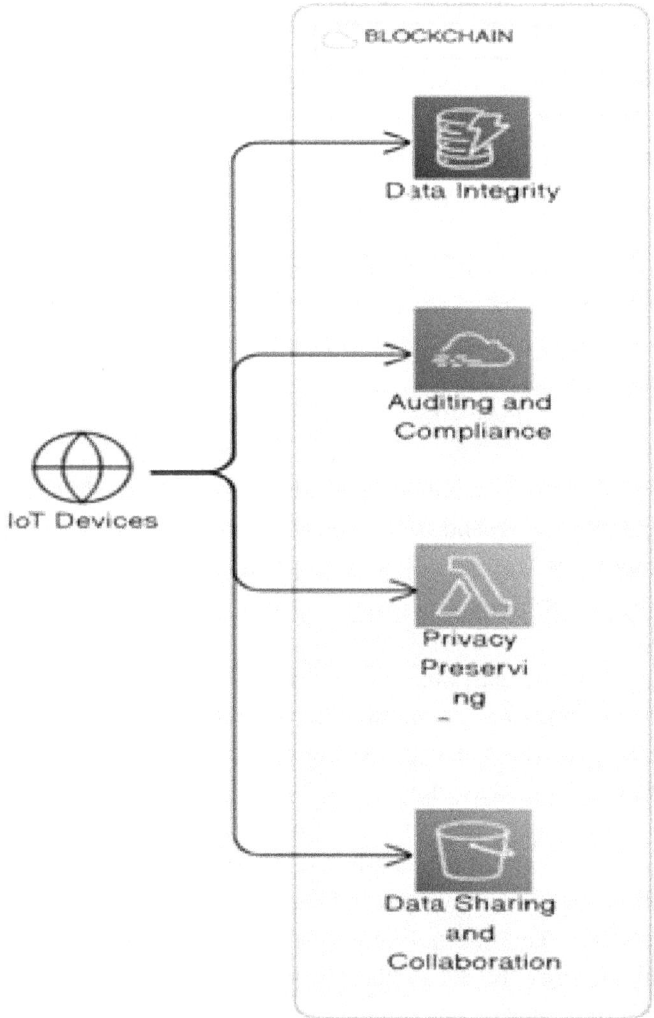

FUTURE TRENDS AND EMERGING TECHNOLOGIES

Future trends and emerging technologies in privacy-preserving machine learning for IoT data in cloud environments hold the promise of revolutionizing the way organizations handle sensitive information while deriving valuable insights. As the IoT ecosystem continues to expand and data privacy becomes an even more critical concern, several noteworthy developments are on the horizon:

a. Federated Learning Advancements: Federated learning, a technique that allows model training on decentralized data while preserving privacy, is poised to evolve further. We can anticipate enhanced federated learning frameworks that provide better model convergence, more efficient communication, and support for a broader range of machine learning algorithms. These advancements will enable collaborative model training across IoT devices and cloud environments with increased efficiency and effectiveness.

b. Improved Differential Privacy: Differential privacy techniques are expected to become more sophisticated and user-friendly. We can expect refinements in noise addition mechanisms, advanced privacy budgets, and better user-centric control over privacy preferences. These improvements will make it easier for organizations to implement differential privacy for IoT data processing without compromising data utility.

c. Blockchain Innovations: Blockchain technology will see further innovations in terms of scalability, interoperability, and energy efficiency. Solutions that strike a balance between data privacy and transparency will emerge, offering improved data integrity and secure execution of privacy-preserving algorithms. Smart contract platforms will gain capabilities to execute machine learning tasks while preserving individual data privacy.

d. Edge Computing Integration: The integration of edge computing with privacy-preserving machine learning will become more prevalent. Edge devices will be equipped with the computational power to execute privacy-preserving algorithms, reducing the need to transmit sensitive data to central cloud environments. This will enhance real-time analytics, reduce latency, and improve privacy by processing data closer to the source.

e. Privacy-Preserving Data Marketplaces: Emerging technologies will facilitate the creation of privacy-preserving data marketplaces. Organizations and individuals will have the option to securely share and monetize their data while maintaining control over their privacy preferences. This will encourage responsible data sharing and collaborative analytics in IoT ecosystems.

f. Hybrid AI-Blockchain Solutions: Hybrid solutions that combine AI and blockchain technologies will gain traction. These solutions will leverage AI for data analytics and blockchain for data integrity and privacy preservation, offering a comprehensive framework for secure and privacy-conscious IoT data processing.

g. Regulatory and Standardization Developments: The regulatory landscape will continue to evolve, with more comprehensive data protection regulations coming into effect. Standardization efforts will also play a crucial role in ensuring that privacy-preserving techniques and technologies adhere to consistent guidelines, fostering trust and compliance in the IoT data processing domain.

The future of privacy-preserving machine learning for IoT data in cloud environments is a dynamic and promising one. Emerging technologies will provide organizations with advanced tools and methodologies to strike the delicate balance between data analytics and privacy preservation. As data privacy and security concerns become more pronounced, these innovations will be crucial in harnessing the full potential of IoT data while maintaining the highest standards of data protection and individual privacy.

CONCLUSION

In conclusion, the adoption of privacy-preserving machine learning techniques for IoT data in cloud environments represents a significant step forward in achieving the delicate balance between data analytics and data privacy. This comprehensive approach ensures that organizations can harness the vast potential of IoT data while preserving the confidentiality, security, and integrity of sensitive information. As we reflect on the key takeaways and the future landscape of privacy-preserving machine learning in IoT, several critical points emerge:

Data Privacy as a Fundamental Right: The importance of data privacy has never been more pronounced. As the IoT ecosystem expands, individuals and organizations alike are increasingly concerned about the security and privacy of their data. It is imperative that privacy becomes a fundamental right and a central consideration in any IoT data processing framework.

Ethical Data Handling: Responsible and ethical data handling is essential. Organizations must prioritize ethical data collection, sharing, and analysis. Transparency, consent, and user control over their data should be at the core of data processing practices, aligning with evolving data protection regulations.

Privacy-By-Design Principles: Privacy-by-design principles should guide the development of IoT applications and cloud-based systems. This means integrating privacy-preserving measures from the outset, rather than attempting to bolt on privacy protection as an afterthought.

Regulatory Compliance: Compliance with data protection regulations is non-negotiable. Regulations like the GDPR have set high standards for data privacy. Organizations must commit to adhering to these regulations, ensuring that they implement the necessary technical and organizational measures to protect data subjects' rights.

Collaboration and Standardization: Collaboration between stakeholders, industry players, and regulators is vital for creating a unified approach to privacy-preserving IoT data processing. Standardization efforts are crucial in establishing consistent guidelines for implementing privacy-preserving technologies.

Data Utility and Privacy: Striking the right balance between data utility and privacy is a continuous challenge. Emerging techniques like federated learning, secure multi-party computation, and differential privacy are instrumental in achieving this balance.

Future-Proofing Privacy: As IoT data continues to grow and evolve, organizations must future-proof their privacy-preserving strategies. This involves staying informed about emerging technologies and regulatory changes while continuously adapting and improving privacy measures.

In the coming years, the landscape of IoT data processing will be marked by increased data privacy awareness, a growing emphasis on ethical data practices, and advanced privacy-preserving technologies. The role of blockchain, federated learning, and differential privacy will continue to expand, while edge computing will offer new opportunities for privacy-conscious data processing.

In conclusion, achieving privacy-preserving machine learning in IoT data processing is not only a technical challenge but also a moral and legal imperative. It is a commitment to respecting individuals' rights and building trust in data-driven technologies. By embracing these principles and emerging technologies, organizations can navigate the evolving data privacy landscape and unlock the full potential of IoT data while safeguarding sensitive information and individual privacy.

REFERENCES

Al-Qarafi, A., Alrowais, F., & Alotaibi, S., S., Nemri, N., Al-Wesabi, F. N., Al Duhayyim, M., & Al-Shabi, M. (. (2022). Optimal machine learning based privacy preserving blockchain assisted internet of things with smart cities environment. *Applied Sciences (Basel, Switzerland)*, *12*(12), 5893. doi:10.3390/app12125893

Briggs, C., Fan, Z., & Andras, P. (2021). A review of privacy-preserving federated learning for the Internet-of-Things. *Federated Learning Systems: Towards Next-Generation AI*, 21-50. Springer. doi:10.1007/978-3-030-70604-3_2

Bugshan, N., Khalil, I., Rahman, M. S., Atiquzzaman, M., Yi, X., & Badsha, S. (2022). Toward trustworthy and privacy-preserving federated deep learning service framework for industrial internet of things. *IEEE Transactions on Industrial Informatics*, *19*(2), 1535–1547. doi:10.1109/TII.2022.3209200

Can, Y. S., & Ersoy, C. (2021). Privacy-preserving federated deep learning for wearable IoT-based biomedical monitoring. *ACM Transactions on Internet Technology*, *21*(1), 1–17. doi:10.1145/3428152

Gheisari, M., Wang, G., & Chen, S. (2020). An edge computing-enhanced internet of things framework for privacy-preserving in smart city. *Computers & Electrical Engineering*, *81*, 106504. doi:10.1016/j.compeleceng.2019.106504

Gupta, I., Gupta, R., Singh, A. K., & Buyya, R. (2020). MLPAM: A machine learning and probabilistic analysis based model for preserving security and privacy in cloud environment. *IEEE Systems Journal*, *15*(3), 4248–4259. doi:10.1109/JSYST.2020.3035666

Gupta, R., Gupta, I., Singh, A. K., Saxena, D., & Lee, C. N. (2022). An iot-centric data protection method for preserving security and privacy in cloud. *IEEE Systems Journal*. Advance online publication. doi:10.1109/JSYST.2022.3218894

Kant, R., Sharma, S., Vikas, V., Chaudhary, S., Jain, A. K., & Sharma, K. K. (2023, April). Blockchain–A Deployment Mechanism for IoT Based Security. In *2023 International Conference on Computational Intelligence, Communication Technology and Networking (CICTN)* (pp. 739-745). IEEE. DOI: 10.1109/CICTN57981.2023.10140715

Lakshmanna, K., Kavitha, R., Geetha, B. T., Nanda, A. K., Radhakrishnan, A., & Kohar, R. (2022). Deep learning-based privacy-preserving data transmission scheme for clustered IIoT environment. *Computational Intelligence and Neuroscience*, *2022*, 1–11. doi:10.1155/2022/8927830 PMID:35720880

Lee, C. C., Gheisari, M., Shayegan, M. J., Ahvanooey, M. T., & Liu, Y. (2023). Privacy-Preserving Techniques in Cloud/Fog and Internet of Things. *Cryptography*, *7*(4), 51. doi:10.3390/cryptography7040051

Li, Y., Li, H., Xu, G., Xiang, T., Huang, X., & Lu, R. (2020). Toward secure and privacy-preserving distributed deep learning in fog-cloud computing. *IEEE Internet of Things Journal*, *7*(12), 11460–11472. doi:10.1109/JIOT.2020.3012480

Ma, W., Zhou, T., Qin, J., Xiang, X., Tan, Y., & Cai, Z. (2022). A privacy-preserving content-based image retrieval method based on deep learning in cloud computing. *Expert Systems with Applications*, *203*, 117508. doi:10.1016/j.eswa.2022.117508

Park, J., Kim, D. S., & Lim, H. (2020). Privacy-preserving reinforcement learning using homomorphic encryption in cloud computing infrastructures. *IEEE Access : Practical Innovations, Open Solutions*, *8*, 203564–203579. doi:10.1109/ACCESS.2020.3036899

Ren, W., Tong, X., Du, J., Wang, N., Li, S. C., Min, G., Zhao, Z., & Bashir, A. K. (2021). Privacy-preserving using homomorphic encryption in Mobile IoT systems. *Computer Communications*, *165*, 105–111. doi:10.1016/j.comcom.2020.10.022

Sharma, V., & Kumar, S. (2023, May). Role of Artificial Intelligence (AI) to Enhance the Security and Privacy of Data in Smart Cities. In *2023 3rd International Conference on Advance Computing and Innovative Technologies in Engineering (ICACITE)* (pp. 596-599). IEEE. 10.1109/ICACITE57410.2023.10182455

Will, N. C. (2022, April). A privacy-preserving data aggregation scheme for fog/cloud-enhanced iot applications using a trusted execution environment. In *2022 IEEE International Systems Conference (SysCon)* (pp. 1-5). IEEE. DOI: 10.1109/SysCon53536.2022.9773838

Xu, R., Baracaldo, N., & Joshi, J. (2021). *Privacy-preserving machine learning: Methods, challenges and directions.* arXiv preprint arXiv:2108.04417. https://doi.org//arXiv.2108.04417 doi:10.48550

Zhou, X., Xu, K., Wang, N., Jiao, J., Dong, N., Han, M., & Xu, H. (2021). A secure and privacy-preserving machine learning model sharing scheme for edge-enabled IoT. *IEEE Access : Practical Innovations, Open Solutions*, *9*, 17256–17265. doi:10.1109/ACCESS.2021.3051945

Zhu, L., Tang, X., Shen, M., Gao, F., Zhang, J., & Du, X. (2021). Privacy-preserving machine learning training in IoT aggregation scenarios. *IEEE Internet of Things Journal*, *8*(15), 12106–12118. doi:10.1109/JIOT.2021.3060764

KEY TERMS AND DEFINITIONS

Cloud Computing: Cloud computing is a technology paradigm that enables on-demand access to a shared pool of computing resources, such as servers, storage, and applications, over the internet, offering flexibility and scalability for users and organizations.

Deep Learning: Deep learning is a subfield of machine learning that focuses on teaching computers to learn and make decisions in a way inspired by the human brain. It uses artificial neural networks, which are computational models composed of interconnected nodes called "neurons." These neural networks are structured in multiple layers, hence the term "deep" learning.

General Data Protection Regulation (GDPR): The General Data Protection Regulation (GDPR) is a comprehensive data protection regulation implemented by the European Union (EU) to safeguard individuals' personal data privacy and rights. It establishes rules for collecting, processing, and storing personal data by organizations, ensuring transparency, consent, and control over individuals' data, as well as imposing strict penalties for non-compliance.

Internet of Things (IoT): The Internet of Things (IoT) is a concept that refers to the connection of everyday objects to the internet, allowing them to send and receive data. These objects can include devices like smartphones, thermostats, wearables, home appliances, and even vehicles. The idea behind IoT is to create a network where these objects can communicate with each other, collect and share data, and perform tasks more efficiently.

Natural Language Processing (NLP): Natural Language Processing (NLP) is a branch of artificial intelligence that focuses on enabling computers to understand, interpret, and interact with human language in a natural and meaningful way. NLP involves the development of algorithms and models that allow computers to process, analyze, and generate human language.

Chapter 7
ChatGPT and Ensemble Learning for Mobile Text Misinformation Identification

Sanjaikanth E. Vadakkethil Somanathan Pillai
https://orcid.org/0000-0003-3264-9923
University of North Dakota, USA

Wen-Chen Hu
University of North Dakota, USA

ABSTRACT

According to Pew Research Center, eight-in-ten Americans acquire news from digital devices, favoring mobile devices over desktops and laptops. News is therefore spread faster, wider, and easier. However, many of these mobile messages are at risk of being incorrect or even distorted on purpose. This research aims to mitigate this problem by identifying mobile text misinformation to allow mobile users to accurately judge the messages they receive. The proposed method uses various mobile data mining technologies including ChatGPT and several ensemble learning methods (including recurrent neural networks (RNN) and bagging, boosting, stacking, & voting means) to identify mobile misinformation. In addition, sentiment and emotional analyses are discussed in comparison. Experiment results show the ensemble learning methods provide higher accuracy than standalone ChatGPT or RNN model. Nevertheless, the problem, misinformation identification, is intrinsically difficult. Further refinements are needed before it is put into practical use.

DOI: 10.4018/979-8-3693-0766-3.ch007

INTRODUCTION

Instead of reading newspapers or watching the news on television, more than eight-in-ten Americans acquire news from digital devices (Shearer, 2021), favoring mobile devices over desktops and laptops (Walker, 2019). A major portion of mobile news is sent through short messages by messaging apps like Whatsapp or posted on social media platforms such as X. Through this method, news is spread easier, faster, and broader. However, many of these messages are at risk of being incorrect or even distorted on purpose. During the election year, this problem has become a serious concern due to political misinformation potentially affecting election results or causing great harm to society such as the January 6 US Capitol attack. This research aims to mitigate this problem by identifying mobile text misinformation to allow mobile users to accurately judge the messages they receive.

This research proposes a system that can effectively identify fake information by combining the results from ChatGPT and various learning techniques (including bagging, boosting, stacking, & voting methods, sentiment and emotional analyses, and a recurrent neural network (RNN)). Each message will go through a series of steps: preprocessing (including lexical analysis, stopword removal, and stemming), indexing and storage, and testing (classification) by using a dataflow graph. This is a supervised learning system, so before the system is put into use, it needs training by using a set of text messages with known results. The initial parameters of the system are set by heuristics because the keywords of text messages are unknown in advance and have to be speculated. After the first round of training, better parameters could be found from the test results. Preliminary experiment results show the accuracy of the proposed method meets the expectation, but still has room for improvement. An explanation for this may be because the short messages do not provide much information and small deviation may cause a great impact on the results. Further refinements are needed before it is put into use.

The rest of this chapter is organized as follows. Section 2 shows the background information of this research and related research. Section 3 discusses the proposed system, its work flow and components, and the preprocessing steps such as data preprocessing, stopword removal, and stemming. The proposed methods including ChatGPT, recurrent neural network, and bagging, boosting, voting, & stacking means are given in Section 4. Section 5 describes experiment results including sentiment and emotional analyses. The conclusion and future research directions are given in Section 6 followed by references.

BACKGROUND AND RELATED LITERATURE

A study reveals that misinformation spreads faster than true information. It is crucial to recognize and differentiate between various types of information, particularly during public health crises, as false information can mislead individuals and hinder efforts to mitigate the impact of the pandemic. Misinformation detection is critical and popular in these days because information could be

created and sent by everyone, not just news agencies, and some may distribute misinformation unintentionally or intentionally. Many methods are used to detect all kinds of misinformation like politics, businesses, text messages, emails, or news. This research places the focus on mobile health text misinformation identification. If the results are favorable, the method may be extended to other kinds of information. Related research can be found from the articles (Bozuyla, 2021; Hakak, Alazab, Khan, Gadekallu, Maddikunta, & Khan, 2021; Kaliyar, Goswami, & Narang, 2019).

ChatGPT

This research tries to identify mobile text misinformation, a kind of language, so it is reasonable that NLP (natural language processing) is used to solve this problem. One of natural language processing tools is ChatGPT (Chat Generative Pre-Trained Transformer) (ChatGPT, 2023), which is used by this research to see how well it solves the problem of misinformation detection. Qin et al. (2023) demonstrate the effectiveness and limitations of ChatGPT in different types of NLP tasks. For example, ChatGPT is good at reasoning and dialogue tasks; on the other hand, it still faces challenges when solving specific tasks such as sequence tagging. NewsGuard (2023) reports ChatGPT has the ability to produce misinformation more frequently, and more persuasively, than its predecessor. Huang and Sun (2023) present a thorough exploration of ChatGPT's proficiency in generating, explaining, and detecting fake news. They study their method's detection consistency and then propose a reason-aware prompt method to improve its performance. They also probe into the potential extra information that could bolster its effectiveness in detecting fake news.

Ensemble Learning

This research also uses ensemble learning, which is a federated approach to seek better predictive performance by combining the predictions from multiple models using machine learning. Huang and Chen (2020) employed multiple ensemble methods to detect fake news and utilized four models, namely LSTM, depth LSTM, LIWC CNN, and N-gram CNN. They are able to achieve a highest accuracy of 99.4%. Ahmad et al. (2020) investigated various textual properties and ensemble methods to detect fake news. Similarly, Aslam, et al. (2021) conducted a study using deep learning models in conjunction with ensemble learning to achieve higher accuracy in detecting fake news. Yu, Jiang, Li, Han, and Wu (2020) detected rumor by using a model based on graph convolution network to represent the spreading structure of rumors, with graph convolution operator for node vector updating. The research (Nithya & Sahayadhas. 2023) used Meta-heuristic Searched-Ensemble Learning (MS-EL). In addition, the selected features are extracted by the "Term Frequency-Inverse Document Frequency (TF-IDF)" and also Word2vec features. Finally, the extracted selected features are integrated with the Hybrid Squirrel-Dragonfly Search Optimization (HS-DSO) and is used to optimize the weighted feature selection approach with the fitness function of solving data variance and correlation. Related research can be found from the articles (Li, Ma, Niu, Wang, Ji, Yu, & Chen, 2019; Reddy, Raj, Gala, & Basava, 2020).

Sentiment and Emotional Analyses

As opposed to the studies mentioned next, our research extends to incorporating sentiment, emotional, hate speech, and irony classifiers into the ensemble methods, resulting in higher accuracy than any of the aforementioned research. Ghanem, Rosso, & Rangel (2020) proposed an LSTM neural network model that is emotionally infused to detect false news based on the comparison between the false news and true news from an emotional perspective, considering a set of false information types (propaganda, hoax, clickbait, and satire). A study from Luvembe, Li, Li, Liu, & Xu (2023) utilized dual emotion features to detect fake news. The study proposed a Deep Normalized Attention-based mechanism for enriched extraction of dual emotion features and an Adaptive Genetic Weight Update-Random Forest (AGWu-RF) for classification. Liu, Zhang, & Liu (2023) proposed a framework for detecting fake news, which leverages graph neural network to jointly model the content, emotional information and propagation structure of news conversations. In addition, they proposed an edge-aware method to enhance the news graph representation by using emotion to amplify the spread of fake news. Related research could be found from the articles (Liu, Zhang, Yang, Thompson, Yu, & Ananiadou, 2023; Visser, Lawrence, & Reed, 2020; Savage, 2021).

THE PROPOSED SYSTEM

This research is to identify mobile text misinformation by using ensemble learning. Other than the ChatGPT and RNN (recurrent neural network), this study also utilizes ensemble-learning methods including bagging, boosting, stacking, and voting means. The proposed system is introduced in this section. Details will be given in the next sections.

The Missions

A dataset consisting of more than 45,000 news records collected from various sources on the Internet (Barbieri, Camacho-Collados, Neves, & Espinosa-Anke. 2020) is used in this research. The dataset comprised an equal proportion of true and fake news and had three columns: title, news, and class. To enhance the accuracy of the model, the title and news columns were combined and used as a single entity in the input model. This was done as the title column may be short, sometimes missing, and may not articulate the full meaning of the news. The ultimate objective of this research is to address the following two research questions:

- **RQ1**: Can ensemble learning effectively detect misinformation?
- **RQ2**: Does the addition of ChatGPT or RNN model to the ensemble learning result in improved accuracy compared to standalone ChatGPT or RNN model?
- **RQ3**: Can the inclusion of emotional and sentiment classifiers improve the accuracy of an ensemble learning method?

Characteristics of Input Data

In this study, the input data was analyzed for sentiment content using Hugging Face RoBERTa (Devlin, Chang, Lee, & Toutanova, 2019) based which is a pre-trained transformer based language model. The model classifies the text input into different classes like neutral, negative, and positive. Input data was also analyzed for emotional content using a pre-trained DistilBERT model obtained from Hugging Face. This model classifies the text input into classes such as sadness, joy, love, anger, fear, and surprise. The input data was also analyzed for hate speech and irony detection model. As shown in Figure 1, the input dataset comprises more than 50% of negative data, around 44% of neural data, and only 5.7% of positive data. Emotional classification was conducted by the researchers on the input dataset, which revealed that 56% of the data belongs to the "anger" category, while 23% of the data belongs to "joy," 10% to "fear," 8% to "sadness," 0.6% to "love," and 0.7% to "surprise" categories. The authors used different ensemble learning methods and selected the model that returns the highest accuracy on validation and test data.

Figure 1. (a) Sentiment Classification of Input Dataset and (b) Emotional Classification of Input Dataset

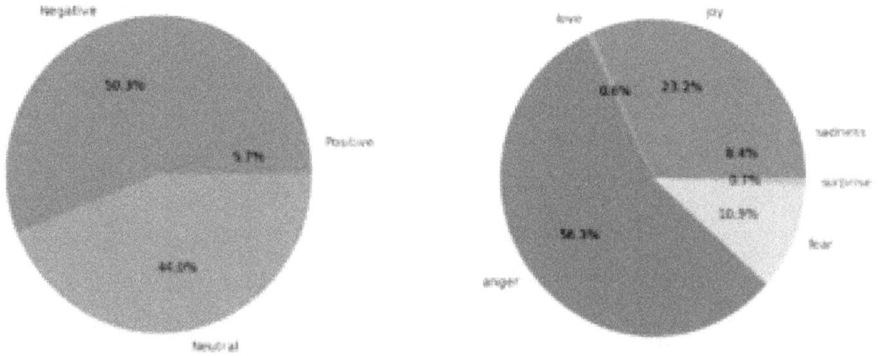

(a) (b)

Data Preprocessing

The input dataset undergoes several preprocessing steps before being passed through various techniques of the proposed ensemble method. The steps involved are (i) data cleanup, (ii) stopword removal, (iii) stemming, (iv) synonym discovery, (v) tokenization, and (vi) padding. Figure 2 shows the stages of the data preprocessing. Data cleanup involves removing unwanted characters, URLs, and extra spaces etc. from the input dataset. Stopword removal is the process of eliminating meaningless, repetitive data called stopwords. These words do not convey significant information and can negatively impact message classification accuracy. Common stopwords include “is,” “has,” “an,” etc. Removing these words can speed up execution time and improve accuracy. Stemming is the process of reducing inflected words to their base or root form, and it helps related words to map to the same stem even if the stem is not a valid root. Tokenization converts the input text into integers. Padding refers to the technique of adding extra elements or symbols to a sequence to make it a fixed length, typically in cases where the original sequence lengths are variable. This ensures that all sequences have the same length, which is required for many machine learning algorithms to process the data efficiently. After all the preprocessing steps are completed, an array of integers is obtained, which is then fed into various ensemble methods to determine the accuracy of the dataset. The model with the highest accuracy is selected.

Figure 2. Steps of Data Preprocessing

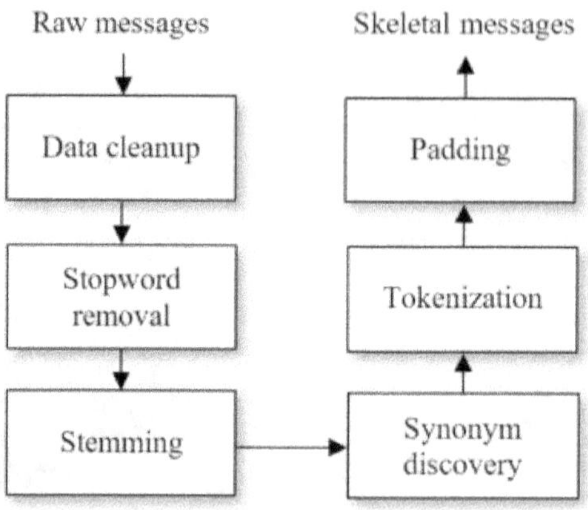

Work Flow of the Proposed System

The study utilized an ensemble learning method to identify the most accurate model for the dataset based on the validation and test results. Other than the ChatGPT and RNN (recurrent neural network) models, the learning means used in the proposed ensemble method include: (1) bagging means, (2) boosting means, (3) stacking means, and (4) voting means where

(1) *Bagging means*, which creates a more accurate result from different subsamples of the training dataset,
(2) *Boosting means*, which combines the predictions of several different models and then adjusting the weights of the models so that the better models have more influence on the final prediction,
(3) *Stacking means*: which is "stacked" on top of each other, and the predictions from each model are combined to produce a final prediction, and
(4) *Voting means*, which builds multiple models and simple statistics are used to combine predictions.

The resulting model was then compared to the standalone RNN model, and the final model with the highest accuracy was chosen using Decision Rules Engine. The dataset was then subjected to different learning means, and the results were compared. Figure 3 shows the work flow of the proposed method.

Figure 3. The Work Flow of the Proposed Method

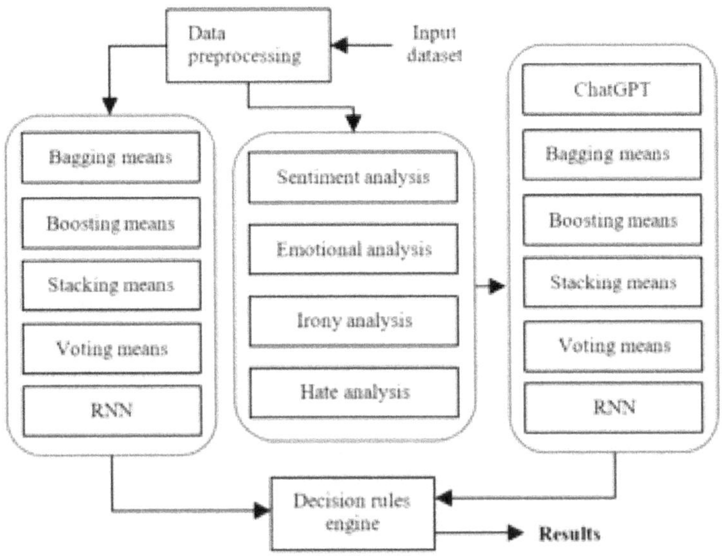

THE PROPOSED METHOD

The study utilizes an ensemble learning method to identify the most accurate model for the dataset based on the validation and test results. Other than the ChatGPT and RNN models, the learning means used in the proposed ensemble method include: (1) bagging means, (2) boosting means, (3) stacking means, and (4) voting means. In addition, sentiment and emotional analyses will be used in comparison. The resulting model was then compared to the standalone ChatGPT and RNN models, and the final model with the highest accuracy was chosen using Decision Rules Engine.

ChatGPT

ChatGPT, an acronym denoting Chat Generative Pre-Trained Transformer, epitomizes a prodigious instantiation of a large language model (LLM) chatbot, artfully devised under the aegis of OpenAI. The focal point of our scholarly inquiry revolves around harnessing the formidable capabilities of ChatGPT in the realm of misinformation detection. To execute this endeavor, we availed ourselves of the ChatGPT API, a portal graciously proffered by OpenAI, granting us unfettered access to the panoply of ChatGPT functionalities. Notably, the deployment of ChatGPT obviated the necessity for laborious data pre-processing routines, obviating the traditional training and testing phases. Instead, we seamlessly injected our verity-seeking input data into the ChatGPT API. Our tool of choice for this noble quest was the venerable ChatGPT 3.5 turbo model (ChatGPT, 2023). In our quest to unearth the veracity of the input news and ferret out any lurking misinformation, ChatGPT responds with an extensive discourse. However, discerning the accuracy of such prolix responses can prove to be an arduous endeavor. To mitigate this challenge, we introduced the concept of Misinformation Adjectives (MA). These adjectives serve as a semantic compass, succinctly delineating the specific categories of misinformation we aim to pinpoint. For instance, an exemplar of an MA is: "Is it true? Provide a response of True, False, Unable to Verify, or No Knowledge, and nothing else." Once we furnish ChatGPT with these Misinformation Adjectives, the responses emanating from the ChatGPT API predominantly assume the form of either True, False, Unable to Verify, or No Knowledge. The residual classifications necessitate manual intervention and categorization, thus culminating in a holistic approach to misinformation detection. Figure 4 shows ChatGPT is used for misinformation identification.

Bagging Learning Means

Bagging means (Kurama, 2023) is a technique in which bootstrapped samples are created first. These samples are generated by randomly drawing the data points from the input samples with replacement as shown in Equation 1.

$$\widehat{f_{bag}} = \widehat{f_1}(X) + \widehat{f_2}(X) + \ldots + \widehat{f_b}(X) \tag{1}$$

where the term on the left hand side is the bagged prediction, and terms on the right hand side are the individual learners. Algorithm I shows the steps used by the bagging learning means.

Figure 4. Misinformation Identification using ChatGPT

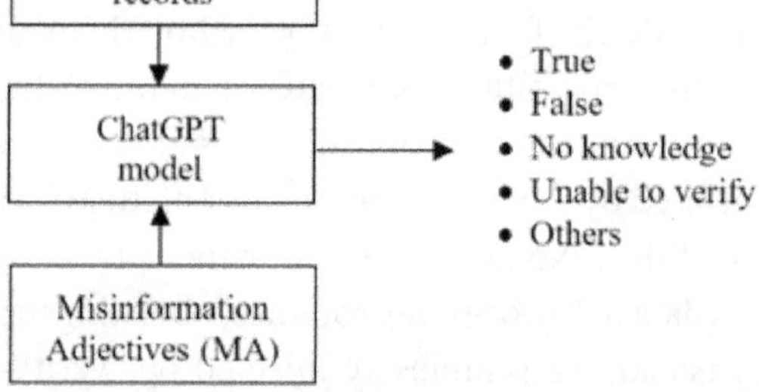

Algorithm I: Bagging Means

```
Bagging -Learning

(1) Initialize the number of base models to be trained (n_
estimators).

(2) For each base model:

(a) Randomly select a subset of the training data with
replacement (bootstrap sampling).

(b) Train the base model on the selected subset of data.

(c) Store the trained base model for later use.

(3) To make a prediction on a new data point:

(a) Pass the data point through each of the trained base
models.

(b) Aggregate the predictions of all base models to obtain the
final prediction. For classification problems, use majority
voting to determine the final prediction.

(4) Repeat steps 2-3 for n_iterations (a hyperparameter that
determines the number of iterations to perform).

(5) Return the final Bagging Classifier model.
```

Boosting Learning Means

Boosting learning technique (Ferreira & Figueiredo. 2012) involves building a strong model by combining several weak models in a series. The process starts by building a model from the training data, and then a second model is built that attempts to correct the errors in the first model. This process continues, and new models are added until either the complete training data set is accurately predicted, or the maximum number of models is reached. As part of their study, the authors incorporated boosting classifiers and specifically utilized the AdaBoostClassifier algorithm. Algorithm II shows the Boosting means.

Stacking Learning Means

Stacking (Dey & Mathur, 2023) is a method of ensemble learning where multiple classification or regression models are combined using a meta-classifier or meta-regressor. The base models are first trained using the complete training set. Then, the meta-model is trained on the predictions produced by the base models. This helps in creating a more accurate model by taking the output of each model as input to the next one. To create the stacking classifier, the authors used KNeighborsClassifier, SVC, DecisionTreeClassifier, and RNN models as base classifiers, and LogisticRegression as the meta model. It is worth mentioning that the same RNN model was used for the above methods to eliminate the variation in results due to different parameters. Algorithm III shows the stacking means.

Voting Learning Means

A voting means (Rojarath, Songpan, & Pong-inwong, 2016) is a type of ensemble learning in which the predictions of multiple models are combined to improve the overall performance of the final model. The voting classifier means involves combining the predictions of multiple base estimators to improve overall model performance. Specifically, we incorporated the KNeighborsClassifier, SVC, DecisionTreeClassifier, and RNN models as the base estimators for our voting classifier. Soft voting was employed, which involves taking the average of the predicted probabilities of each class from each estimator and selecting the class with the highest probability as the final prediction. Algorithm IV shows the voting means.

A Summary

This research proposes a system for detecting misinformation by performing the following tasks:

Algorithm II: Boosting Means

```
Boosting -Learning

(1) Start by building a weak model from the training data.

(2) Use this weak model to predict the outcome.

(3) Identify the cases where the prediction was incorrect.

(4) Build a second weak model that will focus on these
incorrect predictions and try to correct them.

(5) Combine the predictions from the first and second models,
giving more weight to the second model's predictions for the
incorrectly predicted cases.

(6) Repeat the process and building more weak models.

(7) Continue this process until either the complete training
data set is predicted correctly or a predefined maximum number
of models are built.

(8) The final output is the combination of all the weak
models.nitialize the number of base models to be trained (n_
estimators).
```

- The detection accuracy of using different ensemble learning techniques including bagging, boosting, stacking, & voting means, RNN, and ChatGPT was determined.

Algorithm III: Stacking Means

```
Stacking-Learning

(1) Divide the training data into two parts.

(2) Choose a set of diverse base models, such as decision
trees, random forests, and support vector machines.

(3) Train each base model on the first part of the data.

(4) Use these models to predict the outcomes of the second part
of the training data.

(5) Use the predictions from each of the base models as input
features.

(6) Combine these features with the actual outcomes of the
second part of the training data.

(7) Choose a meta-model, and train the meta-model on the new
training data set created in Step 3.

(8) Make predictions on new data.
```

- The results were compared, and the best learning models were found by using decision rules engine.

It shows the better results are achieved by complementing the model with ChatGPT or RNN compared to using individual ensemble means.

Algorithm IV: Voting Means

```
Voting -Learning

(1) Collect multiple models that have been trained on the same
dataset but use different algorithms or settings.

(2) For each model, input the same data and obtain their
individual predictions.

(3) Combine the predictions from all models.

(4) For classification tasks, choose the label with the
majority vote as the final prediction.

(5) For regression tasks, use the combined predictions as the
final prediction.

(6) Evaluate the performance of the voting ensemble using a
test set or other validation method.
```

EXPERIMENT RESULTS

This research is to propose a system, which can be found at the GitHub (Vadakkethil Somanathan Pillai. 2023) to identify misinformation. The experiment results are given in this section to show the effectiveness of this research.

Experiment Data

This study shows promising results, indicating that the accuracy of the ensemble classifiers improve when ChatGPT or RNN (recurrent neural network) is used as one of the base classifiers compared to when it is not included. Table 1 shows the accuracy of different ensemble methods. The learning techniques for the proposed ensemble method, including voting, stacking, & bagging means, when combined with ChatGPT or RNN, have shown to achieve higher accuracy than standalone ChatGPT or RNN model. This is because ensemble learning places emphasis on achieving accuracy through the use of multiple models. The bagging classifier was found to achieve the highest accuracy, with a score of 99.27%. These results are quite remarkable, considering that achieving high accuracy rates beyond 90% is challenging.

All the models that employed RNN achieved an accuracy level of above 99%. However, the boosting ensemble method did not allow the integration of RNN, which is why it exhibited a lower accuracy level as expected. ChatGPT is able to achieve an accuracy of 92.38%. This level of ChatGPT accuracy is promising because it does not require any kind of data model training and can be plugged in as and when it is required. In addition, including sentiment, emotional, hate speech, and irony classifiers into the ensemble methods results in higher accuracy. Other than using the previous methods, we also complement them with sentimental analyses. The confusion matrix, which is a matrix that summarizes the performance of a machine learning model on a set of test data, for bagging, boosting, stacking, & voting means, and RNN is given in Table 2. Additionally, the authors reviewed the results obtained by adding sentiment, emotion, irony and hate speech analysis to the input, and the findings were quite promising. All of the learning techniques of the proposed ensemble method demonstrated a significant improvement in accuracy and were able to achieve near-perfect accuracy levels of 99.88% as shown in Table 2.

In addition, the inclusion of sentiment and emotional classifiers in the input has resulted in a significant improvement in the accuracy of all the ensemble learning methods employed as shown in Figure 5. Specifically, the accuracy rates have increased to 99.88%, compared to the results obtained without the sentiment and emotional classifiers. Additionally, the average accuracy rate of all the learning techniques for the proposed ensemble method has improved from 97.31% to 98.83%. The average accuracy of ensemble learning methods that employ RNN increased

Table 1. Ensemble Learning Accuracy

Ensemble Technique	Accuracy
Standalone ChatGPT	92.38%
Standalone RNN (recurrent neural network)	98.99%
Bagging means	99.26%
Boosting means	90.06%
Stacking means	99.19%
Voting means	99.02%

Table 2. Ensemble Learning Accuracy with Sentiment, Emotion, Irony, and Hate Speech Classifiers

Ensemble Technique	Accuracy
Bagging means	99.86%
Boosting means	94.71%
Stacking means	99.86%
Voting means	99.84%
Standalone RNN (recurrent neural network)	99.88%

from 99.12% to 99.86% when adding emotional and sentiment classifiers. These results are quite remarkable, considering that achieving high accuracy rates beyond 90% is challenging. All the models that employed RNN achieved an accuracy level of above 99%. However, the boosting ensemble method did not allow the integration of RNN, which is why it exhibited a lower accuracy level as expected.

The confusion matrix for bagging, boosting, stacking, & voting means, and RNN with sentiment and emotional analyses is given presented in Table 3.

Figure 5. Accuracy Improvement with and without Sentiment Analysis

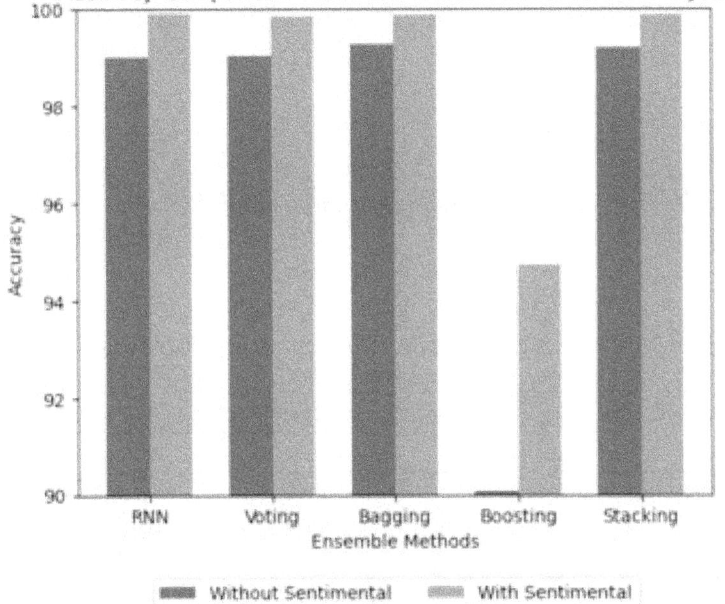

Table 3. Confusion Matrix with Sentiment and Emotional Analyses

Method	Class	Correctly Predicted	Incorrectly Predicted
Bagging means	True	4307	4
	Fake	11	4658
Boosting means	True	3996	153
	Fake	322	4509
Stacking means	True	4305	0
	Fake	13	4662
Voting means	True	4308	4
	Fake	10	4658
Standalone RNN	True	4308	1
	Fake	10	4661

In the field of data analysis and machine learning, performance metrics such as *accuracy*, *precision*, *recall*, and *F1-score* are crucial in evaluating the effectiveness of models. These metrics can be obtained from a confusion matrix, which summarizes the performance of a classification algorithm by comparing the predicted and actual labels of a dataset. The results are given in Table 4. To compute these metrics, the following formulas can be used:

$$A\chi\chi\upsilon\rho\alpha\chi\psi = (T\Pi + TN) / (T\Pi + \Phi\Pi + TN + \Phi N) \qquad (2)$$

$$\Pi\rho\varepsilon\chi\iota\sigma\iota o\upsilon = T\Pi / (T\Pi + \Phi\Pi) \qquad (3)$$

$$P\varepsilon\chi\alpha\lambda\lambda = T\Pi / (T\Pi + \Phi N) \qquad (4)$$

$$\Phi 1\ \sigma\chi o\rho\varepsilon = 2 \times \Pi\rho\varepsilon\chi\iota\sigma\iota o\upsilon \times P\varepsilon\chi\alpha\lambda\lambda / (\Pi\rho\varepsilon\chi\iota\sigma\iota o\upsilon + P\varepsilon\chi\alpha\lambda\lambda) \qquad (5)$$

Table 4. Ensemble Learning Accuracy with Sentiment Classifiers

Method	Accuracy	Precision	Recall	F1 Score
Bagging means	99.83	99.75	99.91	99.83
Boosting means	94.71	92.54	96.31	94.39
Stacking means	99.86	99.70	100.00	99.85
Voting means	99.84	99.77	99.91	99.84
RNN (standalone)	99.88	99.77	99.98	99.87

Discussions

The primary objective of this research is to answer the research questions mentioned previously:

- **RQ1**: *Can ensemble learning effectively detect misinformation?* In this research, we utilized various learning techniques, such as bagging, boosting, stacking, and voting, to detect misinformation. The results are satisfactory as the accuracy is around 99% mostly.
- **RQ2**: *Does the addition of ChatGPT or RNN model to the ensemble learning result in improved accuracy compared to standalone ChatGPT or RNN model?* The experiment results demonstrate that incorporating ChatGPT or RNN model into different learning techniques enhances the accuracy of the system, compared to using standalone ChatGPT or RNN model.
- **RQ3**: *Can the inclusion of emotional and sentiment classifiers improve the accuracy of an ensemble learning method?* Our findings reveal that integrating emotional and sentiment classifiers contributes to improved accuracy of ensemble learning method. In fact, we were able to achieve near 100% accuracy using this approach.

To answer these research questions, we conducted a series of experiments using a dataset of misinformation samples. We trained and tested various models, including learning means for the proposed ensemble method with and without ChatGPT or RNN. The outcomes of this research provide valuable insights into the effectiveness of learning techniques for the proposed ensemble method, as well as the roles of ChatGPT and RNN in improving misinformation detection accuracy. These findings have important implications for the development of more accurate and reliable misinformation detection models in the future.

CONCLUSION

Smartphones are indispensable devices for people in these days, and tens or even hundreds of messages are sent to each device every day. All kinds of information can be found from the messages such as news, greetings from family members or friends, advertisements, promotions, weather reports, etc. People are overwhelmed by the sheer amount of information and they spend much time to sort out a way to find relevant information from the messages. Even worse is some messages give false or fake information and mislead the viewers consequently. The problem becomes more serious especially during the election year. This research tries to automatically identify the mobile text misinformation by using various mobile text/data mining technologies. The dataset used includes 45,000 news articles, which may not represent the most recent news. This limitation could affect the generalizability of our system to more recent news articles. Furthermore, there are many other machine learning models available that we did not include in our research. It is possible that these models may have higher accuracy compared to our model. Also, we only considered the title and text of the news dataset content and did not consider the authenticity of the news publisher. Assigning weight for authenticity could potentially improve the performance of our model. However, our research was solely focused on checking the effectiveness of our misinformation detection system using various ensemble learning methods including the trendy ChatGPT. Our research found that including these classifiers in the input significantly increased the accuracy of the model, and we were able to achieve near-perfect accuracy of 99.87%.

Future Research Directions

In conclusion, our research has demonstrated the potential of ensemble learning methods in improving the accuracy of misinformation detection. This work opens up new avenues for developing more effective strategies for identifying and combating the spread of misinformation in the future. This problem, mobile text misinformation identification, could be classified as one of the NLP (natural language processing) problems. We will consider a variety of DL (deep learning) methods and adapt them to our problem, and see whether the problems are mitigated. Besides, there has been a rising interest in proactive intervention strategies to counter the spread of misinformation and its impact on society. Methods to mitigate the ill effects caused by misinformation will be investigated too.

REFERENCES

Ahmad, I., Yousaf, M., Yousaf, S., & Ahmad, M. O. (2020). Fake news detection using machine learning ensemble methods. *Complexity*, *2020*, 1–11. doi:10.1155/2020/8885861

Arvanitis, L., Sadeghi, M., & Brewster, J. (2023). Despite OpenAI's promises, the company's new AI tool produces misinformation more frequently, and more persuasively, than its predecessor. *NewsGuard Technologies, Inc.* https://www.newsguardtech.com/misinformation-monitor/march-2023/

Aslam, N., Khan, I. U., Alotaibi, F. S., Aldaej, L. A., & Aldubaikil, A. K. (2021). Fake detect: A deep learning ensemble model for fake news detection. *Complexity, 2021*, 1–8. doi:10.1155/2021/5557784

Barbieri, F., Camacho-Collados, J., Neves, L., & Espinosa-Anke, L. (2020). *TweetEval: Unified benchmark and comparative evaluation for Tweet classification*. arXiv. / arXiv.2010.12421 doi:10.18653/v1/2020.findings-emnlp.148

Bozuyla, M. (2021). AdaBoost ensemble learning on top of naive Bayes algorithm to discriminate fake and genuine news from social media. *European Journal of Science and Technology*, *5*(4), 499–513. doi:10.31590/ejosat.1005577

ChatGPT. (2024, January 13). *ChatGPT models*. OpenAI. https://platform.openai.com/docs/models/chatgpt

Devlin, J., Chang, M.-W., Lee, K., & Toutanova, K. (2019). *BERT: Pre-training of deep bidirectional transformers for language understanding*. In 2019 Conference of the North American Chapter of the Association for Computational Linguistics: Human Language Technologies, Minneapolis, Minnesota.

Dey, R., & Mathur, R. (2023). Ensemble learning method using stacking with base learner, a comparison. In Nabendu Chaki, Nilanjana Dutta Roy, Papiya Debnath, and Khalid Saeed (Eds). *Proceedings of International Conference on Data Analytics and Insights, ICDAI 2023*. Springer, Singapore. 10.1007/978-981-99-3878-0_14

Ferreira, A. J., & Figueiredo, M. A. T. (2012). Boosting algorithms: A review of methods, theory, and applications. In C. Zhang & Y. Ma (Eds.), *Ensemble Machine Learning*. Springer. doi:10.1007/978-1-4419-9326-7_2

Ghanem, B., Rosso, P., and Rangel, F. (2020, April 19). An emotional analysis of false information in social media and news articles. *ACM Transactions on Internet Technology*, *20*(2), 19, 1-18. doi:10.1145/3381750

Hakak, S., Alazab, M., Khan, S., Gadekallu, T. R., Maddikunta, P. K. R., & Khan, W. Z. (2021). An ensemble machine learning approach through effective feature extraction to classify fake news. *Future Generation Computer Systems*, *117*, 47–58. doi:10.1016/j.future.2020.11.022

Huang, Y., & Sun, L. (2023). *TweetEval: Harnessing the power of ChatGPT in fake news: An in-depth exploration in generation, detection and explanation*. arXiv. https://doi.org//arXiv.2310.05046 doi:10.48550

Huang, Y.-F., & Chen, P.-H. (2020). Fake news detection using an ensemble learning model based on self-adaptive harmony search algorithms. *Expert Systems with Applications*, *159*, 113584. doi:10.1016/j.eswa.2020.113584

Kaliyar, R. K., Goswami, A., & Narang, P. (2019). Multiclass fake news detection using ensemble machine learning. In *Proceedings of 2019 IEEE 9th International Conference on Advanced Computing (IACC)*, (pp. 103-107). IEEE. https:// doi:10.1109/IACC48062.2019.8971579

Kurama, V. (2023). *Introduction to bagging and ensemble methods*. Paperspace. https://blog.paperspace.com/bagging-ensemble-methods/

Li, S., Ma, K., Niu, X., Wang, Y., Ji, K., Yu, Z., & Chen, Z. (2019). Stacking-based ensemble learning on low dimensional features for fake news detection. In *Proceedings of 2019 IEEE 21st International Conference on High Performance Computing and Communications; IEEE 17th International Conference on Smart City; IEEE 5th International Conference on Data Science and Systems (HPCC/SmartCity/DSS)*, Zhangjiajie, China.10.1109/HPCC/SmartCity/DSS.2019.00383

Liu, F., Zhang, X., & Liu, Q. (2023). Q. (2023). An emotion-aware approach for fake news detection. *IEEE Transactions on Computational Social Systems*, 1–9. doi:10.1109/TCSS.2023.3335269

Liu, L., Zhang, T., Yang, K., Thompson, P., Yu, Z., & Ananiadou, S. (2023, April 30 – May 01). Emotion detection for misinformation: A review. In *Proceedings of the 15th ACM Web Science Conference* (*WebSci 2023*). ACM. https://arxiv.org/pdf/2311.00671.pdf

Luvembe, A. M., Li, W., Li, S., Liu, F., & Xu, G. (2023). Dual emotion based fake news detection: A deep attention-weight update approach. *Information Processing & Management*, *60*(4), 4. doi:10.1016/j.ipm.2023.103354

Nithya, S. H., & Sahayadhas, A. (2023). Meta-heuristic searched-ensemble learning for fake news detection with optimal weighted feature selection approach. *Data & Knowledge Engineering*, *144*, 102124. doi:10.1016/j.datak.2022.102124

Qin, C., Zhang, A., Zhang, Z., Chen, J., Yasunaga, M., & Yang, D. (2023). *Is ChatGPT a general-purpose natural language processing task solver*? arXiv. / arXiv.2302.06476 doi:10.18653/v1/2023.emnlp-main.85

Reddy, H., Raj, N., Gala, M., & Basava, A. (2020). Textmining-based fake news detection using ensemble methods. *International Journal of Automation and Computing*, *17*(2), 210–221. doi:10.1007/s11633-019-1216-5

Rojarath, A., Songpan, W., & Pong-inwong, C. (2016). Improved ensemble learning for classification techniques based on majority voting. In *Proceeding of the 7th IEEE International Conference on Software Engineering and Service Science (ICSESS)*, (pp. 107-110). IEEE. 10.1109/ICSESS.2016.7883026

Savage, N. (2021, March 1). Fact-finding missions. *Communications of the ACM*, *64*(3), 18–19. doi:10.1145/3446879

Shearer, E. (2021, January 12). *More than eight-in-ten Americans get news from digital devices*. Pew Research Center. https://www.pewresearch.org/short-reads/2021/01/12/more-than-eight-in-ten-americans-get-news-from-digital-devices/

Vadakkethil Somanathan Pillai, E. S. (2023). *Misinformation with sentiment*. GitHub. https://github.com/sanjaikanth/MisInformationWithSentiment

Visser, J., Lawrence, J., & Reed, C. (2020, October 22). Reason-checking fake news. *Communications of the ACM*, *63*(11), 38–40. doi:10.1145/3397189

Walker, M. (2019, November 19). *Americans favor mobile devices over desktops and laptops for getting news*. Pew Research Center. https://www.pewresearch.org/short-reads/2019/11/19/americans-favor-mobile-devices-over-desktops-and-laptops-for-getting-news/

World Health Organization. (2023). *WHO coronavirus dashboard*. WHO. https://covid19.who.int/

Yu, K., Jiang, H., Li, T., Han, S., & Wu, X. (2020). Data fusion oriented graph convolution network model for rumor detection. *IEEE Transactions on Network and Service Management*, *17*(4), 2171–2181. doi:10.1109/TNSM.2020.3033996

Chapter 8
Analyzing the Efficacy of Machine Learning Algorithms on Intrusion Detection Systems

Swanand Arun Yamgar
Vellore Institute of Technology, Chennai, India

Bhuvaneswari Amma N. G.
https://orcid.org/0000-0003-3660-380X
Vellore Institute of Technology, Chennai, India

ABSTRACT

Internet security has been a problem for businesses around the world. Encryption, authentication, and virtual private networks have been used to safeguard the network infrastructure and communications over the whole process of data protection. Intrusion detection systems (IDSs) are an advancement in network security that safeguards organizational data. System detecting intrusions into computer networks is known as IDS. Throughout their life, information cannot be guaranteed to be secured. An IDS's task is to find if there is any danger or security breach. The IDS identifies deliberate attempts by authorized users or by third parties to take advantage of security flaws as well as actual abuse. In this study, the authors used classifiers such as decision trees, support vector machines, Naive Bayes, random forests, and logistic regression. The authors also used machine learning algorithms to calculate accuracy, precision, recall, and false positives. They can conclude that this model suggested decision trees with the highest accuracy of 82.3%.

DOI: 10.4018/979-8-3693-0766-3.ch008

INTRODUCTION

Internet security has been a problem for businesses in the world. Encryption, Authentication, and virtual private networks have been used to safeguard the network infrastructure and communications over the whole process of data protection. IDSs are an advancement in network security that safeguards organizational data. Managers of networks can easily get to know the malicious activities on their respective networks with the use of IDS which alerts administrators to take appropriate measures to protect data against these attacks. Any entity that tries to access information without any permission cause harm is referred to as an attacker or an intruder. Thus, an intrusion detection system keeps an eye on computer systems and network traffic to detect possible malicious attacks from outside the organization or attacks internal to the organization. Many find it difficult to protect the privacy and integrity of resources and procedures they use available to protect their systems and networks from the intrusions. Although these technologies offer a certain level of security, like any other technology, they have their drawbacks. Many organizations use firewalls. A firewall is a security policy that generally blocks or controls traffic of the. Firewall policies determine what traffic is allowed to pass through each layer. It enforces restrictions on inbound and outbound network traffic of the private network Antivirus software also helps maintain network integrity, but it provides no meaningful data indicating whether any intrusion has occurred (Chebrolu, 2004; Debar, 2009; Kumar, 2007). As more computers come online, many of their resources become unauthorized to access, attacks, and more.

Security of these systems are critical, requiring active system monitoring and vigilance. An unprotected system can have significant negative effects on an organization. This is where Intrusion Detection System plays a vital role. As mentioned earlier, an intrusion prevention system may not be sufficient to help an organization, but with an effective intrusion detection system, attacks can be detected. Many organizations will always need the best network and good surroundings that is free from threats and malware of all kinds. The development of internet has helped a wide range of purposes. As the development has occurred there are several obstacles which should be achieved so that to make stable, secured, and dependable. To increase the security of the system which includes various dynamic techniques and firewalls and software's we should use Intrusion Detection System for identifying the threats. The importance of this study lies in the reduction of unauthorized results in network systems. This allows network administrators to focus on more diligent opportunities, also the cloud computing which has been developed for hosting and providing services with the help of internet is already making use of virtualization and distributed computing. Virtualization is a technology used by the platforms to fulfil their objective of offering utility. This research paper is developed for those who want to know the security goals and the mechanism of the intrusion detection system also the other references are provided for the ones who want in detail advices on the intrusion detection system.

RELATED WORK

The possibility for incorporating digital gadgets into our daily lives over the Internet evolves as a result of advancement of technology which exposes us to various threats. In this situation intrusion detection system is required to thwart these attacks. The main mechanism used for connected devices is the Intrusion Detection System. Various studies have been done related to the design and development of intrusion detection system. Ferhat K, Sevcan A, have researched the continuous changes and the high calculation volume in the network data and to determine if the network traffic is normal of an attack, they have used k-Means clustering algorithm which divides a large data into small clusters. It consisted KDD 99 dataset and 400 thousand network data were used for this research (Ferhat & Sevcan, 2018).

Peng K, Leung VC, Huang Q. introduced a method of comparison of Chi-SVM and Chi-Logistic Regression which resulted dataset to train and test model and built an IDS using SVM on Apache platform (Peng et al., 2018). Manzoor MA, Morgan Y, they built an intrusion detection system on high volume data traffic using Apache Storm framework by using C-SVM methodology and KDD 99 dataset (Manzoor & Morgan, 2016).

Vimal Kumar K, Radhika N developed an intrusion detection system on the base of Neural network, Decision trees, Naive Bayes, and random forest for the smart grid by using Apache spark platform and, they used Synchro phasor as a dataset for analysis of big data (Vimalkumar & Radhika, 2017). Dahiya P, Srivastava DK built an intrusion detection system with the help of various algorithms such as Naive Bayes, Random Forest and Random Committee and proposed a framework for the intrusion using Spark (Dahiya & Srivastava, 2018).

Wang H, Xiao Y, Long Y adopted the way to build the intrusion detection system using SVM algorithm and KDD99 dataset for the reduction depending on Bagging (Wang et al., 2017). Natesan P, et al. developed the intrusion detection system by using Parallel Naïve Bayes and KDD99 dataset to propose if the detection rate is improved and the time is reduced (Natesan et al., 2017).

Misuse or Signature-Based Detection

Searching of set of malicious bytes from the network traffic is a vital part of searching based detection. They are very easy to build and comprehend signatures which is the main advantage of this detection system. The cause of alerts can be communicated through the events developed by the signature-based IDS. Due to little amount of power matching of patterns the modern systems can do matching more efficiently and also all other signatures can be disregarded for a instance if the network system that needs to be secured only communicates over SMTP, ICMP and DNS. When a user employs sophisticated technologies like payload encoders, encrypted data channels, signature based detection does not perform effectively (Hazem, 2008). The reason is because every alteration needs a very new signature, signature-based systems are significantly less efficient. The performance declines as the number of signatures rises. To avoid the attacks on the system, IDS developers came up with new signatures before the attacker does. The effectiveness of the system is to determine at which rate the developers and attackers produce the new signatures (Allen et al., 2000; Debar et al., 2000; Roesch, 1999).

Anomaly-Based Detection

Anomaly-based detection is a system that provides the foundation to the network-based system. If certain activity network based relates or matches to the particular behavior then the anomaly-based detection system will trigger or will be accepted. The intrusion detection system engine can break through various levels of protocols is crucial in characterizing of the network activity. Its engine must understand its purpose and process the protocols. This analysis of the protocol will be a good advantage for the anomaly-based detection system to reduce false positive alarms. Building the rule for this detection is one of the biggest drawbacks. The effectiveness of the system depends on how efficiently the system is put into use and tested against all the procedures. The main benefit of anomaly-based detection over signature-based engines is to detect and identify the fresh attacks for which there is no signature if they deviate from the usual traffic patterns. Table 1 tabulates the characteristics of various intrusion detection systems.

PROPOSED METHODOLOGY

The development of this system is dependent on the effective use of the model which also is an aid to the overcoming practical difficulties. Figure 1 depicts the block schematic of the proposed model.

The following steps describe the working model:

Step 1: Complete the data collection, then transfer the actual data from the combined data.

Table 1. Characteristics of intrusion detection system

Characteristics	Anomaly-Based Detection	Misuse-Based Detection
Attacks discovered	Any type of attacks can be detected by Anomaly based system	Attacks that are known are detected easily
Recognised backdrop of an attack	No attack type background needed	Yes, attack type of background needed
False alarm rate	False alarm rate is high.	False alarm rate is low
If needed any update	No update needed	Update needed
Type of attacks	Attack type is not defined	Attack type is defined
Identification of the protection tool	No	Yes

Step 2: The actual data is then passed to data pre-processing, which converts the data from the exception class to a class.

Step 3: After pre-processing, data reduction is performed and then sent to feature selection.

Step 4: We begin each model and store in the dictionary by the names before performing data splitting.

Step 5: Finally, we got some accurate results (Pearson, 2020).

The system was developed on models, and a lot of research has been done on different types of machine-learning algorithms. The proposed study focuses on these six models, namely Logistic Regression, Support Vector Machines, Decision Trees, Random Forests, Naive Bayes, and K Nearest Neighbours (Daya, 2013). Therefore, in this work, all these previous methods are further investigated using the respective techniques to make the proposed model more efficient.

Firstly, we felt the need to improve current research in this area is to analyzing previous models to determine what might be missing, after which we proactively sought a solution that would give us accuracy and would be suitable for practical execution. We believe that one of the reasons for the lack of performance is that these systems cannot recognize important system features.

Figure 2 is based on 10 highly correlated heatmaps. The eigenvalues (from 1.0 to -0.4) are displayed. From the figure, it is clear which features have a strong correlation with feature 1.0, with the lowest correlation being -0.4.

The most important step in applying machine learning is to gather data suitable for finding the attacks. Therefore, we took the data set from NSL KDD. The two-detection method used by IDS are misuse and Anomaly which help in finding the attack patterns. If any attacks are known to be detected by the misuse detection system but if there are any changes noticed in the regularity of the pattern then the anomaly detection system plays a vital role in identifying the threat or attack (K.

Figure 1. Flow diagram of proposed approach

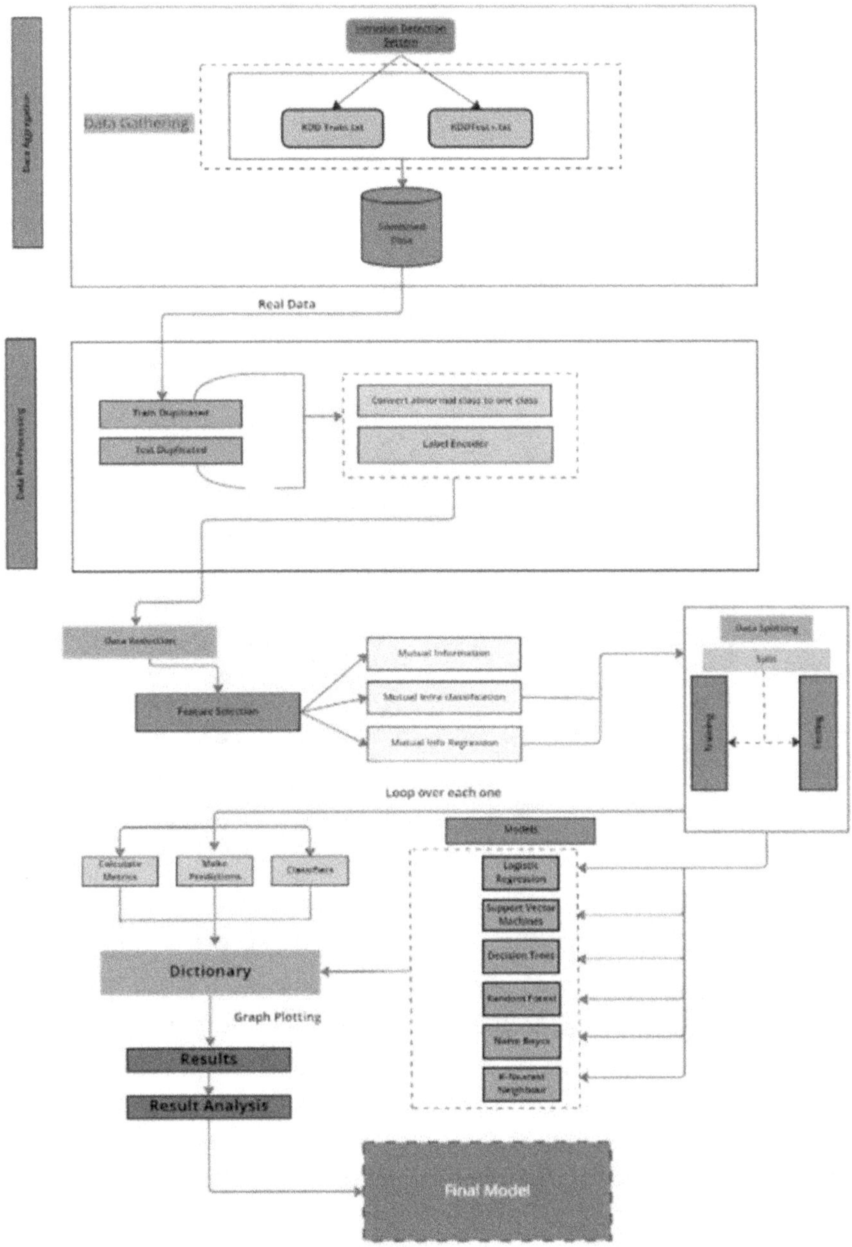

D. D. Cup, 1999). In today's world IDS are mostly dependent on the abilities and

Figure 2. Heat map of proposed approach

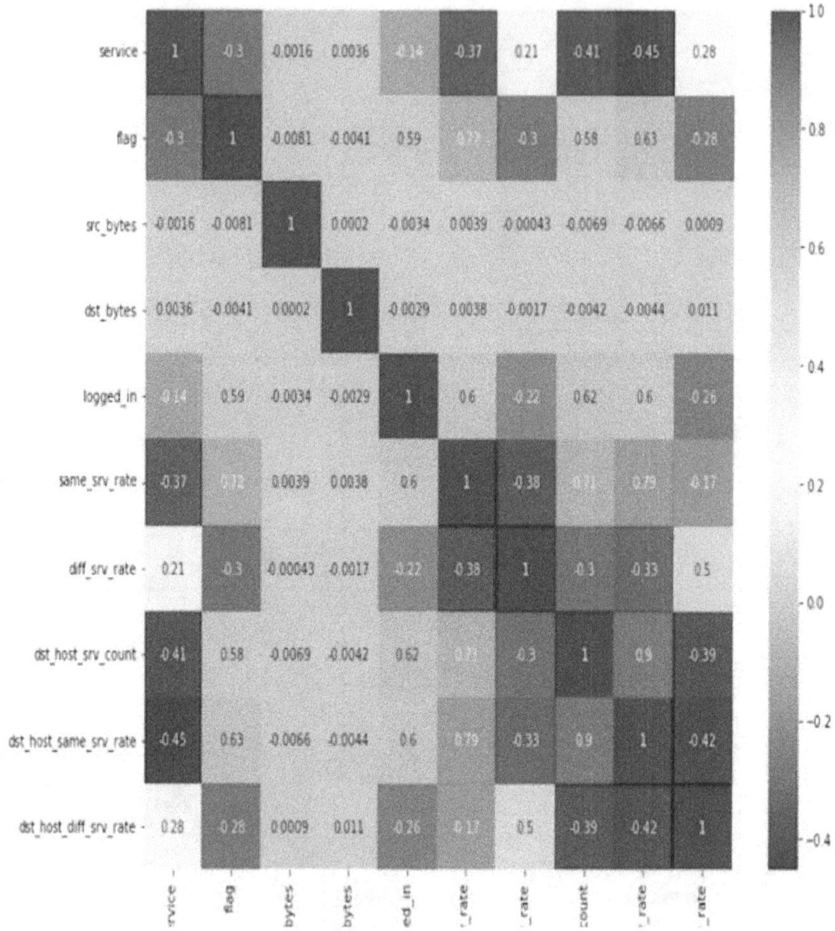

the skills of the security professionals who help them to train. In the upcoming years, the IDS will be dependent on the development of false-positive alarms but the current one can only recognize the attack types that is why techniques such as data mining and machine learning are used as cheaper and consume less time as compared to other costly and labor-intensive human input (Byunghae, 2005; Lee et al., 1999; Mukkamala et al., 2002). The techniques used extract all the data that is useful about the attacks or normal behavior profiles of the network traffic (Ajith et al., 2005; Byunghae, 2005; Quinlan, 1993; Susan & Rayford, 2000). The first wise technique used was based on the models for intrusion detection systems and also many of these models worked on the development of IDS such as to know the connection between input and output vectors which depends on the degree of membership to generalize them to extract the new and developed relationship between input and output vectors (Adetunmbi, Falaki, Adewale et al, 2007; Zhang et al., 2005; Pavel et al., 2005; Susan & Rayford, 2000; Zhang et al., 2004). For the raw data to be compiled they should be connected with various information like service, duration, and machine learning techniques. To make this work there should be (Adetunmbi, Alese, Ogundele et al, 2007; Adetunmbi et al., 2008; Sanjay et al., 2005) a set of rules produced by rough sets to concise and comprise the elements that are necessary for detecting anomalies and threats. In knowing this accuracy process it reduces the computing cost, and size of the overfitting model which leads to improvement of the accuracy of the models (Amor et al., 2004; Axelsson, 1999).

NSL-KDD Dataset

The NSL-KDD is a dataset used for the assessment of research on detection systems. The KDD 99 datasets are included which are linked and are covered by the 41 characteristics of NSLKDD datasets. Out of which seven are symbolic or discrete and the remaining 34 are numerical. In these 17 types were added for the work (Li,, 2020). It is a raw collection of TCP dump datasets that were collected across the network (Kayacik et al., 2006; Sung & Mukkamala, 2003).

Ranking of Features Based on Information Gain Ratio

The thought of entropy is a piece of impureness of data that is used in information gain (IG). And when the entropy is low and all the data items belong to a single class then the distribution of classes is uneven. The higher the classes a data item possesses or the entropy number the more uniform the distribution of the class. Information gain evaluates the decline in a particular attribute's average in a comparison with the whole collection of the data components' outcome of the property which provides the information to be seen as the most helpful for categorizing the data components. A good method for evaluating the usefulness of a feature based on data is the information gain ratio (IGR). The information gain ratio is used to know the value of each feature. The IGR is defined in the given Figure 3 (Canavan, 2000).

Proposed Method for Classifying Model

The sub-discipline branch of artificial intelligence is known as machine learning which deals with developing and designing algorithms that allow computers to learn behavior based on information like sensor data or databases. The use of ML is to know the patterns and with the help of patterns decode and drive out to the conclusions of research. Medical diagnostics, text and handwriting recognition facial recognition, or biometric scanning are a few areas where ML is implemented. In the year 1994, ML was first used for Internet business brackets for intrusion detection. This section discusses the machine literacy styles used in this study to induce an intelligent intrusion discovery system.

1) LOGISTIC REGRESSION

Occasionally we prefer to prognosticate a separate variable e.g., prognosticate if a grid of pixel intensities represents figures' 0' or' 1'. This is a bracket problem. Logistic retrogression is a simple bracket algorithm for learning how to make similar opinions. Using this algorithm, we got a delicacy of 71.7, but it isn't the most accurate among other algorithms.

2) SUPPORT MACHINE VECTOR

SVM is a classifier for the pattern recognition activities. It is also used for intrusion detection in information security. Because of the sound design and ability to disappear the dimensionality curse, the SVM has been one of the most widely used for finding anomaly intrusions. The SVM generalizes the kernel technique which has high dimensional training samples that are rarely conditioned, it assists in the global minimization of danger via structural threat minimization. SVM can choose applicable tuning parameters because it does not calculate on traditional empirical threats like networks. Speed is the key benefit of using SVM for IDS because the capacity to detect interference in real-time is very difficult (Yinka-Banjo, 2022). As the bracket complexity is not dependent on the point of space the SVMs may train bigger and do better measurements. SVMs can also substantially update the learned models emerging during postprocessing.

3) DECISION TREE

A decision tree is a type of tree illustration. It assigns groups predicated on rules applied from the root to the leaves. The inner knot is the test, the branch is the test result, and the flake knot is assigned a type. Handpick the data with the least impurities. This impurity is measured in terms of entropy. Advanced entropy means farther impurities.

Decision Tree Algorithms

1) Handpick a point from the data.
2) Meaning of attributes calculated during data partitioning.
3) Divide the data by the swish particularity value.

4) Go back to step 1

Gini impurity standard is used for type trees. It is the advised entropy change for a decision tree. The Gini impurity is the probability that an item will be misclassified if it is classified according to the marker distribution. Gini impurity characterizes the frequency at which a randomly chosen element is set incorrectly and is determined by the distribution of the labels in the subset. Its measure is defined as the standard description for defining AI, the advantage of the decision tree is that no parameters need to be defined (Aleksandar et al., 2017). It also evaluates all possible issues and makes the decision.

4) RANDOM FOREST

Random Forest is a classifier used to meliorate delicacy. Arbitrary timber consists of multiple decision trees. Compared to other traditional type algorithms, Random Forest has lower type errors. The number of trees, smallest knot size, and attributes utilized to untangle each knot.

The advantages of RF are

1)The performing timber can be saved for future reference
2)Random Forest overcomes the matching problem.
3)Automatically induce perfection and variable significance in RF.

When erecting a single tree in Random Forest, apply randomness to choose the swish knot to resolve. This value is equal to sqrt A, where A is a reality not present in the dataset. still, RF produces truly noisy trees, affecting delicacy and thus leading to poor opinions on new samples.

5) NAIVE BAYES

A Bayesian probability model which has been greatly simplified is called the Naïve Bayesian model, also the foundation of the classifiers is the strong assumption of independence. This indicates the likelihood that one particularity does not influence the likelihood of another particularity.

The Naïve Bayesian classifier gets 2n when provided with a list of n characteristics. The classifier's results are still consistently accurate under independent hypotheticals. The research displayed looks at why Naïve Bayes classifiers perform effectively. They claim that three things such as prejudice, noise, and disunion of the training data are the reasons causing crimes. The machinery knowledge algorithm must classify into the categories of training data (Manu, 2016). The genuinely brought mistakes in the training data are known as bias because the reason is the insufficient size of the groupings and the disunion results.

6) K- CLOSEST NEIGHBOR

The k-nearest neighbor method which is also known as KNN or k-NN is a nonparametric supervised classifier that uses contiguity to categorize or forecast clusters that have individual data points. This is a frequently assigned type algorithm, presuming which can group similar points, even if it may be analyzed in the regression or type issues.

Benefits

-Ease of performance, given the simplicity and delicacy of the algorithm.
-An easily adaptable algorithm that adjusts all new data when new training samples are provided since all training data is kept in memory.
Many hyperparameters of KNN's requirements are less in comparison to other machine learning algorithms, which need a simple value of k and a distance metric.

Disadvantages

- Does not measure up well as KNN requires more data and memory storage than others since it is also a slow algorithm.

As the algorithm reaches the feature that is ideal for counting new characteristics it may cause an increase in the frequency of specific attacks especially if the size of the sample is small. This is frequently referred to as the peak phenomenon (Ibrahim & Kemal, 2013).

RESULTS AND DISCUSSION

Libraries such as Panda, Pyplot, and Scikit-Learn are used in the NSL KDD Notebook to create the implemented models.

Figure 3 and Figure 4 depict the results of the most important algorithms used in this study. We found the most predictive algorithm in the form of a decision tree with an accuracy of 82.3% also to predict we calculate metrics and save each index in a dictionary.

The following steps will show you how we calculate precision, accuracy, and recall:

1) Fit a classifier:

Figure 3. Performance analysis of machine learning classifiers for intrusion detection

	Accuracy	Precision	Recall
Logistic Regression	0.717042	0.943569	0.611111
Support Vector Machines linear	0.723873	0.955617	0.615630
Support Vector Machines polynomial	0.764372	0.962723	0.653822
Support Vector Machines RBf	0.772933	0.957368	0.663977
Decision Trees	0.823013	0.840902	0.769579
Random Forest	0.757541	0.970446	0.645347
Naive Bayes	0.546265	0.440634	0.471463
K-Nearest Neighbor	0.788946	0.962002	0.680358

Figure 4. Comparative analysis

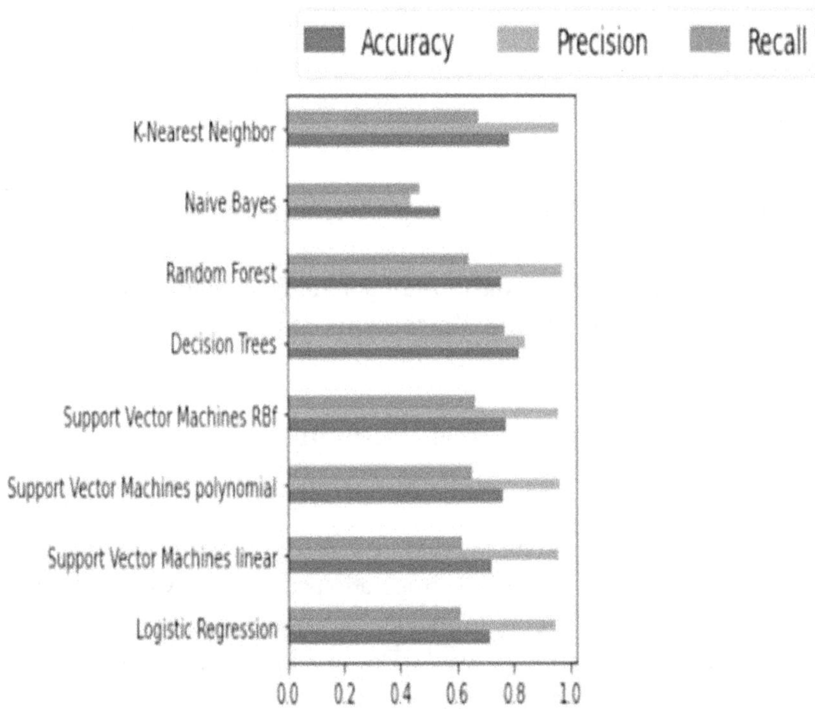

```
model{key}. fit (x_train, y_train)
```

2) To make predictions:

```
predictions = model{key}. predict (x_test)
```

3) Calculation indicators:

```
Precision{key}=accuracy_score(predictions, y_test)
Precision{key}=precision_score(predictions, y_test)
Recall{key}=recall_score(predictions),
```

Comparison Between Different Styles Predicated on Delicacy

Other performance measures analogous as delicacy are also used to estimate the performance of classifiers and crossbred algorithms. Naive Bayes had the lowest delicacy (44.06), while Random Forest and SVC had the topmost delicacy (96). All the other different models have delicacy scores between those numbers.

Comparison Between Different Recall-Predicated Styles

Recall score is an important performance decider because it is important for relating attacks. The table shows different recall scores for different models. Naive Bayes (47) and other algorithms had truly low recall scores between (60 and 70), but decision trees had the topmost recall scores (76.9).

Comparison of Different Delicacy-Predicated Styles

Delicacy is generally considered the most important fashion for assessing machine knowledge algorithms. Considering all algorithms, decision trees scored the topmost (82.3) and Naive Bayes the lowest score (54.6).

Comparison of Different Styles Predicated on False Positive Rates

Intrusion discovery is an important countermeasure for utmost operations, especially client- garçon operations analogous as web operations and web services. multitudinous newer technologies are beginning to include integrated services, analogous as a single appliance that includes a firewall, IDS, and limited IPS functionality. The maturity of operations does not descry the attack and do their swish to acclimatize to the attacker.

The shortage of intrusion discovery gives an attacker an opportunity to attempt an attack till it succeeds. Intrusion discovery helps identify attacks long before they are likely to succeed. It is not so difficult for web-operations to know if there is any certain attack business. Simple rule is that if the app's legit stoners can't nicely induce business, it's nearly easily an attack. Once an IDS cautions and identifies an attack, security professionals can respond rightly. Generally, this means logging stoners out, vacating their accounts or doctoring the cause of vulnerability.

There are certain types of requests an operation can admit

- nearly easily an attack
- nearly easily a legit input
- the safest rule is to assuming that all but legit business is an attack.

Figure 5 depicts the ROC analysis of various classifiers. It is evident that the area under the ROC curve is high for both decision tree classifier and random forest classifier compared to Gaussian Naïve Bayes and KNN classifiers.

Figure 5. ROC analysis

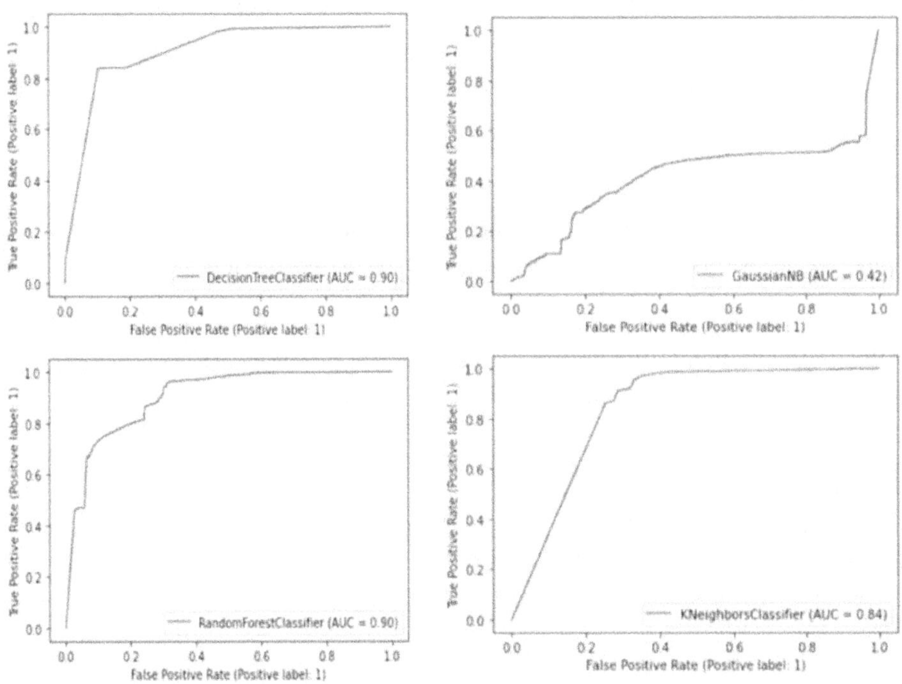

CONCLUSION

As we can see, the decision tree classifier and random forest classifier have the same false positive rate, but the accuracy of the decision tree is higher than random forest classifier. Early detection is an important step in achieving this goal. Studies have attempted to find attacks before using machine learning. This study follows a similar line but with the help of new and improved methods and a larger data set to train this model.

REFERENCES

Adetunmbi, A. O., Alese, B. K., Ogundele, O. S., & Falaki, S. O. (2007). A Data Mining Approach to Network Intrusion Detection. *Journal of Computer Science & Its Applications*, *14*(2), 24–37.

Adetunmbi, A. O., Falaki, S. O., Adewale, O. S., & Alese, B. K. (2007). A Rough Set Approach for Detecting known and novel Network intrusion. In *Second International Conference on Application of Information and Communication Technologies to Teaching, Research and Administrations (AICTTRA, 2007*). Research Gate.

Adetunmbi, A. O., Falaki, S. O., Adewale, O. S., & Alese, B. K. (2008). Intrusion Detection based on Rough Set and k-Nearest Neighbour. *International Journal of Computing and ICT Research*, *2*, 61–66.

Aickelin, U. (2020). Julie Green smith, Jamie Twycross. *Immune System Approaches to Intrusion Detection - A Review*. http://eprints.nottingham.ac.uk/619/1/04icaris_ids review.pdf

Ajith, A., Ravi, J., Johnson, T., & Sang, Y.H. (2005). D-SCIDS: Distributed soft computing intrusion detection system. *Journal of Network and Computer Applications*.

Aleksandar, M., Marco, V., Samuel, K., Alberto, A., & Bryan, D. P. (2017). Evaluating Computer Intrusions Detection Systems: A Survey of Common Practices. *Research Group of the Standard Performance Evaluation Corporaion*, *48*(1), 12. doi:10.1145/2808691

Allen, J., Christie, A., Fithen, W., & McHugh, J. (2000). State of the practice of intrusion detection technologies. *Technical Report CMU/SEI-99TR- 028*. Carnegie-Mellon University - Software Engineering Institute.

Amor, N. B., Beferhat, S., & Elouedi, Z. (2004). Naïve Bayes vs Decision Trees in Intrusion Detection Systems. In *ACM Symposium on Applied Computing* (pp. 420 – 424). ACM. 10.1145/967900.967989

Axelsson, S. (1999). The Base –rate Fallacy and Its Implication for the Difficulty of Intrusion Detection, In *Proceeding of the 6th ACM Conference on Computer and Communication Security* (pp. 127 -141). ACM.

Bace, R. (2001). *Intrusion detection systems*. Research Gate.

Byung-Joo, K., & Il-Kon, K. (2005). Article. In S. Zhang & R. Jarvis (Eds.), *Machine Learning Approach to Real time Intrusion Detection System in Lecture Note in Artificial Intelligence* (Vol. 3809, pp. 153–163). Springer-Verlag Berline.

Byunghae, C. (2005) *Neural Networks Techniques for Host Anomaly Intrusion Detection using Fixed Pattern Transformation in ICCSA*. LNCS.

Canavan, J. E. (2000). *Fundamentals of Network Security*. Artech House Telecommunications Library.

Chebrolu, S. (2004). *Feature deduction and ensemble design of intrusion detection systems*. Elsevier Ltd. . doi:10.1016/j.cose.2004.09.008

Dahiya, P., & Srivastava, D. K. (2018). Network intrusion detection in big dataset using Spark. *Procedia Computer Science*, *132*, 253–262. doi:10.1016/j.procs.2018.05.169

Daya, B. (2013). *Network Security: History, Importance, and Future*. University of Florida Department of Electrical and Computer Engineering. http://web.mit.edu/~bdaya/www/Network%20Security.pdf

Debar, H. (2009). *An Introduction to Intrusion-Detection Systems*. Research Gate.

Debar, H., Dacier, M., & Wespi, A. (2000). A Revised Taxonomy of Intrusion-Detection Systems. *Annales des Télécommunications*, *55*(7–8), 361–378. doi:10.1007/BF02994844

Ferhat, K., & Sevcan, A. (2018). Big Data: Controlling fraud by using machine learning libraries on Spark. *Int J Appl Math Electron Comput.*, *6*(1), 1–5. doi:10.18100/ijamec.2018138629

Hazem M. (2008). Real-Time Intrusion Detection Algorithm for Network Security. *WSEAS Transactions on Communications, 12*(7).

Ibrahim, K., & Kemal, H. (2013). Open Source Intrusion Detection System Using Snort. *The 4th International Symposium on Sustainable Development*, (pp 1-6). Research Gate.

IntechOpen. (n.d.). https://www.intechopen.com/download/get/type/pdfs/id/86

K. D. D. Cup. (1999). *Data*. KDD. http://kdd.ics.uci.edu/databases/ kddcup99/

Kayacik, H.G., Zincir-Heywood, A.N., & Heywood, M.L. (2006). *Selecting Features for Intrusion Detection: A Feature Analysis on KDD 99 Intrusion Detection Datasets*. Research Gate.

Kumar, S. (2007). *Survey of Current Network Intrusion Detection Techniques*. CSE. https://www.cse.wustl.edu/~jain/cse571-07/ftp/ids.pdf

Lee, W., Stolfo, S. J., & Mok, K. (1999). Data Mining in work flow environments: Experiments in intrusion detection. In *Proceedings of the 1999 Conference on Knowledge Discovery and Data Mining*. Research Gate.

Li, C. (2020). *Web Security: Theory And Applications*. School of Software, Sun Yat-sen University.

Manu, B. (2016). A Survey on Secure Network: Intrusion Detection and Prevention Approaches. *The African Journal of Information Systems*, *4*(3), 69–88. doi:10.12691/ajis-4-3-2

Manzoor, M. A., & Morgan, Y. (2016). Real-time support vector machine based network intrusion detection system using Apache Storm. In *IEEE 7th annual information technology, electronics and mobile communication conference (IEMCON)*. IEEE. 10.1109/IEMCON.2016.7746264

Mukkamala, S., Janoski, G., & Sung, A. (2002). Intrusion detection using neural networks and support vector machines. In *Proceedings of IEEE International Joint Conference on Neural Networks* (pp. 1702–1707). IEEE. 10.1109/IJCNN.2002.1007774

Natesan, P., Rajalaxmi, R. R., Gowrison, G., & Balasubramanie, P. (2017). Hadoop based parallel binary bat algorithm for network intrusion detection. *International Journal of Parallel Programming*, *45*(5), 1194–1213. doi:10.1007/s10766-016-0456-z

Pavel, L., Patrick, D., Christia, S., & Konrad, R. (2005). Learning Intrusion Detection: Supervised or Unsupervised? In *International Conference on image analysis and processing (ICAP)* (pp. 50-57). IEEE.

Pearson. (2020). *Working With Snort Rules*. Pearson Education Inc.

Peng, K., Leung, V. C., & Huang, Q. (2018). Clustering approach based on mini batch Kmeans for intrusion detection system over Big Data. *IEEE Access : Practical Innovations, Open Solutions*, *6*, 11897–11906. doi:10.1109/ACCESS.2018.2810267

Quinlan, J. L. (1993). *C4.5 Program for Machine Learning*. Morgan Kaufmam Publishers, Inc.

Roesch, M. (1999). Snort - Lightweight Intrusion Detection for Networks. *13th USENIX Conference on System Administration.*

Sabahi, F., & Movaghar, A. (2008). Intrusion detection: A survey. *Proc. 3rd Int. Conf. Syst. Netw. Commun.*

Sanjay, R., Gulati, V. P., & Arun, K. P. (2005). A Fast Host-Based Intrusion Detection System Using Rough Set Theory in Transactions on Rough Sets IV. *LNCS, 3700*, 144–161.

Scarfon, K. & Mell, P. (2007). Guide to Intrusion Detection and Prevention Systems (IDPS). *Standard NIST SP 800-90.*

Sung, A. H., & Mukkamala, S. (2003) Identifying Important Features for Intrusion Detection using Support Vector Machines and Neural Networks. *IEEE Proceedings of the 2003 Symposium on Applications and the Interne*t.

Susan, M. B., & Rayford, B. V. (2000). Intrusion detection via fuzzy data mining. *Proceedings of the 12th Annual Canadian Information Technology Security Symposium.*

The Snort Project. (2013). *Snort User Manual.* Sourcefire, Inc.

Tiwari, M., Kumar, R., Bharti, A., & Kishan, J. (2017). Intrusion Detection System. *International Journal of Technical Research and Applications.*, *5*, 2320–8163.

Vimalkumar, K., & Radhika, N. (2017). A big data framework for intrusion detection in smart grids using Apache Spark. In In*ternational conference on advances in computing, communications and informatics (ICACCI)*. IEEE. 10.1109/ICACCI.2017.8125840

Wang, H., Xiao, Y., & Long, Y. (2017). Research of intrusion detection algorithm based on parallel SVM on Spark. In *7th IEEE International conference on electronics information and emergency communication (ICEIEC)*. IEEE. 10.1109/ICEIEC.2017.8076533

Yinka-Banjo. (2022). Intrusion Detection Using Anomaly Detection Algorithm and Snort. Springer. doi:10.1007/978-3-030-93453-8_3

Zhang, L., Zhang, G., Yu, L., Zhang, J., & Bai, Y. (2004). Intrusion detection using Rough Set Classification. *Journal of Zhejiang University. Science*, *5*(9), 1076–1086. doi:10.1631/jzus.2004.1076 PMID:15323002

Chapter 9
Secure Communication Protocols for Cloud and IoT:
A Comprehensive Review

Pawan Kumar Goel
https://orcid.org/0000-0003-3601-102X
Raj Kumar Goel Institute of Technology, Ghaziabad, India

ABSTRACT

Secure communication protocols are paramount in ensuring the integrity, confidentiality, and availability of data in the interconnected landscapes of cloud computing and the internet of things (IoT). This comprehensive review explores the significance of these protocols, beginning with an introduction to cloud computing, IoT, and the challenges they pose to security. The exploration of security threats in both ecosystems lays the foundation for in-depth discussions on communication protocols tailored for Cloud and IoT environments.

The review provides an exhaustive analysis of communication protocols for cloud security, including TLS/SSL and IPsec, unraveling their strengths, weaknesses, and use cases. Transitioning to IoT, the exploration delves into protocols such as MQTT and CoAP, evaluating their suitability across diverse IoT scenarios. Integration challenges in Cloud and IoT environments, real-world case studies, and emerging technologies like blockchain further enrich the discussion.

Looking to the future, trends such as zero trust architecture and edge computing are examined, along with the potential impact of blockchain on security. Practical recommendations for implementing secure communication protocols and best practices for ongoing security in Cloud and IoT systems are presented. The conclusion underscores the critical role of secure communication protocols in navigating the evolving digital landscape.

DOI: 10.4018/979-8-3693-0766-3.ch009

INTRODUCTION

In the rapidly evolving landscape of modern information technology, the amalgamation of Cloud Computing and the Internet of Things (IoT) has revolutionized the way we interact with and harness data. This transformation, however, brings forth a host of security challenges, making the implementation of secure communication protocols paramount. This introduction sets the stage for an in-depth exploration of the significance of secure communication protocols within the realms of Cloud and IoT, delving into their growing importance in contemporary society.

Significance of Secure Communication Protocols

Secure communication protocols serve as the linchpin in ensuring the confidentiality, integrity, and availability of data transmitted across diverse networks. In the context of Cloud and IoT, where data is ubiquitously generated, processed, and shared, the need for robust security measures is more critical than ever. As organizations and individuals increasingly rely on Cloud services for storage and processing and integrate an ever-expanding array of IoT devices into their daily lives, the potential vulnerabilities and security risks magnify exponentially.

Growing Importance of Cloud and IoT Technologies

Cloud Computing has emerged as a cornerstone of contemporary computing architecture, offering unparalleled scalability, flexibility, and cost-effectiveness. Simultaneously, the proliferation of IoT devices, ranging from smart home appliances to industrial sensors, has created an interconnected ecosystem that permeates our daily lives. The synergy between Cloud and IoT is reshaping industries, optimizing processes, and enhancing user experiences. However, this transformative power also exposes a broad attack surface, demanding a comprehensive and nuanced approach to security.

The utilization of Cloud services and the integration of IoT devices are no longer speculative trends but integral components of our digital existence. Businesses leverage the Cloud to streamline operations, while consumers benefit from IoT-driven conveniences. This chapter explores the inseparable relationship between secure communication protocols and the sustained growth and evolution of Cloud and IoT technologies.

Purpose and Structure of the Chapter

The primary purpose of this chapter is to conduct a meticulous examination of secure communication protocols within the context of Cloud and IoT. By exploring the existing landscape, identifying potential threats, and evaluating the effectiveness of various protocols, this chapter aims to equip readers with a comprehensive understanding of the challenges and solutions associated with securing communication in these dynamic environments.

The chapter unfolds in a structured manner, starting with an overview of Cloud Computing and IoT, progressing to an exploration of the significance of secure communication protocols. Subsequent sections delve into the intricacies of security threats, the protocols designed to mitigate these threats in both Cloud and IoT settings, and the challenges associated with their integration. Real-world case studies illustrate the practical implementation of these protocols, while a forward-looking perspective explores emerging technologies and trends. The chapter concludes by providing actionable recommendations and best practices for ensuring the security of communication in Cloud and IoT environments. (Atzori et al., 2010).

In essence, this chapter serves as a comprehensive guide, offering insights, analyses, and practical strategies for safeguarding communication channels in the ever-expanding realms of Cloud and IoT technologies.

CLOUD COMPUTING AND IOT OVERVIEW

Define Cloud Computing and its Key Characteristics

Cloud Computing is a paradigm shift in computing that leverages the power of networked servers to deliver computing resources—such as storage, processing power, and applications—over the Internet (Mell et al., 2011). The National Institute of Standards and Technology (NIST) defines Cloud Computing with five essential characteristics:

- **On-Demand Self-Service:** Users can provision computing resources as needed, without requiring human intervention from the service provider.
- **Broad Network Access**: Cloud services are accessible over the network and can be accessed through standard mechanisms, promoting device independence.
- **Resource Pooling:** Computing resources are pooled to serve multiple consumers, allowing for efficient resource utilization and economies of scale.
- **Rapid Elasticity**: Resources can be rapidly and elastically provisioned and released to scale with demand, providing flexibility and cost-efficiency.
- **Measured Service:** Cloud systems automatically control and optimize resource use, and users pay for only the resources they consume.

Define IoT and Discuss its Integration With Cloud Computing

The Internet of Things (IoT) refers to the network of interconnected physical devices embedded with sensors, software, and other technologies, enabling them to collect and exchange data. IoT devices span various domains, from consumer electronics and healthcare devices to industrial sensors and smart infrastructure. The integration of IoT with Cloud Computing is symbiotic, where IoT devices generate vast amounts of data, and Cloud services provide the necessary infrastructure for storage, processing, and analysis (Stallings, 2017).

The integration offers several benefits:

- Scalability: Cloud resources can scale dynamically to accommodate the growing number of IoT devices and the data they generate.
- Data Storage and Processing: Cloud services provide centralized storage and processing capabilities for the massive volumes of data produced by IoT devices.
- Analytics and Insights: Cloud platforms facilitate advanced analytics, enabling organizations to derive meaningful insights from IoT-generated data.
- Remote Monitoring and Control: Cloud-based IoT solutions allow remote monitoring and control of devices, enhancing efficiency and responsiveness.

This section elucidates the synergistic relationship between Cloud Computing and IoT, emphasizing how their integration amplifies the capabilities of both technologies.

Challenges and Security Considerations Associated With Cloud and IoT

While Cloud Computing and IoT offer numerous advantages, they also introduce a set of challenges and security considerations:

- **Data Privacy and Ownership**: Cloud services involve entrusting data to third-party providers, raising concerns about data privacy, ownership, and compliance with regulations.
- **Network Security**: The interconnectivity of IoT devices increases the attack surface, making networks susceptible to breaches and unauthorized access.
- **Scalability Challenges**: As the number of IoT devices grows, managing and securing a vast and dynamic network becomes a logistical challenge.
- **Data Integrity and Authenticity**: Ensuring the integrity and authenticity of data in transit and at rest is critical, especially in environments where sensitive data is involved.

This section explores the multifaceted challenges and security considerations inherent in the integration of Cloud Computing and IoT, laying the groundwork for the subsequent examination of secure communication protocols (Hossain et al., 2015).

IMPORTANCE OF SECURE COMMUNICATION PROTOCOLS

Role of Secure Communication in Ensuring Data Integrity, Confidentiality, and Availability

Secure communication protocols play a pivotal role in upholding the fundamental tenets of information security: data integrity, confidentiality, and availability.

- **Data Integrity:** Secure communication protocols safeguard data from unauthorized tampering or alterations during transmission. Through cryptographic mechanisms such as hash functions and digital signatures, these protocols ensure that the data received is identical to what was originally sent, maintaining its accuracy and reliability.
- **Confidentiality:** Encryption, a cornerstone of secure communication, ensures that sensitive information remains confidential during transit. By transforming plaintext data into ciphertext using complex algorithms, secure communication protocols prevent eavesdroppers from deciphering the content, preserving the confidentiality of the information.
- **Availability:** Denial-of-service (DoS) and distributed denial-of-service (DDoS) attacks pose threats to the availability of services. Secure communication protocols implement measures to mitigate these attacks, ensuring that legitimate users can access resources without interruption. Techniques such as load balancing and redundancy contribute to maintaining service availability.

Emphasizing the Need for Robust Security Protocols in Cloud and IoT

In the context of Cloud Computing and the Internet of Things (IoT), the need for robust security protocols becomes paramount due to the unique challenges presented by these environments.

- **Cloud Computing:** Cloud services involve the transmission of sensitive data over networks, often across geographical boundaries. Robust security protocols protect this data from interception, tampering, or unauthorized access. Additionally, as organizations entrust their data to external cloud providers, security protocols ensure the confidentiality and integrity of the data stored in the cloud.

- **Internet of Things:** The vast and interconnected nature of IoT introduces a multitude of security challenges. IoT devices, ranging from smart home gadgets to industrial sensors, communicate with each other and with cloud services. Secure communication protocols prevent malicious actors from exploiting vulnerabilities in these communications, safeguarding the integrity of data exchanged and the functioning of IoT ecosystems (Al-Fuqaha et al., 2015).

Ensuring Trust in Communication Systems

Trust is a cornerstone of secure communication, especially in Cloud and IoT environments where diverse entities interact. Robust security protocols establish and maintain this trust by:

- **Authentication:** Verifying the identity of communicating parties ensures that data is exchanged between legitimate entities.
- **Authorization:** Security protocols enforce access control policies, allowing only authorized entities to access specific resources.
- **Non-Repudiation:** Secure communication protocols provide mechanisms for proving the origin or delivery of a message, preventing entities from denying their involvement in a communication.

By emphasizing the importance of trust in communication systems, this section underscores the critical role played by secure communication protocols in building and preserving a secure digital environment.

SECURITY THREATS IN CLOUD AND IOT

Common Security Threats in Cloud Computing and IoT Ecosystems

Cloud Computing Threats:

- Data Breaches: Unauthorized access to sensitive information stored in the cloud, whether due to inadequate security measures or compromised credentials.
- Insecure APIs: Vulnerabilities in Application Programming Interfaces (APIs) can expose data and functionalities, allowing attackers to exploit weaknesses.

- Insufficient Identity and Access Management (IAM): Weak or misconfigured IAM practices may result in unauthorized access to critical resources.
- Data Loss: Accidental deletion, corruption, or theft of data, either due to human error or malicious activities (Mather et al., 2009).

IoT Ecosystem Threats:

- Device Compromises: IoT devices may be vulnerable to attacks, leading to unauthorized control or manipulation of connected devices.
- Insecure Network Connectivity: Weaknesses in the communication links between IoT devices and cloud services can be exploited for unauthorized access.
- Lack of Device Management: Inadequate management of IoT devices, including patching and updates, can leave vulnerabilities unaddressed.
- Privacy Concerns: The extensive data collection capabilities of IoT devices can raise privacy issues if not appropriately managed (Miorandi et al., 2012).

Potential Consequences of Security Breaches

Consequences in Cloud Computing:

- Data Exposure: Breaches can result in the exposure of sensitive data, including personally identifiable information (PII) and corporate intellectual property.
- Financial Loss: Organizations may face financial repercussions, including regulatory fines, legal costs, and a loss of customer trust, leading to decreased revenue.
- Reputation Damage: Public perception of an organization's trustworthiness can be significantly impacted, affecting customer relationships and partnerships.

Consequences in IoT Ecosystems:

- Device Manipulation: Unauthorized access to IoT devices can lead to manipulation, disruption, or misuse of functionalities, posing risks to safety and security.
- Data Manipulation: Altered data from compromised IoT devices can lead to incorrect decisions and actions, affecting various applications, from healthcare to industrial processes.
- Privacy Violations: Breaches involving IoT devices may result in the unauthorized collection and misuse of personal information, violating user privacy (Gubbi et al., 2013).

COMMUNICATION PROTOCOLS FOR CLOUD SECURITY

In-depth Review of Communication Protocols

Communication protocols are integral to securing data in transit within cloud environments.

Understanding the strengths, weaknesses, and use cases of these communication protocols is crucial for selecting the most appropriate solutions to address specific security requirements in cloud environments. The subsequent sections will extend this analysis to communication protocols specifically tailored for securing IoT devices and explore the challenges and solutions associated with their integration.

Table 1. In-depth review of communication protocols for cloud security

TLS/SSL (Transport Layer Security/Secure Sockets Layer)	Strengths	• Provides robust encryption. • Supports mutual authentication. • Widespread adoption.
	Weaknesses	• Vulnerabilities such as POODLE and BEAST. • Introduces some latency.
	Use Cases	• Web applications for securing user data. • E-commerce transactions for securing payment information.
IPsec (Internet Protocol Security)	Strengths	• Operates at the network layer. • Offers both authentication and encryption. • Suitable for site-to-site VPNs.
	Weaknesses	• Configuration complexity. • Compatibility issues, especially with NAT.
	Use Cases	• Site-to-site VPNs for secure communication between offices. • Remote access VPNs for secure connectivity for remote employees.
SSH (Secure Shell)	Strengths	SSH provides secure, encrypted communication over an insecure network, often used for secure remote access to systems.
	Weaknesses	SSH is typically used for command-line access, and its use in broader application scenarios may be limited.
DNS over HTTPS (DoH) and DNS over TLS (DoT)	Strengths	These protocols encrypt DNS queries, enhancing privacy and preventing potential eavesdropping.
	Weaknesses	While securing DNS, they may introduce some additional latency.
HTTPS (Hypertext Transfer Protocol Secure)	Strengths	An extension of HTTP, HTTPS uses TLS/SSL to secure data transmission over the web, widely employed to protect sensitive web communications.
	Weaknesses	Similar to TLS/SSL, HTTPS may introduce some latency due to the encryption and decryption processes.
MQTT (Message Queuing Telemetry Transport)	Strengths	MQTT is a lightweight protocol suitable for resource-constrained devices and scenarios with intermittent connectivity.
	Weaknesses	Security concerns include the potential for eavesdropping and unauthorized access.

COMMUNICATION PROTOCOLS FOR IOT SECURITY

Exploration of Communication Protocols for IoT Devices

IoT devices operate in diverse and resource-constrained environments, necessitating specialized communication protocols (Miorandi et al., 2012).

Table 2. Some communication protocols for IoT devices

MQTT (Message Queuing Telemetry Transport)	Overview	MQTT is a lightweight and open-source messaging protocol designed for scenarios with intermittent connectivity and limited bandwidth. It follows a publish-subscribe model, allowing devices to communicate asynchronously.
	Strengths	• Efficiency: Due to its lightweight nature, MQTT is suitable for low-bandwidth and high-latency networks. • Scalability: Its publish-subscribe model facilitates efficient communication between a large number of devices.
	Weaknesses	Security Concerns: MQTT, when used without security measures, may be vulnerable to eavesdropping and unauthorized access.
	Use Cases	Smart Home Applications: MQTT is commonly used in smart home scenarios for efficient communication between various devices, such as sensors and actuators.
CoAP (Constrained Application Protocol)	Overview	CoAP is a lightweight and RESTful protocol designed for resource-constrained devices. It is tailored for environments where devices may have limited processing power and memory.
	Strengths	• Efficiency: CoAP minimizes overhead and is well-suited for low-power devices with limited bandwidth. • Scalability: Its simplicity makes it suitable for scenarios with a large number of devices.
	Weaknesses	Reliability: CoAP relies on the User Datagram Protocol (UDP), which may not guarantee reliable delivery of messages.
	Use Cases	Industrial IoT (IIoT): CoAP is often used in industrial settings where devices need to communicate in a resource-efficient manner.
AMQP (Advanced Message Queuing Protocol)	Overview	AMQP is a messaging protocol designed for real-time communication between devices. It supports both message queuing and publish-subscribe models.
	Strengths	• Interoperability: AMQP promotes interoperability between different systems and languages. • Reliability: It ensures reliable message delivery.
	Weaknesses	Complexity: AMQP may be more complex to implement compared to lightweight protocols like MQTT.
	Use Cases	Smart Grids: AMQP can be applied in scenarios where reliable communication between smart grid devices is critical.

Table 3. Suitability in Different IoT Scenarios

MQTT Suitability	Scenarios	Ideal for scenarios with intermittent connectivity, such as remote monitoring in agriculture or environmental sensing.
	Devices	Well-suited for devices with limited processing power and memory.
CoAP Suitability	Scenarios	Suitable for environments with resource-constrained devices, like building automation systems.
	Devices	Well-suited for low-power devices that need to communicate efficiently.
AMQP Suitability	Scenarios	Applicable in scenarios requiring real-time communication, such as industrial control systems.
	Devices	Suited for devices with sufficient processing capabilities.

Evaluation of Suitability in Different IoT Scenarios

Understanding the strengths, weaknesses, and use cases of these communication protocols is crucial for selecting the most appropriate solutions for securing communication in IoT environments.

INTEGRATION CHALLENGES

Examination of Challenges in Integrating Secure Communication Protocols

Table 4. Integrating secure communication protocols in cloud and IoT environments presents specific challenges

Diversity of Devices and Platforms	Issue	The wide variety of IoT devices and platforms may not uniformly support all secure communication protocols.
	Challenge	Ensuring that selected protocols are compatible with the diverse ecosystem of IoT devices.
Scalability	Issue	As the number of IoT devices grows, ensuring that secure communication scales seamlessly becomes a significant challenge.
	Challenge	Implementing solutions that can handle the dynamic nature of IoT environments.
Interoperability	Issue	Different protocols may not seamlessly interoperate, leading to communication breakdowns.
	Challenge	Standardizing communication protocols and ensuring interoperability across different devices and platforms.

Discussion on Interoperability Issues and Potential Solutions

Table 5. Interoperability issues

Incompatibility Between Protocols	Issue	Some protocols may not be compatible with others, creating communication silos.
	Challenge	Finding common ground or standardizing protocols to enhance interoperability.

Table 6. Potential Solutions

Standardization Efforts	**Solution**	**Industry-wide standardization efforts can help establish common communication protocols.**
	Benefits	**Improved interoperability and a more cohesive IoT ecosystem.**
Adoption of Open Protocols	Solution	Embracing open communication protocols can mitigate interoperability challenges.
	Benefits	Increased flexibility and reduced dependence on proprietary solutions.
Development of Middleware Solutions	Solution	Middleware solutions can act as intermediaries, translating between different protocols.
	Benefits	Facilitates communication between devices using different protocols.

CASE STUDIES

Presentation of Real-World Case Studies

Real-world case studies provide valuable insights into the successful implementations of secure communication protocols in Cloud and IoT environments. Below are two illustrative examples:

Case Study 1: Securing Cloud-Based Healthcare Data

- **Overview:**

A leading healthcare provider implemented a robust secure communication protocol to safeguard patient data stored in the cloud. The organization faced challenges related to regulatory compliance and the need to ensure patient confidentiality while leveraging the benefits of cloud services.

- **Implementation:**

The healthcare provider adopted TLS/SSL as the primary secure communication protocol for data in transit. This decision was driven by TLS/SSL's proven track record in ensuring encryption, authentication, and data integrity. Additionally, the organization implemented stringent access controls and identity management practices within the cloud environment.

- **Outcomes:**
    - Enhanced Data Confidentiality: TLS/SSL encryption ensured that patient data remained confidential during transmission between healthcare facilities and the cloud.
    - Regulatory Compliance: The implementation aligned with healthcare data protection regulations, demonstrating the organization's commitment to compliance.
    - Improved Interoperability: TLS/SSL's widespread support enabled seamless integration with various healthcare systems and applications.

Case Study 2: IoT Security in Smart City Infrastructure

- **Overview:**

A city municipality embarked on a project to create a smart city infrastructure using IoT devices for efficient resource management and citizen services. The challenge was to ensure secure communication among diverse IoT devices while addressing privacy concerns and potential cyber threats.

- **Implementation:**

The municipality opted for a combination of MQTT and CoAP as communication protocols for different sets of IoT devices. MQTT was chosen for real-time monitoring of critical infrastructure, while CoAP was applied to resource-constrained devices like environmental sensors. Security measures included end-to-end encryption, device authentication, and regular firmware updates.

- **Outcomes:**
    - Efficient Communication: MQTT facilitated efficient and real-time communication among devices, ensuring optimal performance for critical applications.

- ◦ Resource Optimization: CoAP's lightweight nature minimized resource usage on constrained devices, contributing to prolonged device lifetimes.
- ◦ Privacy Protection: The implemented secure communication protocols protected citizen privacy by encrypting sensitive data collected by IoT devices.
- ◦ Resilience Against Cyber Threats: Regular updates and authentication measures mitigated the risk of cyber threats, ensuring the integrity of the smart city infrastructure.

Analysis of Implementation Success and Lessons Learned

Implementation Success:

Thorough Risk Assessment: Both organizations conducted thorough risk assessments to identify potential threats and vulnerabilities before selecting and implementing secure communication protocols.

User Education and Training: Successful implementations included user education programs to ensure that employees and stakeholders understood the importance of secure communication practices.

Lessons Learned:

- Continuous Monitoring: Both cases emphasized the importance of continuous monitoring of the security landscape and prompt adjustments to protocols or configurations in response to emerging threats.
- Scalability Planning: The smart city infrastructure case highlighted the need for scalability planning, ensuring that the chosen protocols could accommodate the growing number of IoT devices without compromising security.

FUTURE TRENDS AND EMERGING TECHNOLOGIES

Upcoming Trends in Secure Communication for Cloud and IoT

As technology continues to evolve, several trends and emerging technologies are expected to shape the future of secure communication in Cloud and IoT environments:

Zero Trust Architecture:

- **Overview:**

Zero Trust Architecture (ZTA) represents a paradigm shift in security, moving away from traditional perimeter-based models. ZTA assumes that no entity, whether inside or outside the network, should be trusted by default. Instead, continuous verification and validation of users and devices are required, even after they have gained initial access.

- **Potential Impact:**

ZTA can enhance the security posture of Cloud and IoT environments by adopting a more granular and dynamic approach to access control. This ensures that entities are continuously verified, reducing the risk of unauthorized access and minimizing the impact of compromised credentials.

Edge Computing:

- **Overview:**

Edge Computing involves processing data closer to the source of generation rather than relying solely on centralized cloud servers. This approach reduces latency, enhances real-time processing, and minimizes the need for data transit to centralized cloud data centers.

- **Potential Impact:**

In the context of secure communication, Edge Computing can contribute to improved data privacy and reduced exposure to potential security threats. By processing sensitive data closer to its source, there's less reliance on transmitting data over networks, reducing the attack surface and minimizing the risk of interception.

Potential Impact of Technologies like Blockchain on Security

Blockchain:

- **Overview:**

Blockchain is a decentralized and distributed ledger technology that enables secure, transparent, and tamper-resistant record-keeping. It operates on a consensus mechanism, ensuring that data stored on the blockchain is immutable and trustworthy.

- **Potential Impact:**

In the realm of secure communication, blockchain can be leveraged to enhance the integrity and authenticity of transmitted data. By creating a decentralized and unalterable record of communication events, blockchain technology can provide a robust foundation for secure and transparent transactions in Cloud and IoT environments.

RECOMMENDATIONS AND BEST PRACTICES

Practical Recommendations for Implementing Secure Communication Protocols

Recommendations:

Conduct Comprehensive Risk Assessments:

- Organizations should conduct thorough risk assessments to identify potential threats and vulnerabilities specific to their Cloud and IoT environments.

Select Protocols Based on Use Cases:

- Choose communication protocols based on the specific use cases, considering factors such as device types, network characteristics, and security requirements.

Implement Strong Authentication Mechanisms:

- Utilize robust authentication mechanisms to verify the identities of entities involved in communication, reducing the risk of unauthorized access.

Regularly Update and Patch Systems:

- Keep communication systems and devices up to date with the latest security patches to address known vulnerabilities and enhance overall security.

Best Practices for Ensuring Ongoing Security of Cloud and IoT Systems

Best Practices:

Implement Regular Security Audits:

- Conduct regular security audits to assess the effectiveness of implemented secure communication protocols and identify areas for improvement.

Educate Users and Stakeholders:

- Provide ongoing education and training for users and stakeholders to raise awareness of security best practices and promote a security-conscious culture.

Establish Incident Response Plans:

- Develop comprehensive incident response plans to ensure a swift and effective response to security incidents, minimizing potential damages.

Monitor and Analyze Network Traffic:

- Implement continuous monitoring of network traffic to detect anomalies and potential security threats, allowing for proactive mitigation.

CONCLUSION

The comprehensive review has delved into the intricate landscape of secure communication protocols in the realms of Cloud Computing and the Internet of Things (IoT). Summarizing the key findings reveals the critical importance of these protocols in mitigating security risks and ensuring the integrity, confidentiality, and availability of data.

Key Findings:

I. Diverse Security Threats:

The examination of common security threats in both Cloud Computing and IoT ecosystems revealed a spectrum of challenges, including data breaches, insecure APIs, device compromises, and privacy concerns. Understanding these threats is fundamental for developing effective security strategies.

II. Communication Protocols for Cloud Security:

The in-depth review of communication protocols for securing cloud environments highlighted the strengths and weaknesses of prominent protocols such as TLS/SSL and IPsec. These protocols play a crucial role in encrypting data in transit, authenticating communication, and ensuring the secure exchange of information.

III. Communication Protocols for IoT Security:

The exploration of communication protocols tailored for IoT devices, including MQTT and CoAP, emphasized the need for specialized solutions to address the unique challenges of resource-constrained environments. The evaluation of these protocols showcased their suitability in various IoT scenarios.

IV. Integration Challenges:

Examining challenges associated with integrating secure communication protocols in Cloud and IoT environments underscored issues related to the diversity of devices, scalability, and interoperability. Solutions such as standardization efforts and the development of middleware were discussed to address these challenges.

V. Real-World Case Studies:

The presentation of real-world case studies demonstrated successful implementations of secure communication protocols. These cases showcased the practical application of protocols like TLS/SSL, MQTT, and CoAP in securing healthcare data in the cloud and enabling IoT in smart city infrastructure.

VI. Future Trends and Emerging Technologies:

Discussion on upcoming trends highlighted the significance of Zero Trust Architecture and Edge Computing in shaping the future of secure communication. The potential impact of technologies like blockchain on security was explored, showcasing their role in enhancing data integrity and authenticity.

VII. Recommendations and Best Practices:

Practical recommendations emphasized the importance of comprehensive risk assessments, protocol selection based on use cases, and the implementation of strong authentication mechanisms. Best practices for ongoing security included regular audits, user education, incident response planning, and continuous monitoring of network traffic.

Emphasis on the Critical Role:

The critical role of secure communication protocols in mitigating security risks cannot be overstated. They form the backbone of a resilient security posture, providing a secure conduit for data transmission in environments that are increasingly interconnected and dynamic.

In the face of evolving cyber threats, these protocols act as a first line of defense, safeguarding sensitive information from unauthorized access, data breaches, and manipulation. The case studies illustrated how well-implemented protocols contribute to the confidentiality, integrity, and availability of data, reinforcing the importance of strategic protocol selection and robust security measures.

As Cloud Computing and IoT technologies continue to advance, the need for secure communication will only intensify. The findings from this comprehensive review emphasize the ongoing commitment required from organizations to stay abreast of emerging trends, adopt innovative technologies, and adhere to best practices. Secure communication protocols serve as a cornerstone in building a resilient and trustworthy digital infrastructure, protecting the foundations of modern information systems.

REFERENCES

Al-Fuqaha, A., Guizani, M., Mohammadi, M., Aledhari, M., & Ayyash, M. (2015). Internet of Things: A survey on enabling technologies, protocols, and applications. *IEEE Communications Surveys and Tutorials*, *17*(4), 2347–2376. doi:10.1109/COMST.2015.2444095

Armando, A., Costa, G., Merlo, A., & Verderame, L. (2018). A survey of security in fog computing. *ACM Computing Surveys*, *51*(5), 1–35.

Atzori, L., Iera, A., & Morabito, G. (2010). The Internet of Things: A survey. *Computer Networks*, *54*(15), 2787–2805. doi:10.1016/j.comnet.2010.05.010

Chowdhury, M. H., Uddin, M. Z., Sarker, I. H., & Gani, A. (2018). Internet of Things (IoT) for Cloud-based healthcare: A survey. *Future Generation Computer Systems*, *78*, 641–658.

Cisco. (2018). Cisco Global Cloud Index: Forecast and Methodology, 2016–2021 White Paper. https://www.cisco.com/c/en/us/solutions/collateral/service-provider/global-cloud-index-gci/white-paper-c11-738085.html

Dastjerdi, A. V., & Buyya, R. (2016). Fog computing: Helping the Internet of Things realize its potential. *Computer*, *49*(8), 112–116. doi:10.1109/MC.2016.245

Dijk, M. V., Juels, A., Mohassel, P., Ristenpart, T., & Tromer, E. (2010). On the impossibility of cryptography alone for privacy-preserving cloud computing. In *Proceedings of the 2010 ACM Workshop on Cloud Computing Security Workshop* (pp. 1-6). ACM.

Dinh, H. T., Lee, C., Niyato, D., & Wang, P. (2013). A survey of mobile cloud computing: Architecture, applications, and approaches. *Wireless Communications and Mobile Computing*, *13*(18), 1587–1611. doi:10.1002/wcm.1203

Gubbi, J., Buyya, R., Marusic, S., & Palaniswami, M. (2013). Internet of Things (IoT): A vision, architectural elements, and future directions. *Future Generation Computer Systems*, *29*(7), 1645–1660. doi:10.1016/j.future.2013.01.010

Hossain, M. S., & Fotouhi, M. (2015). Cloud-based RFID framework for traceability and anti-counterfeiting. *Journal of Network and Computer Applications*, *55*, 65–80.

IBM. (2020). *Blockchain: A technical overview*. IBM. https://www.ibm.com/cloud/learn/blockchain-a-technical-overview

ISO/IEC. (2016). *ISO/IEC 27002:2013 - Information technology -- Security techniques -- Code of practice for information security controls*. ISO.

Kahn, R. E., & Cerf, V. G. (1974). A Protocol for Packet Network Intercommunication. *IEEE Transactions on Communications*, *22*(5), 637–648. doi:10.1109/TCOM.1974.1092259

Karagiannis, G., Altintas, O., Ekici, E., Heijenk, G., Jarupan, B., Lin, K., & Weil, T. (2010). Vehicular networking: A survey and tutorial on requirements, architectures, challenges, standards and solutions. *IEEE Communications Surveys and Tutorials*, *13*(4), 584–616. doi:10.1109/SURV.2011.061411.00019

Kent, S., & Seo, K. (2005). Security Architecture for the Internet Protocol. *IETF RFC 4301*.

Mather, T., Kumaraswamy, S., & Latif, S. (2009). *Cloud Security and Privacy: An Enterprise Perspective on Risks and Compliance*. O'Reilly Media.

Mell, P., & Grance, T. (2011). *The NIST Definition of Cloud Computing*. National Institute of Standards and Technology. https://csrc.nist.gov/publications/detail/sp/800-145/final

Microsoft. (2021). *IoT security best practices*. Microsoft. https://docs.microsoft.com/en-us/azure/iot/security-best-practices

Miorandi, D., Sicari, S., De Pellegrini, F., & Chlamtac, I. (2012). Internet of things: Vision, applications and research challenges. *Ad Hoc Networks*, *10*(7), 1497–1516. doi:10.1016/j.adhoc.2012.02.016

NIST. (2018). *National Initiative for Cybersecurity Education (NICE) Cybersecurity Workforce Framework*. NIST. https://nvlpubs.nist.gov/nistpubs/specialpublications/nist.sp.800-181r1.pdf

OASIS. (2019). MQTT Version 5.0. OASIS. https://docs.oasis-open.org/mqtt/mqtt/v5.0/os/mqtt-v5.0-os.html

Roman, R., Alcaraz, C., Lopez, J., & Sklavos, N. (2011). Key management systems for sensor networks in the context of the Internet of Things. *Computers & Electrical Engineering*, *37*(2), 147–159. doi:10.1016/j.compeleceng.2011.01.009

Shelby, Z., Hartke, K., & Bormann, C. (2014). The Constrained Application Protocol (CoAP). *IETF RFC 7252. ISO/IEC. (2017). ISO/IEC 27001:2013 - Information technology -- Security techniques -- Information security management systems -- Requirements.*

Stallings, W. (2017). *Cryptography and Network Security: Principles and Practice*. Pearson.

Stojmenovic, I., Wen, S., Huang, X., & Luan, H. (2014). An overview of fog computing and its security issues. *Concurrency and Computation*, *28*(10), 2991–3005. doi:10.1002/cpe.3485

Chapter 10
Landscape of Serverless Computing Technology and IoT Tools in the IT Sectors

D. Dhanya
Department of Artificial Intelligence and Data Science, Mar Ephraem College of Engineering and Technology, Kanyakumari, India

M. Arun Manicka Raja
Department of Computer Science and Engineering, RMK College of Engineering and Technology, Puduvoyal, India

Khasimbee Shaik
Department of Computer Science and Engineering, Aditya College of Engineering, Surampalem, India

L. Sharmila
Department of Computer Science and Engineering, Agni College of Technology, Chennai, India

Maya P. Shelke
https://orcid.org/0000-0001-7171-1545
Department of Information Technology, PCET's Pimpri Chinchwad College of Engineering, Pune, India

S.B. Gokul
YSR Engineering College, India

ABSTRACT

This chapter delves into the challenges of securing sensitive data and systems in the digital landscape, focusing on serverless computing, IoT, and authentication protocols. It discusses best practices for implementing security measures in serverless architectures, including encryption, access control, and monitoring. The rise of IoT devices has revolutionized industries by enabling real-time data collection and analysis, but also presents a significant cyber threat surface. To secure IoT ecosystems, strategies include device authentication, encryption, and intrusion detection systems. Authentication protocols like multi-factor authentication, biometrics, and blockchain-based solutions are crucial. Understanding serverless computing, IoT security, and authentication protocols is essential for businesses to proactively address security gaps and safeguard assets in an evolving threat landscape.

DOI: 10.4018/979-8-3693-0766-3.ch010

INTRODUCTION

This chapter discusses the integration of serverless computing, IoT, and authentication protocols in the digital landscape, highlighting the challenges and opportunities for businesses. Serverless computing offers scalability and cost-effectiveness, but its decentralized nature necessitates a multi-layered security approach. This includes encryption, access control, and continuous monitoring to mitigate risks associated with these platforms. The chapter emphasizes the need for organizations to implement robust security measures across these domains (Cassel et al., 2022). Encryption is crucial in serverless environments to protect data privacy and confidentiality. It prevents unauthorized access and data breaches, while fine-grained access control mechanisms restrict interaction between authorized users and functions. Continuous monitoring is vital for detecting anomalous behavior and identifying security threats. By utilizing monitoring tools and robust logging mechanisms, organizations can respond swiftly to potential breaches. Real-time alerting and automated incident response workflows further enhance the effectiveness of security monitoring in serverless architectures (Ahmadi, 2024).

The rise of IoT devices has revolutionized industries by enabling real-time data collection and decision-making. However, these devices pose significant security challenges. A holistic approach is needed to secure IoT ecosystems, including device authentication, data encryption, and intrusion detection systems. Device authentication mechanisms like certificate-based and mutual TLS validate devices' identities, while end-to-end encryption protocols protect data between devices and cloud-based platforms. Intrusion detection systems monitor network traffic and device behavior to identify potential cyber threats in real-time. Authentication protocols are crucial for verifying user and device identities in digital resources (Golec et al., 2023). Traditional methods, like username/password, are vulnerable to cyber-attacks. Organizations are exploring more robust mechanisms like multi-factor authentication (MFA), biometrics, and blockchain-based solutions. MFA combines multiple factors to enhance security against unauthorized access. Biometrics uses unique biological traits like fingerprints or facial recognition for high accuracy. Blockchain-based solutions use decentralized ledgers to securely authenticate users and devices without relying on centralized authorities. This chapter emphasizes the significance of security in the digital age, emphasizing the need for organizations to implement robust security measures and stay updated on evolving threats and best practices to protect their digital assets and mitigate risks associated with emerging technologies (Kumar & others, 2018).

Organizations face numerous challenges in securing sensitive data and systems due to rapid technological advancements and evolving cyber threats. Cybercriminals exploit vulnerabilities in software, hardware, and network infrastructure to gain unauthorized access to sensitive information and commit malicious activities. The threat landscape is vast and multifaceted, from phishing attacks to sophisticated nation-state cyber espionage. To avoid potential security breaches, organizations must remain vigilant and proactive in detecting and mitigating emerging threats. The rise of connected devices and the Internet of Things (IoT) has significantly impacted digital security (Shafiei et al., 2022). Insecure IoT devices, lacking robust security controls and firmware updates, pose significant risks to individuals and organizations. Compromised IoT devices can be used as entry points into corporate networks or enlisted in large-scale botnet attacks, amplifying cyber threats. The rise of cloud computing and serverless architectures has introduced new security challenges for organizations. Misconfigured storage buckets, inadequate access controls, and insecure APIs can expose sensitive data to unauthorized access or breaches. The decentralized nature of serverless platforms also complicates securing event-driven architectures and serverless functions (Y. Li et al., 2022).

Organizations face challenges in maintaining robust digital security due to data privacy and compliance regulations like GDPR and CCPA. These laws impose stringent requirements on data collection, processing, and storage, with non-compliance leading to financial penalties and reputational damage. Therefore, comprehensive data protection measures are crucial for maintaining digital security. The cybersecurity talent gap is widening as organizations struggle to recruit and retain qualified professionals in areas like threat intelligence, incident response, and security operations (Benedict, 2020). Addressing this requires public and private sectors to invest in cybersecurity education, training, and workforce development initiatives. Organizations must remain vigilant, adaptive, and proactive in navigating the complex landscape of digital security by investing in robust security technologies, implementing best practices, and fostering a culture of security awareness to mitigate risks and safeguard digital assets in an increasingly interconnected world (Golec et al., 2023).

In the digital age, sensitive data is crucial for organizations across industries, including proprietary information, financial records, customer data, and intellectual property. Securing sensitive data is essential to maintain trust and confidence, as a single breach can lead to reputational damage, customer attrition, and loss of business opportunities. By implementing robust security measures, organizations can demonstrate their commitment to protecting the privacy and confidentiality of their stakeholders' information, enhancing trust and fostering long-term relationships. The repercussions of a security breach can be devastating for businesses, individuals, and entire economies (Scheuner & Leitner, 2020).

Securing sensitive data is crucial for compliance with regulatory requirements and industry standards. Countries have enacted strict data protection laws, like GDPR in Europe and HIPAA in the US, to protect personal data privacy. Non-compliance can lead to financial penalties, legal liabilities, and reputational damage. Implementing comprehensive data security measures and adhering to regulations can help organizations mitigate compliance risks, safeguard operations, and preserve their reputation (Lynn et al., 2017).

Securing sensitive data is crucial to prevent financial losses and intellectual property theft. Cybercriminals often target organizations for financial gain or competitive advantage. Loss of sensitive data can result in legal fees, regulatory fines, remediation costs, and revenue loss. Investing in robust security technologies and practices can reduce the likelihood of data breaches and minimize the financial impact of security incidents. Security breaches can lead to financial losses, operational disruptions, and downtime, affecting productivity, business continuity, and customer satisfaction. The impact extends beyond financial losses, affecting an organization's ability to deliver products, meet contractual obligations, and respond to customer inquiries. Proactively securing sensitive data and systems minimizes these risks and ensures uninterrupted business operations (Scheuner & Leitner, 2020).

Securing sensitive data is crucial for protecting national security, public safety, and critical infrastructure. Cyberattacks on government agencies, healthcare organizations, and energy utilities pose a significant threat, compromising sensitive information and services. Prioritizing cybersecurity and investing in robust defense mechanisms can strengthen resilience to cyber threats and protect critical infrastructure integrity and security (Rajan, 2020). The significance of securing sensitive data and systems cannot be overstated due to the numerous risks associated with security breaches. Prioritizing data security helps organizations protect stakeholders, comply with regulations, mitigate financial losses, ensure operational continuity, and safeguard national security and public safety in an increasingly interconnected world.

SECURING SERVERLESS COMPUTING ENVIRONMENTS

Serverless architecture, a future of cloud computing, is a paradigm shift in application development, deployment, and management. It abstracts underlying servers, allowing developers to focus on code writing. Serverless architecture is event-driven, with functions executed in response to specific triggers like HTTP requests, database changes, or file uploads. One of the important components of serverless architecture is Function as a Service (FaaS), which enables developers to deploy individual functions or snippets of code without having to manage the underlying infrastructure (Lynn et al., 2017; Rajan, 2020). This pay-as-you-go model offers scalability, cost-efficiency, and agility, as resources are automatically provisioned and scaled based on demand. Additionally, serverless platforms typically offer built-in integrations with other cloud services, such as databases, storage, and authentication, further simplifying application development and deployment (Christidis et al., 2020; Enes et al., 2020).

However, the decentralized nature of serverless computing introduces unique security considerations and challenges. Unlike traditional server-based architectures where security measures are applied at the infrastructure level, serverless environments require a shift towards securing code and application logic. With functions being executed in ephemeral containers on shared infrastructure, organizations must implement robust security measures to mitigate the risk of unauthorized access, data breaches, and other security threats. One of the primary security challenges in serverless computing is ensuring the integrity and confidentiality of sensitive data. With functions processing and manipulating data in memory, organizations must implement encryption mechanisms to protect data both at rest and in transit (Kumari et al., 2021; Somu et al., 2020). Additionally, access controls and authentication mechanisms are crucial for preventing unauthorized access to sensitive resources and functions. By implementing fine-grained access controls and least privilege principles, organizations can minimize the attack surface and mitigate the risk of privilege escalation attacks.

Another security consideration in serverless environments is the risk of injection attacks, such as SQL injection and code injection. With functions often accepting input from external sources, such as HTTP requests or event triggers, developers must sanitize and validate input data to prevent malicious payloads from executing arbitrary code or accessing unauthorized resources. Additionally, implementing runtime protections, such as runtime application self-protection (RASP) and function-level firewalls, can help detect and mitigate injection attacks in real-time (Koschel et al., 2021).

Furthermore, securing serverless environments requires comprehensive monitoring and logging capabilities to detect and respond to security incidents in a timely manner. By collecting and analyzing logs, organizations can gain visibility into function invocations, resource usage, and potential security threats. Real-time alerting and automated incident response workflows enable organizations to respond swiftly to security incidents, minimizing the impact and severity of breaches (Edlund, 2022).

Serverless architecture, a future of cloud computing, is a paradigm shift in application development, deployment, and management. It abstracts underlying servers, allowing developers to focus on code writing. Serverless architecture is event-driven, with functions executed in response to specific triggers like HTTP requests, database changes, or file uploads.

SECURITY CHALLENGES IN SERVERLESS COMPUTING

Serverless computing offers scalability, cost-effectiveness, and simplified management, but it also presents unique security challenges that organizations must address to effectively safeguard their data and systems, making understanding and mitigating these challenges crucial (Lin & Khazaei, 2020). Figure 1 outlines various factors that pose security challenges in serverless computing.

- **Lack of Visibility and Control**: One of the primary security challenges in serverless computing is the limited visibility and control over the underlying infrastructure. Unlike traditional server-based architectures, where organizations have full control over the server environment, serverless platforms abstract away the infrastructure layer, making it challenging to monitor and manage security configurations effectively. This lack of visibility can hinder threat detection and response efforts, leaving organizations vulnerable to security breaches and unauthorized access.
- **Inadequate Authentication and Authorization**: Serverless architectures rely heavily on APIs (Application Programming Interfaces) for interaction between services and functions. However, ensuring secure authentication and authorization mechanisms for these APIs presents a significant challenge. Without robust authentication controls in place, malicious actors may exploit vulnerabilities in exposed APIs to gain unauthorized access to sensitive data or execute malicious code. Implementing strong authentication and authorization mechanisms, such as API keys, OAuth tokens, and role-based access control (RBAC), is essential for mitigating these risks.

Figure 1. Factors for security challenges in serverless computing

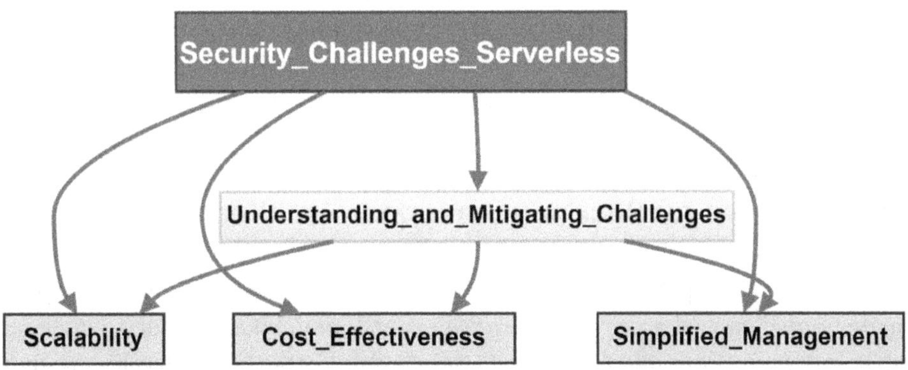

- **Data Security and Privacy Concerns**: Serverless applications often process and store sensitive data in third-party cloud environments, raising concerns about data security and privacy. In a serverless architecture, data may traverse multiple services and functions, increasing the risk of data exposure or leakage. Additionally, inadequate data encryption and access control measures can leave data vulnerable to interception or unauthorized access. Organizations must implement robust encryption mechanisms, such as TLS (Transport Layer Security) for data in transit and encryption-at-rest for data storage, to protect sensitive information from unauthorized access or disclosure.
- **Injection and Code Vulnerabilities**: Serverless functions are susceptible to common security vulnerabilities, such as injection attacks and code vulnerabilities. Malicious actors may exploit vulnerabilities in serverless functions to execute arbitrary code, inject malicious payloads, or escalate privileges within the environment. Vulnerabilities in third-party dependencies or libraries used in serverless functions can also pose significant risks. Implementing secure coding practices, such as input validation, parameterized queries, and regular code reviews, is essential for mitigating these vulnerabilities and reducing the risk of security breaches.
- **Denial of Service (DoS) Attacks**: Serverless architectures are inherently scalable, allowing them to handle fluctuations in workload demand effectively. However, this scalability also makes them attractive targets for Denial of Service (DoS) attacks. Malicious actors may attempt to overwhelm serverless functions with excessive requests or trigger infinite loops to consume resources and disrupt service availability. Implementing rate limiting, throttling, and anomaly detection mechanisms can help mitigate the impact of DoS attacks and ensure the availability and reliability of serverless applications.

Securing serverless computing environments involves addressing security challenges like limited visibility, authentication issues, data security concerns, code vulnerabilities, and DoS attacks. By implementing robust security measures, adopting secure coding practices, and utilizing advanced tools and technologies, organizations can improve their serverless applications' security and mitigate risks associated with serverless architecture deployment.

Best Practices for Securing Serverless Architectures

Implementing a comprehensive approach to serverless architecture security, including encryption techniques, access control measures, and continuous monitoring strategies, can help organizations mitigate security risks and protect sensitive data and systems.

Figure 2 illustrates best practices for implementing secure serverless architectures (Cinar, 2023).

Encryption Techniques

- Data Encryption: Encrypt sensitive data both at rest and in transit to protect it from unauthorized access. Use industry-standard encryption algorithms and robust main management practices to ensure the confidentiality and integrity of data.
- Client-Side Encryption: Implement client-side encryption to encrypt data before it is transmitted to serverless functions or stored in backend databases. This ensures that data remains encrypted throughout its lifecycle and reduces the risk of exposure during transmission or storage.
- Secure Key Management: Implement secure management practices to protect encryption keys from unauthorized access or compromise. Use hardware security modules (HSMs) or cloud-based management services to securely generate, store, and rotate encryption keys.

Access Control Measures

- Role-Based Access Control (RBAC): Implement RBAC to enforce least privilege access controls and limit the permissions granted to serverless functions. Assign roles and permissions based on the principle of least privilege, ensuring that each function has access only to the resources and data necessary for its intended purpose (X. Li et al., 2022).
- API Gateway Authentication: Use API gateway authentication mechanisms, such as API keys, OAuth tokens, or AWS IAM (Identity and Access

Figure 2. Best practices for implementing -secured serverless architectures

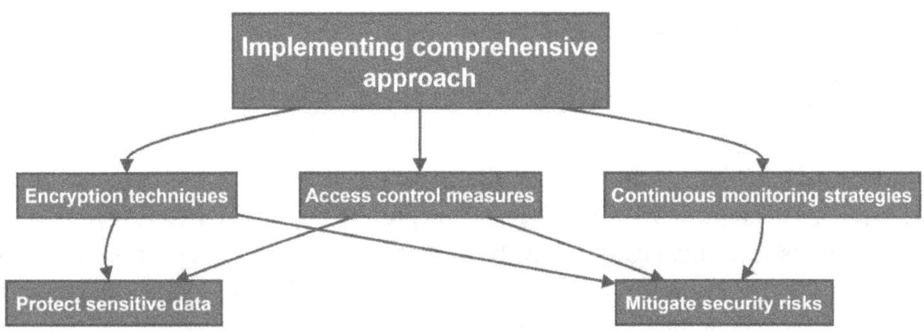

Management) policies, to authenticate and authorize incoming requests to serverless functions. Enforce strict access controls based on user identity, IP address, or other contextual factors to prevent unauthorized access.

- Least Privilege Execution: Restrict the execution privileges of serverless functions to minimize the potential impact of security breaches or code vulnerabilities. Limit the runtime environment's capabilities and permissions to only those necessary for the function to perform its intended tasks.

Continuous Monitoring Strategies

Securing serverless architectures requires a multi-layered approach involving encryption techniques, access control measures, and continuous monitoring strategies. By adopting best practices and utilizing advanced security tools, organizations can improve their serverless environments and reduce risks (de Oliveira, n.d.).

- Real-Time Logging and Monitoring: Implement real-time logging and monitoring solutions to capture and analyze events, logs, and metrics generated by serverless functions. Monitor for suspicious activities, anomalies, or deviations from expected behavior that may indicate security incidents or unauthorized access attempts.
- Intrusion Detection Systems (IDS): Deploy intrusion detection systems to monitor network traffic and serverless function executions for signs of malicious activity or unauthorized access. Implement rule-based or machine learning-based IDS to detect and respond to security threats in real-time.
- Automated Incident Response: Develop automated incident response workflows to respond swiftly to security incidents or anomalies detected within serverless environments. Integrate with existing security tools and orchestration platforms to automate incident triage, investigation, and remediation processes.

MANAGING SECURITY RISKS IN IOT ENVIRONMENTS

Impact of IoT on Industries

The Internet of Things (IoT) has revolutionized industries by promoting innovation, efficiency, and connectivity. However, it also presents significant security risks that organizations must manage effectively to protect their IoT ecosystems, requiring proactive identification and resolution (Thilakarathne, 2020). Figure 3 depicts the significant impact of the Internet of Things (IoT) on various industries. The Internet of Things (IoT) is transforming industries by promoting innovation, efficiency, and connectivity. However, managing security risks is crucial to protect critical infrastructure, sensitive data, and public safety. Organizations can leverage IoT's transformative power by understanding unique security challenges and implementing robust cybersecurity measures, ensuring the integrity and resilience of their IoT ecosystems (Tawalbeh et al., 2020).

- **Healthcare Industry:** Remote Patient Monitoring: IoT devices enable remote monitoring of patient vitals and health data, improving patient care and outcomes. However, the proliferation of connected medical devices increases the risk of security breaches and unauthorized access to sensitive patient information. Patient Privacy Concerns: Protecting patient privacy is paramount in healthcare IoT environments. Data encryption, access controls, and secure communication protocols are essential for safeguarding sensitive health data and complying with healthcare regulations such as HIPAA.
- **Manufacturing Sector:** Industrial IoT (IIoT) Adoption: IIoT technologies, such as sensors, actuators, and smart machinery, enhance operational efficiency and productivity in manufacturing environments. However, insecure IoT devices and communication channels pose cybersecurity risks, including data tampering, equipment malfunction, and supply chain disruptions. Operational Resilience: Ensuring the resilience of manufacturing operations against cyber

Figure 3. Impact of IoT on industries

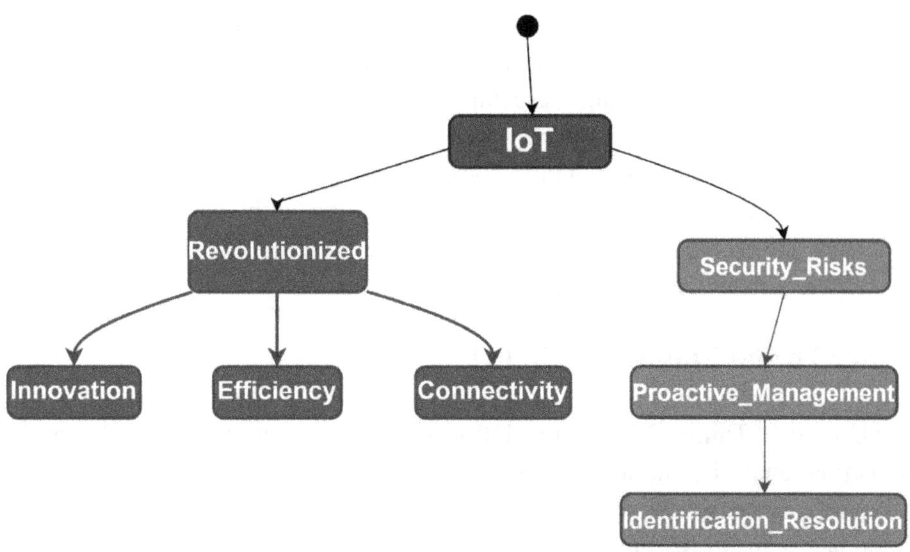

threats requires implementing robust security measures, including network segmentation, anomaly detection systems, and secure firmware updates for IoT devices.

- **Transportation and Logistics:** Connected Vehicles: IoT-enabled sensors and telematics systems enhance vehicle performance monitoring, route optimization, and fleet management in the transportation industry. However, cybersecurity vulnerabilities in connected vehicles can compromise passenger safety and privacy, leading to potential accidents or data breaches. Supply Chain Security: IoT technologies play a crucial role in optimizing logistics operations and tracking goods throughout the supply chain. Securing IoT-enabled supply chain processes is essential for preventing unauthorized access, tampering, or theft of valuable cargo and ensuring the integrity of goods in transit.
- **Smart Cities:** Urban Infrastructure Management: IoT sensors and smart city initiatives enable municipalities to monitor and manage critical infrastructure, including utilities, transportation systems, and public services. However, interconnected IoT devices create a vast attack surface for cyber threats, ranging from traffic signal manipulation to power grid disruptions. Citizen Privacy and Surveillance: Balancing the benefits of smart city technologies with citizen privacy concerns is a important challenge. Implementing privacy-preserving IoT solutions, transparent data governance policies, and robust cybersecurity measures is essential for building trust and ensuring the ethical use of smart city data.
- **Energy and Utilities:** Smart Grids and Energy Management: IoT devices facilitate real-time monitoring of energy consumption, grid stability, and renewable energy integration in the utility sector. However, insecure IoT devices pose risks of unauthorized access, data manipulation, and disruption of critical energy infrastructure. Resilience Against Cyber Attacks: Strengthening the resilience of energy and utility systems against cyber threats requires deploying intrusion detection systems, network segmentation, and incident response protocols. Collaborating with industry stakeholders and government agencies is crucial for developing and implementing cybersecurity best practices in the energy sector.

Cyber Threat Landscape in IoT

The Internet of Things (IoT) has revolutionized industries by enabling real-time data collection, analysis, and automation. However, this has also expanded the attack surface for cyber threats, necessitating a comprehensive understanding of the cyber threat landscape in IoT environments (Velmurugadass et al., 2021).

- **Botnets and DDoS Attacks**: One of the primary cyber threats in IoT environments is the proliferation of botnets, comprising compromised IoT devices recruited into vast networks controlled by malicious actors. These botnets are often used to launch Distributed Denial of Service (DDoS) attacks, overwhelming target systems with massive volumes of traffic and disrupting service availability. Mirai and Reaper are examples of notorious IoT botnets that have been used to orchestrate large-scale DDoS attacks, highlighting the severity of this threat.
- **Device Compromise and Data Breaches**: Insecure IoT devices with inadequate security controls and firmware vulnerabilities are prime targets for cybercriminals seeking to compromise devices and steal sensitive data. Unauthorized access to IoT devices can lead to data breaches, exposing personal information, financial records, and proprietary data to unauthorized parties. Furthermore, compromised IoT devices may be leveraged as entry points into corporate networks, facilitating lateral movement and escalating the impact of cyber-attacks.
- **Privacy Concerns and Data Misuse**: IoT devices often collect vast amounts of personal and sensitive data, raising concerns about privacy and data misuse. Inadequate data encryption, insecure communication protocols, and lax access controls can result in unauthorized access to sensitive information, leading to privacy violations and regulatory non-compliance. Malicious actors may exploit these vulnerabilities to harvest personal data for identity theft, fraud, or targeted advertising without users' consent.
- **Firmware and Software Vulnerabilities**: Vulnerabilities in IoT device firmware and software present significant security risks, as they can be exploited by attackers to gain unauthorized access, execute arbitrary code, or perform remote code execution attacks. Insecure firmware update mechanisms and lack of patch management practices exacerbate the risk of exploitation, leaving IoT devices vulnerable to known security vulnerabilities and zero-day exploits.
- **Supply Chain Attacks**: Supply chain attacks targeting IoT ecosystems pose a growing threat to organizations, as attackers seek to compromise devices at various stages of the manufacturing, distribution, or deployment process. Malicious actors may inject backdoors, tamper with firmware, or install malicious implants in IoT devices, compromising their integrity and security. These supply chain attacks can have far-reaching consequences, undermining the trustworthiness of IoT devices and eroding consumer confidence in the IoT ecosystem.

The cyber threat landscape in IoT environments is constantly evolving, encompassing botnets, DDoS attacks, device compromise, data breaches, privacy concerns, firmware vulnerabilities, and supply chain attacks. To effectively manage security risks, organizations must implement robust measures like secure device provisioning, firmware integrity verification, continuous monitoring, and threat intelligence sharing to safeguard the integrity and security of IoT ecosystems.

Security Strategies for IoT Ecosystems

Device Authentication Mechanisms

The figure 4 depicts the implementation factors for device authentication mechanisms. Implementing robust device authentication mechanisms, data encryption protocols, and intrusion detection and prevention systems in IoT ecosystems is crucial for mitigating security risks, safeguarding sensitive data, and enhancing the resilience of IoT deployments against various cyber threats (Azrour, Mabrouki, Guezzaz, & Kanwal, 2021; Velmurugadass et al., 2021).

Figure 4. Implementation factors for device authentication mechanisms

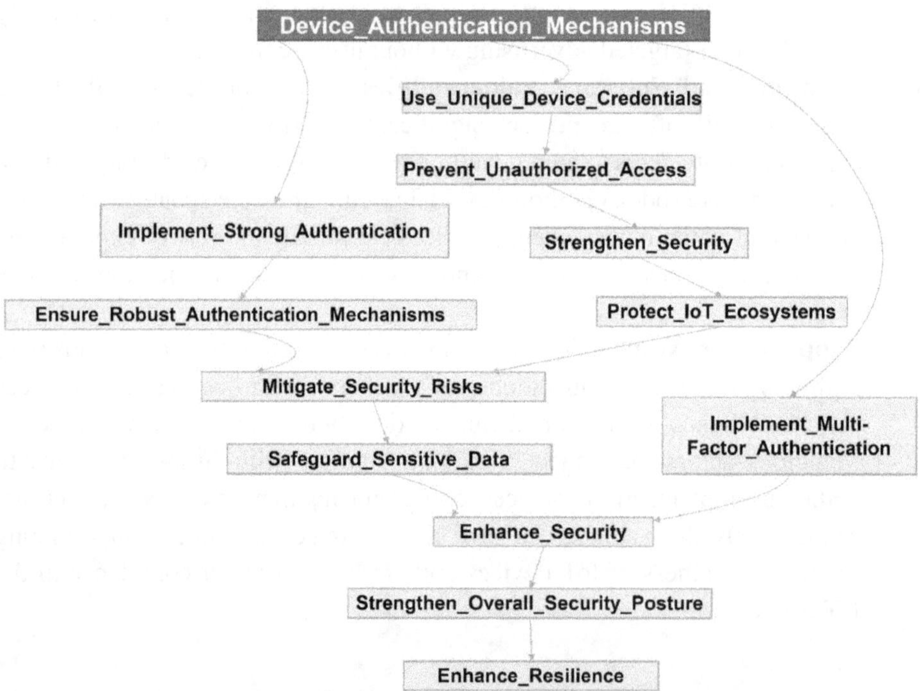

i. Implement Strong Authentication: Utilize robust authentication mechanisms to verify the identity of IoT devices before granting access to network resources or sensitive data. This may include cryptographic methods such as mutual authentication, where both the device and the server authenticate each other using digital certificates or shared secrets.
ii. Use Unique Device Credentials: Assign unique credentials, such as device certificates or authentication tokens, to each IoT device to prevent unauthorized access and impersonation attacks. Ensure that these credentials are securely stored and cannot be easily compromised or intercepted.
iii. Implement Multi-Factor Authentication (MFA): Enhance security by requiring multiple authentication factors, such as passwords, biometric data, or one-time passcodes, before granting access to IoT devices or services. MFA adds an additional layer of protection against unauthorized access and strengthens overall security posture.

Data Encryption Protocols

i. Encrypt Data in Transit and at Rest: Utilize encryption protocols, such as Transport Layer Security (TLS) for data in transit and Advanced Encryption Standard (AES) for data at rest, to protect sensitive information exchanged between IoT devices and backend systems. Encrypting data ensures that it remains confidential and integrity-protected, even if intercepted by malicious actors.
ii. Implement End-to-End Encryption: Securely transmit data between IoT devices and cloud-based platforms using end-to-end encryption protocols. This ensures that data remains encrypted throughout its entire journey, from the device sensors to the data storage systems, protecting it from unauthorized access or tampering.
iii. Use Strong Encryption Keys: Generate and manage encryption keys securely to prevent unauthorized decryption of encrypted data. Employ industry-standard cryptographic algorithms and management practices to ensure the confidentiality and integrity of encryption keys used to protect IoT data.

Intrusion Detection and Prevention Systems (IDPS)

i. Deploy Network-Based IDPS: Implement network-based intrusion detection and prevention systems to monitor network traffic and detect suspicious or malicious activities in real-time. IDPS can analyze network packets, detect known attack patterns, and block or mitigate potential threats before they can cause harm to IoT devices or systems.

ii. Utilize Host-Based IDPS: Install host-based intrusion detection and prevention agents on IoT devices to monitor system logs, file integrity, and process activity for signs of unauthorized access or malicious behavior. Host-based IDPS can detect anomalies, such as unauthorized file modifications or privilege escalation attempts, and trigger alerts or automated responses to mitigate security risks.
iii. Employ Anomaly Detection Techniques: Utilize machine learning algorithms and anomaly detection techniques to identify abnormal patterns of behavior within IoT ecosystems. Anomaly detection can help detect zero-day attacks, previously unknown threats, and insider threats that may evade traditional signature-based detection methods.

ENHANCING AUTHENTICATION PROTOCOLS FOR ROBUST SECURITY

Importance of Authentication in Digital Security

Authentication is the foundation of digital security, ensuring the identity of users and devices accessing digital resources. In today's digital world, robust authentication protocols are crucial for protecting sensitive data, preventing unauthorized access, and safeguarding digital system integrity. Authentication serves as the first line of defense against security threats and vulnerabilities (Azrour, Mabrouki, Guezzaz, & Farhaoui, 2021). Figure 5 emphasizes the importance of improving authentication protocols for robust security.

i. **Preventing Unauthorized Access**: Authentication protocols play a crucial role in preventing unauthorized access to digital resources, such as databases, applications, and network resources. By requiring users and devices to authenticate themselves before gaining access, organizations can ensure that only authorized individuals or entities are granted permission to access sensitive information or perform privileged actions. This helps mitigate the risk of data breaches, insider threats, and unauthorized use of resources, thereby preserving the confidentiality and integrity of digital assets.
ii. **Protecting Sensitive Data**: Authentication is paramount for protecting sensitive data from unauthorized disclosure or manipulation. Strong authentication mechanisms, such as multi-factor authentication (MFA) and biometric authentication, help verify the identity of users and devices with a high degree of certainty, reducing the risk of unauthorized data access or data theft. By enforcing strict authentication requirements, organizations can safeguard

sensitive data, such as personal information, financial records, and intellectual property, from malicious actors and cybercriminals.

iii. **Mitigating Identity Theft and Fraud**: Authentication protocols help mitigate the risk of identity theft and fraud by ensuring that only legitimate users are granted access to digital resources. Password-based authentication, for example, requires users to provide a unique combination of credentials to prove their identity, making it harder for attackers to impersonate legitimate users and gain unauthorized access. Advanced authentication methods, such as biometric authentication and behavioral biometrics, offer even greater security by leveraging unique physiological or behavioral characteristics to verify user identities with a high degree of accuracy.

iv. **Ensuring Regulatory Compliance**: Authentication is essential for ensuring regulatory compliance with data protection laws, industry regulations, and privacy standards. Many regulatory frameworks, such as the General Data Protection Regulation (GDPR) and the Payment Card Industry Data Security Standard (PCI DSS), require organizations to implement robust authentication measures to protect sensitive data and ensure the privacy and security of personal information. Failure to comply with these regulations can result in severe financial penalties, legal liabilities, and reputational damage.

v. **Building Trust and Confidence**: Effective authentication mechanisms help build trust and confidence among users, customers, and stakeholders. By demonstrating a commitment to robust security practices, organizations can reassure users that their personal information is safe and secure, enhancing customer loyalty, brand reputation, and business credibility. Trustworthy authentication processes also foster a positive user experience, reducing friction and frustration associated with security measures while maintaining a high level of security.

Authentication is a crucial aspect of digital security, protecting sensitive data, preventing unauthorized access, and mitigating security risks. Advanced features like multi-factor authentication, biometric authentication, and behavioral analytics can strengthen organizations' security posture against cyber threats. Investing in robust authentication measures is essential for building trust, ensuring regulatory compliance, and safeguarding digital systems in an interconnected world (Ali et al., 2020).

Authentication Protocols

Authentication protocols are essential for digital security, verifying user and device identities for secure access to sensitive data and applications. Password-Based

Figure 5. Enhancing authentication protocols for robust security

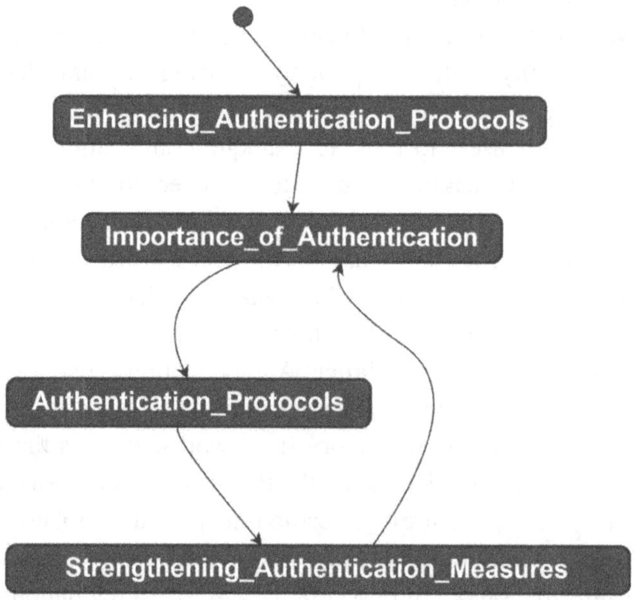

Authentication Protocol, a common method, uses a unique combination of username and password to authenticate users. However, this method has limitations, including vulnerability to brute-force attacks and password reuse (Panda & Chattopadhyay, 2020).

Multi-Factor Authentication (MFA) and Biometric Authentication are two methods of authentication that enhance security by requiring users to provide multiple authentication factors, such as passwords, biometric data, or one-time passcodes. MFA reduces the risk of unauthorized access by requiring multiple factors to be compromised. Biometric authentication, on the other hand, uses unique physiological or behavioral characteristics, offering high security and convenience.

OAuth and OpenID Connect are popular authentication protocols for secure web-based applications and APIs. OAuth allows users to grant third-party applications limited access without disclosing their credentials, while OpenID Connect provides identity verification services. Security Assertion Markup Language (SAML) is a protocol used for exchanging authentication and authorization data between identity providers and service providers, enabling single sign-on (SSO) functionality.

Authentication protocols are crucial for digital system security and integrity by verifying user and device identities. Robust authentication measures protect sensitive data, prevent unauthorized access, and build trust with users and stakeholders.

Strengthening Authentication Measures

Multi-factor, biometric, and blockchain-based authentication methods enhance security measures, mitigate unauthorized access risks, protect sensitive data, and build trust with users and stakeholders by enhancing security posture in digital environments (Ali et al., 2020).

- ***Multi-factor Authentication (MFA):*** Multi-factor authentication (MFA) enhances security by requiring users to provide multiple authentication factors to verify their identity. These factors typically include something the user knows (e.g., password), something they have (e.g., smartphone or security token), or something they are (e.g., biometric data). By combining multiple factors, MFA significantly reduces the risk of unauthorized access, as attackers would need to compromise multiple authentication methods to gain entry. Organizations can implement MFA across various systems and applications to provide an additional layer of security beyond traditional password-based authentication.
- ***Biometric Authentication:*** Biometric authentication leverages unique physiological or behavioral characteristics, such as fingerprints, facial features, iris patterns, or voiceprints, to verify user identities. Biometric authentication offers a high level of security and convenience, as it is based on traits that are inherently difficult to replicate or steal. By capturing and comparing biometric data during the authentication process, organizations can ensure that only authorized individuals are granted access to sensitive systems and resources. Biometric authentication can be integrated into various devices and applications, including smartphones, laptops, and physical access control systems, to enhance security while improving user experience.
- ***Blockchain-based Authentication Solutions:*** Blockchain-based authentication solutions leverage decentralized ledger technology to securely verify and authenticate user identities without relying on centralized authorities. By distributing authentication data across a network of nodes, blockchain-based authentication solutions provide enhanced security, transparency, and immutability. Each authentication event is cryptographically recorded on the blockchain, making it tamper-proof and resistant to unauthorized modifications. Blockchain-based authentication can be particularly beneficial in scenarios where traditional authentication methods are vulnerable to central points of failure or single points of compromise. These solutions offer decentralized and trustless authentication mechanisms, empowering users to control their digital identities while mitigating the risk of identity theft and fraud.

INTEGRATING SECURITY MEASURES ACROSS EMERGING TECHNOLOGIES

Organizations are increasingly adopting technologies like serverless computing, IoT, and advanced authentication protocols to enhance their security posture. These technologies offer scalability, cost-effectiveness, and simplified application workload management, while IoT enables real-time data collection and analysis from interconnected devices. Authentication protocols like multi-factor authentication and biometric authentication ensure secure access to digital resources. However, the convergence of these technologies also introduces new security considerations and potential attack vectors that must be addressed to mitigate potential risks and vulnerabilities. The figure 6 demonstrates the integration of security measures across emerging technologies (Lau, 2020).

Integrating serverless computing, IoT, and authentication protocols presents a security challenge due to the abstraction of underlying infrastructure, vulnerability of IoT devices to compromise due to lack of built-in security features and firmware updates, and the need for innovative approaches to verify device identities, as traditional authentication methods may not be suitable for IoT devices (Saxena et al., 2021).

Organizations must implement comprehensive security strategies to address security gaps in emerging technologies, including main components (Laufs et al., 2020).

i. Secure Development Practices: Implement secure coding practices and threat modeling techniques to identify and mitigate security vulnerabilities in serverless applications, IoT devices, and authentication protocols, and conduct code reviews, static analysis, and security testing throughout the development lifecycle.

Figure 6. Integrating security measures across emerging technologies

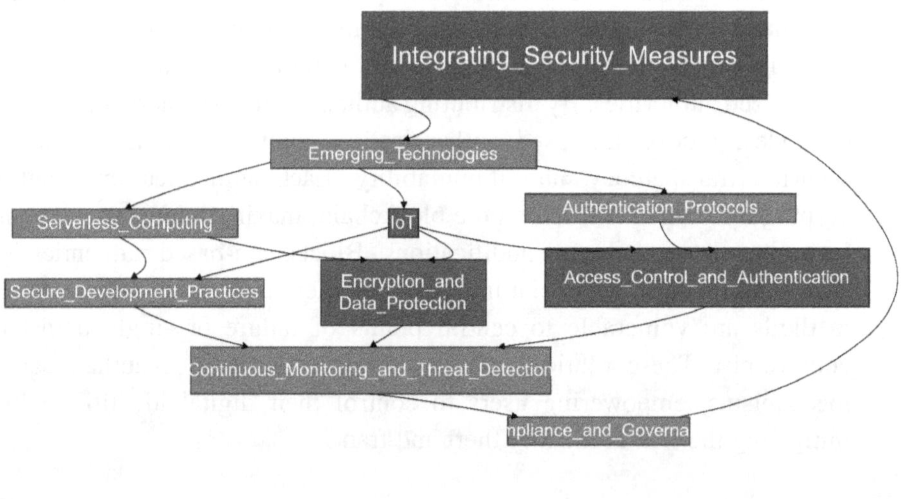

ii. Encryption and Data Protection: To protect sensitive data from unauthorized access, it is crucial to use strong encryption algorithms and management practices, as well as secure communication protocols like TLS for data transmission between IoT devices, serverless functions, and backend systems.
iii. Access Control and Authentication: Implement robust access control mechanisms to restrict sensitive resources based on user roles, permissions, and device identities. Implement multi-factor authentication and biometric authentication solutions to securely verify user and device identities, reducing unauthorized access and identity theft.
iv. Continuous Monitoring and Threat Detection: Implement monitoring and logging solutions to analyze events, logs, and metrics from serverless functions, IoT devices, and authentication systems, and utilize intrusion detection and prevention systems to monitor network traffic and respond to potential security incidents.
v. Compliance and Governance: The organization must adhere to regulatory standards like GDPR, HIPAA, and PCI DSS, and establish risk management policies, incident response, and security awareness training to foster a secure culture.

Integrating security measures across emerging technologies can help organizations mitigate risks, protect sensitive data, and enhance digital ecosystem resilience. By adopting a proactive approach, organizations can utilize serverless computing, IoT, and authentication protocols while addressing potential security challenges and ensuring digital asset integrity and confidentiality.

CONCLUSION

This chapter explores the integration of emerging technologies like serverless computing, IoT, and advanced authentication protocols, emphasizing the need for comprehensive security strategies. As organizations adopt these technologies for innovation, efficiency, and customer experience, it's crucial to prioritize security and mitigate potential risks. The convergence of these technologies presents both opportunities and challenges, including scalability, flexibility, and convenience, but also introduces new security concerns like data privacy, access control, and threat detection.

The chapter discusses security measures for serverless architectures, IoT ecosystems, and authentication protocols. It emphasizes the need for a multi-layered approach, including encryption techniques, access control, continuous monitoring, and threat detection strategies. Integrating security measures across emerging technologies is crucial for holistic protection and resilience. Implementing secure development practices, encryption, data protection mechanisms, robust access control, continuous monitoring, threat detection solutions, and compliance frameworks can enhance security posture and minimize security breaches.

The integration of security measures across emerging technologies necessitates a proactive, collaborative approach involving stakeholders from IT, security, development, and compliance. By prioritizing security, adopting best practices, and fostering a culture of security awareness, organizations can effectively utilize these technologies, address security challenges, and safeguard their digital assets.

ABBREVIATIONS

AES - Advanced Encryption Standard
API - Application Programming Interface
AWS - Amazon Web Services
CCPA - California Consumer Privacy Act
DD - Denial of Service
DSS - Data Security Standard
GDPR - General Data Protection Regulation
HIPAA - Health Insurance Portability and Accountability Act
HSM - Hardware Security Module
HTTP - Hypertext Transfer Protocol
IAM - Identity and Access Management
ID - Identity
IDPS - Intrusion Detection and Prevention System
IDS - Intrusion Detection System
II - Information Infrastructure
IP - Internet Protocol
IT - Information Technology
MFA - Multi-Factor Authentication
OA - Open Authorization
PCI - Payment Card Industry
RASP - Runtime Application Self-Protection
RBAC - Role-Based Access Control
SAML - Security Assertion Markup Language
SQL - Structured Query Language
SSO - Single Sign-On
TLS - Transport Layer Security
US - United States

REFERENCES

Ahmadi, S. (2024). Challenges and Solutions in Network Security for Serverless Computing. *International Journal of Current Science Research and Review*, *7*(01), 218–229. doi:10.47191/ijcsrr/V7-i1-23

Ali, Z., Ghani, A., Khan, I., Chaudhry, S. A., Islam, S. H., & Giri, D. (2020). A robust authentication and access control protocol for securing wireless healthcare sensor networks. *Journal of Information Security and Applications*, *52*, 102502. doi:10.1016/j.jisa.2020.102502

Azrour, M., Mabrouki, J., Guezzaz, A., & Farhaoui, Y. (2021). New enhanced authentication protocol for internet of things. *Big Data Mining and Analytics*, *4*(1), 1–9. doi:10.26599/BDMA.2020.9020010

Azrour, M., Mabrouki, J., Guezzaz, A., & Kanwal, A. (2021). Internet of things security: Challenges and key issues. *Security and Communication Networks*, *2021*, 1–11. doi:10.1155/2021/5533843

Benedict, S. (2020). Serverless blockchain-enabled architecture for iot societal applications. *IEEE Transactions on Computational Social Systems*, *7*(5), 1146–1158. doi:10.1109/TCSS.2020.3008995

Cassel, G. A. S., Rodrigues, V. F., da Rosa Righi, R., Bez, M. R., Nepomuceno, A. C., & da Costa, C. A. (2022). Serverless computing for Internet of Things: A systematic literature review. *Future Generation Computer Systems*, *128*, 299–316. doi:10.1016/j.future.2021.10.020

Christidis, A., Moschoyiannis, S., Hsu, C.-H., & Davies, R. (2020). Enabling serverless deployment of large-scale ai workloads. *IEEE Access : Practical Innovations, Open Solutions*, *8*, 70150–70161. doi:10.1109/ACCESS.2020.2985282

Cinar, B. (2023). The Rise of Serverless Architectures: Security Challenges and Best Practices. *Asian Journal of Research in Computer Science*, *16*(4), 194–210. doi:10.9734/ajrcos/2023/v16i4382

de Oliveira, A. (n.d.). *Securing Weak Points in Serverless Architectures*. Research Gate.

Edlund, E. (2022). *Creating a Serverless Application Using the Serverless Framework and React: Deploying a serverless back-end to different cloud providers*. Research Gate.

Enes, J., Expósito, R. R., & Touriño, J. (2020). Real-time resource scaling platform for big data workloads on serverless environments. *Future Generation Computer Systems*, *105*, 361–379. doi:10.1016/j.future.2019.11.037

Golec, M., Gill, S. S., Golec, M., Xu, M., Ghosh, S. K., Kanhere, S. S., Rana, O., & Uhlig, S. (2023). BlockFaaS: Blockchain-enabled serverless computing framework for AI-driven IoT healthcare applications. *Journal of Grid Computing*, *21*(4), 63. doi:10.1007/s10723-023-09691-w

Koschel, A., Klassen, S., Jdiya, K., Schaaf, M., & Astrova, I. (2021). Cloud computing: Serverless. *2021 12th International Conference on Information, Intelligence, Systems & Applications (IISA)*, (pp. 1–7). Research Gate.

Kumar, M. (2018). *Serverless computing for the Internet of Things*. Research Gate.

Kumari, A., Sahoo, B., Behera, R. K., Misra, S., & Sharma, M. M. (2021). Evaluation of integrated frameworks for optimizing qos in serverless computing. *Computational Science and Its Applications–ICCSA 2021: 21st International Conference, Cagliari, Italy, September 13–16, 2021. Proceedings*, *21*(Part VII), 277–288.

Lau, A. (2020). New technologies used in COVID-19 for business survival: Insights from the Hotel Sector in China. *Information Technology & Tourism*, *22*(4), 497–504. doi:10.1007/s40558-020-00193-z

Laufs, J., Borrion, H., & Bradford, B. (2020). Security and the smart city: A systematic review. *Sustainable Cities and Society*, *55*, 102023. doi:10.1016/j.scs.2020.102023

Li, X., Leng, X., & Chen, Y. (2022). Securing Serverless Computing: Challenges, Solutions, and Opportunities. *IEEE Network*.

Li, Y., Lin, Y., Wang, Y., Ye, K., & Xu, C. (2022). Serverless computing: State-of-the-art, challenges and opportunities. *IEEE Transactions on Services Computing*, *16*(2), 1522–1539. doi:10.1109/TSC.2022.3166553

Lin, C., & Khazaei, H. (2020). Modeling and optimization of performance and cost of serverless applications. *IEEE Transactions on Parallel and Distributed Systems*, *32*(3), 615–632. doi:10.1109/TPDS.2020.3028841

Lynn, T., Rosati, P., Lejeune, A., & Emeakaroha, V. (2017). A preliminary review of enterprise serverless cloud computing (function-as-a-service) platforms. *2017 IEEE International Conference on Cloud Computing Technology and Science (CloudCom)*, (pp. 162–169). IEEE. 10.1109/CloudCom.2017.15

Panda, P. K., & Chattopadhyay, S. (2020). A secure mutual authentication protocol for IoT environment. *Journal of Reliable Intelligent Environments*, *6*(2), 79–94. doi:10.1007/s40860-020-00098-y

Rajan, A. P. (2020). A review on serverless architectures-function as a service (FaaS) in cloud computing. [Telecommunication Computing Electronics and Control]. *Telkomnika*, *18*(1), 530–537. doi:10.12928/telkomnika.v18i1.12169

Saxena, S., Bhushan, B., & Ahad, M. A. (2021). Blockchain based solutions to secure IoT: Background, integration trends and a way forward. *Journal of Network and Computer Applications*, *181*, 103050. doi:10.1016/j.jnca.2021.103050

Scheuner, J., & Leitner, P. (2020). Function-as-a-service performance evaluation: A multivocal literature review. *Journal of Systems and Software*, *170*, 110708. doi:10.1016/j.jss.2020.110708

Shafiei, H., Khonsari, A., & Mousavi, P. (2022). Serverless computing: A survey of opportunities, challenges, and applications. *ACM Computing Surveys*, *54*(11s), 1–32. doi:10.1145/3510611

Somu, N., Daw, N., Bellur, U., & Kulkarni, P. (2020). Panopticon: A comprehensive benchmarking tool for serverless applications. *2020 International Conference on COMmunication Systems & NETworkS (COMSNETS)*, (pp. 144–151). IEEE. 10.1109/COMSNETS48256.2020.9027346

Tawalbeh, L., Muheidat, F., Tawalbeh, M., & Quwaider, M. (2020). IoT Privacy and security: Challenges and solutions. *Applied Sciences (Basel, Switzerland)*, *10*(12), 4102. doi:10.3390/app10124102

Thilakarathne, N. N. (2020). Security and privacy issues in iot environment. *International Journal of Engineering and Management Research*, *10*(1), 10. doi:10.31033/ijemr.10.1.5

Velmurugadass, P., Dhanasekaran, S., Anand, S. S., & Vasudevan, V. (2021). Enhancing Blockchain security in cloud computing with IoT environment using ECIES and cryptography hash algorithm. *Materials Today: Proceedings*, *37*, 2653–2659. doi:10.1016/j.matpr.2020.08.519

Chapter 11
Enhancing Cloud and IoT Security:
Leveraging IoT Technology for Multi-Factor User Authentication

C. V. Suresh Babu
https://orcid.org/0000-0002-8474-2882
Hindustan Institute of Technology and Science, India

Abhinaba Pal
https://orcid.org/0009-0004-1727-7628
Hindustan Institute of Technology and Science, India

A. Vinith
Hindustan Institute of Technology and Science, India

Venkatraman Muralirajan
Hindustan Institute of Technology and Science, India

Sriram Gunasekaran
Hindustan Institute of Technology and Science, India

ABSTRACT

As the world becomes increasingly reliant on cloud computing and the internet of things (IoT), ensuring the security of sensitive data and access to cloud resources is paramount. This chapter focuses on innovative approaches to user authentication within the context of "security frameworks for cloud and IoT systems." The proposed chapter discusses how IoT technology can be harnessed to develop a robust, multi-factor authentication system tailored to manage cloud computing interfaces. The chapter explores the vulnerabilities of traditional single-factor authentication methods, emphasizing the critical need for enhanced security measures. It highlights the integration of biometric authentication, secure communication protocols, and the use of IoT devices for secure user authentication. The chapter also covers topics like behavioral analytics, user-friendly interfaces, and compliance with data privacy regulations to create a comprehensive approach to enhancing security in cloud and IoT environments.

DOI: 10.4018/979-8-3693-0766-3.ch011

INTRODUCTION

In an era characterized by increasing digitization and the ever-expanding digital landscape, the security of our online interactions and data has become a paramount concern. The rapid expansion of cloud computing and the Internet of Things (IoT) has transformed the landscape of data storage, access, and processing (Suresh Babu, Simon, & Kumar, 2023). Nevertheless, the heightened reliance on cloud-based services has raised substantial concerns about safeguarding sensitive information. The need for robust and sophisticated authentication methods is more critical than ever before. A primary vulnerability inherent in single-factor authentication lies in its proneness to password-related attacks. Malicious actors frequently deploy diverse techniques, such as brute force attacks, dictionary attacks, and credential phishing, to exploit weak or easily guessable passwords. Furthermore, users commonly recycle passwords across multiple accounts, compounding the potential harm if one set of credentials is compromised. This chapter begins by highlighting the vulnerabilities of single-factor authentication, underscoring the prevalent risks posed by common attacks and emphasizing the security challenges associated with password-related breaches and password reuse. It then pivots towards the exploration of IoT technology as a multifaceted solution to these issues, offering insights into how IoT can bolster authentication security. We then delve into the intricacies of multi-factor or (2FA) authentication which requires a user to provide at least two or more authentication factors to prove their identity so that even if one credential becomes compromised, unauthorized users will be unable to meet the second authentication requirement and hence be unable to gain access to a facility or system. Our subject matter then encompasses the integration of biometric authentication into IoT-based systems, presenting a detailed examination of its advantages and challenges. Additionally, we address the pivotal role of secure communication protocols in IoT authentication, showcasing the implementation of encryption and secure channels. Moreover, we explore the significance of user-friendly interfaces and user education in the context of IoT-based authentication, offering design principles and educational strategies. The chapter then transitions to the importance of compliance and regulation adherence, emphasizing the need to align with data privacy and security regulations and providing case studies to illustrate practical compliance. Lastly, it concludes with strategies for large-scale networking in constarined environments and their reletive merits.

CHAPTER OBJECTIVES

The chapter "Integration of the Internet of Things and Cloud: Security Challenges and Solutions – A Review" delves into a multifaceted exploration of security concerns and solutions within the realm of cloud and Internet of Things (IoT) systems (Suresh Babu, 2023). The following points outline the key objectives of this review, each contributing to a comprehensive understanding of the subject matter.Firstly, the chapter aims to scrutinize the vulnerabilities inherent in traditional single-factor authentication methods when applied to cloud and IoT systems. This analysis will shed light on the limitations of relying solely on passwords or other single means of authentication, which are often insufficient to protect sensitive data in the complex and interconnected cloud and IoT environments.Secondly, it seeks to uncover the pivotal role of IoT technology in elevating security through multi-factor authentication in cloud computing interfaces. IoT can offer unique identifiers and secure channels for multi-factor authentication, providing an added layer of security that is essential in today's digital landscape.The chapter also explores the integration of biometric authentication and secure communication protocols within IoT-based authentication mechanisms. By examining the advantages of biometrics and robust communication, the review aims to highlight the potential for enhancing security while providing a more seamless user experience. Furthermore, the chapter addresses the importance of user-friendly interfaces and user education for successful IoT-based authentication. These aspects play a critical role in ensuring that security measures are not only robust but also accessible and understandable for end-users. Lastly, it emphasizes the significance of continuous monitoring, incident response, and compliance with regulations in safeguarding cloud and IoT systems. This section underscores the need for proactive security measures, rapid responses to incidents, and adherence to industry and legal standards to maintain the integrity and security of these interconnected systems.In sum, this chapter offers a comprehensive examination of security challenges and solutions within the context of cloud and IoT systems, highlighting the need for evolving authentication methods, biometrics, user-friendly interfaces, and continuous vigilance to protect the integrity of these increasingly interconnected technologies.

TARGET AUDIENCE

This chapter, "Integration of the Internet of Things and Cloud: Security Challenges and Solutions – A Review," offers invaluable insights and knowledge for a diverse range of readers, catering to the needs and interests of various professional and educational backgrounds. For researchers and practitioners engaged in the fields of cloud computing, IoT, and cybersecurity, this chapter serves as a critical resource. It provides a comprehensive analysis of security challenges and innovative solutions within the context of these rapidly evolving technologies. By exploring vulnerabilities, authentication methods, and incident response strategies, it equips professionals with a deeper understanding of how to secure cloud and IoT systems effectively. Information technology professionals seeking innovative solutions for securing cloud and IoT systems will find this chapter to be a practical guide. It presents real-world strategies and best practices for implementing security measures that are tailored to the unique demands of interconnected systems. By delving into multi-factor authentication, biometrics, and continuous monitoring, this chapter offers actionable insights to enhance their security efforts. Educators and students interested in emerging technologies and security in cloud and IoT environments will benefit from this chapter as well. It provides a structured overview of the evolving security landscape in these domains, making it an excellent resource for academic purposes. Furthermore, it introduces students to the practical applications of security principles, enhancing their understanding of real-world security challenges and solutions. In summary, "Integration of the Internet of Things and Cloud: Security Challenges and Solutions – A Review" is a valuable resource that caters to a wide audience. It empowers researchers and practitioners with in-depth knowledge, offers actionable insights to IT professionals, and provides educational material for students and educators. By addressing the security concerns and solutions in cloud and IoT systems, this chapter contributes to a deeper understanding of the critical intersections of technology, security, and innovation in our interconnected digital world.

INTRODUCTION TO CLOUD AND IoT SECURITY CHALLENGES

In the world of cloud computing and the Internet of Things (IoT), the intertwining of technologies has ushered in a new era of connectivity and convenience. However, with this evolution comes a host of intricate security challenges that organizations must grapple with. In this pivotal chapter of our exploration, we shine a light on the multifaceted dimensions of Cloud and IoT security. One of the central themes of this chapter is the perpetual evolution of threats and vulnerabilities. Cyber adversaries are becoming increasingly sophisticated, constantly adapting their tactics to exploit weaknesses in cloud and IoT systems (Aldowah et al., 2019). From data breaches to DDoS attacks, the threat landscape is diverse and ever-changing. But it's not all doom and gloom. We also delve into the solutions and strategies that are reshaping the security landscape. Organizations are deploying robust encryption, multi-factor authentication, and advanced intrusion detection systems to fortify their defenses (Al-Fuqaha et al., 2015). Moreover, the adoption of proactive security measures, threat intelligence, and constant monitoring are essential components of mitigating risks. As we journey through this chapter, you'll gain valuable insights into how organizations are navigating this dynamic ecosystem. Learn about the best practices and real-world case studies that demonstrate how cloud and IoT security challenges are being addressed, ensuring the confidentiality, integrity, and availability of data and devices in an interconnected world and for that we must need to know about cloud computing architecture.

Overview of the Security Challenges in Cloud and IoT Systems

Security challenges in cloud and IoT systems within real-time applications are a critical concern, impacting data privacy, integrity, and availability. These systems face vulnerabilities like data breaches, unauthorized entry, and distributed denial of service (DDoS) attacks. For instance, a smart city application employing IoT devices and cloud infrastructure for traffic monitoring and streetlight control can be exploited, leading to accidents or traffic jams through manipulated data or unauthorized access. Robust security measures, including authentication, encryption, and intrusion detection, are essential to safeguard data and control systems in real-time, preventing potential disasters. Continuous monitoring and updates are necessary to address evolving threats in cloud and IoT environments (Ometov, Bezzateev, Mäkitalo, Andreev, Mikkonen, & Koucheryavy, 2018). Some of the security challenges in cloud and IoT systems:

- **Data Manipulation Risks:**
    - Manipulated data from IoT devices can lead to false traffic information.

Figure 1. Cloud architecture (Sadeeq et al., 2021)

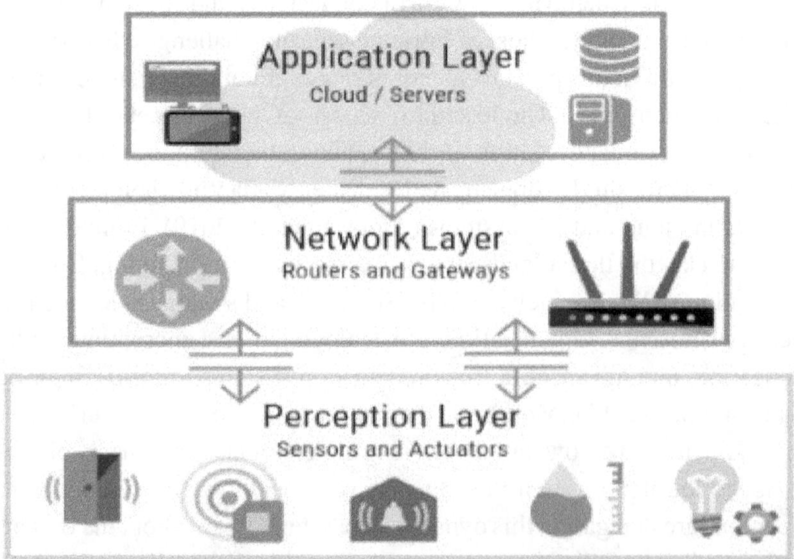

- ○ False data can result in traffic accidents and congestion.
- **Unauthorized Access Threats:**
    - ○ Inadequate security can permit unauthorized access to control systems.
    - ○ Unauthorized access can disrupt streetlights and traffic management.
- **Authentication Protocols:**
    - ○ Strong authentication methods ensure only authorized personnel can access systems.
    - ○ Examples include multi-factor authentication, biometric recognition, and secure access tokens.
- **Data Encryption:**
    - ○ Encrypting data in transit and at rest protects data integrity and confidentiality.
    - ○ It prevents data manipulation and unauthorized access.
- **Intrusion Detection Systems (IDS):**
    - ○ IDS continuously monitor for unusual activities or intrusion attempts.
    - ○ Prompt detection and response mitigate potential security breaches.
- **Continuous Updates:**
    - ○ Regular updates for software, security protocols, and IoT device firmware are crucial.
    - ○ Updates patch vulnerabilities and adapt to evolving threats.

Figure 2. Types of attacks (Balogh et al., 2021)

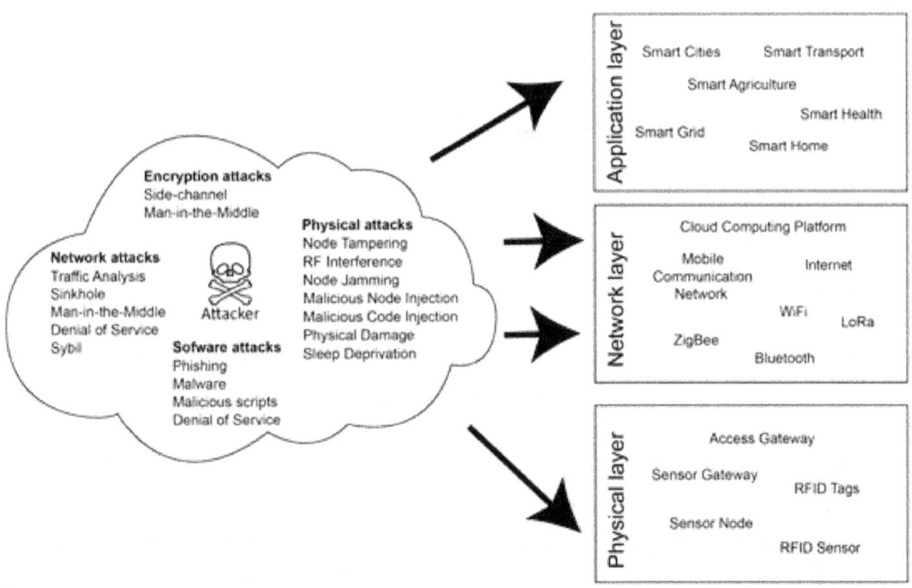

The Need for Enhanced User Authentication in Such Environments

Enhanced user authentication is imperative in contemporary digital environments due to the escalating threats to personal and sensitive data (Ometov, Petrov, Bezzateev, Andreev, Koucheryavy, & Gerla, 2019). As technology continues to advance, so do the techniques employed by malicious actors seeking unauthorized access to systems and information. In this context, traditional username-password combinations fall short in providing robust protection. Enhanced user authentication methods, such as multi-factor authentication (MFA) and biometrics, play a pivotal role in fortifying security (Ometov, Petrov, Bezzateev, Andreev, Koucheryavy, & Gerla, 2019). MFA demands multiple forms of verification, making it significantly more challenging for unauthorized users to gain entry (Das et al., 2020). Meanwhile, biometrics leverages unique physical traits like fingerprints or facial recognition, rendering it nearly impossible for fraudsters to mimic. Moreover, with the increasing reliance on online services, such as e-commerce, banking, and healthcare, ensuring user identity becomes paramount (Suresh Babu, Akshayah, & Janapriyan, 2023). These services handle sensitive information, including financial data and medical records, making the need for robust authentication practices essential to prevent data breaches and identity theft.

In summary, the need for enhanced user authentication in digital environments stems from the ever-evolving landscape of cyber threats and the increasing value of personal data (Suresh Babu & Akshara, 2023). By embracing advanced authentication methods, organizations can bolster security and protect the integrity of their systems and the privacy of their users.

VULNERABILITIES IN SINGLE-FACTOR AUTHENTICATION

Single-factor authentication, a widely adopted method for confirming a user's identity, is deceptively simple yet riddled with inherent vulnerabilities that can undermine digital security (Ometov, Bezzateev, Mäkitalo, Andreev, Mikkonen, & Koucheryavy, 2018). In this conventional approach, access to systems and accounts relies solely on something the user knows, often a password. However, this simplicity renders it susceptible to an array of threats and weaknesses, rendering it inadequate for protecting sensitive information in our interconnected digital landscape.

Password-based single-factor authentication is vulnerable to various forms of attack, including brute force, phishing, and password leaks. Users, too, often fall victim to common pitfalls such as using weak or easily guessable passwords, or even reusing them across multiple accounts (Fernando et al., 2023). These vulnerabilities can result in unauthorized access, data breaches, and compromised personal information.

Recognizing these risks, it becomes evident that a transition to more resilient authentication methods, like multi-factor authentication (MFA), is imperative. MFA's additional layers of verification enhance security by demanding multiple forms of proof, significantly reducing the likelihood of unauthorized access (Das et al., 2020). This exploration delves into the vulnerabilities of single-factor authentication, emphasizing the critical need to adopt MFA for robust security and risk mitigation in the digital age.

Exploration of Common Attacks on Single-Factor Authentication

Single-factor authentication, particularly when relying solely on passwords, is susceptible to a range of common attacks, which can compromise digital security and expose sensitive information. Understanding these threats is crucial for organizations and individuals to better protect themselves (Ometov, Bezzateev, Mäkitalo, Andreev, Mikkonen, & Koucheryavy, 2018). Here, we explore some of the most prevalent attacks on single-factor authentication:

- **Brute Force Attacks:** These are malicious attempts to gain access to a system or account by systematically trying all possible combinations of passwords or passphrases until the correct one is found. These attacks are time-consuming but can succeed if passwords are weak or not adequately protected.

Figure 3. Authentication examples (Ometov, Bezzateev, Mäkitalo, Andreev, Mikkonen, & Koucheryavy, 2018)

- **Phishing:** It is a deceptive online tactic where attackers impersonate trusted entities via email, websites, or messages to trick individuals into revealing personal information, such as login credentials or financial data. These fraudulent communications aim to exploit trust and manipulate recipients into unwittingly sharing sensitive details.
- **Keyloggers:** These are malicious software or hardware tools designed to clandestinely record and monitor keystrokes on a computer or mobile device. These programs capture everything a user types, including passwords, credit card numbers, and other sensitive information. Attackers can then access the collected data, compromising the user's privacy and security. Keyloggers are often used in cyberattacks, espionage, or by malicious actors seeking unauthorized access to personal or financial information (Suresh Babu & Srisakthi, 2023).
- **Man-in-the-Middle (MitM):** These are cybersecurity threats where an attacker secretly intercepts or alters communications between two parties without their knowledge. By inserting themselves into the data flow, the attacker can eavesdrop, modify, or steal sensitive information exchanged between the legitimate parties. MitM attacks are commonly executed on public Wi-Fi networks and can jeopardize the confidentiality and integrity of data, making encryption and secure connections vital for protection.

Risks Associated With Password-Related Attacks and Password Reuse

Password-related attacks and password reuse pose significant risks to individuals and organizations in the digital age. Password-related attacks encompass various threats,

Figure 4. Dictionary attack (Chen et al., 2019)

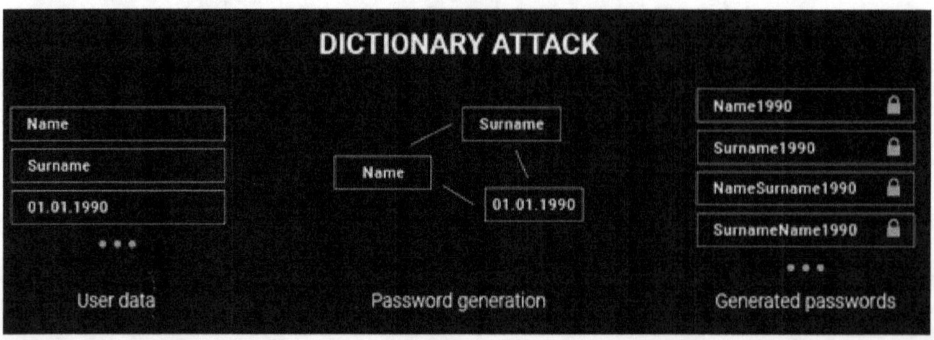

including brute force attacks, phishing, and credential stuffing, which can lead to unauthorized access, data breaches, and compromised security (Nigam et al., 2022).

One key risk is the vulnerability of weak or easily guessable passwords, which make it relatively simple for attackers to breach accounts. Password reuse exacerbates this risk, as compromised credentials from one service can be leveraged to infiltrate other accounts if users employ the same passwords across multiple platforms (Karthick Kumar et al., 2022). Additionally, the human tendency to choose memorable but insecure passwords and not frequently update them further compounds the problem.

Furthermore, attackers often obtain password databases from data breaches and use these credentials for malicious purposes. When users reuse passwords, they create a domino effect where a breach in one system can potentially lead to unauthorized access to numerous other accounts (Al-Doori & Al-Gailani, 2023).

MULTI-FACTOR AUTHENTICATION (MFA) w.r.t IoT

The integration of MFA into IoT technology has the potential to significantly bolster security and user experience in today's interconnected world. IoT devices, such as smartphones, smartwatches, and biometric sensors, can play a pivotal role in reinforcing MFA (Das et al., 2020). The absence of robust authentication mechanisms has led to several high-profile incidents in the past, underscoring the critical need for a layered security approach in IoT ecosystems, few of which has been stated as follows:

(a) ***Case Study 1:*** *Mirai Botnet Attack (2016):* One of the most notorious incidents illustrating the vulnerabilities of IoT devices without MFA is the Mirai botnet attack in 2016. Mirai exploited default usernames and passwords on insecure IoT devices, gaining control over a vast network of compromised devices to launch large-scale Distributed Denial of Service (DDoS) attacks (Antonakakis et al., 2017). MFA implementation could have thwarted the attack by requiring an additional authentication factor whose absence directly lead to:

- *Default Credentials Exploitation:* Mirai capitalized on the prevalent use of default usernames and passwords on IoT devices. These devices often had unchanged, easily guessable credentials, making them susceptible to Mirai's scanning and exploitation tactics.
- *Lack of Device Identity Verification:* Mirai's success was partially due to the absence of robust device identity verification. IoT devices often lacked mechanisms to ensure that only legitimate, authorized devices could access and communicate within the network.

Mirai's propagation method involved scanning a broad range of IP addresses, attempting to connect to IoT devices using a predefined list of username and password combinations. Once a vulnerable device was identified, Mirai employed a variety of exploits to gain access and install its malware payload. Mirai also employed a decentralized C2 infrastructure using a peer-to-peer network (Poblete, 2018), making it challenging to dismantle. This structure enabled the botnet to persist even if certain nodes were taken down. The C2 servers orchestrated coordinated DDoS attacks by instructing infected devices to flood targeted servers with traffic.

(b) ***Case Study 2:*** *Jeep Cherokee Hack (2015):* This was not a full-blown catastrophe but rather an experiment conducted within a black-box which ended up being quite illuminating. In July 2015, cybersecurity researchers Charlie Miller and Chris Valasek demonstrated the potential dangers of insecure connected vehicles by remotely compromising a Jeep Cherokee's sophisticated infotainment system (designed to receive over-the-air updates), allowing remote access and control (Poblete, 2018). Miller and Valasek identified a vulnerability in the Uconnect system, which provided a gateway for unauthorized access to the vehicle's Controller Area Network (CAN) bus. This critical flaw widened the attack surface, enabling the compromise of essential vehicle functions.

- *Vulnerability exploitation and Remote Attack Vector:* The researchers exploited a flaw in the Uconnect system that allowed them to remotely gain control over the vehicle's entertainment system. Subsequently, they pivoted to the CAN bus, manipulating the vehicle's electronic control units (ECUs) responsible for crucial functions such as steering, brakes, and transmission (Bajpai & Enbody, 2020). This demonstrated the potential for a malicious actor to take command of the vehicle's core systems. By leveraging the internet connectivity of the Uconnect system, the researchers demonstrated the feasibility of a remote attack. This scenario highlighted the risks associated with vehicles being constantly connected to the internet without adequate security measures.

With regards to prevention mechanisms in this particular case, implementing MFA for communication channels between the Uconnect system and external networks and authentication within the in-vehicle Controller Area Network (CAN) could have bolstered the overall security posture significantly.

The above incidents have prompted a collective effort to mitigate the overaching impact of such oversights and prevent similar future attacks. Manufacturers have begun emphasizing improved default security settings, while security professionals have started advocating for regular updates, strong authentication mechanisms, and network segmentation to minimize the attack surface.

Now in terms of implementing MFA from a top-down approach, one such solution involves IoT devices- themselves behaving as physical authentication tokens. They generate one-time passwords or codes that users need to enter, adding an extra layer of security (Kondoro et al., 2021). These tokens can be synchronized with various services, ensuring seamless and secure access (Ometov, Petrov, Bezzateev, Andreev, Koucheryavy, & Gerla, 2019). IoT devices, such as smartphones, smartwatches, and biometric sensors, can themselves play a pivotal role (Hammad et al., 2018) in reinforcing MFA as alluded to previously. Another application of IoT in MFA is through biometric authentication. Devices equipped with biometric features, such as fingerprint scanners and facial recognition, can serve as a robust authentication factor. Users can verify their identity through these unique biometric markers, making it considerably more challenging for unauthorized individuals to gain access to accounts and systems.

A Lightweight Solution to MFA

In recent times, a focus of MFA development has involved coming up wth more "lightweight" solutions which compensates for its time and resource utilization disadvantage as compared to its single-factor counterpart. Such proposals have involved the configuration of a Physically Unclonable Function (PUF) as part of the first factor of the MFA protocol (Noura et al., 2019). A PUF is a security primitive that leverages minuscule manufacturing variations in physical hardware to create unique digital fingerprints, making it immune to reverse engineering techniques. PUFs are used to securely generate and store cryptographic keys, allowing for the highest level of security for integrated circuits (ICs) and system-on-chips (SoCs). These unique device-specific measurements are obtained from silicon, and due to the inherent variations in silicon processing, every IC produced differs from one another, providing a reliable and unpredictable security solution. Now, this again happens to used in conjuction with a pseudo-random number (known as a "nonce") generated to prevent replay attacks and ensure the uniqueness of data (McGinthy et al., 2019). Nonces are commonly used in in the SSL/TLS handshake, where unique nonce values are exchanged between the client and the server to protect each connection from attacks or interventions. Additionally, nonces may be used as initialization vectors and in cryptographic hash functions to ensure the security of messages and data.

The system follows that- each IoT device is provisioned with a unique secret identifier, securely stored on the server. This identifier serves as the foundation for device-specific authentication. Then a random channel-derived nonce is generated and passed into the PUF contained in the IoT device. The PUF leverages the physical properties of the device to produce a unique response. This initial correspondance establishes the baseline for the device's authentication and forms the foundation for subsequent interactions. Following a round of substanciation, a new set of channel-derived parameters is generated parallely in an isolated manner. The updated correpondance values introduce variability into the authentication process for the next cycle, aligning with the dynamic nature of wireless channels all the while attaining the followng session key, which is in turn required to form the secret keys for the purpose of encryption. As for the 2nd factor of the MFA protocol, non-crytographic and non-sensitive parameters (still unique to individual hardware devices) such as power consumption, network packet transmission characterstics, signal-to-noise ratio (SNR), and propagation delay can be used to create a unique device idntity that is authenticated using ML algorithms. During the training phase, we feed model with labeled data, utilizing a random forest regressor, associating specific feature sets with known device identities. The model then learns to differentiate between legitimate and unauthorized devices based on the stated parameters.

Regulatory and Legal Compliances

Sensory subsystems are the building blocks of any large scale IoT network such as an Industrial IoT (IIoT) deployment and the integration of these sophisticated technologies have enhanced physical-security accross the industry from smart homes to manufacturing facilities (Ometov, Bezzateev, Mäkitalo, Andreev, Mikkonen, & Koucheryavy, 2018). One prime example is the utilization of smart cameras equipped with motion and facial recognition sensors. These devices can instantly detect unauthorized access or unusual activities, sending alerts to homeowners or security personnel in real-time. Moreover, environmental sensors, such as smoke and carbon monoxide detectors, play a crucial role in safeguarding homes and buildings by providing early warnings of potentially life-threatening situations. On a broader scale, IIoT devices like access control systems (ACS) and perimeter sensors are indispensable for protecting critical infrastructure. Access control systems manage and monitor entry points, ensuring that only authorized personnel gain access, while perimeter sensors can detect breaches and potential security threats in real-time (Wang et al., 2019). Physical access control systems (PACS) are a sub-catagory of ACS and refer to a collection of technologies that control physical access at federal agency buildings. These systems grant access to employees, contractors, and visitors, typically using identification cards, card readers, and other technologies to confirm identities and access rights (Yanushkevich et al., 2008). There are various types of PACS, including cloud-based access control, video management systems, biometric access, and proximity access control.

It is paramount for Government organizations to protect their physical security systems from cybersecurity risks. This includes recognizing the risks that can exist in physical security devices such as cameras, door controllers, and their monitoring systems and as these systems are increasingly connected to networks and IT infrastructure which is both a boon and a curse as alluded to before, they can be vulnerable to breaches. In the USA, the Interagency Security Committee (ISC) is responsible for setting policies and recommendations that govern physical security at nonmilitary federal facilities. Additionally, there are specific standards and regulations related to physical access control systems in federal buildings, such as the Federal Identity, Credential, and Access Management (FICAM)-compliant PACS and the Security Control Overlay of Special Publication 800-53 Revision 5 (Kurii & Opirskyy, 2022). The use of MFA in PACS is mandated by federal regulations, such as the NIST SP 800-171 (Toth & Toth, 2017), which requires all contractors to implement MFA on all network devices.

The integration of MFA into PACS aligns with the government's commitment to modernizing federal identities and access controls, as outlined in the various federal initiatives related to Federal Identity, Credential, and Access Management (FICAM).

The MFA Dilemma: Essential Privacy, Endless Hassle

Different industries have specific regulations that mandate the use of MFA to ensure data privacy and protection. For example, the Gramm–Leach–Bliley Act, which is an U.S federal law requires financial institutions to inform their customers about how they protect their data, and MFA is a crucial component of how they do so. The Act consists of three sections: the Financial Privacy Rule, the Safeguards Rule, and the Pretexting provisions (Karpf, 2017). The Safeguards Rule, in particular, requires covered companies to develop, implement, and maintain an information security program with administrative, technical, and physical safeguards designed to protect customer information. The GLBA's Safeguards Rule has been updated to strengthen financial institutions' privacy and security measures, including the implementation of multi-factor authentication (MFA) to access any information system or the handling of customer data. Also, with regards to other industry-specific regulations:

(a) Sarbanes-Oxley Act (SOX): for financial reporting, primarily deals with corporate accountability and financial transparency. Here, MFA helps enforce the requirement of SOX's passwords and acess credentials protection (Karpf, 2017). Noncompliance can result in fines, imprisonment, or both. While SOX does not lay down password policy requirements, security experts recommend that organizations follow password management best practices. Additionally, the principle of least privilege mandates that users are granted only the minimum level of access. By maintaining minimal access rights and removing unused or unnecessary permissions, organizations can use JIT (Just-in-Time) to further align with the least privilege principles for SOX compliance.

(b) PCI-DSS (Payment Card Industry Data Security Standard): is a set of security controls designed to ensure the secure processing, storage, or transmission of credit card information and was created by the PCI Security Standards Council, an independent body founded by major payment card brands including Visa, MasterCard, American Express, Discover, and JCB International (Rizvi et al., 2020). With relevance to the scope of our subject matter, PCI-DSS Requirement 8 specifically addresses authentication measures (Pilewski & Pilewski, 2010). PCI DSS Requirement 8.4.1 mandates the implementation of multi-factor authentication (MFA) for all non-console access into the cardholder data environment (CDE) for personnel with administrative access. Additionally, Requirement 8.4.2 requires MFA for all access into the CDE, and Requirement 8.4.3 mandates MFA for all remote network access originating from outside the entity's network, including remote access by all personnel, third parties, and vendors. PCI DSS Requirement 8.3 also requires strong authentication for users and administrators, and passwords must be changed at least once every 90 days. Processes for identifying users and authenticating access to system components must be defined and consistently monitored and updated whenever required, and all involved personnel must understand their responsibilities. This requiremnt is ultimately designed to ensure that users are responsible for their actions and that transactions on critical data and systems can be performed and monitored by known and authorized individuals.

BIOMETRIC AUTHENTICATION INTEGRATION

The integration of biometric authentication into various systems and applications has emerged as a robust and highly secure solution for identity verification. Biometrics, which include fingerprint recognition, facial recognition, iris scanning, and voice authentication, offer a personalized and nearly foolproof means of ensuring that only authorized individuals gain access to sensitive data or physical locations. This technology enhances security by eliminating the need for passwords or PINs, which can be easily compromised (Nigam et al., 2022). Biometric authentication is particularly valuable in financial institutions, healthcare, and government sectors, as it not only ensures data protection but also simplifies user access, leading to a seamless and convenient user experience. Its precision and reliability make it an indispensable tool in our increasingly digital and security-conscious world (Hammad et al., 2018). However, challenges exist, such as concerns regarding privacy and data security, as biometric data is sensitive and needs strong protection. Additionally, the cost of implementing biometric systems and potential hardware limitations can be barriers to adoption. Striking a balance between security and privacy, and addressing implementation costs are ongoing challenges in harnessing the full potential of biometric authentication.

Novel Approaches to Biometric Authentication

Recent innovations in biometric authentication have moved beyond traditional methodologies to incorporate diverse physiological and behavioral characteristics of individuals. Emerging behavioral biometric techniques include analyzing keystroke dynamics (Raul et al., 2020) during typing activities and tracking mouse movement patterns. Novel vascular biometric methodologies examine vein configurations in palms and fingers. Other techniques leverage the distinctive anatomical properties of the human ear or employ electrocardiogram analysis to examine unique cardiac rhythms. Although still in early research stages, analysis of specific genomic sequences shows promise for future DNA-based biometrics (Zahid et al., 2019). Identification based on individual body odors utilizes scent chemical compounds and compositions, while gait recognition focuses on an individual's unique walking patterns and mechanics. Multiple brainwave-based techniques utilize electroencephalogram (EEG) recordings to discern authentication based on an individual's neural oscillations (Belgacem et al., 2015). Infrared thermography of facial heat patterns also shows potential as a biometric modality.

Intersetingly, EEG and Electrocardiogram (ECG) based biometric authentication can play an important role in IoT security despite being more cumbersome than some traditional MFA techniques for a few key reasons:

- *Sensitivity:* EEG and ECG biometrics offer very sensitive and difficult to spoof authentication factors related to an individual's physiology and health state. This makes them well suited to high security IoT applications in healthcare, finance, etc.
- *Passiveness:* EEG and ECG biometrics can operate passively without requiring active user participation once sensors are attached. This makes them suitable for continuous and implicit authentication in environments where active participation is difficult.
- *Difficult to Imitate:* Vital sign biometrics like EEG and ECG are very difficult to copy or mimic compared to passwords, fingerprints, or tokens. This can be highlighted with a study from Yokohama National University (Matsumoto et al., 2002) where they used "gummy" fingers or artificial fingers made of cheap and readily available gelatin and other materials that can be used to spoof fingerprint recognition systems.

Biometric authentication using ECG and EEG signals involves distinct processes for each physiological parameter. In ECG authentication, signals are acquired from the individual's chest, and relevant features like P-wave, QRS complex, and T-wave patterns (Sufi et al., 2010) are extracted to form a unique biometric template. This template is securely stored, and during authentication, newly acquired ECG signals are compared to verify the individual's identity. EEG authentication, on the other hand, requires recording brainwave activity using electrodes on the scalp. After pre-processing to eliminate noise, features such as frequency bands and spectral patterns are extracted for biometric template creation, which is securely stored. Subsequent authentication involves comparing newly recorded EEG signals with the stored template. These methods ultimately offer inherent uniqueness, continuous authentication, and resistance to spoofing attempts but the recording of such intimate biological information could lead to concerns about the protection and secure storage of the data itslef and such privacy concerns must be carefully addressed.

SECURE COMMUNICATION PROTOCOLS FOR IoT

As established abundantly in the preceding excerpts, the establishment of secure communication protocols is of paramount importance- not just in the realm of IoT, but for all communication channels in general. Several key protocols spearhead this notion, one of them being the Transport Layer Security (TLS), which ensures end-to-end encryption and authentication, making it exceptionally difficult for malicious actors to intercept or manipulate data transmissions. Another vital protocol is the Datagram Transport Layer Security (DTLS), which is optimized for IoT devices and provides secure communication in resource-constrained environments (Kondoro et al., 2021). Additionally, the Message Queuing Telemetry Transport (MQTT) protocol, when used with TLS, offers efficient and secure data exchange. These protocols collectively enable the protection of sensitive information and the integrity of IoT and IIoT ecosystems, ensuring their resilience against evolving cybersecurity threats (Siddiqui et al., 2018).

Solutions for Bandwidth-Constrained Environments

It just so happens that a sizable proportion of IoT deployments ocuur in bandwidth-limited environments, e.g. agricultural IoT for sustainable farming, where the deployment often involves a multitude of distributed sensor nodes across vast landscapes. These nodes are responsible for collecting diverse data points, ranging from soil moisture levels to weather conditions. The inherent challenge lies in the remoteness of these locations, which calls for a balancing act between optimizing network-load and the utilization of compute-intensive protocols- tailored for such environments.

Given the limitations of bandwidth in remote areas, traditional cloud-centric IoT architectures may prove impractical. In response, edge computing emerges as an optimal solution. This involves decentralizing computing resources, distributing processing capabilities closer to the data source (Nguyen et al., 2018). In this paradigm, nodes at the edge of the network, often embedded within the IoT devices themselves, perform preliminary data processing and analysis, facilitating real-time, localized decision-making. Centralized nodes, traditionally present in cloud-centric models, handle complex processing, storage, and management tasks. This not only reduces the need for extensive data transmission to centralized cloud servers but also minimizes latency and bandwidth usage.

The Constrained Application Protocol (CoAP) emerges as a key communication protocol for large-scale IoT deployments, especially in scenarios with bandwidth constraints. CoAP is designed to be lightweight, employing a simple request-response model similar to HTTP but tailored for resource-constrained devices (Arvind & Narayanan, 2019). Its efficiency is underscored by features like its compact binary message format, and support for asynchronous communication. Its key characteristics include:

- *Lightweight Header:* CoAP's header is designed to be concise, reducing overhead in communication and making it suitable for environments with limited bandwidth.
- *Resource Discovery:* CoAP allows for observing resources, enabling devices to receive notifications when the state of a resource changes. This is particularly useful in scenarios where real-time data updates are critical.
- *UDP as Transport Protocol:* CoAP uses DTLS as a secure protocol and UDP as a transfer protocol rather than TCP, hence reducing the communication overhead. (To implement a secure CoAP service, it is recommended to use DTLS, not to implement a custom authentication/encryption mechanism, and to utilize all 8-byte to generate random Tokens for Requests (Azzawi, 2017))

Access Management and Authentication Framework of CoAP

(a) Authentication Mechanisms:
   - *Pre-Shared Keys (PSK):* In CoAP, pre-shared keys can be employed for device authentication. Each device and server share a secret key, ensuring mutual authentication (Pérez et al., 2019). PSK is lightweight and suitable for such resource-constrained IoT devices.

- *Raw Public Key (RPK) and X.509 Certificates:* More robust authentication can be achieved using asymmetric cryptography. Devices can present raw public keys or X.509 certificates during the handshake process for mutual verification.
- *OAuth and Token-Based Authentication:* Leveraging OAuth 2.0 and token-based authentication mechanisms enhances CoAP security. Devices can obtain access tokens, and the CoAP server validates these tokens to grant or deny access.

(b) Access Control Framework:

- *Resource-Level Access Control:* CoAP resources can be protected at the granular level. Access control policies define which devices or users are allowed to perform specific operations on particular resources.
- *Role-Based Access Control (RBAC):* Implementing RBAC allows administrators to assign specific roles to devices or users (Hemdi & Deters, 2016). Each role carries a set of permissions, streamlining access control management.
- *Scopes and Groups:* Introducing scopes or groups categorizes devices with similar access requirements. Access control policies can then be applied at the scope or group level, reducing the complexity of managing individual permissions.

CONCLUSION AND FUTURE DIRECTIONS

The integration of of the diverse biometric authentication techniques in IoT-based systems has proven to be substantially benefitial for security and user convenience. It ensures reliable identity verification and eliminates the need for cumbersome passwords, enhancing the overall user experience. However, challenges, such as privacy concerns and implementation costs, must be addressed. Striking a balance between security and privacy and finding cost-effective solutions will be crucial.

Looking to the future, the ongoing development of biometric technology, including advancements in accuracy and the ability to handle diverse biometric traits, promises to expand its applications within IoT. Techniques such as emerging nailbed biometric approaches focus visual analysis on nailbed patterns and combining traditional palmprint analysis with examination of unique palm vein structures constitutes another novel direction. The distinctive blood vessel patterns of the human retina also provides identification potential. Additionally, the integration of artificial intelligence and machine learning can enhance biometric systems' adaptability and resilience against potential threats. Moreover, addressing privacy issues through robust regulations and ethical considerations will be pivotal. The fusion of biometrics and IoT is poised to revolutionize authentication methods, with innovations on the horizon that will further strengthen security while maintaining user-friendly experiences. As this field continues to evolve, collaboration among technology experts, regulators, and industry stakeholders will be essential in shaping a secure and privacy-conscious future.

Recapitulation of Key Findings and Takeaways

This chapter has navigated the multifaceted realm of cloud and IoT security and has involved the exploration of MFA within IoT ecosystems, which highlights its pivotal role in fortifying security, where the integration of diverse authentication factors, ranging from biometrics and physical parameters to non-cryptographic features, emerges as a comprehensive strategy to safeguard devices and networks. The chapter has delved into the pervasive security challenges intrinsic to the IoT landscape, encompassing device vulnerabilities, communication protocols, and key management issues, underscoring the imperative of comprehensive security measures to ensure the integrity, confidentiality, and availability of IoT systems. Real-life case studies, including the Mirai Botnet attack and the repercussions of lacking MFA, has helped us understand the urgency of robust security measures in the IoT domain, emphasizing the potential impact of security lapses and the need for proactive defenses. Aligning IoT security practices with regulatory frameworks such as SOX, PCI-DSS, HIPAA, and NIST guidelines have been explored, with a recognition that some regulations explicitly mandate MFA while others underscore the broader importance of access controls and robust security measures. Solutions, such as the proposal for PUFs and non-cryptographic parameters for authentication in IoT devices, offer innovative approaches that address key management challenges and improve system scalability. Exploring biometric authentication through ECG and EEG signals opens avenues for cutting-edge possibilities, providing unique and secure methods of user identification, particularly in healthcare and sensitive environments. The discussion on the CoAP protocol's lightweight design and compatibility with edge computing in large-scale IoT projects, such as agriculture, illustrates the strategic use of edge nodes for local processing, optimizing resource utilization alongside centralized nodes. The excerpt on the Authentication and Access Control Framework for CoAP elucidates the importance of securing IoT communication, integrating authentication mechanisms, access controls, secure channels, and key management to ensure a robust defense against cyber threats. In conclusion, this chapter contributes significantly to the discourse on enhancing cloud and IoT security, offering a overarching analysis of authentication strategies, security challenges, regulatory considerations, and innovative solutions to fortify the complex landscape of Cloud and IoT deployments.

REFERENCES

Al-Doori, M. J., & Al-Gailani, M. F. (2023). Securing IoT Networks with NTRU Cryptosystem: A Practical Approach on ARM-based Devices for Edge and Fog Layer Integration. *International Journal of Intelligent Engineering & Systems*, *16*(5).

Al-Fuqaha, A., Guizani, M., Mohammadi, M., Aledhari, M., & Ayyash, M. (2015). Internet of things: A survey on enabling technologies, protocols, and applications. *IEEE Communications Surveys and Tutorials*, *17*(4), 2347–2376. doi:10.1109/COMST.2015.2444095

Aldowah, H., Ul Rehman, S., & Umar, I. (2019). Security in internet of things: issues, challenges and solutions. In *Recent Trends in Data Science and Soft Computing: Proceedings of the 3rd International Conference of Reliable Information and Communication Technology (IRICT 2018)* (pp. 396-405). Springer International Publishing. 10.1007/978-3-319-99007-1_38

Antonakakis, M., April, T., Bailey, M., Bernhard, M., Bursztein, E., Cochran, J., & Zhou, Y. (2017). Understanding the mirai botnet. In *26th USENIX security symposium (USENIX Security 17)* (pp. 1093-1110). Research Gate.

Arvind, S., & Narayanan, V. A. (2019, March). An overview of security in CoAP: attack and analysis. In *2019 5th international conference on advanced computing & communication systems (ICACCS)* (pp. 655-660). IEEE. 10.1109/ICACCS.2019.8728533

Azzawi, M. A. (2017). *Enhanced Light Weight And Robust Authentication Mechanism For Internet Of Things (IoT) Environment* [Doctoral dissertation]. Universiti Kebangsaan Malaysia.

Bajpai, P., & Enbody, R. (2020, March). Towards effective identification and rating of automotive vulnerabilities. In *Proceedings of the Second ACM Workshop on Automotive and Aerial Vehicle Security* (pp. 37-44). ACM. 10.1145/3375706.3380556

Balogh, S., Gallo, O., Ploszek, R., Špaček, P., & Zajac, P. (2021). IoT security challenges: Cloud and blockchain, postquantum cryptography, and evolutionary techniques. *Electronics (Basel)*, *10*(21), 2647. doi:10.3390/electronics10212647

Belgacem, N., Fournier, R., Nait-Ali, A., & Bereksi-Reguig, F. (2015). A novel biometric authentication approach using ECG and EMG signals. *Journal of Medical Engineering & Technology*, *39*(4), 226–238. doi:10.3109/03091902.2015.1021429 PMID:25836061

Chen, C. M., Wang, K. H., Yeh, K. H., Xiang, B., & Wu, T. Y. (2019). Attacks and solutions on a three-party password-based authenticated key exchange protocol for wireless communications. *Journal of Ambient Intelligence and Humanized Computing*, *10*(8), 3133–3142. doi:10.1007/s12652-018-1029-3

Das, S., Wang, B., Kim, A., & Camp, L. J. (2020). *Mfa is a necessary chore!: Exploring user mental models of multi-factor authentication technologies*. Research Gate.

Fernando, W. P. K., Dissanayake, D. A. N. P., Dushmantha, S. G. V. D., Liyanage, D. L. C. P., & Karunatilake, C. (2023). *Challenges and Opportunities in Password Management: A Review of Current Solutions*. Research Gate.

Hammad, M., Liu, Y., & Wang, K. (2018). Multimodal biometric authentication systems using convolution neural network based on different level fusion of ECG and fingerprint. *IEEE Access : Practical Innovations, Open Solutions*, *7*, 26527–26542. doi:10.1109/ACCESS.2018.2886573

Hemdi, M., & Deters, R. (2016, October). Using REST based protocol to enable ABAC within IoT systems. In *2016 IEEE 7th Annual Information Technology, Electronics and Mobile Communication Conference (IEMCON)* (pp. 1-7). IEEE. 10.1109/IEMCON.2016.7746297

Karpf, B. A. (2017). *Dead reckoning: where we stand on privacy and security controls for the Internet of Things* [Doctoral dissertation]. Massachusetts Institute of Technology.

Karthick Kumar, A., Vadivukkarasi, K., Dayana, R., & Malarvezhi, P. (2022). Botnet Attacks Detection Using Embedded Feature Selection Methods for Secure IOMT Environment. In Pervasive Computing and Social Networking. *Proceedings of ICPCSN*, *2022*, 585–599.

Kondoro, A., Dhaou, I. B., Tenhunen, H., & Mvungi, N. (2021). Real time performance analysis of secure IoT protocols for microgrid communication. *Future Generation Computer Systems*, *116*, 1–12. doi:10.1016/j.future.2020.09.031

Kurii, Y., & Opirskyy, I. (2022). Analysis and Comparison of the NIST SP 800-53 and ISO/IEC 27001: 2013. *NIST Spec. Publ*, *800*(53), 10.

Matsumoto, T., Matsumoto, H., Yamada, K., & Hoshino, S. (2002, April). Impact of artificial "gummy" fingers on fingerprint systems. In *Optical security and counterfeit deterrence techniques IV* (Vol. 4677, pp. 275–289). SPIE. doi:10.1117/12.462719

McGinthy, J. M., Wong, L. J., & Michaels, A. J. (2019). Groundwork for neural network-based specific emitter identification authentication for IoT. *IEEE Internet of Things Journal*, *6*(4), 6429–6440. doi:10.1109/JIOT.2019.2908759

Nguyen, T. D., Huh, E. N., & Jo, M. (2018). Decentralized and revised content-centric networking-based service deployment and discovery platform in mobile edge computing for IoT devices. *IEEE Internet of Things Journal*, *6*(3), 4162–4175. doi:10.1109/JIOT.2018.2875489

Nigam, D., Patel, S. N., Vincent, D. R., Srinivasan, K., & Sinouvassane, A. (2022). Biometric authentication for intelligent and Privacy-Preserving healthcare systems. *Journal of Healthcare Engineering*, *2022*, 1–15. doi:10.1155/2022/1789996 PMID:35368929

Noura, H. N., Melki, R., & Chehab, A. (2019, September). Secure and lightweight mutual multi-factor authentication for IoT communication systems. In *2019 IEEE 90th Vehicular Technology Conference (VTC2019-Fall)* (pp. 1-7). IEEE. 10.1109/VTCFall.2019.8891082

Ometov, A., Bezzateev, S., Mäkitalo, N., Andreev, S., Mikkonen, T., & Koucheryavy, Y. (2018). Multi-factor authentication: A survey. *Cryptography*, *2*(1), 1. doi:10.3390/cryptography2010001

Ometov, A., Petrov, V., Bezzateev, S., Andreev, S., Koucheryavy, Y., & Gerla, M. (2019). Challenges of multi-factor authentication for securing advanced IoT applications. *IEEE Network*, *33*(2), 82–88. doi:10.1109/MNET.2019.1800240

Pérez, S., Garcia-Carrillo, D., Marín-López, R., Hernández-Ramos, J. L., Marín-Pérez, R., & Skarmeta, A. F. (2019). Architecture of security association establishment based on bootstrapping technologies for enabling secure IoT infrastructures. *Future Generation Computer Systems*, *95*, 570–585. doi:10.1016/j.future.2019.01.038

Pilewski, B. G., & Pilewski, C. A. (2010). Achieving PCI DSS Compliance: A Compliance Review. *Information Security Management Handbook*, *4*(4), 149–167. doi:10.1201/EBK1439819029-c10

Poblete, J. (2018). *Connected Automobiles and Cybersecurity*. Research Gate.

Raul, N., Shankarmani, R., & Joshi, P. (2020). A comprehensive review of keystroke dynamics-based authentication mechanism. In *International Conference on Innovative Computing and Communications: Proceedings of ICICC 2019*, Volume 2 (pp. 149-162). Springer Singapore. 10.1007/978-981-15-0324-5_13

Rizvi, S., Campbell, S., & Alden, K. (2020, October). Why Compliance is needed for Internet of Things? In *2020 International Conference on Software Security and Assurance (ICSSA)* (pp. 66-71). IEEE. 10.1109/ICSSA51305.2020.00019

Sadeeq, M. M., Abdulkareem, N. M., Zeebaree, S. R., Ahmed, D. M., Sami, A. S., & Zebari, R. R. (2021). IoT and Cloud computing issues, challenges and opportunities: A review. *Qubahan Academic Journal, 1*(2), 1–7. doi:10.48161/qaj.v1n2a36

Siddiqui, Z., Tayan, O., & Khan, M. K. (2018). Security analysis of smartphone and cloud computing authentication frameworks and protocols. *IEEE Access : Practical Innovations, Open Solutions, 6*, 34527–34542. doi:10.1109/ACCESS.2018.2845299

Sufi, F., Khalil, I., & Hu, J. (2010). ECG-based authentication. Handbook of information and communication security, 309-331.

Suresh Babu, C. V. (2023). *IoT and its Applications*. Anniyappa Publication.

Suresh Babu, C. V., & Akshara, P. M. (2023). Virtual Threats and Asymmetric Military Challenges. In Cyber Security Policies and Strategies of the World's Leading States (pp. 49-68). IGI Global. doi:10.4018/978-1-6684-8846-1.ch004

Suresh Babu, C. V., Akshayah, N. S., & Janapriyan, R. (2023). IoT-Based Smart Accident Detection and Alert System. In Handbook of Research on Deep Learning Techniques for Cloud-Based Industrial IoT (pp. 322-337). IGI Global.

Suresh Babu, C. V., Simon, P. A., & Kumar, S. B. (2023). The Future of Cyber Security Starts Today, Not Tomorrow. In Malware Analysis and Intrusion Detection in Cyber-Physical Systems (pp. 348-375). IGI Global.

Suresh Babu, C. V., & Srisakthi, S. (2023). Cyber Physical Systems and Network Security: The Present Scenarios and Its Applications. In Cyber-Physical Systems and Supporting Technologies for Industrial Automation (pp. 104-130). IGI Global.

Toth, P., & Toth, P. (2017). *NIST MEP cybersecurity self-assessment handbook for assessing NIST SP 800-171 security requirements in response to DFARS cybersecurity requirements*. US Department of Commerce, National Institute of Standards and Technology. doi:10.6028/NIST.HB.162

Wang, G., Nixon, M., & Boudreaux, M. (2019). Toward cloud-assisted industrial IoT platform for large-scale continuous condition monitoring. *Proceedings of the IEEE, 107*(6), 1193–1205. doi:10.1109/JPROC.2019.2914021

Yanushkevich, S. N., Boulanov, O., Stoica, A., & Shmerko, V. P. (2008). Support of interviewing techniques in physical access control systems. *Computational Forensics: Second International Workshop, IWCF 2008, Washington, DC, USA, August 7-8, 2008 Proceedings*, *2*, 147–158.

Zahid, A. Z. G., Al-Kharsan, I. H. M. S., Bakarman, H. A., Ghazi, M. F., Salman, H. A., & Hasoon, F. N. (2019, December). Biometric authentication security system using human DNA. In *2019 First International Conference of Intelligent Computing and Engineering (ICOICE)* (pp. 1-7). IEEE. 10.1109/ICOICE48418.2019.9035151

Chapter 12
SISA En-Decryption Algorithm for Multilingual Data Privacy and Security in IoT

Sivasakthi Kannan
https://orcid.org/0009-0005-8053-7856
Tata Elxsi Ltd., India

Manju C. Thayammal
https://orcid.org/0000-0002-2838-8022
Ponjesly College of Engineering, India

Sherly Alphonse
Vellore Institute of Technology, Chennai, India

Priyanga
Ponjesly College of Engineering, India

S. Abinaya
https://orcid.org/0000-0001-7957-7934
Vellore Institute of Technology, Chennai, India

ABSTRACT

Because of worldwide integration, multilingual databases and document transfers are quite widespread, which raises the requirement for data security against hackers. Without regard to Unicode, the suggested SISA En-De-Cryption (SEDC) method is capable of encrypting any language. The multilingual data and documents in the devices are secured using the proposed SEDC method in this work. Because the proposed SEDC technique has no size or language restrictions on the key, it is substantially more secure than current encryption algorithms in the literature. The brute force attack is also decreased by this SEDC trait. The SEDC algorithm's design is so straightforward that it may be created in any computer language. The suggested SEDC algorithm may also be fused with several other technologies like cloud-based web applications, IoT, block chain etc. and can be utilized for data security in multiple areas like healthcare, smart agriculture and mobile communication etc. When compared to other existing algorithms, the suggested SEDC method performs better.

DOI: 10.4018/979-8-3693-0766-3.ch012

INTRODUCTION

Data security is very important because it protects the data from hackers and unauthorized access (Abdel & Mohamed, 2018). The data regarding transactions, knowledge, databases and infrastructure are an important asset of an organization (Adams & Tavares, 1990). In ancient period king Caesar share secret data of their kingdom by encrypting it. From the period of king Caesar to till now countries require security for their data and every human needs to secure their personal data (Gnanasekar, 2016). Many encryption and decryption algorithms were proposed in literature. Some of the generally used techniques are Triple DES, RSA, Blowfish, Twofish and AES. The AES (Advance Encryption Standard) is considered as the most secure algorithm and it is trusted by U.S. Government. The encryption algorithms use either symmetric key or asymmetric key for the processing of data. The AES algorithm uses symmetric key encryption. Previously AES – 128 and AES – 192 were used in many works in literature and nowadays AES – 256 is commonly used. Because of worldwide integration, multilingual databases and document transfers are quite widespread, which raises the requirement for data security against hackers. While using the data, there are many approaches to protect user privacy. Each technique, nevertheless, is only suitable for specific data types and situations; for instance, data suppression is suitable for some data release operations, but not for those that call for the processing of genuine or specific data. None of the aforementioned methods can guarantee the privacy of language score information while enabling the most accurate calculation. The problem is that fully secure computation or decryption alone are insufficient to protect user scores from other agents because the calculations are quite complex, and there is a chance that an agent could infer the user's level of linguistic proficiency. The monolingual data and documents can be supported by the existing algorithms, which are not effective for the multilingual documents.

Most of the encryption algorithms can encrypt only monolingual data. The symmetric key encryption algorithms get key for security but their key size leads to brute force attack and they are programmatically complex. To overcome the problems created by Monolingual Encryption Techniques (MULET) was proposed. MULET provides security on the table alone and it can encrypt only the data with Unicode. The proposed SEDC algorithm overcomes above all drawbacks. SEDC algorithm is capable of encrypting any language irrespective of the Unicode. Even if the character is not present in the SEDC table, the encryption operation will be performed but it is considered as a bad cipher. The existing algorithms like symmetric key encryption algorithm tends to brute force attack. The proposed SEDC algorithm is much secure than other encryption algorithms in literature, because of the no size restriction and no language restriction for key. This characteristic of SEDC reduces the brute force attack. The design of the SEDC algorithm is very simple that it can be developed using any programming language. The contributions of the proposed work include that the input and key have no size restriction and language restriction. The user defined language table is used (Balajee & Gnanasekar, 2016).

MOTIVATION FOR THE PROPOSED WORK

UNICODE is used to represent the multilingual data in various countries (Bhoge & Chatur, 2014). The characters should be represented using some standard approaches before using for computing. In 1963, IBM have uniform EBCDIC for mainframes. Concurrently, the ASCII is represented as a 7-bit of character. The 8th bit is used for registered resolves. The computers are used in many countries with this standard character encoding. The deviation in these adapted characters sets created some problems in due time. So, there was the need for modified character encoding and the International Organization for Standardization (ISO) created the ISO-8859-character set in the initial 1980s. It has supported various languages, but not the symbols such as ligatures. Therefore, UNICODE came into existence. The plan of UNICODE was initiated in 1980. Concurrently, ISO had in progress the Universal Character Set (UCS) or ISO 10646. UNICODE 1.0 was out in 1991. Then UNICODE has functioned closely with ISO and UCS to safeguard parallel purposes. The existing algorithms mostly support monolingual data and documents. The proposed SISA En-De-Cryption (SEDC) algorithm secures multilingual data and documents.

LITERATURE SURVEY

Several algorithms are proposed in literature for encryption and decryption of data. The algorithms have several disadvantages and shortcomings. The AES algorithm is a widely used techniques. But it has several disadvantages. In AES algorithm while using a 256-bit key, each recipient should accept the key through a dissimilar channel compared to the message. This is a primary disadvantage of the AES algorithm. There is also a need for an asymmetric encryption algorithm to encrypt the key sent to the recipient through the separate channel. Also, the AES algorithm uses an algebraic structure which is very difficult to implement in a software. All the blocks in AES are encrypted using the same method. If the key used in the AES algorithm is not encrypted properly it will create a cryptanalytical attack. To improve the security in AES algorithms there is a need to increase the count of rounds or the block size which is not a best solution. AES algorithms are designed for working in 32-bit platforms and they are not capable of working in 64-bit platforms which is a negative factor. Other than the 128-bit length key all the other keys are having unreal length. The XOR operation with the state matrix creates an increase in the likelihood of search space in the remaining rounds. The decryption process in AES algorithm is much gentler compared to the encryption process. AES with 128-bit key is not appropriate for the big data applications (Changder et al., 2010).

The k-nearest neighbours from encrypted data and an encrypted query are employed in the novel symmetric encryption system Wong et al. (2009) presented. A pair of encryption functions with an inner-product preserving property were utilised in the technique. The pair of encryption functions were employed in many encryption methods, including ranked multi-keyword search in apps, as a result of this characteristic. When the attacker obtains plaintext-ciphertext combinations, the pair of encryption functions becomes insecure. Some preventive measures, such as randomising plaintexts before encryption, were included in the programmes to stop this attack. They examined the inner product's security while still maintaining encryption features. They talked about the defences against application attacks. The second encryption mechanism is not utilised in this attack (Ogata et al. 2019).

A multi-user multi-keyword ranked search technique that may be used to any language was proposed by Liu et al. (2019). It is a brand-new multi-keyword rank searchable encryption (MRSE) method based on PCTD and the Paillier Cryptosystem. The k-nearest neighbour searchable encryption (KNN-SE) technique can minimise the limitations and achieve higher performance in terms of usefulness and effectiveness in previous MRSE systems. Additionally, it allows for the input of keywords in any language and does not require a specified keyword list. However, multilingual search is limited to each language and cannot be studied across languages due to the pattern of matching of keywords in the new MRSE scheme. In this research, a Cross-Lingual Multi-Keyword Rank Search (CLRSE) scheme that overcomes language barriers and achieves semantic extension using the Open Multilingual Wordnet is proposed. Through flexible term and language choice options, the CLRSE scheme also comprehends intelligent and tailored search. Through extensive experiments, they assess the presentation of the scheme in terms of security, usability, accuracy, and competence. A single human-memorisable password was used to outsource encrypted data with associated keywords to a number of servers using the Password Authenticated Searchable Encryption (PASE) method provided by Chen et al. (2020) (Hernández et al., 2002). The data was eventually located using an encrypted keyword search procedure (Mroczkowski et al., 2009). PASE ensures that these procedures can only be completed by a real user who can identify the initially registered password. PASE specifically guarantees that no one server may utilise the user's password in an offline attack or research any information regarding the encrypted keywords. By removing the requirement for the client to store high-entropy keys, the concept underlying PASE protocols expands the ideas behind searchable encryption and gives users protocol device doubt. They offered an efficient direct construction in a two-server environment after modelling PASE's capabilities along with two security criteria. Under the Decisional Diffie-Hellman presumption, they demonstrated the model. They employed a number of keywords and permitted password changes by users without requiring any that were crucial for re-encrypting the data that was outsourced. In response to a data user's request for a multi-keyword search over encrypted data, Yang et al. (2017) proposed a multi-keyword rank searchable encryption (MRSE), which proceeds the top-k results (Cvetanovic et al., 2019). With this technique, cloud storage systems' data privacy is efficiently protected without losing the usability of the data. The foundation of many current MRSE systems is an algorithm known as k-nearest neighbour for searchable encryption (KNN-SE). KNN-SE is deficient in a number of ways that restrict the applications it can be used for. They introduced a unique MRSE system in this study that virtually eliminates all of the flaws of the KNN-SE based MRSE systems. In fact, this system provides keywords in any language and does not require a specified keyword list. This system, which supports many users, prioritizes flexible search clearance, time-controlled cancellation, and improved data protection. Another planning assessment approach based on an arbitrary number generator was proposed by Russia et al. (2017) to examine the laboriousness of the actualized square code symmetric cryptography calculations (Hernández et al., 2003). Distinctive Plaintexts in a Similar Key (DPSK) is the only assessing mode included in this assessment model. The plaintext and the reporter key, which serve as the basis of the assessment model, are both generated by irrational integers. In comparison to this DPSK working model, AES, DES, Blow-Fish, and IDEA, TripleDES is many hundred times slower. The quantity of plaintexts and keys is typically a factor in the time-consuming cryptographic calculation, whereas irregular numbers are a factor in the evaluation model. This working model does not show increased efficacy in their suggested model.

By taking into consideration the adaptive syntax design of Indian languages (Hussain et al., 2015), Changder et al. (2017) provide another phonetic technique of Indian languages. By contrasting the message bits and the image's pixel estimates, the initial message is transformed to an irrelevant two-stream in order to increase the framework's security rather than being hidden. The fragments of this double stream are then codified into a grammatical form. The computation also looks for the same grammatical structure in the first word of each sentence and locates the piece-stream of the intended grammatical characteristic to recover the modified message. The first message from the cover document was eliminated by the calculation. On several Indian languages, such as Bengali, the suggested technique yields satisfactory results. Using Arabic material, Taha et al. (2017) provided a formula for data concealing (Hussain et al., 2011). The new computation extends the amount of cryptic information that can be inserted into an Arabic content repository without degrading the material's quality. The proposed calculation makes use of a variety of Arabic language traits and characteristics. It makes use of both tiny space characters and the Arabic expansion character (Kashida). The tiniest of details can be concealed by each present Kashida, and three pieces can be shrouded by each current area. The suggested calculation was tested for stego-instant messages of varied lengths. In comparison to the most relevant Kashida-based techniques and spaces-based procedures, it shows superiority in achieving high limit concealing percentage. A framework using Arabic calligraphy to conceal data was proposed by Hamzah et al. (2014) (Kazlauskas & Kazlauskas, 2009). The planning, installing, and extraction phases make up the structure's lifecycle. String is used in the implanting step to create stego text and letter forms that correspond to a cryptic message. A contextual research was conducted using the Arabic textual style Naskh. As a dataset, a collection of proverbs and verses in Arabic was used. The system's security and cap were evaluated. The security in this system is good because, in any stego-framework, the visual contrast between the cover and the stego-cover should be indiscernible to the human eye. Telugu is an Indian language that was successfully encoded by Bharati and Prasad in 2016 (Kazlauskas, 2015). The suggested method makes use of the Telugu text and its characteristics to obscure the secret message. It depends on how the request for credit in the text doesn't interfere with the record's existence. This asking can be effectively used to hide the unexplained messages. The key record age, concealing cycle, and eliminating measure are the three main components of the suggested technique. The age of the Cover Message is a key component of the plan. Basically, the Cover Message is a collection of essential mixes arranged in lines and parts. These mixtures are created by encrypting the text records that have been saved. The Cover Message is created using the ascribes mixes found in the text. In "Odia Offline Typewritten Character recognition with template Matching with Unicode Mapping" (Panda & Tripath, 2015) (Patidar et al., 2013), a method utilising offline Odia character recognition is demonstrated. In "MULET: A Multilanguage Encryption Technique" (Kumar et al., 2010), a novel encryption algorithm utilising a number of languages was developed. The UNICODE character set was being handled by this algorithm for a number of different languages. "Universal Encryption Algorithm using Logical Operations and Bits Shuffling for Unicode" (Tandon et al., 2015) describes a novel cryptographic technique that uses UNICODE to encode and decrypt the data.

Machine translation (MT) is a helpful technique in multilingual communication to break down linguistic barriers. There are numerous MT services with varying levels of quality accessible, but if the MT quality is too low, occasionally users' proficiency in a foreign language might lead to better communication outcomes. For instance, if there are two users and they both speak English, but at varying levels of ability, they can decide whether to communicate via MT or English. It might be more effective to communicate in English if the MT services they utilize are of poor quality. Making choices about which languages and services to employ becomes more challenging as there are more users with a variety of language abilities. It already uses a 2018 fix known as the best-balanced machine translation technique. Since it is difficult for a human to choose which languages should be used when there is a group of people who speak different languages and have varying levels of expertise, the method suggests which languages should be used in multilingual communication when machine translation services are available. To compute and recommend the best languages to employ, Personal Agents and an Optimising Agent must exchange data about MT quality and user language exam scores, such as TOEIC and TOEFL.

Due to the first idea, customers were hesitant to share their test results for fear that it would reflect poorly on the service. Even if language scores don't necessarily represent users, some users don't feel comfortable disclosing their results. It is crucial to safeguard the confidentiality of test results, just like with any personal information. The issue of releasing each user's test results has been brought up, and many organizations prioritize maintaining the privacy of test results. In certain systems the users are required to reveal their language test results in the original approach of determining the best-balanced machine translation combinations. The results of language tests should be classified as private information since some users may not want their results to be made public. This research proposed a method to determine the most balanced language mix while keeping the user's language scores private. They combined cryptographic methods with a multi-agent system to create a 3-agent-type system with a privacy-aware protocol because existing privacy protection strategies are insufficient for implementing the best-balanced machine translation (Pituxcoosuvarn et al., 2020).

There are numerous ways to safeguard data privacy while using the data. However, each technique is only appropriate for particular data types and circumstances; for example, data suppression is appropriate for some data release procedures, but not those that require real or specific data to be processed data. None of the strategies mentioned are acceptable for maintaining the confidentiality of language score data while permitting best-balanced calculation. The issue is that relying solely on data encryption because fully secure computation or decryption alone are insufficient to keep user scores secret from other agents as a result of the procedures calculations are quite intricate, and there is a potential that an agent can infer the user's linguistic proficiency.

PROPOSED SYSTEM FOR MULTILINGUAL DATA SECURITY

In this section, the encryption functions are discussed. The SEDC algorithm and SEDC language table formation are discussed in detail.

SEDC Algorithm

SEDC Algorithm is an abbreviation of SISA (SIvaSAkthi's) En-De-Cryption algorithm (Mroczkowski, 2009) (Dawood et al.,2019). This SEDC algorithm is the new generation of cryptography where it has ability to encrypt and decrypt multilingual data and it has two types of security enabled while encrypting data. Previously proposed algorithms like AES, DES, Twofish, Blowfish etc. are having ability to encrypt and decrypt monolingual data mostly English and also each algorithm is having size restriction for key value. The proposed SEDC Algorithm overcomes all these drawbacks of such algorithms. SEDC Algorithm works with following requirements, Input Text/Plain Text, Key Value, SEDC Lang Table, Min Max Value, SEDC Formulas.

SEDC Lang Table

Before starting encryption and decryption SEDC Lang table are needed to be designed. The SEDC Lang table consist of all required language characters with its SEDC number. In SEDC Lang table you can create single table for all languages or can create separate table for every language. The SEDC number can start with any digit (for example A = 1 or A = 32) but the number won't start with 0. Also, the SEDC number must be in ascending order and in correct sequence. For example, if SEDC number starts with 32 then the sequence must be 32, 33, 34, and so on. At the same time the characters can be arranged in any order. For example, the characters can be arranged as M, A, b, C, q, Q and so on. SEDC Value is the decimal number assigned for the character in SEDC Lang table. Designing one's own SEDC Lang table improve security. And if single table is designed for all languages, then there is no any need of detecting languages, rather than checking the presence of character in table. But if tables are separately created for each language, then there is a need to detect language as in tables 1 and 2.

Above tables are sample table, similarly one can create their own table to encrypt or decrypt data to improve security.

Table 1. Same table for every language

A	M	N	B	C	.....	அ	எ	°	....
32	33	34	35	36	.....	123	124	125	....

Table 2. Different table for every language

English									
A	M	N	B	C	D	a	e	1	....
1	**2**	**3**	**4**	**5**	**6**	**7**	**8**	**9**	**....**
Tamil									
அ	ீ	ஶ	எ	ண	◌ொ	ஹ	ு	ா	....
10	**11**	**12**	**13**	**14**	**15**	**16**	**17**	**18**	**....**

Min Max Value

Min Max value is found out by the help of Min Max Algorithm from SEDC Lang table. If the table is created for every language separately then Min Max value will differ for every language, else if single table is created for every language, then Min Max value is common for all languages. The Max value is the SEDC value in the place of total number of characters in the table. The Min value is the SEDC value in the place of the half of total number of characters in the table. SEDC Algorithm works with 4 formulas.

SEDC CC and PC

Equation (1) is used for encryption and Equation (2) used for decryption.

1. SEDC CC Formula

CC (Cipher Character) formula is used to encrypt plain character into cipher character.

$$C= (A+B)-C \tag{1}$$

2. SEDC PC Formula

PC (Plain Character) formula is used to decrypt cipher character into plain character.

$$PC= (A-B)+C \tag{2}$$

Where A is the Decimal value of first character, B is the Decimal complement value of 2nd character and C is Decimal value of 3rd character.

SEDC LV and GV

Equation (3) and (4) are used in encryption and decryption.

1.SEDC LV

LV (Least Value) formula is used when the final decimal value of calculation in encryption and decryption is less than the starting value of table.

$$V= SV-LV \text{ (or) } FDV \tag{3}$$

$$AV= (EV \text{ (or) } MV +1)-V \tag{4}$$

2.SEDC GV

GV (Greatest Value) formula is used when the final decimal value of calculation in encryption and decryption is greater than the ending value (or) maximum value of table.

$$V-GV \text{ (or) } FDV-EV \text{ (or) } MV \tag{5}$$

$$AV=(SV-1)+V \tag{6}$$

Where V is the Value, AV is the Actual Value, SV is the Starting Value, LV is the Least Value, EV is the Ending Value, MV is the Maximum Value, GV is the Greatest Value, FDV is the Final Decimal Value.Input Text may be a Plain Text to encrypt or Cipher Text to decrypt of any language. Key value is to encrypt or decrypt data. Key value has no size limit or no language restriction.

Workflow Diagram and Steps for SEDC Algorithms

The workflow of SEDC algorithm is given in Fig.1.

Figure 1. Flow diagram for SEDC algorithms

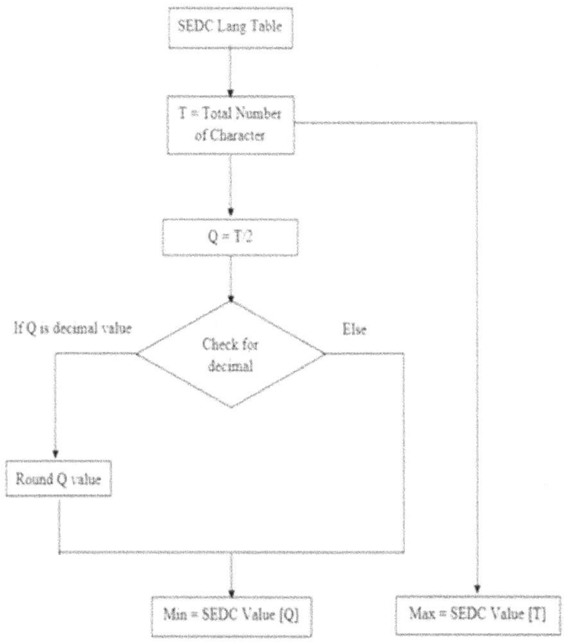

Min Max Algorithm

The steps in Min Max algorithm is given below

Step 1: Start
Step 2: Get SEDC LANG TABLE
Step 3: Get total number of characters in table (T = Total number of characters in table)
Step 4: Divide T by 2 (N = T/2)
  a. If N is float value then round it
Step 5: Assume SEDC value in Nth place of table as minimum value (Min = SEDC value in Nth place in SEDC Table)
Step 6: Assume SEDC value of last character as maximum value (Max = SEDC value of last character in SEDC TABLE)
Step 7: End

Figure 2. Encryption

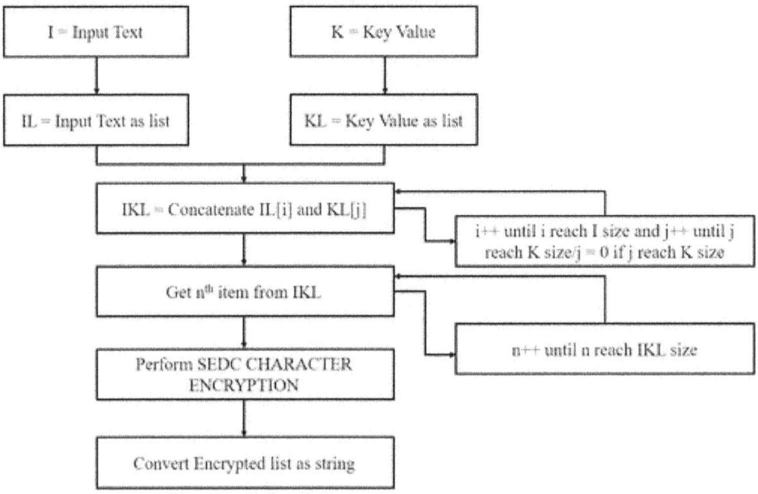

SEDC Algorithm

SEDC Encryption

SEDC Encryption converts plain text into cipher text by concatenating input characters and encrypted characters. SEDC CC Formula, GV Formula, LV Formula were used for encrypting the characters in plain text. Finally, SEDC Encryption provide secure encrypted text as in Fig.2.The steps for SEDC encryption are given below.

Step 1: Start
Step 2: Get Input Text (I = Input Text)
Step 3: Get Key Value (K = Key Value)
Step 4: Convert Input Text as list (IL = I as list)
Step 5: Convert Key Value as list (KL = K as list)
Step 6: Join ith item of IL and jth item of KL (IKL = IL[i] + KL[j])

a. j++ until j reach KL size/j = 0 if j reach KL size and i++ until i reach IL size

Step 7: Create empty encryption list
Step 8: Get nth item of IKL list (N = IKL [n])

------------ SEDC CHARACTER ENCRYPTION STARTS------------

Step 9: Get minimum value and maximum value of 1st character from lang table
Step 10: Check n

a. If nth is first item, concatenate minimum value with nth item

b. Else, concatenate last encrypted character from encryption list with nth item

Step 11: Check language of 1st, 2nd, and 3rd characters/Presence of character

a. If language table or character is not present then assume minimum value as 2nd character

Step 12: Get SEDC value of 1st, 2nd, and 3rd characters from SEDC Lang Table

Step 13: Convert 2nd SEDC value as binary value and find the complement value

Step 14: Convert above complement binary value as decimal value

Step 15: Check decimal value

a. If decimal value is greater than minimum value, assume minimum value as decimal complement of 2nd value

Step 16: Perform SEDC CC Formula (M = SEDC CC Formula)

a. If M is greater than maximum value, perform SEDC GV Formula (M = SEDC GV Formula)

b. If M is lesser than starting value, perform SEDC LV Formula (M = SEDC LV Formula)

Step 17: Find Character of M from SEDC Lang Table and store it in encryption list

------------ SEDC CHARACTER ENCRYPTION ENDS------------

Step 18: Increment nth and continue from 8th step

Step 19: Convert encryption list as string

Step 20: Stop

SEDC Decryption

SEDC Decryption convert cipher text into plain text by concatenating input characters, key characters and next i+1th input characters. SEDC PC Formula, LV Formula were used for decrypting the characters in cipher text. Finally, SEDC Decryption provides perfect decrypted data as in Fig.3.The steps in SEDC decryption are given below.

Step 1: Start

Step 2: Get Input Text (I = Input Text)

Step 3: Get Key Value (K = Key Value)

Step 4: Convert Input Text as list (IL = I as list)

Step 5: Convert Key Value as list (KL = K as list)

Step 6: Join ith item of IL and jth item of KL (IKL = IL[i] + KL[j])

Figure 3. Decryption

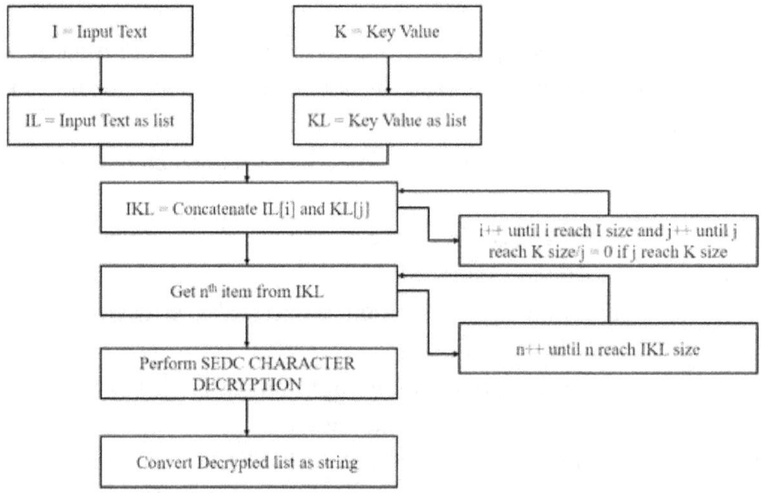

j++ until j reach KL size/j = 0 if j reach KL size and i++ until i reach IL size

Step 7: Create empty decryption list

Step 8: Get nth item of IKL list (N = IKL [n])

------------ SEDC CHARACTER DECRYPTION STARTS------------

Step 9: Get minimum value and maximum value of 1st character from lang table

Step 10: Check n

If nth is first item, concatenate minimum value with nth item

Else, concatenate i^{th} item from input list with nth item and increment i

Step 11: Check language of 1st, 2nd, and 3rd characters/Presence of character

If language table or character is not present then assume minimum value as 2nd character

Step 12: Get SEDC value of 1st, 2nd, and 3rd characters from SEDC Lang Table

Step 13: Convert 2nd SEDC value as binary value and find the complement value

Step 14: Convert above complement binary value as decimal value

Step 15: Check decimal value

If decimal value is greater than minimum value, assume minimum value as decimal complement of 2nd value

Step 16: Perform SEDC PC Formula (M = SEDC PC Formula)

If M is greater than maximum value, perform SEDC GV Formula (M = SEDC GV Formula)

If M is lesser than starting value, perform SEDC LV Formula (M = SEDC LV Formula)

Step 17: Find Character of M from SEDC Lang Table and store it in decryption list

------------ SEDC CHARACTER DECRYPTION ENDS------------

Step 18: Increment n and continue from 8th step

Step 19: Convert decryption list as string

Step 20: Stop

RESULTS AND DISCUSSION

Sample Input

Input Language: English, Key Language: English

a. Input/Plain Text: Over the years, I will come, who will nostrud aliquip out of her the advantage of exercise, so that stimulus efforts if the school district and longevity.
b. Key Value Text: Try me Hai Hello World!!! 123@
c. Encrypted Text: *8qO!Lj0L"2df^~OH]hLqTK8Wd-* 5\^e`YkOee^cF%BsZ U=zB%>RMB"~,m6rAhXwUa9Cr@kNqT[Z1=}:?FR3.a3j8|NiT{Qe1@4. {FxNlWB,%3- b0d]NFJr+)!MvEq39(FSnVoQf#@+(@D[1-m%jIIvG5
d. Decrypted Text: Over the years, I will come, who will nostrud aliquip out of her the advantage of exercise, so that stimulus efforts if the school district and longevity.
e. Accuracy: 100%

Input Language: English, Key Language: Tamil

a. Input/Plain Text: Over time, I'll meet people who will advise her on the benefits of exercise in order to support the school district's efforts to promote longevity.
b. Key Value Text: என்னை முயர்ச்சி செய் ஹெலோ வேல்ட்!!! 123@
c. Encrypted Text: O[ZL):]dI]X,7_+C)NWbX8?OrID>l[Kt+l|>ZPHd] Kw2(FJ~x&@Lt.@$sc:|Q;"{Vl$8r?cc}p$,g)!,)++"9(j[FL0rQA=&eSO!AW i/9"{N\YKk$n&<o%kQq++)@q&FWB.Y`6=$hRP 0bYQmPFwxNYk.
d. Decrypted Text: Over time, I'll meet people who will urge her to exercise so that the school district's efforts to promote longevity are stimulated.
e. Accuracy: 100%

Input Language: Tamil, Key Language: Tamil

a. Input/Plain Text: கூறைந்தபட்சம், வனெியம், வினகோதமான உடற்பயிற்சி உல்லாம்ககோ தகொழிலாளர் நிசி உட் அலிகிப் எக்ஸ் ஈ காமகோடகோ விளவை.
b. Key Value Text: என்னை முயர்ச்சி சயெ் ஹலெகோ வலேட்!!! 123
c. Encrypted Text: கீ□□□ச□□ஐகொ□றகௌB<vாகூ□□சூ□5uஓகூ□□உரு ஊQ□னேரஅழநைஙற□3வ□□□ஈ□நீகோஃ[ந□இெ□□க□ஆL□□□ஆ J□□□Q□□மகூளயிஜwகீஷ□7□^இ□தபளள+□சூஷஜன□I
d. Decrypted Text: கூறைந்தபட்சம், வனெியம், வினகோதமான உடற்பயிற்சி உல்லாம்ககோ தகொழிலாளர் நிசி உட் அலிகிப் எக்ஸ் ஈ காமகோடகோ விளவை.
e. Accuracy: 100%

Input Language: Hindi, Key Language: English

a. Input/Plain Text: यूट एनमि एड मनिमिम वेनयिम, क्वसि नॉस्ट्रुड एक्सरसाइज ड्यूस ऑटे यूरेअर डोलर रीप्लेन्ड्रटि इन वॉलपेक्टेट वेलटि एसेल सलिम डोलोर यूआर फुगयिा नुल्ला पैराइटुर।
b. Key Value Text: Try me Hai Hello World!!! 123@
c. Encrypted Text: ज़औौ^य़टत8फव_धॉऐढ़ऐत*ढयिब,ठषछभशmचय़ऑग़हॐऔद्दो mअेनौ१ब्र४इxॉऑ४।य़[अवSfनोञर२लyइख़ऑॐ`ञलृौबऱेचळ८य़ऐ९[ऱैbग¨ककआ य़धऍKISणज़ोcअॖऄऐत[?ँSज्ञ[ॡलDृाढ़एEऑालमाoय़ऐ़ऱॲ{ौसऔँ॰ग़ाँइ
d. Decrypted Text: यूट एनमि एड मनिमिम वेनयिम, क्वसि नॉस्ट्रुड एक्सरसाइज ड्यूस ऑटे यूरेअर डोलर रीप्लेन्ड्रटि इन वॉलपेक्टेट वेलटि एसेल सलिम डोलोर यूआर फुगयिा नुल्ला पैराइटुर।
e. Accuracy: 100%

Input Language: Mixed, Key Language: Mixed

a. Input/Plain Text: Over the years கூறைந்தபட்சம், வனெியம் लॉरेम इप्सम डोलर अमेट കോൺസക്റ്ററ്റർ അഡിപിസിംഗ് ડરિક્ટર ઇન ધ الووسم صخشلا
b. Key Value Text: Loremலகோரமெ்लॉरेमലോറൊtમેعل
c. EncryptedText:23}M#|>T#&0\j6@□ை□ஹமஸ□□ாை□ஞு□6:□□□ஓ□ல□. ऱा'ॡब्र]उढौ॰+धृऋढ़Rफ़ुंअे+L ജഒള□ሆൽം൳ൽ൴ലv□ീസഃൻന്ധ-ശ്ഴവ്യ□{ □ઐૃઅ।□ILઐધ'ઙUبيٍ٢اا ءقيوبنٰ
e. Accuracy: 100%

d. Decrypted Text: Over the years குறைந்தபட்சம், வெனியம் लॉरेम इप्सम डोलर अमेट കോൺസെക്റ്റർ അഡിപിസിംഗ് ડરિક્ટર ઇન ધ الشخص المسؤول
e. Accuracy: 100%

DISCUSSION ON SECURITY PARAMETERS

Security Analysis

The secrecy of data is estimated by the variance between the actual and the agitated values as given by the following Equation (7).

$$S=(VAR(S-S')/(VAR(S)) \tag{7}$$

Avalanche Effect

When a single bit changes the input, the avalanche effect—a cryptography property—occurs, which is when a single bit changes the input results in a modification in more than half of the output bits (Khan & Verma, 2015; Maram et al., 2019). A single change in the network's input causes an avalanche of modifications when S-box is used to construct an S-P network. Python is used to implement the algorithm. Hindi, French, Spanish, Mandarin, and Telugu are among the languages used in the simple text. Depending on the language employed, the smallest avalanche effect obtained in this case is 6.2%, and the highest avalanche effect is 100%.

The performance of the SEDC algorithm's avalanche effect is shown in Figure 4 and table 3. Python has been used to implement the requested task. The languages used for the plain text are English, Tamil, Malayalam, Gujarati, and Hindi. It demonstrates that the SEDC algorithm achieves an avalanche effect that is nearly 100% higher than the avalanche effect produced by the present technique. Based on the presence of characters in the SEDC Lang Table and changes to characters in the cypher text, the SEDC algorithm's avalanche effect is produced.

From the results achieved above in Fig.4 it is proved that the SEDC algorithm achieves better performance than the existing algorithms.

Hamming Distance

The Hamming distance (Tandon et al.,2015) among two strings of equal length is the total number of positions at which the corresponding characters are different as in table 4.

Accuracy

Accuracy is calculated as the total number of characters than can be correctly decrypted from the encrypted text. This is represented by the formula as in equation (8). The accuracy is 100% for the proposed approach.

Table 3. Avalanche effect

Input Number	Plain text/ Cipher text	Plain-text (PT) /cipher-text (CT) & 1-bit change plain-text (PT1) /cipher-text (CT1) (UNICODE format)	Avalanche effect (%)
1	Plain text	Over the years, I'll visit her and explain the benefits of exercising to her.	100%
	Cipher Text	*8qO!Lj0L"2df^~OH]hLqTK8Wd-* 5\^e`YkOee^cF%BsZU=zB% >RMB"~,m6rAhXwUa9Cr@kNqT[Z1=}:?FR3.a3j8	
	1-bit change of plaintext	over the years, I'll visit her and explain the benefits of exercising to her.	
	Cipher text	Jw2/A,+olaRD'>?/h=),24kwwDMi@t|>&@yKoE&>$&E"4:u|;" E}r-ba?k.u3!)885"xcR`KnQt;zp]]Z~f2Sm"r+w	
2	Plain text	I will eventually arrive who will advise her on the benefits of exercise throughout the years.	74.5%
	Cipher Text	*8qO!Lj0L"2df^~OH]hLqTK8Wd-* 5\^e`YkOee^cF%BsZU=zB% >RMB"~,m6rAhXwUa9Cr@kNqT[Z1=}:?FR3.a3j8	
	1-bit change of plaintext	i will eventually arrive who will advise her on the benefits of exercise throughout the years.	
	Cipher text	*8qO!Lj0L"2df^~OH]hLqTKwwDMi@t|>&@yKoE&>$&E"4:u|; "E}r-ba?k.u3!)885"xcR`KnQt;zp]]Z~f2Sm"r+w	
3	Plain text	உழைப்பு மற்றும் டோலரோர் மகேனா அலிகா. கூறநைந்தபட்சம், வனெியம், வினோதமான உடற்பயிற்சி	6.2%
	Cipher Text	□□□உமீ அஔ# க□எஸு ஞூ□□வ எஉ□மQ□ொஊ□□□n°□ெ □86ஔளந□□ல□□மீ□ஈ□த9@கறஷெஆவ □□US□ஶல□ஓ□ரூ கூ&ூ தூஊ இ□உஞூ ஹ□□	
	1-bit change of plaintext	உழைப்பு மற்றும் டோலரோர் மகேனா கலிகா. கூறநைந்தபட்சம், வனெியம், வினோதமான உடற்பயிற்சி	
	Cipher text	□□□உமீ அஔ# க□எஸு ஞூ□ □வ எஉ□மQ□ொஊ□□□nஓ □□□ய86 ஔளந□□ல□□மீ□ஈ□த9@கறஷெஆவ□ □US□ஶல□ஓ□ரூ கூ&ூதூ ஊ இ□உஞூ ஹ□□	
4	Plain text	உழைப்பு மற்றும் டோலரோர் மகேனா அலிகா. கூறநைந்தபட்சம், வனெியம், வினோதமான உடற்பயிற்சி	27.2%
	Cipher Text	□□□உமீ அஔ# க□எஸு ஞூ□ □வ எஉ□மQ□ொஊ□□□n°□ெ□86 ஔளந□□ல□□மீ□ஈ□த9@கறஷெஆவ□□ US□ஶல□ஓ□ரூ கூ&ூதூ ஊ இ□உஞூ ஹ□□	
	1-bit change of plaintext	அழைப்பு மற்றும் டோலரோர் மகேனா அலிகா. கூறநைந்தபட்சம், வனெியம், வினோதமான உடற்பயிற்சி	
	Cipher text	□ஐ□□யதூள'□ஊ□□□□Q□த□□□□Q□ொஊ□□□n°□ெ□86ஔள ந□□ல□'□மீ□ஈ□த9@கறஷெஆவ□□US□ ஶல□ ஓ□ரூ கூ&ூ தூஊ இ□உஞூ ஹ□□	

continued on following page

Table 3. Continued

<table>
<tr><th>Input Number</th><th>Plain text/ Cipher text</th><th>Plain-text (PT) /cipher-text (CT) & 1-bit change plain-text (PT1) /cipher-text (CT1) (UNICODE format)</th><th>Avalanche effect (%)</th></tr>
<tr><td rowspan="4">5</td><td>Plain text</td><td>लॉरेम इप्सम डोलर अमेट, कंसेटेटुर एडपिसि्किगि इलीट, सेड डू आइज़्मोड अस्थायी इनडिडिंट यूट लैबर एट डोलोर मैग्ना एलकि। यूट एनमि एड</td><td rowspan="4">95.3%</td></tr>
<tr><td>Cipher Text</td><td>ज़ुरुड़पऴ$़?लृऋएँ(फसद(:ख़ङष.qाहचऐगुौलृ8शछड़ऐँभ्ं़ृ#लड़िp`ऱखऋt लूH.र३ऐृऊNखषुइअुाप'ऱथख़ाटभआु-ढठाMऐूइलxज़:Mबफ़३ञेgजुअैंृजलृ W3आुङवउज़$४ोC3नूऐ>डस</td></tr>
<tr><td>1-bit change of plaintext</td><td>लॉरेम एप्सम डोलर अमेट, कंसेटेटुर एडपिसि्किगि इलीट, सेड डू आइज़्मोड अस्थायी इनडिडिंट यूट लैबर एट डोलोर मैग्ना एलकि। यूट एनमि एड</td></tr>
<tr><td>Cipher text</td><td>ज़ुरुड़पऴ$ीऔऔक़क ख़णीञ0गुलृऑि&ÿऱढड़ीॅअुऄ@ मर्णकविौड़ीॅ८ग़Vबुअॅज़)Hॉड़ुण\तप`ॐधफय़अॅ*ओअुृचपुोbअुऋञउ।रोएँr ढ़॥ज़ीॅअुूh५अ"ुळऔअं ॖsऋअुृचkअॅ५ऑऔ९Qsऑड़pड़ॅकsp९४</td></tr>
<tr><td rowspan="4">6</td><td>Plain text</td><td>ലേ ാറം ഇപ്സം ഡേ ാളർ സിറ്റ് അമേറ്റ്, കേ ാൺസെക്റ്ററർ അഡിപിസിംഗ് എലൈറ്റ്</td><td rowspan="4">60.4%</td></tr>
<tr><td>Cipher Text</td><td>ർൺ൰ഠം"∫ബശഭഔ!ഡ്തീർ ായഭ□ങഴKന്മഓീർ൰ ണ്ണ);ഹൂധഇമ്മൽ്ന്റഫമ൳ൄvധ്ഡഃൂവമ്മക്കsധ്ഡമ്മയ്X൰ ഹ്മൗക്ക്ധ്ഡഔ</td></tr>
<tr><td>1-bit change of plaintext</td><td>ഡേ ാറം ഇപ്സം ഡേ ാളർ സിറ്റ് അമേറ്റ്, കേ ാൺസെക്റ്ററർ അഡിപിസിംഗ് എലൈറ്റ്</td></tr>
<tr><td>Cipher text</td><td>ഒളൂൈ ാഹ്മ"∫ബശഭഔ!ഡ്തീർ ായഭ□ങഴKന്മഓീർ൰ ണ്ണ);ഹൂധഇമ്മൽ്ന്റഫമ൳ൄvധ്ഡഃൂവമ്മക്കsധ്ഡമ്മയ്X൰ ഹ്മൗക്ക്ധ്ഡഔ</td></tr>
<tr><td rowspan="4">7</td><td>Plain text</td><td>તમે કામ કરી શકો છો, આશ્રય માટે યોગ્ય છે, પરંતુ કામદાર અને મેગા મેગા જેવા કામ કરે છે. તે જ સમયે, તમે પણ</td><td rowspan="4">98.1%</td></tr>
<tr><td>Cipher Text</td><td>૮પ□Nગ઼ા□□'□ચ□fનઝ□O૬૬47૬□ૅલૅ □એચ□>ળણ□ઍAએ□2<ણે૮૧ઈ F□ૢ□ંMQ□ઑીJ□□□ટ%૨ઍીsWs□ચ૬~૨ઇ□X□#□□_@ૃઐzીPઔ ૠ.J૬ઊ઼ૹ&ૣ□</td></tr>
<tr><td>1-bit change of plaintext</td><td>તપ કામ કરી શકો છો, આશ્રય માટે યોગ્ય છે, પરંતુ કામદાર અને મેગા મેગા જેવા કામ કરે છે. તે જ સમયે, તમે પણ</td></tr>
<tr><td>Cipher text</td><td>૮૧ૂૅ૯□ પૂલ{ં□ટ2ષ□>0s□ીં@િંભતxૠખથ૧□*ૐલ્ટ\w□ળઇ□ત*□ૃ ૯□3Q□□લY□ૢ□|□ઐષ□ૢ૬ો□`ઍૢ□ □ૢઓ8□ૈA^0૬k□ૈ-૯પ□Zuઇ0□. ૐ□</td></tr>
<tr><td>8</td><td>Plain text</td><td>Lorem ipsum dolor sit amet, consectetur adipiscing elit, sed tempor and vitality, so that the labor and sorrow</td><td>89.1%</td></tr>
</table>

Accuracy= (count of the number of characters correctly displayed from encrypted text/length of original plaintext) ×100 (8)

The above graph in Fig. 5 and table 5 represents the approximate time taken for encryption or decryption depends on the number of input characters and number of key characters. Thus, the proposed approach achieves good performance compared to the other existing algorithms.

Figure 4. Avalanche effect

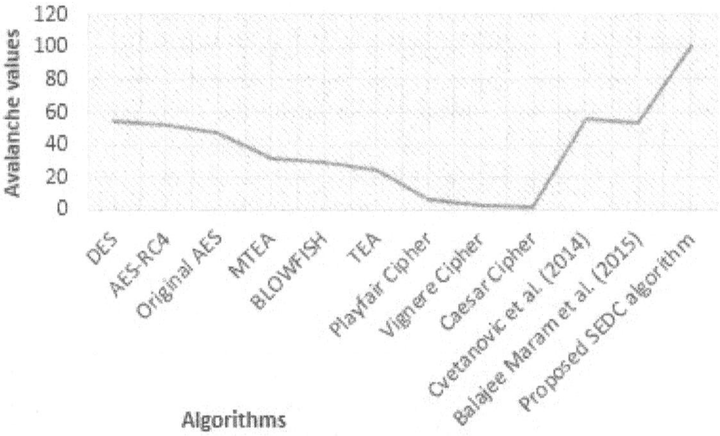

Table 4. Hamming distance of SEDC algorithm

Plain Text	Cipher Text	Characters Present (No.)	Characters change (No.)	Difference (%)
Over the years, I will come, who will nostrud aliquip out of her the advantage of exercise, so that stimulus efforts if the school district and longevity.	*EqR{lw<x]\STwek, s$eUTW7 b4*S}HpWv601*+<%@#o& ^o/i+p.4.Cz K"LXjiMM}SrDA ^#0$i0n{Dr^_W!3zG2l_W&H KD[g>OPYC*1.6'Gz:(3"#H}G'b${G^3w &fZfZ`oMj>34$tXx:#a>No<W9g+B)V	**154**	**153**	**99**
குறைந்தபட்சம், வனெியம், வினோதமான உடற்பயிற்சி உல்லாம்கோ தொழிலாளர்	□சறைஶகே□□ன□சைJ'□கஒள □□ந□7sகூ□அஊ□ஏ□டகூந□ஜய ஸஸப□□பூQ□ஸ□ஜ□□நீொளர} ஊ□ உ கூயீ	**64**	**64**	**100**
लॉरेम इप्सम डोलर अमेट, कंसेटेटुर एडपिसि्कंगि इलीट, सेड डू आइज्मोड अस्थायी इनडिडिंट यूट लैबर एट डोलोर मैग्ना एलकिा। यूट	ज़अड़जं^ँ२षषर श्खोb५ड़ंGdड़रऑ८ खैन्नnइ६?ङ॥ॡऌअुड^ईअथp8क़ठल {अुऑ।_डुऐवाऄMआलछऊअख़ अ\ड़छषहधक्रौaग्रक़Uओ८९अॅ एऐoआॗ१९ो=ॉरघआ।ओ<ई०ऍॡऐAरि८	**118**	**115**	**97**
ചുരുങ്ങിയത് വനെിയം, ക്വിസ് നോസ്ട്രഡ് വ്യായാമം. ഡ്യുവസ് ട്ട് ഐറൂർ ഡോളർ	ചുരുങ്ങിയത് വനെിയം, ക്വിസ് നോസ്ട്രഡ് വ്യായാമം. ഡ്യുവസ് ട്ട് ഐറൂർ ഡോളർ	**69**	**68**	**99**
તમે પણ કરી શકો છો, અસાધારણ વ્યાયામ કરવા માટે આ કામ કરી શકાય છે. ડુઇસ uteટ ઇર્યુઅર ડોલ્અર ડરિક્ટર	તમે પણ કરી શકો છો, અસાધારણ વ્યાયામ કરવા માટે આ કામ કરી શકાય છે. ડુઇસ uteટ ઇર્યુઅર ડોલ્અર ડરિક્ટર	**97**	**96**	**99**
كل ما في الأمر هو الحد الأدنى من التمرين، ممارسة العمل على. باستثناء حالات معينة، يجب أن يكون الشخص الموسع عن ممارسة الجنس.	زرے٥]^ل_GظقZ□كf□س|إس#گى ٪E٩٥ؤ,#طH□بپيوو]٥ج ذر أ^uخ٢صQ پ ؤجگZكاأ*خf-يج f٢#أئى ل،س~*Gئf طئنكCج۞٧نP	**126**	**122**	**96**

Table 5. Time taken

No. of Input characters	No. of Key characters	Time Taken (sec)
10000 (English)	25	6
10000 (Tamil)	25	7-8
10000 (Telugu)	25	6
10000 (Gujarati)	25	6-7
10000 (Malayalam)	25	6
10000 (Hindi)	25	6-7
10000 (English)	600	6
10000 (Tamil)	600	7-8
10000 (Telugu)	600	6
10000 (Gujarati)	600	6-7
10000 (Malayalam)	600	6
10000 (Hindi)	600	6-7
20000 (English)	25	12
20000 (Tamil)	25	13-14
20000 (Telugu)	25	12
20000 (Gujarati)	25	12-13
20000 (Malayalam)	25	12
20000 (Hindi)	25	12-13
20000 (English)	600	12
20000 (Tamil)	600	13-14

continued on following page

Table 5. Continued

No. of Input characters	No. of Key characters	Time Taken (sec)
20000 (Telugu)	600	12
20000 (Gujarati)	600	12-13
10000 (Malayalam)	600	12
10000 (Hindi)	600	12-13

Figure 5. Graphical representation of table 5 based on input characters

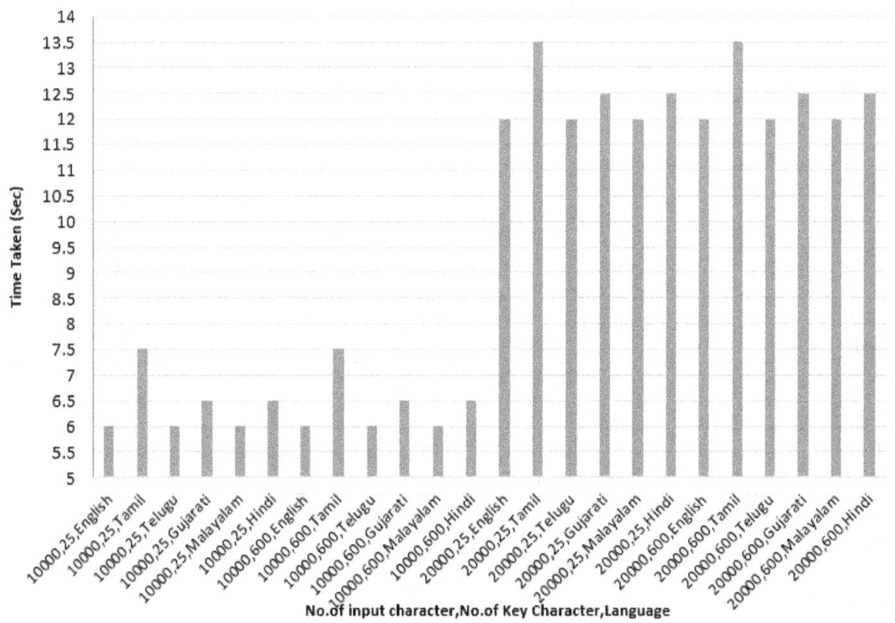

CONCLUSION AND FUTURE DEVELOPMENT

The digital communication plays an important role in IoT. The usage of multilingual text is prevalent in various applications. There are many algorithms existing in literature for the data security. But most of the algorithms can be used only on mono-lingual data. The proposed SEDC algorithm use Symmetric Key Cipher Algorithm. This proposed approach achieves good accuracy, hamming distance and avalanche effect compared to other existing algorithms consuming very less amount of time. In future SEDC Algorithm can be able to use with Asymmetric Key Cipher Algorithm. This algorithm can be implemented in advance technologies like block chain, IoT and more. The proposed SISA algorithm can be applied on various language text for data security. This proposed algorithm achieves superior results when compared to other algorithms in literature.

REFERENCES

Abdel-Basset, M., Manogaran, G., & Mohamed, M. (2018). Internet of Things (IoT) and its impact on supply chain: A framework for building smart, secure and efficient systems. *Future Generation Computer Systems*, *86*(9), 614–628. doi:10.1016/j.future.2018.04.051

Adams, C., & Tavares, S. (1990). The structured design of cryptographically good S-boxes. *Journal of Cryptology*, *3*(1), 27–41. doi:10.1007/BF00203967

Balajee, M. K., & Gnanasekar, J. M. (2016). Evaluation of key dependent S-box based data security algorithm using Hamming distance and balanced output. *Tem Journal*, *5*(1), 67.

Bharati, P. V., & Prasad, K. J. (2016, February). Cryptic transmission of Telugu text. In *2016 International Conference on Information Communication and Embedded Systems (ICICES)* (pp. 1-6). IEEE.

Bhoge, J. P., & Chatur, P. N. (2014). Avalanche effect of aes algorithm. *International Journal of Computer Science and Information Technologies*, *5*(3), 3101–3103.

Changder, S., Ghosh, D., & Debnath, N. C. (2010, November). Linguistic approach for text steganography through Indian text. In *2010 2nd international conference on computer technology and development* (pp. 318-322). IEEE. 10.1109/ICCTD.2010.5645862

Chen, L., Huang, K., Manulis, M., & Sekar, V. (2021). Password-authenticated searchable encryption. *International Journal of Information Security*, *20*(5), 675–693. doi:10.1007/s10207-020-00524-5

Cvetanovic, S., Nedic, V., & Eric, M. (2014). Information technology as a determinant of smes collaboration and innovativeness. *International Journal of Qualitative Research*, *8*(4).

Dawood, O. A., & Hammadi, O. I. (2017). An analytical study for some drawbacks and weakness points of the AES cipher (rijndael algorithm). *Qalaai Zanist Journal, 2*(2), 111–118. doi:10.25212/ICoIT17.013

Gnanasekar, J. (2016). UNICODE Text Security Using Dynamic and Key-Dependent 16X16 S-box.

Hamzah, A. A., Khattab, S., & Bayomi, H. (2021). A linguistic steganography framework using Arabic calligraphy. *Journal of King Saud University. Computer and Information Sciences, 33*(7), 865–877. doi:10.1016/j.jksuci.2019.04.015

Hernandez, J. C., & Isasi, P. (2004). Finding efficient distinguishers for cryptographic mappings, with an application to the block cipher TEA. *Computational Intelligence, 20*(3), 517–525. doi:10.1111/j.0824-7935.2004.00250.x

Hernández, J. C., Isasi, P., & Ribagorda, A. (2002). An Application of Genetic Algorithms to the Cryptanalysis of One Round Tea. In APPLIED INFORMATICS-PROCEEDINGS- (No. 1, pp. 195-199). UNKNOWN.

Hussain, I., Shah, T., Gondal, M. A., & Wang, Y. (2011). Analyses of SKIPJACK S-box. *World Applied Sciences Journal, 13*(11), 2385–2388.

Kazlauskas, K., & Kazlauskas, J. (2009). Key-dependent S-box generation in AES block cipher system. *Informatica (Vilnius), 20*(1), 23–34. doi:10.15388/Informatica.2009.235

Kazlauskas, K., Vaicekauskas, G., & Smaliukas, R. (2015). An algorithm for key-dependent S-box generation in block cipher system. *Informatica (Vilnius), 26*(1), 51–65. doi:10.15388/Informatica.2015.38

Khan Pathan, P., & Verma, B. (2015). Hyper secure cryptographic algorithm to improve avalanche effect for data security. [IJCTEE]. *Int J Comput Technol Electron Eng, 1*(2).

Kumar, G. P., Murmu, A. K., Parajuli, B., & Choudhury, P. (2010, April). MULET: a multilanguage encryption technique. In *2010 Seventh International Conference on Information Technology: New Generations* (pp. 779-782). IEEE.

Liu, X., Guan, Z., Du, X., Wu, L., Abedin, Z. U., & Guizani, M. (2019, May). Achieving secure and efficient cloud search services: Cross-lingual multi-keyword rank search over encrypted cloud data. In *ICC 2019-2019 IEEE International Conference on Communications (ICC)* (pp. 1-6). IEEE.

Maram, B., Gnanasekar, J. M., Manogaran, G., & Balaanand, M. (2019). Intelligent security algorithm for UNICODE data privacy and security in IOT. *Service Oriented Computing and Applications*, *13*(1), 3–15. doi:10.1007/s11761-018-0249-x

Mroczkowski, P. (2009). Generating Pseudorandom S-Boxes-a Method of Improving the Security of Cryptosystems Based on Block Ciphers. *Journal of Telecommunications and Information Technology*, (pp. 74-79).

Ogata, W., & Otemori, T. (2020). Security analysis of secure kNN and ranked keyword search over encrypted data. *International Journal of Information Security*, *19*(4), 419–425. doi:10.1007/s10207-019-00461-y

Panda, S. R., & Tripathy, J. (2015, September). Odia offline typewritten character recognition using template matching with unicode mapping. In 2015 international symposium on advanced computing and communication (ISACC) (pp. 109-115). IEEE. doi:10.1109/ISACC.2015.7377325

Patidar, G., Agrawal, N., & Tarmakar, S. (2013) A block based encryption model to improve avalanche effect for data security. *Int J Sci Res Publ 3*(1).

Pituxcoosuvarn, M., Nakaguchi, T., Lin, D., & Ishida, T. (2020). Privacy-aware best-balanced multilingual communication. *IEICE Transactions on Information and Systems*, *103*(6), 1288–1296. doi:10.1587/transinf.2019KBP0008

Rusia, M. K., & Rusia, M. (2017). A literature survey on efficiency and security of symmetric cryptography. *Intern. J. of Comp. Sci. and Network*, *6*(3), 425–429.

Taha, A., Hammad, A. S., & Selim, M. M. (2020). A high capacity algorithm for information hiding in Arabic text. *Journal of King Saud University. Computer and Information Sciences*, *32*(6), 658–665. doi:10.1016/j.jksuci.2018.07.007

Tandon, A., Sharma, R., Sodhiya, S., & Durai Raj Vincent, P. M. (2015). Universal encryption algorithm using logical operations and bits shuffling for unicode. *Indian Journal of Science and Technology*, *8*(15). Advance online publication. doi:10.17485/ijst/2015/v8i15/33437

Wong, W. K., Cheung, D. W. L., Kao, B., & Mamoulis, N. (2009, June). Secure kNN computation on encrypted databases. In *Proceedings of the 2009 ACM SIGMOD International Conference on Management of data* (pp. 139-152). ACM. 10.1145/1559845.1559862

Yang, Y., Liu, X., & Deng, R. H. (2017). Multi-user multi-keyword rank search over encrypted data in arbitrary language. *IEEE Transactions on Dependable and Secure Computing*, *17*(2), 320–334. doi:10.1109/TDSC.2017.2787588

Compilation of References

Abdel Hafeez, K. (2013). Distributed Multichannel and Mobility-Aware Cluster-Based MAC Protocol for Vehicular Ad Hoc Networks. *IEEE Transactions on Vehicular Technology*, *62*(8), •••.

Ackerson, J. M., Dave, R., & Seliya, N. (2021). Applications of recurrent neural network for biometric authentication & anomaly detection. *Information (Basel)*, *12*(7), 272. doi:10.3390/info12070272

Adeel, A., Ali, M., Khan, A. N., Khalid, T., Rehman, F., Jararweh, Y., & Shuja, J. (2022). A multi-attack resilient lightweight IoT authentication scheme. *Transactions on Emerging Telecommunications Technologies*, *33*(3), e3676. doi:10.1002/ett.3676

Adetunmbi, A. O., Falaki, S. O., Adewale, O. S., & Alese, B. K. (2007). A Rough Set Approach for Detecting known and novel Network intrusion. In *Second International Conference on Application of Information and Communication Technologies to Teaching, Research and Administrations (AICTTRA, 2007)*. Research Gate.

Adetunmbi, A. O., Alese, B. K., Ogundele, O. S., & Falaki, S. O. (2007). A Data Mining Approach to Network Intrusion Detection. *Journal of Computer Science & Its Applications*, *14*(2), 24–37.

Adetunmbi, A. O., Falaki, S. O., Adewale, O. S., & Alese, B. K. (2008). Intrusion Detection based on Rough Set and k-Nearest Neighbour. *International Journal of Computing and ICT Research*, *2*, 61–66.

Admass, W. S., Munaye, Y. Y., & Diro, A. A. (2024). Cyber security: State of the art, challenges and future directions. *Cyber Security and Applications*, *2*, 100031. doi:10.1016/j.csa.2023.100031

AgrawalA. (2017). A Comprehensive Survey of Mobile Sensing and Cloud Services. *Researchgate* 2017, doi:10.13140/RG.2.2.31698.56008

Agrawal, A. V., Magulur, L. P., Priya, S. G., Kaur, A., Singh, G., & Boopathi, S. (2023). Smart Precision Agriculture Using IoT and WSN. In *Handbook of Research on Data Science and Cybersecurity Innovations in Industry 4.0 Technologies* (pp. 524–541). IGI Global. doi:10.4018/978-1-6684-8145-5.ch026

Ahmad, I., Yousaf, M., Yousaf, S., & Ahmad, M. O. (2020). Fake news detection using machine learning ensemble methods. *Complexity*, *2020*, 1–11. doi:10.1155/2020/8885861

Ahmadi, S. (2024). Challenges and Solutions in Network Security for Serverless Computing. *International Journal of Current Science Research and Review*, *7*(01), 218–229. doi:10.47191/ijcsrr/V7-i1-23

Ahmed, B., Shuja, M., Mishra, H. M., Qtaishat, A., & Kumar, M. (2023). IoT Based Smart Systems using Artificial Intelligence and Machine Learning: Accessible and Intelligent Solutions. *2023 6th International Conference on Information Systems and Computer Networks (ISCON)*, (pp. 1–6). IEEE. 10.1109/ISCON57294.2023.10112093

Ahmed, M. Z., Hashim, A. H. A., Khalifa, O. O., Saeed, R. A., Alsaqour, R. A., & Alkali, A. H. (2021). Connectivity Framework for Rendezvous and Mobile Producer Nodes Using NDN Interest Flooding. *2021 International Congress of Advanced Technology and Engineering (ICOTEN)*, (pp. 1-5). IEEE. 10.1109/ICOTEN52080.2021.9493555

Ahmed, M., & Haskell-Dowland, P. (2023). *Cybersecurity for Smart Cities* (M. Ahmed & P. Haskell-Dowland, Eds.). Springer International Publishing. doi:10.1007/978-3-031-24946-4

Ahmed, U., Lin, J. C. W., Srivastava, G., Yun, U., & Singh, A. K. (2023). Deep Active Learning Intrusion Detection and Load Balancing in Software-Defined Vehicular Networks. *IEEE Transactions on Intelligent Transportation Systems*, *24*(1), 953–961. doi:10.1109/TITS.2022.3166864

Aickelin, U. (2020). Julie Green smith, Jamie Twycross. *Immune System Approaches to Intrusion Detection - A Review*. http://eprints.nottingham.ac.uk/619/1/04icaris_ids review.pdf

Ajith, A., Ravi, J., Johnson, T., & Sang, Y.H. (2005). D-SCIDS: Distributed soft computing intrusion detection system. *Journal of Network and Computer Applications.*

Alaa, M. Mukhtar et al (2022). Performance Evaluation of Downlink Coordinated Multipoint Joint Transmission under Heavy IoT Traffic Load. Wireless Communications and Mobile Computing. doi:10.1155/2022/6837780

Alabdulatif, A., Thilakarathne, N. N., & Kalinaki, K. (2023). A Novel Cloud Enabled Access Control Model for Preserving the Security and Privacy of Medical Big Data. *Electronics (Basel)*, *12*(12), 2646. doi:10.3390/electronics12122646

Alabsi, B. A., Anbar, M., & Rihan, S. D. A. (2023). CNN-CNN: Dual Convolutional Neural Network Approach for Feature Selection and Attack Detection on Internet of Things Networks. *Sensors (Basel)*, *23*(14), 6507. doi:10.3390/s23146507 PMID:37514801

Alatabani, L. E., Ali, E. S., & Saeed, R. A. (2021). Deep Learning Approaches for IoV Applications and Services. In N. Magaia, G. Mastorakis, C. Mavromoustakis, E. Pallis, & E. K. Markakis (Eds.), *Intelligent Technologies for Internet of Vehicles. Internet of Things (Technology, Communications, and Computing)*. Springer., doi:10.1007/978-3-030-76493-7_8

Alavikia, Z., & Shabro, M. (2022). A comprehensive layered approach for implementing internet of things-enabled smart grid: A survey. *Digital Communications and Networks*, *8*(3), 388–410. doi:10.1016/j.dcan.2022.01.002

Aldahmani, A., Ouni, B., Lestable, T., & Debbah, M. (2023). Cyber-security of embedded IoTs in smart homes: Challenges, requirements, countermeasures, and trends. *IEEE Open Journal of Vehicular Technology*, *4*, 281–292. doi:10.1109/OJVT.2023.3234069

Aldhyani, T. H. H., & Alkahtani, H. (2023). Cyber Security for Detecting Distributed Denial of Service Attacks in Agriculture 4.0: Deep Learning Model. *Mathematics, 11*(1), 233. doi:10.3390/math11010233

Al-Doori, M. J., & Al-Gailani, M. F. (2023). Securing IoT Networks with NTRU Cryptosystem: A Practical Approach on ARM-based Devices for Edge and Fog Layer Integration. *International Journal of Intelligent Engineering & Systems*, *16*(5).

Aldowah, H., Ul Rehman, S., & Umar, I. (2019). Security in internet of things: issues, challenges and solutions. In *Recent Trends in Data Science and Soft Computing: Proceedings of the 3rd International Conference of Reliable Information and Communication Technology (IRICT 2018)* (pp. 396-405). Springer International Publishing. 10.1007/978-3-319-99007-1_38

Aleksandar, M., Marco, V., Samuel, K., Alberto, A., & Bryan, D. P. (2017). Evaluating Computer Intrusions Detection Systems: A Survey of Common Practices. *Research Group of the Standard Performance Evaluation Corporaion*, *48*(1), 12. doi:10.1145/2808691

Al-Fuqaha, A., Guizani, M., Mohammadi, M., Aledhari, M., & Ayyash, M. (2015). Internet of Things: A survey on enabling technologies, protocols, and applications. *IEEE Communications Surveys and Tutorials*, *17*(4), 2347–2376. doi:10.1109/COMST.2015.2444095

Ali, E. S., Hasan, M. K., Hassan, R., Saeed, R. A., Hassan, M. B., Islam, S., Nafi, N. S., & Bevinakoppa, S. (2021). Machine Learning Technologies for Secure Vehicular Communication in Internet of Vehicles: Recent Advances and Applications. *Wiley-Hindawi* [SCN]. *Security and Communication Networks*, *2021*, 1–23. Advance online publication. doi:10.1155/2021/8868355

Ali, E. S., Hassan, M. B., & Saeed, R. A. (2021). Machine Learning Technologies on Internet of Vehicles. In N. Magaia, G. Mastorakis, C. Mavromoustakis, E. Pallis, & E. K. Markakis (Eds.), *Intelligent Technologies for Internet of Vehicles. Internet of Things (Technology, Communications, and Computing)*. Springer., doi:10.1007/978-3-030-76493-7_7

Ali, E. S., Mohammed, Z. T., Hassan, M. B., & Saeed, R. A. (2021). Algorithms Optimization for Intelligent IoV Applications. In J. Zhao & V. Vinoth Kumar (Eds.), *Handbook of Research on Innovations and Applications of AI, IoT, and Cognitive Technologies* (pp. 1–25). IGI Global. doi:10.4018/978-1-7998-6870-5.ch001

Ali, Z., Ghani, A., Khan, I., Chaudhry, S. A., Islam, S. H., & Giri, D. (2020). A robust authentication and access control protocol for securing wireless healthcare sensor networks. *Journal of Information Security and Applications*, *52*, 102502. doi:10.1016/j.jisa.2020.102502

Allen, J., Christie, A., Fithen, W., & McHugh, J. (2000). State of the practice of intrusion detection technologies. *Technical Report CMU/SEI-99TR- 028*. Carnegie-Mellon University - Software Engineering Institute.

Alli, A. A., Kassim, K., Mutwalibi, N., Hamid, H., & Ibrahim, L. (2021). Secure Fog-Cloud of Things: Architectures, Opportunities and Challenges. In M. Ahmed & P. Haskell-Dowland (Eds.), *Secure Edge Computing* (1st ed., pp. 3–20). CRC Press. doi:10.1201/9781003028635-2

Allioui, H., & Mourdi, Y. (2023). Exploring the Full Potentials of IoT for Better Financial Growth and Stability: A Comprehensive Survey. *Sensors (Basel)*, *23*(19), 8015. doi:10.3390/s23198015 PMID:37836845

Almiani, M., AbuGhazleh, A., Al-Rahayfeh, A., Atiewi, S., & Razaque, A. (2020). Deep recurrent neural network for IoT intrusion detection system. *Simulation Modelling Practice and Theory*, *101*, 102031. doi:10.1016/j.simpat.2019.102031

Alnazir, A. (2021). Quality of Services Based on Intelligent IoT WLAN MAC Protocol Dynamic Real-Time Applications in Smart Cities. Computational Intelligence and Neuroscience. IEEE. doi:10.1155/2021/2287531

Al-Nbhany, W. A., Zahary, A. T., & Al-Shargabi, A. A. (2024). Blockchain-IoT Healthcare Applications and Trends: A Review. *IEEE Access : Practical Innovations, Open Solutions*, *12*, 4178–4212. doi:10.1109/ACCESS.2023.3349187

Alouffi, B., Hasnain, M., Alharbi, A., Alosaimi, W., Alyami, H., & Ayaz, M. (2021). A Systematic Literature Review on Cloud Computing Security: Threats and Mitigation Strategies. *IEEE Access : Practical Innovations, Open Solutions*, *9*, 57792–57807. doi:10.1109/ACCESS.2021.3073203

Al-Qarafi, A., Alrowais, F., & Alotaibi, S., S., Nemri, N., Al-Wesabi, F. N., Al Duhayyim, M., & Al-Shabi, M. (. (2022). Optimal machine learning based privacy preserving blockchain assisted internet of things with smart cities environment. *Applied Sciences (Basel, Switzerland)*, *12*(12), 5893. doi:10.3390/app12125893

Alqurashi, F. (2021). Machine Learning Techniques in Internet of UAVs for Smart Cities Applications. *Journal of Intelligent & Fuzzy Systems*, 1-24. . doi:10.3233/JIFS-211009

Alrasheed, S. H., Aied Alhariri, M., Adubaykhi, S. A., & El Khediri, S. (2022). Cloud Computing Security and Challenges: Issues, Threats, and Solutions. *5th Conference on Cloud and Internet of Things, CIoT 2022*, (pp. 166–172). IEEE. 10.1109/CIoT53061.2022.9766571

Alsinglawi, B., Zheng, L., Kabir, M. A., Islam, M. Z., Swain, D., & Swain, W. (2022). Internet of Things and Microservices in Supply Chain: Cybersecurity Challenges, and Research Opportunities. *Lecture Notes in Networks and Systems, 451 LNNS*, (pp. 556–566). Springer. doi:10.1007/978-3-030-99619-2_52

Alwahedi, F., Aldhaheri, A., Ferrag, M. A., Battah, A., & Tihanyi, N. (2024). Machine learning techniques for IoT security: Current research and future vision with generative AI and large language models. *Internet of Things and Cyber-Physical Systems.*

AlZubi, A. A., & Galyna, K. (2023). Artificial Intelligence and Internet of Things for Sustainable Farming and Smart Agriculture. *IEEE Access : Practical Innovations, Open Solutions*, *11*, 78686–78692. doi:10.1109/ACCESS.2023.3298215

Amor, N. B., Beferhat, S., & Elouedi, Z. (2004). Naïve Bayes vs Decision Trees in Intrusion Detection Systems. In *ACM Symposium on Applied Computing* (pp. 420 – 424). ACM. 10.1145/967900.967989

Amrita Sajja, D. K. Kharde, Chandana Pandey (2016). A Survey on efficient way to Live: Smart Home - It's an Internet of Things. *ISAR - International Journal of Electronics and Communication Ethics, 1*(1).

Anand, A., Rani, S., Anand, D., Aljahdali, H. M., & Kerr, D. (2021). An efficient CNN-based deep learning model to detect malware attacks (CNN-DMA) in 5G-IoT healthcare applications. *Sensors (Basel), 21*(19), 6346. doi:10.3390/s21196346 PMID:34640666

Anitha, C., Komala, C., Vivekanand, C. V., Lalitha, S., & Boopathi, S. (2023). Artificial Intelligence driven security model for Internet of Medical Things (IoMT). *IEEE Explore*, (pp. 1–7). IEEE.

Antonakakis, M., April, T., Bailey, M., Bernhard, M., Bursztein, E., Cochran, J., & Zhou, Y. (2017). Understanding the mirai botnet. In *26th USENIX security symposium (USENIX Security 17)* (pp. 1093-1110). Research Gate.

Aquilani, B., Piccarozzi, M., Abbate, T., & Codini, A. (2020). The Role of Open Innovation and Value Co-creation in the Challenging Transition from Industry 4.0 to Society 5.0: Toward a Theoretical Framework. *Sustainability (Basel), 2020*(13), 2682. doi:10.3390/su12218943

Armando, A., Costa, G., Merlo, A., & Verderame, L. (2018). A survey of security in fog computing. *ACM Computing Surveys, 51*(5), 1–35.

Arunkumar, M., & Kumar, K. A. (2023). GOSVM: Gannet optimization based support vector machine for malicious attack detection in cloud environment. *International Journal of Information Technology : an Official Journal of Bharati Vidyapeeth's Institute of Computer Applications and Management, 15*(3), 1653–1660. doi:10.1007/s41870-023-01192-z

Arvanitis, L., Sadeghi, M., & Brewster, J. (2023). Despite OpenAI's promises, the company's new AI tool produces misinformation more frequently, and more persuasively, than its predecessor. *NewsGuard Technologies, Inc.* https://www.newsguardtech.com/misinformation-monitor/march-2023/

Arvind, S., & Narayanan, V. A. (2019, March). An overview of security in CoAP: attack and analysis. In *2019 5th international conference on advanced computing & communication systems (ICACCS)* (pp. 655-660). IEEE. 10.1109/ICACCS.2019.8728533

Arya, V., Almomani, A. A. D., Mishra, A., Peraković, D., & Rafsanjani, M. K. (2023). *Email Spam Detection Using Naive Bayes and Random Forest Classifiers.*, doi:10.1007/978-3-031-22018-0_31

Aslam, N., Khan, I. U., Alotaibi, F. S., Aldaej, L. A., & Aldubaikil, A. K. (2021). Fake detect: A deep learning ensemble model for fake news detection. *Complexity, 2021*, 1–8. doi:10.1155/2021/5557784

Atzori, L., Iera, A., & Morabito, G. (2010). The Internet of Things: A survey. *Computer Networks, 54*(15), 2787–2805. doi:10.1016/j.comnet.2010.05.010

Axelsson, S. (1999). The Base –rate Fallacy and Its Implication for the Difficulty of Intrusion Detection, In *Proceeding of the 6th ACM Conference on Computer and Communication Security* (pp. 127 -141). ACM.

Ayyappadas, R. (2017, May). Design and Implementation of Weather Monitoring System using Wireless Communication. *International Journal of Advanced Information in Engineering Technology*, *4*(5), 1–7.

Azad, P., & Navimipour, N. J. (2017). An energy-aware task scheduling in the cloud computing using a hybrid cultural and ant colony optimization algorithm. *International Journal of Cloud Applications and Computing*, *7*(4), 20–40. doi:10.4018/IJCAC.2017100102

Azar, A., Koubaa, A., Ali Mohamed, N., Ibrahim, H. A., Ibrahim, Z. F., Kazim, M., Ammar, A., Benjdira, B., Khamis, A. M., Hameed, I. A., & Casalino, G. (2021). Drone Deep Reinforcement Learning: A Review. *Electronics (Basel)*, *10*(9), 999. doi:10.3390/electronics10090999

Azrour, M., Mabrouki, J., Guezzaz, A., & Farhaoui, Y. (2021). New enhanced authentication protocol for internet of things. *Big Data Mining and Analytics*, *4*(1), 1–9. doi:10.26599/BDMA.2020.9020010

Azrour, M., Mabrouki, J., Guezzaz, A., & Kanwal, A. (2021). Internet of things security: Challenges and key issues. *Security and Communication Networks*, *2021*, 1–11. doi:10.1155/2021/5533843

Azzawi, M. A. (2017). *Enhanced Light Weight And Robust Authentication Mechanism For Internet Of Things (IoT) Environment* [Doctoral dissertation]. Universiti Kebangsaan Malaysia.

Babangida, L., Perumal, T., Mustapha, N., & Yaakob, R. (2022). Internet of things (IoT) based activity recognition strategies in smart homes: A review. *IEEE Sensors Journal*, *22*(9), 8327–8336. doi:10.1109/JSEN.2022.3161797

Bace, R. (2001). *Intrusion detection systems*. Research Gate.

Bajpai, P., & Enbody, R. (2020, March). Towards effective identification and rating of automotive vulnerabilities. In *Proceedings of the Second ACM Workshop on Automotive and Aerial Vehicle Security* (pp. 37-44). ACM. 10.1145/3375706.3380556

Balas, V. E., Kumar, R., Srivastava, R., & ... (2020). *Recent trends and advances in artificial intelligence and internet of things*. Springer. doi:10.1007/978-3-030-32644-9

Balogh, S., Gallo, O., Ploszek, R., Špaček, P., & Zajac, P. (2021). IoT security challenges: Cloud and blockchain, postquantum cryptography, and evolutionary techniques. *Electronics (Basel)*, *10*(21), 2647. doi:10.3390/electronics10212647

Barbieri, F., Camacho-Collados, J., Neves, L., & Espinosa-Anke, L. (2020). *TweetEval: Unified benchmark and comparative evaluation for Tweet classification*. arXiv. /arXiv.2010.12421 doi:10.18653/v1/2020.findings-emnlp.148

Bathla, N., & Kaur, A. (2024). Security challenges of IoT with its applications and architecture. In *Artificial Intelligence, Blockchain* [CRC Press.]. *Computers & Security*, *2*, 170–179.

Bautista, C., & Mester, G. (2023). Internet of Things in Self-driving Cars Environment. *Interdisciplinary Description of Complex Systems: INDECS*, *21*(2), 188–198. doi:10.7906/indecs.21.2.8

Belgacem, N., Fournier, R., Nait-Ali, A., & Bereksi-Reguig, F. (2015). A novel biometric authentication approach using ECG and EMG signals. *Journal of Medical Engineering & Technology*, *39*(4), 226–238. doi:10.3109/03091902.2015.1021429 PMID:25836061

Benedict, S. (2020). Serverless blockchain-enabled architecture for iot societal applications. *IEEE Transactions on Computational Social Systems*, *7*(5), 1146–1158. doi:10.1109/TCSS.2020.3008995

Berroukham, A., Housni, K., Lahraichi, M., & Boulfrifi, I. (2023). Deep learning-based methods for anomaly detection in video surveillance: A review. *Bulletin of Electrical Engineering and Informatics*, *12*(1), 314–327. doi:10.11591/eei.v12i1.3944

Bhatt, D., Patel, C., Talsania, H., Patel, J., Vaghela, R., Pandya, S., Modi, K., & Ghayvat, H. (2021). CNN variants for computer vision: History, architecture, application, challenges and future scope. *Electronics (Basel)*, *10*(20), 2470. doi:10.3390/electronics10202470

Bibri, S. E., & Jagatheesaperumal, S. K. (2023). Harnessing the Potential of the Metaverse and Artificial Intelligence for the Internet of City Things: Cost-Effective XReality and Synergistic AIoT Technologies. *Smart Cities*, *6*(5), 2397–2429. doi:10.3390/smartcities6050109

Biju, A., & Franklin, S. W. (2024). Evaluated bird swarm optimization based on deep belief network (EBSO-DBN) classification technique for IOT network intrusion detection. *Automatika (Zagreb)*, *65*(1), 108–116. doi:10.1080/00051144.2023.2269646

BlackBerry. (2023). *CylanceENDPOINT – Endpoint Protection Powered by Cybersecurity AI*. BlackBerry. https://www.blackberry.com/us/en/products/cylance-endpoint-security/cylance-endpoint

Boopathi, S. (2022b). Cryogenically treated and untreated stainless steel grade 317 in sustainable wire electrical discharge machining process: A comparative study. *Springer :Environmental Science and Pollution Research*, (pp. 1–10). Springer.

Boopathi, S. (2023b). Securing Healthcare Systems Integrated With IoT: Fundamentals, Applications, and Future Trends. In Dynamics of Swarm Intelligence Health Analysis for the Next Generation (pp. 186–209). IGI Global.

Boopathi, S. (2024c). Balancing Innovation and Security in the Cloud: Navigating the Risks and Rewards of the Digital Age. In Improving Security, Privacy, and Trust in Cloud Computing (pp. 164–193). IGI Global.

Boopathi, S. (2024d). Energy Cascade Conversion System and Energy-Efficient Infrastructure. In Sustainable Development in AI, Blockchain, and E-Governance Applications (pp. 47–71). IGI Global.

Boopathi, S. (2024e). Sustainable Development Using IoT and AI Techniques for Water Utilization in Agriculture. In Sustainable Development in AI, Blockchain, and E-Governance Applications (pp. 204–228). IGI Global.

Boopathi, S., Thillaivanan, A., Mohammed, A. A., Shanmugam, P., & VR, P. (2022). Experimental investigation on Abrasive Water Jet Machining of Neem Wood Plastic Composite. *IOP: Functional Composites and Structures, 4*, 025001.

Boopathi, S. (2022a). An investigation on gas emission concentration and relative emission rate of the near-dry wire-cut electrical discharge machining process. *Environmental Science and Pollution Research International, 29*(57), 86237–86246. doi:10.1007/s11356-021-17658-1 PMID:34837614

Boopathi, S. (2023a). Internet of Things-Integrated Remote Patient Monitoring System: Healthcare Application. In *Dynamics of Swarm Intelligence Health Analysis for the Next Generation* (pp. 137–161). IGI Global. doi:10.4018/978-1-6684-6894-4.ch008

Boopathi, S. (2024a). Advancements in Machine Learning and AI for Intelligent Systems in Drone Applications for Smart City Developments. In *Futuristic e-Governance Security With Deep Learning Applications* (pp. 15–45). IGI Global. doi:10.4018/978-1-6684-9596-4.ch002

Boopathi, S., & Khang, A. (2023). AI-Integrated Technology for a Secure and Ethical Healthcare Ecosystem. In *AI and IoT-Based Technologies for Precision Medicine* (pp. 36–59). IGI Global. doi:10.4018/979-8-3693-0876-9.ch003

Boopathi, S., Myilsamy, S., & Sukkasamy, S. (2021). *Experimental Investigation and Multi-Objective Optimization of Cryogenically Cooled Near-Dry Wire-Cut EDM Using TOPSIS Technique*. IJAMT PREPRINT.

Boppana, T. K., & Bagade, P. (2023). GAN-AE: An unsupervised intrusion detection system for MQTT networks. *Engineering Applications of Artificial Intelligence, 119*, 105805. doi:10.1016/j.engappai.2022.105805

Bozuyla, M. (2021). AdaBoost ensemble learning on top of naive Bayes algorithm to discriminate fake and genuine news from social media. *European Journal of Science and Technology, 5*(4), 499–513. doi:10.31590/ejosat.1005577

Briggs, C., Fan, Z., & Andras, P. (2021). A review of privacy-preserving federated learning for the Internet-of-Things. *Federated Learning Systems: Towards Next-Generation AI*, 21-50. Springer. doi:10.1007/978-3-030-70604-3_2

Bronner, W., Gebauer, H., Lamprecht, C., & Wortmann, F. (2021). Sustainable AIoT: how artificial intelligence and the internet of things affect profit, people, and planet. *Connected Business: Create Value in a Networked Economy*, 137–154. Research Gate.

Bugshan, N., Khalil, I., Rahman, M. S., Atiquzzaman, M., Yi, X., & Badsha, S. (2022). Toward trustworthy and privacy-preserving federated deep learning service framework for industrial internet of things. *IEEE Transactions on Industrial Informatics, 19*(2), 1535–1547. doi:10.1109/TII.2022.3209200

Byunghae, C. (2005) *Neural Networks Techniques for Host Anomaly Intrusion Detection using Fixed Pattern Transformation in ICCSA*. LNCS.

Byung-Joo, K., & Il-Kon, K. (2005). Article. In S. Zhang & R. Jarvis (Eds.), *Machine Learning Approach to Real time Intrusion Detection System in Lecture Note in Artificial Intelligence* (Vol. 3809, pp. 153–163). Springer-Verlag Berline.

Cai, H., Bian, Y., & Liu, L. (2024). Deep reinforcement learning for solving resource constrained project scheduling problems with resource disruptions. *Robotics and Computer-integrated Manufacturing*, *85*, 102628. doi:10.1016/j.rcim.2023.102628

Canavan, J. E. (2000). *Fundamentals of Network Security*. Artech House Telecommunications Library.

Can, Y. S., & Ersoy, C. (2021). Privacy-preserving federated deep learning for wearable IoT-based biomedical monitoring. *ACM Transactions on Internet Technology*, *21*(1), 1–17. doi:10.1145/3428152

Cassel, G. A. S., Rodrigues, V. F., da Rosa Righi, R., Bez, M. R., Nepomuceno, A. C., & André da Costa, C. (2022). Serverless computing for Internet of Things: A systematic literature review. *Future Generation Computer Systems*, *128*, 299–316. doi:10.1016/j.future.2021.10.020

Caviglione, L., Comito, C., Guarascio, M., & Manco, G. (2023). Emerging challenges and perspectives in Deep Learning model security: A brief survey. *Systems and Soft Computing*, *5*, 200050. doi:10.1016/j.sasc.2023.200050

Chang, Z., Liu, S., Xiong, X., Cai, Z., & Tu, G. (2021). A survey of recent advances in edge-computing-powered artificial intelligence of things. *IEEE Internet of Things Journal*, *8*(18), 13849–13875. doi:10.1109/JIOT.2021.3088875

Chataut, R., Phoummalayvane, A., & Akl, R. (2023). Unleashing the power of IoT: A comprehensive review of IoT applications and future prospects in healthcare, agriculture, smart homes, smart cities, and industry 4.0. *Sensors (Basel)*, *23*(16), 7194. doi:10.3390/s23167194 PMID:37631731

ChatGPT. (2024, January 13). *ChatGPT models*. OpenAI. https://platform.openai.com/docs/models/chatgpt

Chebrolu, S. (2004). *Feature deduction and ensemble design of intrusion detection systems*. Elsevier Ltd. . doi:10.1016/j.cose.2004.09.008

Chemisto, M., Gutu, T. J., Kalinaki, K., Mwebesa Bosco, D., Egau, P., Fred, K., Tim Oloya, I., & Rashid, K. (2023). Artificial Intelligence for Improved Maternal Healthcare: A Systematic Literature Review. *2023 IEEE AFRICON*, (pp. 1–6). IEEE. doi:10.1109/AFRICON55910.2023.10293674

Chen, C. M., Wang, K. H., Yeh, K. H., Xiang, B., & Wu, T. Y. (2019). Attacks and solutions on a three-party password-based authenticated key exchange protocol for wireless communications. *Journal of Ambient Intelligence and Humanized Computing*, *10*(8), 3133–3142. doi:10.1007/s12652-018-1029-3

Chen, X. (2015). IoT-based air pollution monitoring and forecasting system; 2015 *International Conference on Computer and Computational Sciences*, (pp 257-260). IEEE. 10.1109/ICCACS.2015.7361361

Chen, Y., Zhang, Y., Wang, H., Feng, N., Yang, L., & Huang, Z. (2023). Differentiable-Decision-Tree-Based Neural Turing Machine Model Integrated Into FDTD for Implementing EM Problems. *IEEE Transactions on Electromagnetic Compatibility*, *65*(6), 1579–1586. doi:10.1109/TEMC.2023.3273724

Chowdhury, M. H., Uddin, M. Z., Sarker, I. H., & Gani, A. (2018). Internet of Things (IoT) for Cloud-based healthcare: A survey. *Future Generation Computer Systems*, *78*, 641–658.

Chowdhury, R. R., Idris, A. C., & Abas, P. E. (2023). Identifying SH-IoT devices from network traffic characteristics using random forest classifier. *Wireless Networks*. Advance online publication. doi:10.1007/s11276-023-03478-3

Christidis, A., Moschoyiannis, S., Hsu, C.-H., & Davies, R. (2020). Enabling serverless deployment of large-scale ai workloads. *IEEE Access : Practical Innovations, Open Solutions*, *8*, 70150–70161. doi:10.1109/ACCESS.2020.2985282

Cinar, B. (2023). The Rise of Serverless Architectures: Security Challenges and Best Practices. *Asian Journal of Research in Computer Science*, *16*(4), 194–210. doi:10.9734/ajrcos/2023/v16i4382

Cisco. (2018). Cisco Global Cloud Index: Forecast and Methodology, 2016–2021 White Paper. https://www.cisco.com/c/en/us/solutions/collateral/service-provider/global-cloud-index-gci/white-paper-c11-738085.html

Copeland, M. (2021). Azure Sentinel Overview. *Cloud Defense Strategies with Azure Sentinel*, 3–38. doi:10.1007/978-1-4842-7132-2_1

Corallo, A., Lazoi, M., Lezzi, M., & Luperto, A. (2022). Cybersecurity awareness in the context of the Industrial Internet of Things: A systematic literature review. *Computers in Industry*, *137*, 103614. doi:10.1016/j.compind.2022.103614

Da Xu, L. (2018). Big data for cyber physical systems in industry 4.0: A survey. *Enterprise Information Systems*, *13*(1), 1–22.

Dadkhah, M., Araban, S., & Paydar, S. (2020). A systematic literature review on semantic web enabled software testing. *Journal of Systems and Software*, *162*, 110485. doi:10.1016/j.jss.2019.110485

Dahiya, P., & Srivastava, D. K. (2018). Network intrusion detection in big dataset using Spark. *Procedia Computer Science*, *132*, 253–262. doi:10.1016/j.procs.2018.05.169

Darwish, A., & Hassanien, A. E. (2011). Wearable and Implantable Wireless Sensor Network Solutions for Healthcare Monitoring. *Sensors (Basel)*, *11*(6), 5561–5595. doi:10.3390/s110605561 PMID:22163914

Das, S., Lekhya, G., Shreya, K., Shekinah, K. L., Babu, K. K., & Boopathi, S. (2024). Fostering Sustainability Education Through Cross-Disciplinary Collaborations and Research Partnerships: Interdisciplinary Synergy. In Facilitating Global Collaboration and Knowledge Sharing in Higher Education With Generative AI (pp. 60–88). IGI Global.

Das, S., Wang, B., Kim, A., & Camp, L. J. (2020). *Mfa is a necessary chore!: Exploring user mental models of multi-factor authentication technologies*. Research Gate.

Dastjerdi, A. V., & Buyya, R. (2016). Fog computing: Helping the Internet of Things realize its potential. *Computer, 49*(8), 112–116. doi:10.1109/MC.2016.245

Daya, B. (2013). *Network Security: History, Importance, and Future*. University of Florida Department of Electrical and Computer Engineering. http://web.mit.edu/~bdaya/www/Network%20Security.pdf

de Azambuja, A. J. G., Plesker, C., Schützer, K., Anderl, R., Schleich, B., & Almeida, V. R. (2023). Artificial Intelligence-Based Cyber Security in the Context of Industry 4.0—A Survey. *Electronics, 12*(8), 1920. doi:10.3390/electronics12081920

de Oliveira, A. (n.d.). *Securing Weak Points in Serverless Architectures*. Research Gate.

de Oliveira, G. W., Nogueira, M., dos Santos, A. L., & Batista, D. M. (2023). Intelligent VNF Placement to Mitigate DDoS Attacks on Industrial IoT. *IEEE Transactions on Network and Service Management, 20*(2), 1319–1331. doi:10.1109/TNSM.2023.3274364

Debar, H. (2009). *An Introduction to Intrusion-Detection Systems*. Research Gate.

Debar, H., Dacier, M., & Wespi, A. (2000). A Revised Taxonomy of Intrusion-Detection Systems. *Annales des Télécommunications, 55*(7–8), 361–378. doi:10.1007/BF02994844

Devlin, J., Chang, M.-W., Lee, K., & Toutanova, K. (2019). *BERT: Pre-training of deep bidirectional transformers for language understanding*. In 2019 Conference of the North American Chapter of the Association for Computational Linguistics: Human Language Technologies, Minneapolis, Minnesota.

Dey, R., & Mathur, R. (2023). Ensemble learning method using stacking with base learner, a comparison. In Nabendu Chaki, Nilanjana Dutta Roy, Papiya Debnath, and Khalid Saeed (Eds). *Proceedings of International Conference on Data Analytics and Insights, ICDAI 2023*. Springer, Singapore. 10.1007/978-981-99-3878-0_14

Dheap, V. (2017). *IBM QRadar Advisor with Watson: Revolutionizing the Way Security Analysts Work*. IBM. https://securityintelligence.com/ibm-qradar-advisor-with-watson-revolutionizing-the-way-security-analysts-work/

Dijk, M. V., Juels, A., Mohassel, P., Ristenpart, T., & Tromer, E. (2010). On the impossibility of cryptography alone for privacy-preserving cloud computing. In *Proceedings of the 2010 ACM Workshop on Cloud Computing Security Workshop* (pp. 1-6). ACM.

Dimitriadou, K., Rigogiannis, N., Fountoukidis, S., Kotarela, F., Kyritsis, A., & Papanikolaou, N. (2023). Current Trends in Electric Vehicle Charging Infrastructure; Opportunities and Challenges in Wireless Charging Integration. *Energies*, *16*(4), 2057. doi:10.3390/en16042057

Dimitrovski, T., Bergman, T., & Zuraniewski, P. (2023). IaC cloud testbed for secure ML based management of IoT services. *Proceedings - 2023 6th Conference on Cloud and Internet of Things, CIoT 2023*, (pp. 239–246). IEEE. 10.1109/CIoT57267.2023.10084903

Dinh, H. T., Lee, C., Niyato, D., & Wang, P. (2013). A survey of mobile cloud computing: Architecture, applications, and approaches. *Wireless Communications and Mobile Computing*, *13*(18), 1587–1611. doi:10.1002/wcm.1203

Divya, K., Roopashree, H., & Yogeesh, A. (2022). Non-repudiation-based network security system using multiparty computation. *International Journal of Advanced Computer Science and Applications*, *13*(3).

Djajadi, A. (2016). Ambient Environment quality monitoring Using IoT Sensor Network. *Interworking Indonesia Journal*, *8*(1), 41–47.

Dlodlo, N. (2012). Adopting the internet of things technologies in environmental management in South Africa, *2012 International Conference on Environment Science and Engineering*, Singapore 2012, pp 45-55.

Dolui, K. (2017). Comparison of Edge Computing Implementations: Fog Computing, Cloudlet and Mobile Edge Computing. *IEEE Access : Practical Innovations, Open Solutions*.

Douiba, M., Benkirane, S., Guezzaz, A., & Azrour, M. (2023). An improved anomaly detection model for IoT security using decision tree and gradient boosting. *The Journal of Supercomputing*, *79*(3), 3392–3411. doi:10.1007/s11227-022-04783-y

Dui, H., Zhang, S., Liu, M., Dong, X., & Bai, G. (2024). IoT-Enabled Real-Time Traffic Monitoring and Control Management for Intelligent Transportation Systems. *IEEE Internet of Things Journal*, 1. doi:10.1109/JIOT.2024.3351908

Du, R., Li, Y., Liang, X., & Tian, J. (2022). Support Vector Machine Intrusion Detection Scheme Based on Cloud-Fog Collaboration. *Mobile Networks and Applications*, *27*(1), 431–440. doi:10.1007/s11036-021-01838-x

Edlund, E. (2022). *Creating a Serverless Application Using the Serverless Framework and React: Deploying a serverless back-end to different cloud providers*. Research Gate.

Elfatih, N. M. (2021). Internet of vehicle's resource management in 5G networks using AI technologies: Current status and trends. *IET Communications*, *2021*, 1–21.

Elsaeidy, A., Munasinghe, K. S., Sharma, D., & Jamalipour, A. (2019). Intrusion detection in smart cities using Restricted Boltzmann Machines. *Journal of Network and Computer Applications*, *135*, 76–83. doi:10.1016/j.jnca.2019.02.026

Eltahir, A. A., Saeed, R. A., Mukherjee, A., & Hasan, M. K. (2016). Evaluation and Analysis of an Enhanced Hybrid Wireless Mesh Protocol for Vehicular Ad-hoc Network. *EURASIP Journal on Wireless Communications and Networking*, *2016*(1), 1–11. doi:10.1186/s13638-016-0666-5

Enes, J., Expósito, R. R., & Touriño, J. (2020). Real-time resource scaling platform for big data workloads on serverless environments. *Future Generation Computer Systems*, *105*, 361–379. doi:10.1016/j.future.2019.11.037

Ezechina, A. (2015). The Internet of Things (Iot): A Scalable Approach to Connecting Everything. *The International Journal of Engineering and Science*, *4*(1), 09-12.

Ezhilarasi, M., Gnanaprasanambikai, L., Kousalya, A., & Shanmugapriya, M. (2023). A novel implementation of routing attack detection scheme by using fuzzy and feed-forward neural networks. *Soft Computing*, *27*(7), 4157–4168. doi:10.1007/s00500-022-06915-1

Fahim, K. E., Kalinaki, K., & Shafik, W. (2023). Electronic Devices in the Artificial Intelligence of the Internet of Medical Things (AIoMT). In Handbook of Security and Privacy of AI-Enabled Healthcare Systems and Internet of Medical Things (1st Edition, pp. 41–62). CRC Press. https://doi.org/ doi:10.1201/9781003370321-3

Fares, N. Y., & Jammal, M. (2023). AI-Driven IoT Systems and Corresponding Ethical Issues. *AI & Society*, 233–248. doi:10.1201/9781003261247-17

Fatima, F. (2015, December). Internet of things: A Survey on Architecture, Applications, Security, Enabling Technologies, Advantages & Disadvantages. *International Journal of Advanced Research in Computer and Communication Engineering*, *4*(12).

Fazeldehkordi, E., & Grønli, T. M. (2022). A Survey of Security Architectures for Edge Computing-Based IoT. *IoT*, *3*(3), 332–365. doi:10.3390/iot3030019

Ferdin, J. J. J. (2019, April). IoT Based Weather Monitoring System for Effective Analytics. *International Journal of Engineering and Advanced Technology*, *8*(4), 311–315.

Ferhat, K., & Sevcan, A. (2018). Big Data: Controlling fraud by using machine learning libraries on Spark. *Int J Appl Math Electron Comput.*, *6*(1), 1–5. doi:10.18100/ijamec.2018138629

Fernando, W. P. K., Dissanayake, D. A. N. P., Dushmantha, S. G. V. D., Liyanage, D. L. C. P., & Karunatilake, C. (2023). *Challenges and Opportunities in Password Management: A Review of Current Solutions*. Research Gate.

Ferrag, A., Maglaras, L., Janicke, H., Tuyishime, E., Balan, T. C., Cotfas, P. A., Cotfas, D. T., & Rekeraho, A. (2023). Enhancing Cloud Security—Proactive Threat Monitoring and Detection Using a SIEM-Based Approach. *Applied Sciences 2023, Vol. 13, Page 12359, 13*(22), 12359. doi:10.3390/app132212359

Ferreira, A. J., & Figueiredo, M. A. T. (2012). Boosting algorithms: A review of methods, theory, and applications. In C. Zhang & Y. Ma (Eds.), *Ensemble Machine Learning*. Springer. doi:10.1007/978-1-4419-9326-7_2

Furstenau, L. B., Rodrigues, Y. P. R., Sott, M. K., Leivas, P., Dohan, M. S., López-Robles, J. R., Cobo, M. J., Bragazzi, N. L., & Choo, K. K. R. (2023). Internet of things: Conceptual network structure, main challenges and future directions. *Digital Communications and Networks*, *9*(3), 677–687. doi:10.1016/j.dcan.2022.04.027

Gankotiya, A., Agarwal, S. K., Prasad, D., & Kumar, S. (2023). Cloud Computing and IoT Integration: Issues, Challenges and Opportunities. *2023 International Conference on Power, Instrumentation, Control and Computing, PICC 2023.* 10.1109/PICC57976.2023.10142839

Gaurav, A., Gupta, B. B., & Panigrahi, P. K. (2023). A comprehensive survey on machine learning approaches for malware detection in IoT-based enterprise information system. *Enterprise Information Systems*, *17*(3), 2023764. doi:10.1080/17517575.2021.2023764

Ghanem, B., Rosso, P., and Rangel, F. (2020, April 19). An emotional analysis of false information in social media and news articles. *ACM Transactions on Internet Technology*, *20*(2), 19, 1-18. doi:10.1145/3381750

Gheisari, M., Wang, G., & Chen, S. (2020). An edge computing-enhanced internet of things framework for privacy-preserving in smart city. *Computers & Electrical Engineering*, *81*, 106504. doi:10.1016/j.compeleceng.2019.106504

Ghiasi, M., Niknam, T., Wang, Z., Mehrandezh, M., Dehghani, M., & Ghadimi, N. (2023). A comprehensive review of cyber-attacks and defense mechanisms for improving security in smart grid energy systems: Past, present and future. *Electric Power Systems Research*, *215*, 108975. doi:10.1016/j.epsr.2022.108975

Ghorpade S. N et al (2021). Enhanced Differential Crossover and Quantum Particle Swarm Optimization for IoT Applications. *IEEE Access*. IEEE. . doi:10.1109/ACCESS.2021.3093113

Golec, M., Gill, S. S., Golec, M., Xu, M., Ghosh, S. K., Kanhere, S. S., Rana, O., & Uhlig, S. (2023). BlockFaaS: Blockchain-enabled serverless computing framework for AI-driven IoT healthcare applications. *Journal of Grid Computing*, *21*(4), 63. doi:10.1007/s10723-023-09691-w

Golightly, L., Modesti, P., Garcia, R., & Chang, V. (2023). Securing distributed systems: A survey on access control techniques for cloud, blockchain, IoT and SDN. *Cyber Security and Applications*, *1*, 100015. doi:10.1016/j.csa.2023.100015

Gomez, C., Chessa, S., Fleury, A., Roussos, G., & Preuveneers, D. (2019). Internet of Things for enabling smart environments: A technology-centric perspective. *Journal of Ambient Intelligence and Smart Environments*, *11*(1), 23–43. doi:10.3233/AIS-180509

Gong, L.-H., Pei, J.-J., Zhang, T.-F., & Zhou, N.-R. (2024). Quantum convolutional neural network based on variational quantum circuits. *Optics Communications*, *550*, 129993. doi:10.1016/j.optcom.2023.129993

Goyal, M., & Srivastava, D. (2021). A Behaviour-Based Authentication to Internet of Things Using Machine Learning. *Design and Development of Efficient Energy Systems*, 245–263. doi:10.1002/9781119761785.ch14

Gubbia, J. (2013). Internet of Things (IoT): A vision, architectural elements, and future directions. *Future Generation Computer Systems*, *29*(7), 1645–1660. doi:10.1016/j.future.2013.01.010

Guo, D., Liu, Z., & Li, R. (2023). RegraphGAN: A graph generative adversarial network model for dynamic network anomaly detection. *Neural Networks*, *166*, 273–285. doi:10.1016/j.neunet.2023.07.026 PMID:37531727

Gupta, S., Tanwar, S., & Gupta, N. (2022). *A Systematic Review on Internet of Things (IoT): Applications & Challenges*. 2022 10th International Conference on Reliability, Infocom Technologies and Optimization (Trends and Future Directions) (ICRITO), Noida, India. 10.1109/ICRITO56286.2022.9964892

Gupta, A., & Nahar, P. (2023). Classification and yield prediction in smart agriculture system using IoT. *Journal of Ambient Intelligence and Humanized Computing*, *14*(8), 10235–10244. doi:10.1007/s12652-021-03685-w

Gupta, I., Gupta, R., Singh, A. K., & Buyya, R. (2020). MLPAM: A machine learning and probabilistic analysis based model for preserving security and privacy in cloud environment. *IEEE Systems Journal*, *15*(3), 4248–4259. doi:10.1109/JSYST.2020.3035666

Gupta, P., Gupta, H., Ushasukhanya, S., & Vijayaragavan, E. (2023). Telemetry Simulation & Analysis. 2023 International Conference on Networking and Communications (ICNWC), Hammad, M., Abd El-Latif, A. A., Hussain, A., Abd El-Samie, F. E., Gupta, B. B., Ugail, H., & Sedik, A. (2022). Deep learning models for arrhythmia detection in IoT healthcare applications. *Computers & Electrical Engineering*, *100*, 108011.

Gupta, R., Gupta, I., Singh, A. K., Saxena, D., & Lee, C. N. (2022). An iot-centric data protection method for preserving security and privacy in cloud. *IEEE Systems Journal*. Advance online publication. doi:10.1109/JSYST.2022.3218894

Gürfidan, R., Ersoy, M., & Kilim, O. (2023). *AI-Powered Cyber Attacks Threats and Measures*. (pp. 434–444). Springer. doi:10.1007/978-3-031-31956-3_37

Guthi, A. (2016, July). Implementation of an Efficient Noise and Air Pollution Monitoring System Using Internet of Things (IoT). *International Journal of Advanced Research in Computer and Communication Engineering*, *5*(7), 237–242.

Haav, H.-M. (2014). Linked data connections with emerging information technologies: A survey. *International Journal of Computer Science and Applications*, *11*(3), 21–44.

Hadzovic, S., Mrdovic, S., & Radonjic, M. (2023). A Path Towards an Internet of Things and Artificial Intelligence Regulatory Framework. *IEEE Communications Magazine*, *61*(7), 90–96. doi:10.1109/MCOM.002.2200373

Hakak, S., Alazab, M., Khan, S., Gadekallu, T. R., Maddikunta, P. K. R., & Khan, W. Z. (2021). An ensemble machine learning approach through effective feature extraction to classify fake news. *Future Generation Computer Systems*, *117*, 47–58. doi:10.1016/j.future.2020.11.022

Hammad, M., Liu, Y., & Wang, K. (2018). Multimodal biometric authentication systems using convolution neural network based on different level fusion of ECG and fingerprint. *IEEE Access : Practical Innovations, Open Solutions*, *7*, 26527–26542. doi:10.1109/ACCESS.2018.2886573

Hanafi, A. V., Ghaffari, A., Rezaei, H., Valipour, A., & arasteh, B. (2023). Intrusion detection in Internet of things using improved binary golden jackal optimization algorithm and LSTM. *Cluster Computing*, •••, 1–18. doi:10.1007/s10586-023-04102-x

Hansen, E. B., & Bøgh, S. (2021). Artificial intelligence and internet of things in small and medium-sized enterprises: A survey. *Journal of Manufacturing Systems*, *58*, 362–372. doi:10.1016/j.jmsy.2020.08.009

Haribalaji, V., Boopathi, S., & Asif, M. M. (2021). Optimization of friction stir welding process to join dissimilar AA2014 and AA7075 aluminum alloys. *Materials Today: Proceedings*, *50*, 2227–2234. doi:10.1016/j.matpr.2021.09.499

Hassan, M. B., Alsharif, S., Alhumyani, H., Ali, E. S., Mokhtar, R. A., & Saeed, R. A. (2021). An Enhanced Cooperative Communication Scheme for Physical Uplink Shared Channel in NB-IoT. *Wireless Personal Communications*, *120*(3), 2367–2386. doi:10.1007/s11277-021-08067-1

Hazem M. (2008). Real-Time Intrusion Detection Algorithm for Network Security. *WSEAS Transactions on Communications, 12*(7).

Hegde, N., & Manvi, S. S. (2022). Approaches for Detecting and Predicting Attacks Based on Deep and Reinforcement Learning to Improve Information Security. In *Convergence of Deep Learning and Internet of Things* (pp. 113–130). Computing and Technology. doi:10.4018/978-1-6684-6275-1.ch006

Heidari, A., & Jafari Navimipour, N. (2022). Service discovery mechanisms in cloud computing: A comprehensive and systematic literature review. *Kybernetes*, *51*(3), 952–981. doi:10.1108/K-12-2020-0909

Hema, N., Krishnamoorthy, N., Chavan, S. M., Kumar, N., Sabarimuthu, M., & Boopathi, S. (2023). A Study on an Internet of Things (IoT)-Enabled Smart Solar Grid System. In *Handbook of Research on Deep Learning Techniques for Cloud-Based Industrial IoT* (pp. 290–308). IGI Global. doi:10.4018/978-1-6684-8098-4.ch017

Hemdi, M., & Deters, R. (2016, October). Using REST based protocol to enable ABAC within IoT systems. In *2016 IEEE 7th Annual Information Technology, Electronics and Mobile Communication Conference (IEMCON)* (pp. 1-7). IEEE. 10.1109/IEMCON.2016.7746297

Hephzipah, J. J., Vallem, R. R., Sheela, M. S., & Dhanalakshmi, G. (2023). An efficient cyber security system based on flow-based anomaly detection using Artificial neural network. *Mesopotamian Journal of Cyber Security*, 48–56. doi:10.58496/MJCS/2023/009

He, X., He, Q., & Chen, J.-S. (2021). Deep autoencoders for physics-constrained data-driven nonlinear materials modeling. *Computer Methods in Applied Mechanics and Engineering*, *385*, 114034. doi:10.1016/j.cma.2021.114034

Holt, T. J., Griffith, M., Turner, N., Greene-Colozzi, E., Chermak, S., & Freilich, J. D. (2023). Assessing nation-state-sponsored cyberattacks using aspects of Situational Crime Prevention. *Criminology & Public Policy*, *22*(4), 825–848. doi:10.1111/1745-9133.12646

Hossain, M. S., & Fotouhi, M. (2015). Cloud-based RFID framework for traceability and anti-counterfeiting. *Journal of Network and Computer Applications*, *55*, 65–80.

Hosseinnia Shavaki, F., & Ebrahimi Ghahnavieh, A. (2023). Applications of deep learning into supply chain management: A systematic literature review and a framework for future research. *Artificial Intelligence Review*, *56*(5), 4447–4489. doi:10.1007/s10462-022-10289-z PMID:36212799

Houssein, E. H., Gad, A. G., Wazery, Y. M., & Suganthan, P. N. (2021). Task scheduling in cloud computing based on meta-heuristics: Review, taxonomy, open challenges, and future trends. *Swarm and Evolutionary Computation*, *62*, 100841. doi:10.1016/j.swevo.2021.100841

Hua, H., Li, Y., Wang, T., Dong, N., Li, W., & Cao, J. (2023). Edge Computing with Artificial Intelligence: A Machine Learning Perspective. *ACM Computing Surveys*, *55*(9), 1–35. doi:10.1145/3555802

Huang, B., Chaki, D., Bouguettaya, A., & Lam, K.-Y. (2023). A survey on conflict detection in iot-based smart homes. *ACM Computing Surveys*, *56*(5), 1–40. doi:10.1145/3570326

Huang, W., Xie, X., Wang, Z., Feng, J. Y., Han, G., & Zhang, W. (2023). ZT-Access: A combining zero trust access control with attribute-based encryption scheme against compromised devices in power IoT environments. *Ad Hoc Networks*, *145*, 103161. doi:10.1016/j.adhoc.2023.103161

Huang, Y. (2016). Remote Environmental Monitoring Embedded System Design Based on Wireless Sensor Networks. *Chemical Engineering Transactions*, *51*, 223–228. doi:10.3303/CET1651038

Huang, Y.-F., & Chen, P.-H. (2020). Fake news detection using an ensemble learning model based on self-adaptive harmony search algorithms. *Expert Systems with Applications*, *159*, 113584. doi:10.1016/j.eswa.2020.113584

Hussain, Z., Babe, M., Saravanan, S., Srimathy, G., Roopa, H., & Boopathi, S. (2023). Optimizing Biomass-to-Biofuel Conversion: IoT and AI Integration for Enhanced Efficiency and Sustainability. In Circular Economy Implementation for Sustainability in the Built Environment (pp. 191–214). IGI Global.

IBM. (2020). *Blockchain: A technical overview*. IBM. https://www.ibm.com/cloud/learn/blockchain-a-technical-overview

Ibrahim, K., & Kemal, H. (2013). Open Source Intrusion Detection System Using Snort. *The 4th International Symposium on Sustainable Development*, (pp 1-6). Research Gate.

Ibrahim, S. E., Saeed, R. A., & Mukherjee, A. (2021). Resource Management in Vehicular Cloud Computing. *In Research Anthology on Architectures, Frameworks, and Integration Strategies for Distributed and Cloud Computing. edited by Management Association, Information Resources.* IGI Global.

IntechOpen. (n.d.). https://www.intechopen.com/download/get/type/pdfs/id/86

ISO/IEC. (2016). *ISO/IEC 27002:2013 - Information technology -- Security techniques -- Code of practice for information security controls*. ISO.

Jahangir, H., Lakshminarayana, S., Maple, C., & Epiphaniou, G. (2023). A Deep Learning-Based Solution for Securing the Power Grid against Load Altering Threats by IoT-Enabled Devices. *IEEE Internet of Things Journal, 10*(12), 10687–10697. doi:10.1109/JIOT.2023.3240289

Jangjou, M., & Sohrabi, M. K. (2022). A Comprehensive Survey on Security Challenges in Different Network Layers in Cloud Computing. *Archives of Computational Methods in Engineering, 29*(6), 3587–3608. doi:10.1007/s11831-022-09708-9

Jasim, A. F. J., & Kurnaz, S. (2023). New automatic (IDS) in IoTs with artificial intelligence technique. *Optik (Stuttgart), 273*, 170417. doi:10.1016/j.ijleo.2022.170417

Jiang, X., Ma, Z., Yu, F. R., Song, T., & Boukerche, A. (2020). Edge Computing for Video Analytics in the Internet of Vehicles with Blockchain. *In Proceedings of the 10th ACM Symposium on Design and Analysis of Intelligent Vehicular Networks and Applications (DIVANet '20)*. Association for Computing Machinery, New York, NY, USA, 1–7. 10.1145/3416014.3424582

Jin, T., Li, J., Yang, J., Li, J., Hong, F., Long, H., Deng, Q., Qin, Y., Jiang, J., Zhou, X., Song, Q., Pan, C., & Luo, P. (2021). SARS-Cov-2 presented in the air of an intensive car unit (ICU). *Sustainable Cities and Society, 2021*(65), 102446. doi:10.1016/j.scs.2020.102446 PMID:32837871

Jiyi, W., Wenjuan, L., Jian, C., Shiyou, Q., Qifei, Z., & Rajkumar, B. (2021). AIoT: a taxonomy, review and future directions. *Telecommunications Science, 37*(8).

Juan et al (2020). Machine learning applied in production planning and control: a state-of-the-art in the era of industry 4.0. *Journal of Intelligent Manufacturing.* Springer

Juma, M., Alattar, F., & Touqan, B. (2023). Securing Big Data Integrity for Industrial IoT in Smart Manufacturing Based on the Trusted Consortium Blockchain (TCB). *IoT, 4*(1), 27–55. doi:10.3390/iot4010002

Jyoti, K. S., & Chhabra, A. (2023). Machine Learning-Based Threat Identification Systems: Machine Learning-Based IDS Using Decision Tree. In Handbook of Research on Machine Learning-Enabled IoT for Smart Applications Across Industries (pp. 127–151). IGI Global. doi:10.4018/978-1-6684-8785-3.ch007

K. D. D. Cup. (1999). *Data.* KDD. http://kdd.ics.uci.edu/databases/ kddcup99/

Kahn, R. E., & Cerf, V. G. (1974). A Protocol for Packet Network Intercommunication. *IEEE Transactions on Communications, 22*(5), 637–648. doi:10.1109/TCOM.1974.1092259

Kalinaki, K., Fahadi, M., Alli, A. A., Shafik, W., Yasin, M., & Mutwalibi, N. (2023). Artificial Intelligence of Internet of Medical Things (AIoMT) in Smart Cities: A Review of Cybersecurity for Smart Healthcare. In Handbook of Security and Privacy of AI-Enabled Healthcare Systems and Internet of Medical Things (1st Edition, pp. 271–292). CRC Press. https://doi.org/doi:10.1201/9781003370321-11

Kalinaki, K., Shafik, W., Gutu, T. J. L., & Malik, O. A. (2023). Computer Vision and Machine Learning for Smart Farming and Agriculture Practices. In *Artificial Intelligence Tools and Technologies for Smart Farming and Agriculture Practices* (pp. 79–100). IGI Global. doi:10.4018/978-1-6684-8516-3.ch005

Kalinaki, K., Thilakarathne, N. N., Mubarak, H. R., Malik, O. A., & Abdullatif, M. (2023). Cybersafe Capabilities and Utilities for Smart Cities. In *Cybersecurity for Smart Cities* (pp. 71–86). Springer. doi:10.1007/978-3-031-24946-4_6

Kaliyar, R. K., Goswami, A., & Narang, P. (2019). Multiclass fake news detection using ensemble machine learning. In *Proceedings of 2019 IEEE 9th International Conference on Advanced Computing (IACC)*, (pp. 103-107). IEEE. https://doi:10.1109/IACC48062.2019.8971579

Kamil Abed Angesh Anupam, A., & Ali Kamil Abed, C. (2023). Review of security issues in Internet of Things and artificial intelligence-driven solutions. *Security and Privacy*, *6*(3), e285. doi:10.1002/spy2.285

Kanawaday. (2017). Machine learning for predictive maintenance of industrial machines using IoT sensor data. *2017 8th IEEE International Conference on Software Engineering and Service Science (ICSESS)*. IEEE. 10.1109/ICSESS.2017.8342870

Kandhro, I. A., Alanazi, S. M., Ali, F., Kehar, A., Fatima, K., Uddin, M., & Karuppayah, S. (2023). Detection of Real-Time Malicious Intrusions and Attacks in IoT Empowered Cybersecurity Infrastructures. *IEEE Access : Practical Innovations, Open Solutions*, *11*, 9136–9148. doi:10.1109/ACCESS.2023.3238664

Kant, R., Sharma, S., Vikas, V., Chaudhary, S., Jain, A. K., & Sharma, K. K. (2023, April). Blockchain–A Deployment Mechanism for IoT Based Security. In *2023 International Conference on Computational Intelligence, Communication Technology and Networking (CICTN)* (pp. 739-745). IEEE. DOI: 10.1109/CICTN57981.2023.10140715

Karagiannis, G., Altintas, O., Ekici, E., Heijenk, G., Jarupan, B., Lin, K., & Weil, T. (2010). Vehicular networking: A survey and tutorial on requirements, architectures, challenges, standards and solutions. *IEEE Communications Surveys and Tutorials*, *13*(4), 584–616. doi:10.1109/SURV.2011.061411.00019

Karaman, H. (2010). *A Content Based Movie Recommendation System Empowered By Collaborative Missing Data Prediction*. [Master Thesis, The Graduate School Of Natural And Applied Sciences Of Middle East Technical University].

Karpf, B. A. (2017). *Dead reckoning: where we stand on privacy and security controls for the Internet of Things* [Doctoral dissertation]. Massachusetts Institute of Technology.

Karthick Kumar, A., Vadivukkarasi, K., Dayana, R., & Malarvezhi, P. (2022). Botnet Attacks Detection Using Embedded Feature Selection Methods for Secure IOMT Environment. In Pervasive Computing and Social Networking. *Proceedings of ICPCSN, 2022*, 585–599.

Kassab, W., & Darabkh, K. A. (2020). A–Z survey of Internet of Things: Architectures, protocols, applications, recent advances, future directions and recommendations. *Journal of Network and Computer Applications*, *163*, 102663. doi:10.1016/j.jnca.2020.102663

Kattenborn, T., Leitloff, J., Schiefer, F., & Hinz, S. (2021). Review on Convolutional Neural Networks (CNN) in vegetation remote sensing. *ISPRS Journal of Photogrammetry and Remote Sensing*, *173*, 24–49. doi:10.1016/j.isprsjprs.2020.12.010

Kaur, B., Dadkhah, S., Shoeleh, F., Neto, E. C. P., Xiong, P., Iqbal, S., Lamontagne, P., Ray, S., & Ghorbani, A. A. (2023). Internet of things (IoT) security dataset evolution: Challenges and future directions. *Internet of Things : Engineering Cyber Physical Human Systems*, *22*, 100780. doi:10.1016/j.iot.2023.100780

Kayacik, H.G., Zincir-Heywood, A.N., & Heywood, M.L. (2006). *Selecting Features for Intrusion Detection: A Feature Analysis on KDD 99 Intrusion Detection Datasets*. Research Gate.

Kent, S., & Seo, K. (2005). Security Architecture for the Internet Protocol. *IETF RFC 4301*.

Khalifa, O. O., Omar, A. A., Ahmed, M. Z., Saeed, R. A., Hashim, A. H. A., & Esgiar, A. N. (2021). An Automatic Facial Age Progression Estimation System. *2021 International Congress of Advanced Technology and Engineering (ICOTEN)*. Research Gate.

Khan, A. R., Kashif, M., Jhaveri, R. H., Raut, R., Saba, T., & Bahaj, S. A. (2022). Deep learning for intrusion detection and security of Internet of things (IoT): Current analysis, challenges, and possible solutions. *Security and Communication Networks*, *2022*, 2022. doi:10.1155/2022/4016073

Khan, M. F. (2019). *Moth Flame Clustering Algorithm for Internet of Vehicle (MFCA-IoV)*. IEEE., doi:10.1109/ACCESS.2018.2886420

Khan, M., Glavin, F. G., & Nickles, M. (2023). Federated learning as a privacy solution-an overview. *Procedia Computer Science*, *217*, 316–325. doi:10.1016/j.procs.2022.12.227

Khoda Parast, F., Sindhav, C., Nikam, S., Izadi Yekta, H., Kent, K. B., & Hakak, S. (2022). Cloud computing security: A survey of service-based models. *Computers & Security*, *114*, 102580. doi:10.1016/j.cose.2021.102580

Kim, A., Oh, J., Ryu, J., & Lee, K. (2020). A review of insider threat detection approaches with IoT perspective. *IEEE Access : Practical Innovations, Open Solutions*, *8*, 78847–78867. doi:10.1109/ACCESS.2020.2990195

Koblah, D., Acharya, R., Capecci, D., Dizon-Paradis, O., Tajik, S., Ganji, F., Woodard, D., & Forte, D. (2023). A Survey and Perspective on Artificial Intelligence for Security-Aware Electronic Design Automation. *ACM Transactions on Design Automation of Electronic Systems*, *28*(2), 1–57. doi:10.1145/3563391

Kondamudi, S. S. R. (2016, February). IoT based Data Logger System for weather monitoring using Wireless sensor networks. *International Journal of Engineering Trends and Technology*, *32*(2), 71–75. doi:10.14445/22315381/IJETT-V32P213

Kondoro, A., Dhaou, I. B., Tenhunen, H., & Mvungi, N. (2021). Real time performance analysis of secure IoT protocols for microgrid communication. *Future Generation Computer Systems*, *116*, 1–12. doi:10.1016/j.future.2020.09.031

Koohang, A., Sargent, C. S., Nord, J. H., & Paliszkiewicz, J. (2022). Internet of Things (IoT): From awareness to continued use. *International Journal of Information Management*, *62*, 102442. doi:10.1016/j.ijinfomgt.2021.102442

Koschel, A., Klassen, S., Jdiya, K., Schaaf, M., & Astrova, I. (2021). Cloud computing: Serverless. *2021 12th International Conference on Information, Intelligence, Systems & Applications (IISA)*, (pp. 1–7). Research Gate.

Kumar, M. (2018). *Serverless computing for the Internet of Things*. Research Gate.

Kumar, M., Kumar, K., Sasikala, P., Sampath, B., Gopi, B., & Sundaram, S. (2023). Sustainable Green Energy Generation From Waste Water: IoT and ML Integration. In Sustainable Science and Intelligent Technologies for Societal Development (pp. 440–463). IGI Global.

Kumar, P. R., Meenakshi, S., Shalini, S., Devi, S. R., & Boopathi, S. (2023). Soil Quality Prediction in Context Learning Approaches Using Deep Learning and Blockchain for Smart Agriculture. In Effective AI, Blockchain, and E-Governance Applications for Knowledge Discovery and Management (pp. 1–26). IGI Global. doi:10.4018/978-1-6684-9151-5.ch001

Kumar, S. (2007). *Survey of Current Network Intrusion Detection Techniques*. CSE. https://www.cse.wustl.edu/~jain/cse571-07/ftp/ids.pdf

Kumari, A., Sahoo, B., Behera, R. K., Misra, S., & Sharma, M. M. (2021). Evaluation of integrated frameworks for optimizing qos in serverless computing. *Computational Science and Its Applications–ICCSA 2021: 21st International Conference, Cagliari, Italy, September 13–16, 2021. Proceedings*, *21*(Part VII), 277–288.

Kumar, P., Kumar, R., Gupta, G. P., Tripathi, R., Jolfaei, A., & Islam, A. N. (2023). A blockchain-orchestrated deep learning approach for secure data transmission in IoT-enabled healthcare system. *Journal of Parallel and Distributed Computing*, *172*, 69–83. doi:10.1016/j.jpdc.2022.10.002

Kumar, R., Joshi, G., Chauhan, A. K. S., Singh, A. K., & Rao, A. K. (2023). A Deep Learning and Channel Sounding Based Data Authentication and QoS Enhancement Mechanism for Massive IoT Networks. *Wireless Personal Communications*, *130*(4), 2495–2514. doi:10.1007/s11277-023-10389-1

Kunduru, A. R. (2023). ARTIFICIAL INTELLIGENCE USAGE IN CLOUD APPLICATION PERFORMANCE IMPROVEMENT. *CENTRAL ASIAN JOURNAL OF MATHEMATICAL THEORY AND COMPUTER SCIENCES,* *4*(8), 42–47. https://cajmtcs.centralasianstudies.org/index.php/CAJMTCS/article/view/491

Kurama, V. (2023). *Introduction to bagging and ensemble methods*. Paperspace. https://blog.paperspace.com/bagging-ensemble-methods/

Kurii, Y., & Opirskyy, I. (2022). Analysis and Comparison of the NIST SP 800-53 and ISO/IEC 27001: 2013. *NIST Spec. Publ*, *800*(53), 10.

Lakshmanna, K., Kavitha, R., Geetha, B. T., Nanda, A. K., Radhakrishnan, A., & Kohar, R. (2022). Deep learning-based privacy-preserving data transmission scheme for clustered IIoT environment. *Computational Intelligence and Neuroscience*, *2022*, 1–11. doi:10.1155/2022/8927830 PMID:35720880

Langone, R., Alzate, C., Bey-Temsamani, A., & Suykens, J. A. K. (2014). Alarm prediction in industrial machines using autoregressive LS-SVM models, *2014 IEEE Symposium on Computational Intelligence and Data Mining (CIDM)*. IEEE. 10.1109/CIDM.2014.7008690

Lau, A. (2020). New technologies used in COVID-19 for business survival: Insights from the Hotel Sector in China. *Information Technology & Tourism*, *22*(4), 497–504. doi:10.1007/s40558-020-00193-z

Laufs, J., Borrion, H., & Bradford, B. (2020). Security and the smart city: A systematic review. *Sustainable Cities and Society*, *55*, 102023. doi:10.1016/j.scs.2020.102023

Lee, W., Stolfo, S. J., & Mok, K. (1999). Data Mining in work flow environments: Experiments in intrusion detection. In *Proceedings of the 1999 Conference on Knowledge Discovery and Data Mining*. Research Gate.

Lee, C. C., Gheisari, M., Shayegan, M. J., Ahvanooey, M. T., & Liu, Y. (2023). Privacy-Preserving Techniques in Cloud/Fog and Internet of Things. *Cryptography*, *7*(4), 51. doi:10.3390/cryptography7040051

Li, C. (2020). *Web Security: Theory And Applications*. School of Software, Sun Yat-sen University.

Li, J. (2016). Industrial Big Data: Intelligent Transformation and Value Innovation in the Age of Industry 4.0. *CommonWealth Magazine Group*, 90–93.

Liao, H., Murah, M. Z., Hasan, M. K., Aman, A. H. M., Fang, J., Hu, X., & Khan, A. U. R. (2024). A Survey of Deep Learning Technologies for Intrusion Detection in Internet of Things. *IEEE Access : Practical Innovations, Open Solutions*, *12*, 4745–4761. doi:10.1109/ACCESS.2023.3349287

Li, J. (2023). IOT security analysis of BDT-SVM multi-classification algorithm. *International Journal of Computers and Applications*, *45*(2), 170–179. doi:10.1080/1206212X.2020.1734313

Lin, C., & Khazaei, H. (2020). Modeling and optimization of performance and cost of serverless applications. *IEEE Transactions on Parallel and Distributed Systems*, *32*(3), 615–632. doi:10.1109/TPDS.2020.3028841

Liris, C. O., Lahoud, I., El Khoury, H., & Liris, P.-A. C. (2018). Ontology-based Recommender System in Higher Education. *IW3C2 (International World Wide Web Conference Committee)*. ACM. ISBN 978-1-4503-5640-4/18/04.

Li, S. E. (2023). Deep reinforcement learning. In *Reinforcement Learning for Sequential Decision and Optimal Control* (pp. 365–402). Springer. doi:10.1007/978-981-19-7784-8_10

Li, S., Ma, K., Niu, X., Wang, Y., Ji, K., Yu, Z., & Chen, Z. (2019). Stacking-based ensemble learning on low dimensional features for fake news detection. In *Proceedings of 2019 IEEE 21st International Conference on High Performance Computing and Communications; IEEE 17th International Conference on Smart City; IEEE 5th International Conference on Data Science and Systems (HPCC/SmartCity/DSS)*, Zhangjiajie, China.10.1109/HPCC/SmartCity/DSS.2019.00383

Liu, L., Zhang, T., Yang, K., Thompson, P., Yu, Z., & Ananiadou, S. (2023, April 30 – May 01). Emotion detection for misinformation: A review. In *Proceedings of the 15th ACM Web Science Conference* (*WebSci 2023*). ACM. https://arxiv.org/pdf/2311.00671.pdf

Liu, C., & Ke, L. (2023). Cloud assisted Internet of things intelligent transportation system and the traffic control system in the smart city. *Journal of Control and Decision*, *10*(2), 174–187. doi:10.1080/23307706.2021.2024460

Liu, F., Zhang, X., & Liu, Q. (2023). Q. (2023). An emotion-aware approach for fake news detection. *IEEE Transactions on Computational Social Systems*, 1–9. doi:10.1109/TCSS.2023.3335269

Liu, L., & Li, Z. (2022). Permissioned blockchain and deep reinforcement learning enabled security and energy efficient Healthcare Internet of Things. *IEEE Access : Practical Innovations, Open Solutions*, *10*, 53640–53651. doi:10.1109/ACCESS.2022.3176444

Li, X., Leng, X., & Chen, Y. (2022). Securing Serverless Computing: Challenges, Solutions, and Opportunities. *IEEE Network.*

Li, Y., Li, H., Xu, G., Xiang, T., Huang, X., & Lu, R. (2020). Toward secure and privacy-preserving distributed deep learning in fog-cloud computing. *IEEE Internet of Things Journal*, *7*(12), 11460–11472. doi:10.1109/JIOT.2020.3012480

Li, Y., Lin, Y., Wang, Y., Ye, K., & Xu, C. (2022). Serverless computing: State-of-the-art, challenges and opportunities. *IEEE Transactions on Services Computing*, *16*(2), 1522–1539. doi:10.1109/TSC.2022.3166553

Li, Z., Kai, W., & Bo, L. (2013, April). Sensor-Network based Intelligent Water Quality Monitoring and Control. *International Journal of Advanced Research in Computer Engineering and Technology*, *2*(4), 1659–1662.

Lojka, T., Miškuf, M., & Zolotová, I. (2016). Industrial IoT Gateway with Machine Learning for Smart Manufacturing. In I. Nääs, (Eds.), *Advances in Production Management Systems. Initiatives for a Sustainable World. APMS. IFIP Advances in Information and Communication Technology* (Vol. 488). Springer. doi:10.1007/978-3-319-51133-7_89

Luvembe, A. M., Li, W., Li, S., Liu, F., & Xu, G. (2023). Dual emotion based fake news detection: A deep attention-weight update approach. *Information Processing & Management*, *60*(4), 4. doi:10.1016/j.ipm.2023.103354

Lynn, T., Rosati, P., Lejeune, A., & Emeakaroha, V. (2017). A preliminary review of enterprise serverless cloud computing (function-as-a-service) platforms. *2017 IEEE International Conference on Cloud Computing Technology and Science (CloudCom)*, (pp. 162–169). IEEE. 10.1109/CloudCom.2017.15

Maguluri, L. P., Arularasan, A., & Boopathi, S. (2023). Assessing Security Concerns for AI-Based Drones in Smart Cities. In Effective AI, Blockchain, and E-Governance Applications for Knowledge Discovery and Management (pp. 27–47). IGI Global. doi:10.4018/978-1-6684-9151-5.ch002

Mahor, V., Bijrothiya, S., Rawat, R., Kumar, A., Garg, B., & Pachlasiya, K. (2022). IoT and Artificial Intelligence Techniques for Public Safety and Security. *Smart Urban Computing Applications*, 111–126. doi:10.1201/9781003373247-5

Majeed Butt, O., Zulqarnain, M., & Majeed Butt, T. (2021, March). Butt. O. Majeed, M. Zulqarnain and T. Majeed Butt (2020). Recent advancement in smart grid technology: Future prospects in the electrical power network. *Ain Shams Engineering Journal*, *12*(1), 687–695. doi:10.1016/j.asej.2020.05.004

Malathi, J., Kusha, K., Isaac, S., Ramesh, A., Rajendiran, M., & Boopathi, S. (2024a). IoT-Enabled Remote Patient Monitoring for Chronic Disease Management and Cost Savings: Transforming Healthcare. In Advances in Explainable AI Applications for Smart Cities (pp. 371–388). IGI Global.

Malathi, J., Kusha, K., Isaac, S., Ramesh, A., Rajendiran, M., & Boopathi, S. (2024b). IoT-Enabled Remote Patient Monitoring for Chronic Disease Management and Cost Savings: Transforming Healthcare. In Advances in Explainable AI Applications for Smart Cities (pp. 371–388). IGI Global.

Malekmohamadi Faradonbe, S., Safi-Esfahani, F., & Karimian-Kelishadrokhi, M. (2020). A review on neural turing machine (NTM). *SN Computer Science*, *1*(6), 333. doi:10.1007/s42979-020-00341-6

Malik, I., Bhardwaj, A., Bhardwaj, H., & Sakalle, A. (2023). IoT-Enabled Smart Homes: Architecture, Challenges, and Issues. *Revolutionizing Industrial Automation Through the Convergence of Artificial Intelligence and the Internet of Things*, 160-176.

Manikanta Narayana, D. S., Bharadwaj Nookala, S., Chopra, S., & Shanmugam, U. (2023). An Adaptive Threat Defence Mechanism Through Self Defending Network to Prevent Hijacking in WiFi Network. *IEEE International Conference on Advances in Electronics, Communication, Computing and Intelligent Information Systems, ICAECIS 2023 - Proceedings*, (pp. 133–138). IEEE. 10.1109/ICAECIS58353.2023.10170470

Manimurugan, S. (2021). IoT-Fog-Cloud model for anomaly detection using improved Naïve Bayes and principal component analysis. *Journal of Ambient Intelligence and Humanized Computing*, *1*, 1–10. doi:10.1007/s12652-020-02723-3

Manu, B. (2016). A Survey on Secure Network: Intrusion Detection and Prevention Approaches. *The African Journal of Information Systems*, *4*(3), 69–88. doi:10.12691/ajis-4-3-2

Manzoor, M. A., & Morgan, Y. (2016). Real-time support vector machine based network intrusion detection system using Apache Storm. In *IEEE 7th annual information technology, electronics and mobile communication conference (IEMCON)*. IEEE. 10.1109/IEMCON.2016.7746264

Mather, T., Kumaraswamy, S., & Latif, S. (2009). *Cloud Security and Privacy: An Enterprise Perspective on Risks and Compliance*. O'Reilly Media.

Matsumoto, T., Matsumoto, H., Yamada, K., & Hoshino, S. (2002, April). Impact of artificial "gummy" fingers on fingerprint systems. In *Optical security and counterfeit deterrence techniques IV* (Vol. 4677, pp. 275–289). SPIE. doi:10.1117/12.462719

Ma, W., Zhou, T., Qin, J., Xiang, X., Tan, Y., & Cai, Z. (2022). A privacy-preserving content-based image retrieval method based on deep learning in cloud computing. *Expert Systems with Applications, 203*, 117508. doi:10.1016/j.eswa.2022.117508

Mazhar, M. S., Saleem, Y., Almogren, A., Arshad, J., Jaffery, M. H., Rehman, A. U., Shafiq, M., & Hamam, H. (2022). Forensic Analysis on Internet of Things (IoT) Device Using Machine-to-Machine (M2M) Framework. *Electronics, 11*(7), 1126. doi:10.3390/electronics11071126

McClellan, M., Cervelló-Pastor, C., & Sallent, S. (2020). Deep Learning at the Mobile Edge: Opportunities for5G Networks. *Applied Sciences (Basel, Switzerland), 10*(14), 4735. doi:10.3390/app10144735

McGinthy, J. M., Wong, L. J., & Michaels, A. J. (2019). Groundwork for neural network-based specific emitter identification authentication for IoT. *IEEE Internet of Things Journal, 6*(4), 6429–6440. doi:10.1109/JIOT.2019.2908759

Meiryani, J. Fahlevi, M., & Purnomo, A. (2023). The Integration of Internet of Things (IoT) And Cloud Computing in Finance and Accounting: Systematic Literature Review. *2023 8th International Conference on Business and Industrial Research, ICBIR 2023 - Proceedings*, (pp. 525–529). IEEE. 10.1109/ICBIR57571.2023.10147688

Melko, R. G., Carleo, G., Carrasquilla, J., & Cirac, J. I. (2019). Restricted Boltzmann machines in quantum physics. *Nature Physics, 15*(9), 887–892. doi:10.1038/s41567-019-0545-1

Mell, P., & Grance, T. (2011). *The NIST Definition of Cloud Computing*. National Institute of Standards and Technology. https://csrc.nist.gov/publications/detail/sp/800-145/final

Microsoft. (2021). *IoT security best practices*. Microsoft. https://docs.microsoft.com/en-us/azure/iot/security-best-practices

Min, Q., Lu, Y., Liu, Z., Su, C., & Wang, B. (2019). Machine Learning based Digital Twin Framework for Production Optimization in Petrochemical Industry. *International Journal of Information Management, 49*, 502–519. doi:10.1016/j.ijinfomgt.2019.05.020

Miorandi, D., Sicari, S., De Pellegrini, F., & Chlamtac, I. (2012). Internet of things: Vision, applications and research challenges. *Ad Hoc Networks, 10*(7), 1497–1516. doi:10.1016/j.adhoc.2012.02.016

Mishra, S., & Tyagi, A. K. (2022). The Role of Machine Learning Techniques in Internet of Things-Based Cloud Applications. *Internet of Things : Engineering Cyber Physical Human Systems*, 105–135. doi:10.1007/978-3-030-87059-1_4

Misra S. et al (2016). Security Challenges and Approaches in Internet of Things. S*pringer Briefs in Electrical and Computer Engineering*, 2016.

Mohamed, A., Dahl, G. E., & Hinton, G. (2011). Acoustic modeling using deep belief networks. *IEEE Transactions on Audio, Speech, and Language Processing*, *20*(1), 14–22. doi:10.1109/TASL.2011.2109382

Mohamed, D., & Ismael, O. (2023). Enhancement of an IoT hybrid intrusion detection system based on fog-to-cloud computing. *Journal of Cloud Computing (Heidelberg, Germany)*, *12*(1), 1–13. doi:10.1186/s13677-023-00420-y

Mohan, D., Al-Hamid, D. Z., Chong, P. H. J., Sudheera, K. L. K., Gutierrez, J., Chan, H. C., & Li, H. (2024). Artificial Intelligence and IoT in Elderly Fall Prevention: A Review. *IEEE Sensors Journal*, *24*(4), 4181–4198. doi:10.1109/JSEN.2023.3344605

Mohandass, M., Kaliraj, I., Maareeswari, R., & Vimalraj, R. (2023). IoT Based Traffic Management System for Emergency Vehicles. 2023 9th International Conference on Advanced Computing and Communication Systems (ICACCS), Nadhan, A. S., & Jacob, I. J. (2024). Enhancing healthcare security in the digital era: Safeguarding medical images with lightweight cryptographic techniques in IoT healthcare applications. *Biomedical Signal Processing and Control*, *88*, 105511.

Mohanty, A., Venkateswaran, N., Ranjit, P., Tripathi, M. A., & Boopathi, S. (2023). Innovative Strategy for Profitable Automobile Industries: Working Capital Management. In Handbook of Research on Designing Sustainable Supply Chains to Achieve a Circular Economy (pp. 412–428). IGI Global.

Mohd, N. (2015). *A Comprehensive Review of Swarm Optimization Algorithms*. ResearchGate. doi:10.1371/journal.pone.0122827

Molina, D. (2020). Comprehensive Taxonomies of Nature- and Bio-inspired Optimization: Inspiration versus Algorithmic Behavior, *Critical Analysis and Recommendations*.

Mukhopadhyay, S. C., Tyagi, S. K. S., Suryadevara, N. K., Piuri, V., Scotti, F., & Zeadally, S. (2021). Artificial intelligence-based sensors for next generation IoT applications: A review. *IEEE Sensors Journal*, *21*(22), 24920–24932. doi:10.1109/JSEN.2021.3055618

Mukkamala, S., Janoski, G., & Sung, A. (2002). Intrusion detection using neural networks and support vector machines. In *Proceedings of IEEE International Joint Conference on Neural Networks* (pp. 1702–1707). IEEE. 10.1109/IJCNN.2002.1007774

Nagendran, G. A., Raj, R. J. S., Priya, C. S. R., & Singh, H. (2023). IoT Cloud Systems: A Survey. *Proceedings - 5th International Conference on Smart Systems and Inventive Technology, ICSSIT 2023*, (pp. 415–418). IEEE. 10.1109/ICSSIT55814.2023.10060983

Nahr, J. G., Nozari, H., & Sadeghi, M. E. (2021). Green supply chain based on artificial intelligence of things (AIoT). *International Journal of Innovation in Management. Economics and Social Sciences*, *1*(2), 56–63.

Nair, M. M., & Tyagi, A. K. (2023). AI, IoT, blockchain, and cloud computing: The necessity of the future. *Distributed Computing to Blockchain: Architecture, Technology, and Applications*, (pp. 189–206). IEEE. doi:10.1016/B978-0-323-96146-2.00001-2

Nanda, A. K., Sharma, A., Augustine, P. J., Cyril, B. R., Kiran, V., & Sampath, B. (2024a). Securing Cloud Infrastructure in IaaS and PaaS Environments. In Improving Security, Privacy, and Trust in Cloud Computing (pp. 1–33). IGI Global. doi:10.4018/979-8-3693-1431-9.ch001

Nassar, A., & Yilmaz, Y. (2019). Reinforcement learning for adaptive resource allocation in fog RAN for IoT with heterogeneous latency requirements. *IEEE Access : Practical Innovations, Open Solutions*, *7*, 128014–128025. doi:10.1109/ACCESS.2019.2939735

Natesan, P., Rajalaxmi, R. R., Gowrison, G., & Balasubramanie, P. (2017). Hadoop based parallel binary bat algorithm for network intrusion detection. *International Journal of Parallel Programming*, *45*(5), 1194–1213. doi:10.1007/s10766-016-0456-z

Naveeenkumar, N., Rallapalli, S., Sasikala, K., Priya, P. V., Husain, J., & Boopathi, S. (2024). Enhancing Consumer Behavior and Experience Through AI-Driven Insights Optimization. In *AI Impacts in Digital Consumer Behavior* (pp. 1–35). IGI Global. doi:10.4018/979-8-3693-1918-5.ch001

Ndubuaku, M., vid Okereafor (2015). Internet of Things for Africa: Challenges and Opportunities. *2015 International Conference on Cyberspace Governance – Cyber ABUJA*. IEEE.

Neha, G., Gupta, P., & Alam, M. A. (2022). Challenges in the Adaptation of IoT Technology. *Intelligent Systems Reference Library*, *210*, 347–369. doi:10.1007/978-3-030-76653-5_19

Nguyen, T. D., Huh, E. N., & Jo, M. (2018). Decentralized and revised content-centric networking-based service deployment and discovery platform in mobile edge computing for IoT devices. *IEEE Internet of Things Journal*, *6*(3), 4162–4175. doi:10.1109/JIOT.2018.2875489

Nigam, D., Patel, S. N., Vincent, D. R., Srinivasan, K., & Sinouvassane, A. (2022). Biometric authentication for intelligent and Privacy-Preserving healthcare systems. *Journal of Healthcare Engineering*, *2022*, 1–15. doi:10.1155/2022/1789996 PMID:35368929

NIST. (2018*). National Initiative for Cybersecurity Education (NICE) Cybersecurity Workforce Framework*. NIST. https://nvlpubs.nist.gov/nistpubs/specialpublications/nist.sp.800-181r1.pdf

Nithiyanandam, N., Rajesh, M., Sitharthan, R., Shanmuga Sundar, D., Vengatesan, K., & Madurakavi, K. (2022). Optimization of Performance and Scalability Measures across Cloud Based IoT Applications with Efficient Scheduling Approach. *International Journal of Wireless Information Networks*, *29*(4), 442–453. doi:10.1007/s10776-022-00568-5

Nithya, S. H., & Sahayadhas, A. (2023). Meta-heuristic searched-ensemble learning for fake news detection with optimal weighted feature selection approach. *Data & Knowledge Engineering*, *144*, 102124. doi:10.1016/j.datak.2022.102124

Noura, H. N., Melki, R., & Chehab, A. (2019, September). Secure and lightweight mutual multi-factor authentication for IoT communication systems. In *2019 IEEE 90th Vehicular Technology Conference (VTC2019-Fall)* (pp. 1-7). IEEE. 10.1109/VTCFall.2019.8891082

OASIS. (2019). MQTT Version 5.0. OASIS. https://docs.oasis-open.org/mqtt/mqtt/v5.0/os/mqtt-v5.0-os.html

Oladimeji, D., Gupta, K., Kose, N. A., Gundogan, K., Ge, L., & Liang, F. (2023). Smart transportation: An overview of technologies and applications. *Sensors (Basel)*, *23*(8), 3880. doi:10.3390/s23083880 PMID:37112221

Oleiwi, H. W., Mhawi, D. N., & Al-Raweshidy, H. (2022). MLTs-ADCNs: Machine Learning Techniques for Anomaly Detection in Communication Networks. *IEEE Access : Practical Innovations, Open Solutions*, *10*, 91006–91017. doi:10.1109/ACCESS.2022.3201869

Ometov, A., Bezzateev, S., Mäkitalo, N., Andreev, S., Mikkonen, T., & Koucheryavy, Y. (2018). Multi-factor authentication: A survey. *Cryptography*, *2*(1), 1. doi:10.3390/cryptography2010001

Ometov, A., Petrov, V., Bezzateev, S., Andreev, S., Koucheryavy, Y., & Gerla, M. (2019). Challenges of multi-factor authentication for securing advanced IoT applications. *IEEE Network*, *33*(2), 82–88. doi:10.1109/MNET.2019.1800240

Oprea, S.-V., & Bâra, A. (2023). An Edge-Fog-Cloud computing architecture for IoT and smart metering data. *Peer-to-Peer Networking and Applications*, *16*(2), 1–28. doi:10.1007/s12083-022-01436-y

Orfanos, V. A., Kaminaris, S. D., Papageorgas, P., Piromalis, D., & Kandris, D. (2023). A Comprehensive Review of IoT Networking Technologies for Smart Home Automation Applications. *Journal of Sensor and Actuator Networks*, *12*(2), 30. doi:10.3390/jsan12020030

Orrù, P. F., Zoccheddu, A., Sassu, L., Mattia, C., Cozza, R., & Arena, S. (2020). Machine Learning Approach Using MLP and SVM Algorithms for the Fault Prediction of a CentrifugalPump in the Oil and Gas Industry. *Sustainability (Basel)*, *12*(11), 4776. doi:10.3390/su12114776

Ozturk, G. (2010). A *Hybrid Video Recommendation System Based On A Graph-Based Algorithm*. [Master thesis, Computer Engineering Department, Middle East Technical University].

Pachiappan, K., Anitha, K., Pitchai, R., Sangeetha, S., Satyanarayana, T., & Boopathi, S. (2024a). Intelligent Machines, IoT, and AI in Revolutionizing Agriculture for Water Processing. In *Handbook of Research on AI and ML for Intelligent Machines and Systems* (pp. 374–399). IGI Global.

Pal, K., & Yasar, A.-U.-H. (2023). Internet of Things Impact on Supply Chain Management. *Procedia Computer Science*, *220*, 478–485. doi:10.1016/j.procs.2023.03.061

Panda, P. K., & Chattopadhyay, S. (2020). A secure mutual authentication protocol for IoT environment. *Journal of Reliable Intelligent Environments*, *6*(2), 79–94. doi:10.1007/s40860-020-00098-y

Pandey, N. K., Kumar, K., Saini, G., & Mishra, A. K. (2023). Security issues and challenges in cloud of things-based applications for industrial automation. *Annals of Operations Research*. Advance online publication. doi:10.1007/s10479-023-05285-7 PMID:37361100

Park, J., Kim, D. S., & Lim, H. (2020). Privacy-preserving reinforcement learning using homomorphic encryption in cloud computing infrastructures. *IEEE Access : Practical Innovations, Open Solutions*, *8*, 203564–203579. doi:10.1109/ACCESS.2020.3036899

Park, S. H., Yun, S. W., Jeon, S. E., Park, N. E., Shim, H. Y., Lee, Y. R., Lee, S. J., Park, T. R., Shin, N. Y., Kang, M. J., & Lee, I. G. (2022). Performance Evaluation of Open-Source Endpoint Detection and Response Combining Google Rapid Response and Osquery for Threat Detection. *IEEE Access : Practical Innovations, Open Solutions*, *10*, 20259–20269. doi:10.1109/ACCESS.2022.3152574

Patel, A., & Jain, S. (2021). Present and future of semantic web technologies: A research statement. *International Journal of Computers and Applications*, *43*(5), 413–422. doi:10.1080/1206212X.2019.1570666

Pavel, L., Patrick, D., Christia, S., & Konrad, R. (2005). Learning Intrusion Detection: Supervised or Unsupervised? In *International Conference on image analysis and processing (ICAP)* (pp. 50-57). IEEE.

Pearson. (2020). *Working With Snort Rules*. Pearson Education Inc.

Peiris, C., & Pillai, B. (2022). Microsoft Azure Cloud Threat Prevention Framework. In hreat Hunting in the Cloud: Defending AWS, Azure and Other Cloud Platforms Against Cyberattacks (pp. 101–182). Wiley.

Peng, K., Leung, V. C., & Huang, Q. (2018). Clustering approach based on mini batch Kmeans for intrusion detection system over Big Data. *IEEE Access : Practical Innovations, Open Solutions*, *6*, 11897–11906. doi:10.1109/ACCESS.2018.2810267

Pereira, A. G., Lima, T. M., & Charrua-Santos, F. (2020). Industry 4.0 and Society 5.0. *Opportunities and Threats. Int. J. Recent Technol. Eng.*, *2020*(8), 3305–3308.

Pérez, S., Garcia-Carrillo, D., Marín-López, R., Hernández-Ramos, J. L., Marín-Pérez, R., & Skarmeta, A. F. (2019). Architecture of security association establishment based on bootstrapping technologies for enabling secure IoT infrastructures. *Future Generation Computer Systems*, *95*, 570–585. doi:10.1016/j.future.2019.01.038

Pham, C.-H., Huynh-The, T., Sedgh-Gooya, E., El-Bouz, M., & Alfalou, A. (2024). Extension of physical activity recognition with 3D CNN using encrypted multiple sensory data to federated learning based on multi-key homomorphic encryption. *Computer Methods and Programs in Biomedicine*, *243*, 107854. doi:10.1016/j.cmpb.2023.107854 PMID:37865060

Picoto, W. N., Abreu, J. C., & Martins, P. (2023). Integrating the Internet of Things Into E-Commerce: The Role of Trust, Privacy, and Data Confidentiality Concerns in Consumer Adoption. [IJEBR]. *International Journal of E-Business Research*, *19*(1), 1–18. doi:10.4018/IJEBR.321647

Pilewski, B. G., & Pilewski, C. A. (2010). Achieving PCI DSS Compliance: A Compliance Review. *Information Security Management Handbook*, *4*(4), 149–167. doi:10.1201/EBK1439819029-c10

Poblete, J. (2018). *Connected Automobiles and Cybersecurity*. Research Gate.

Popitsch, N., & Haslhofer, B. (2011). DSNotify – A solution for event detection and link maintenance in dynamic datasets. *Journal of Web Semantics*, *9*(3), 266–283. doi:10.1016/j.websem.2011.05.002

Pramila, P., Amudha, S., Saravanan, T., Sankar, S. R., Poongothai, E., & Boopathi, S. (2023). Design and Development of Robots for Medical Assistance: An Architectural Approach. In Contemporary Applications of Data Fusion for Advanced Healthcare Informatics (pp. 260–282). IGI Global.

Preethi, N. (2014). Performance Evaluation of IoT Result for Machine Learning. Transactions on Engineering and Sciences. 2(11).

Qays, M. O., Ahmad, I., Abu-Siada, A., Hossain, M. L., & Yasmin, F. (2023). Key communication technologies, applications, protocols and future guides for IoT-assisted smart grid systems: A review. *Energy Reports*, *9*, 2440–2452. doi:10.1016/j.egyr.2023.01.085

Qin, C., Zhang, A., Zhang, Z., Chen, J., Yasunaga, M., & Yang, D. (2023). *Is ChatGPT a general-purpose natural language processing task solver*? arXiv. /arXiv.2302.06476 doi:10.18653/v1/2023.emnlp-main.85

Qu, H., Jiang, J., Zhao, J., Zhang, Y., & Yang, J. (2020). A novel method for network traffic classification based on robust support vector machine. *Transactions on Emerging Telecommunications Technologies*, *31*(11), e4092. doi:10.1002/ett.4092

Quinlan, J. L. (1993). *C4.5 Program for Machine Learning*. Morgan Kaufmam Publishers, Inc.

Rahamathunnisa, U., Sudhakar, K., Padhi, S., Bhattacharya, S., Shashibhushan, G., & Boopathi, S. (2024). Sustainable Energy Generation From Waste Water: IoT Integrated Technologies. In Adoption and Use of Technology Tools and Services by Economically Disadvantaged Communities: Implications for Growth and Sustainability (pp. 225–256). IGI Global.

Rahamathunnisa, U., Subhashini, P., Aancy, H. M., Meenakshi, S., Boopathi, S., & ... (2023). Solutions for Software Requirement Risks Using Artificial Intelligence Techniques. In *Handbook of Research on Data Science and Cybersecurity Innovations in Industry 4.0 Technologies* (pp. 45–64). IGI Global.

Raj, H., Kumar, M., Kumar, P., Singh, A., & Verma, O. P. (2022). Issues and Challenges Related to Privacy and Security in Healthcare Using IoT, Fog, and Cloud Computing. *Advanced Healthcare Systems: Empowering Physicians with IoT-Enabled Technologies*, 21–32. doi:10.1002/9781119769293.ch2

Rajan, A. P. (2020). A review on serverless architectures-function as a service (FaaS) in cloud computing. [Telecommunication Computing Electronics and Control]. *Telkomnika*, *18*(1), 530–537. doi:10.12928/telkomnika.v18i1.12169

Ramudu, K., Mohan, V. M., Jyothirmai, D., Prasad, D., Agrawal, R., & Boopathi, S. (2023). Machine Learning and Artificial Intelligence in Disease Prediction: Applications, Challenges, Limitations, Case Studies, and Future Directions. In Contemporary Applications of Data Fusion for Advanced Healthcare Informatics (pp. 297–318). IGI Global.

Rao, C. K., Sahoo, S. K., & Yanine, F. F. (2024). Demand side energy management algorithms integrated with the IoT framework in the PV smart grid system. In *Advanced Frequency Regulation Strategies in Renewable-Dominated Power Systems* (pp. 255-277). Elsevier. 10.1007/978-981-99-0838-7_14

Rasool, R. U., Ahmad, H. F., Rafique, W., Qayyum, A., & Qadir, J. (2022). Security and privacy of internet of medical things: A contemporary review in the age of surveillance, botnets, and adversarial ML. *Journal of Network and Computer Applications*, *201*, 103332. doi:10.1016/j.jnca.2022.103332

Rastegari, H., Nadi, F., Lam, S. S., Abdullah, M. I., Kasan, N. A., Rahmat, R. F., & Mahari, W. A. W. (2023). Internet of Things in aquaculture: A review of the challenges and potential solutions based on current and future trends. *Smart Agricultural Technology*, *4*, 100187. doi:10.1016/j.atech.2023.100187

Rath, M., Tripathy, N., Tripathy, S. S., Sharma, V., & Garanayak, M. K. (2023). Development in IoT and Cloud Computing Using Artificial Intelligence. *Integration of Cloud Computing with Emerging Technologies*, 118–129. doi:10.1201/9781003341437-12

Ratnakar, N. C., Prajapati, B. R., Prajapati, B. G., & Prajapati, J. B. (2024). Smart Innovative Medical Devices Based on Artificial Intelligence. In *Handbook on Augmenting Telehealth Services* (pp. 150–172). CRC Press.

Raul, N., Shankarmani, R., & Joshi, P. (2020). A comprehensive review of keystroke dynamics-based authentication mechanism. In *International Conference on Innovative Computing and Communications: Proceedings of ICICC 2019*, Volume 2 (pp. 149-162). Springer Singapore. 10.1007/978-981-15-0324-5_13

Ravi, K. (2016). IoT based smart greenhouse. *IEEE Region 10 Humanitarian Technology Conference (R10-HTC)*. IEEE.

Rebecca, B., Kumar, K. P. M., Padmini, S., Srivastava, B. K., Halder, S., & Boopathi, S. (2024). Convergence of Data Science-AI-Green Chemistry-Affordable Medicine: Transforming Drug Discovery. In *Handbook of Research on AI and ML for Intelligent Machines and Systems* (pp. 348–373). IGI Global.

Reddy, H., Raj, N., Gala, M., & Basava, A. (2020). Textmining-based fake news detection using ensemble methods. *International Journal of Automation and Computing*, *17*(2), 210–221. doi:10.1007/s11633-019-1216-5

Reichert, C. (2017). *Cisco launches IoT Threat Defense*. ZDNET. https://www.zdnet.com/article/cisco-launches-iot-threat-defense/#google_vignette

Rejeb, A., Rejeb, K., Treiblmaier, H., Appolloni, A., Alghamdi, S., Alhasawi, Y., & Iranmanesh, M. (2023). The Internet of Things (IoT) in healthcare: Taking stock and moving forward. *Internet of Things : Engineering Cyber Physical Human Systems*, *22*, 100721. doi:10.1016/j.iot.2023.100721

Renugadevi, N., Saravanan, S., & Sudha, C. N. (2023). IoT based smart energy grid for sustainable cites. *Materials Today: Proceedings*, *81*, 98–104. doi:10.1016/j.matpr.2021.02.270

Ren, W., Tong, X., Du, J., Wang, N., Li, S. C., Min, G., Zhao, Z., & Bashir, A. K. (2021). Privacy-preserving using homomorphic encryption in Mobile IoT systems. *Computer Communications*, *165*, 105–111. doi:10.1016/j.comcom.2020.10.022

Revathi, S., Babu, M., Rajkumar, N., Meti, V. K. V., Kandavalli, S. R., & Boopathi, S. (2024). Unleashing the Future Potential of 4D Printing: Exploring Applications in Wearable Technology, Robotics, Energy, Transportation, and Fashion. In Human-Centered Approaches in Industry 5.0: Human-Machine Interaction, Virtual Reality Training, and Customer Sentiment Analysis (pp. 131–153). IGI Global.

Rhayem, A., Mhiri, M. B. A., & Gargouri, F. (2020). Semantic web technologies for the internet of things: Systematic literature review. *Internet of Things : Engineering Cyber Physical Human Systems*, *11*, 100206. doi:10.1016/j.iot.2020.100206

Rizvi, S., Campbell, S., & Alden, K. (2020, October). Why Compliance is needed for Internet of Things? In *2020 International Conference on Software Security and Assurance (ICSSA)* (pp. 66-71). IEEE. 10.1109/ICSSA51305.2020.00019

Roesch, M. (1999). Snort - Lightweight Intrusion Detection for Networks. *13th USENIX Conference on System Administration.*

Rojarath, A., Songpan, W., & Pong-inwong, C. (2016). Improved ensemble learning for classification techniques based on majority voting. In *Proceeding of the 7th IEEE International Conference on Software Engineering and Service Science (ICSESS)*, (pp. 107-110). IEEE. 10.1109/ICSESS.2016.7883026

Roman, R., Alcaraz, C., Lopez, J., & Sklavos, N. (2011). Key management systems for sensor networks in the context of the Internet of Things. *Computers & Electrical Engineering*, *37*(2), 147–159. doi:10.1016/j.compeleceng.2011.01.009

Romany, F. (2021). Mansour, Nada M. Alfar, Sayed Abdel-Khalek, Maha Abdelhaq, RA Saeed, Raed Alsaqour (2021). Optimal deep learning based fusion model for biomedical image classification. *Expert Systems: International Journal of Knowledge Engineering and Neural Networks*, (June). doi:10.1111/exsy.12764

Rong, G., Xu, Y., Tong, X., & Fan, H. (2021). An edge-cloud collaborative computing platform for building AIoT applications efficiently. *Journal of Cloud Computing (Heidelberg, Germany)*, *10*(1), 1–14. doi:10.1186/s13677-021-00250-w

Sabahi, F., & Movaghar, A. (2008). Intrusion detection: A survey. *Proc. 3rd Int. Conf. Syst. Netw. Commun.*

Sadeeq, M. M., Abdulkareem, N. M., Zeebaree, S. R., Ahmed, D. M., Sami, A. S., & Zebari, R. R. (2021). IoT and Cloud computing issues, challenges and opportunities: A review. *Qubahan Academic Journal*, *1*(2), 1–7. doi:10.48161/qaj.v1n2a36

Safi, M., Dadkhah, S., Shoeleh, F., Mahdikhani, H., Molyneaux, H., & Ghorbani, A. A. (2022). A Survey on IoT Profiling, Fingerprinting, and Identification. *ACM Transactions on Internet of Things*, *3*(4), 1–39. doi:10.1145/3539736

Sagu, A., Gill, N. S., Gulia, P., Singh, P. K., & Hong, W. C. (2023). Design of Metaheuristic Optimization Algorithms for Deep Learning Model for Secure IoT Environment. *Sustainability, 15*(3), 2204. doi:10.3390/su15032204

Sahu, D. K., Pradhan, B. K., Wilczynski, S., Anis, A., & Pal, K. (2023). Development of an internet of things (IoT)-based pill monitoring device for geriatric patients. In *Advanced Methods in Biomedical Signal Processing and Analysis* (pp. 129–158). Elsevier. doi:10.1016/B978-0-323-85955-4.00012-0

Saied, M., Guirguis, S., & Madbouly, M. (2024). Review of artificial intelligence for enhancing intrusion detection in the internet of things. *Engineering Applications of Artificial Intelligence*, *127*, 107231. doi:10.1016/j.engappai.2023.107231

Salman, H., & Arslan, H. (2023). PLS-IoT Enhancement against Eavesdropping via Spatially Distributed Constellation Obfuscation. *IEEE Wireless Communications Letters*, *12*(9), 1508–1512. doi:10.1109/LWC.2023.3279989

Sangeethalakshmi, K., Preethi, U., & Pavithra, S. (2023). Patient health monitoring system using IoT. *Materials Today: Proceedings*, *80*, 2228–2231. doi:10.1016/j.matpr.2021.06.188

Sanjay, R., Gulati, V. P., & Arun, K. P. (2005). A Fast Host-Based Intrusion Detection System Using Rough Set Theory in Transactions on Rough Sets IV. *LNCS*, *3700*, 144–161.

Sapandeep, K. &, Ikvinderpal, S. (2016). A Survey Report on Internet of Things Applications. *International Journal of Computer Science Trends and Technology, 4*(2).

Saranya, C. M., & Nitha, K. P. (2015, April). Analysis of Security methods in Internet of Things. *International Journal on Recent and Innovation Trends in Computing and Communication*, *3*(4).

Sarhan, M., Layeghy, S., Moustafa, N., & Portmann, M. (2023). Cyber Threat Intelligence Sharing Scheme Based on Federated Learning for Network Intrusion Detection. *Journal of Network and Systems Management*, *31*(1), 1–23. doi:10.1007/s10922-022-09691-3

Sarker, I. H., Khan, A. I., Abushark, Y. B., & Alsolami, F. (2022). Internet of things (iot) security intelligence: A comprehensive overview, machine learning solutions and research directions. *Mobile Networks and Applications*, 1–17.

Sarker, I. H., Khan, A. I., Abushark, Y. B., & Alsolami, F. (2023). Internet of Things (IoT) Security Intelligence: A Comprehensive Overview, Machine Learning Solutions and Research Directions. *Mobile Networks and Applications*, *28*(1), 296–312. doi:10.1007/s11036-022-01937-3

Savage, N. (2021, March 1). Fact-finding missions. *Communications of the ACM*, *64*(3), 18–19. doi:10.1145/3446879

Saxena, S., Bhushan, B., & Ahad, M. A. (2021). Blockchain based solutions to secure IoT: Background, integration trends and a way forward. *Journal of Network and Computer Applications*, *181*, 103050. doi:10.1016/j.jnca.2021.103050

Scarfon, K. & Mell, P. (2007). Guide to Intrusion Detection and Prevention Systems (IDPS). *Standard NIST SP 800-90.*

Scheuner, J., & Leitner, P. (2020). Function-as-a-service performance evaluation: A multivocal literature review. *Journal of Systems and Software*, *170*, 110708. doi:10.1016/j.jss.2020.110708

Schiller, E., Aidoo, A., Fuhrer, J., Stahl, J., Ziörjen, M., & Stiller, B. (2022). Landscape of IoT security. *Computer Science Review*, *44*, 100467. doi:10.1016/j.cosrev.2022.100467

Shafiei, H., Khonsari, A., & Mousavi, P. (2022). Serverless computing: A survey of opportunities, challenges, and applications. *ACM Computing Surveys*, *54*(11s), 1–32. doi:10.1145/3510611

Shafik, W. (2023). A Comprehensive Cybersecurity Framework for Present and Future Global Information Technology Organizations. In Effective Cybersecurity Operations for Enterprise-Wide Systems (pp. 56–79). Springer. doi:10.4018/978-1-6684-9018-1.ch002

Shafik, W., & Kalinaki, K. (2023). Smart City Ecosystem: An Exploration of Requirements, Architecture, Applications, Security, and Emerging Motivations. In Handbook of Research on Network-Enabled IoT Applications for Smart City Services (pp. 75–98). IGI Global. doi:10.4018/979-8-3693-0744-1.ch005

Shafiq, D. A., Jhanjhi, N., & Abdullah, A. (2022). Load balancing techniques in cloud computing environment: A review. *Journal of King Saud University. Computer and Information Sciences*, *34*(7), 3910–3933. doi:10.1016/j.jksuci.2021.02.007

Shafi, S., & Mallinson, D. J. (2023). The potential of smart home technology for improving healthcare: A scoping review and reflexive thematic analysis. *Housing and Society*, *50*(1), 90–112. doi:10.1080/08882746.2021.1989857

Shaikh, F. K. (2013). Communication Technology That Suits IoT – A Critical Review. *WSN4DC 2013, CCIS 366. Springer-Verlag Berlin Heidelberg, 2013*, 14–25.

Shamshirband, S., Fathi, M., Chronopoulos, A. T., Montieri, A., Palumbo, F., & Pescapè, A. (2020). Computational intelligence intrusion detection techniques in mobile cloud computing environments: Review, taxonomy, and open research issues. *Journal of Information Security and Applications*, *55*, 102582. doi:10.1016/j.jisa.2020.102582

Shanmuganathan, V., & Suresh, A. (2023). LSTM-Markov based efficient anomaly detection algorithm for IoT environment. *Applied Soft Computing*, *136*, 110054. doi:10.1016/j.asoc.2023.110054

Sharma, D. M., Ramana, K. V., Jothilakshmi, R., Verma, R., Maheswari, B. U., & Boopathi, S. (2024). Integrating Generative AI Into K-12 Curriculums and Pedagogies in India: Opportunities and Challenges. *Facilitating Global Collaboration and Knowledge Sharing in Higher Education With Generative AI*, 133–161.

Sharma, V., & Kumar, S. (2023, May). Role of Artificial Intelligence (AI) to Enhance the Security and Privacy of Data in Smart Cities. In *2023 3rd International Conference on Advance Computing and Innovative Technologies in Engineering (ICACITE)* (pp. 596-599). IEEE. 10.1109/ICACITE57410.2023.10182455

Sharma, A., Singh, P. K., & Kumar, Y. (2020). An integrated fire detection system using IoT and image processing technique for smart cities. *Sustainable Cities and Society*, *61*, 102332. doi:10.1016/j.scs.2020.102332

Sharma, B., Sharma, L., Lal, C., & Roy, S. (2024). Explainable artificial intelligence for intrusion detection in IoT networks: A deep learning based approach. *Expert Systems with Applications*, *238*, 121751. doi:10.1016/j.eswa.2023.121751

Sharma, M., Sharma, M., Sharma, N., & Boopathi, S. (2024a). Building Sustainable Smart Cities Through Cloud and Intelligent Parking System. In *Handbook of Research on AI and ML for Intelligent Machines and Systems* (pp. 195–222). IGI Global.

Sharma, T., & Sharma, P. (2023). AI-Based Cybersecurity Threat Detection and Prevention. In *Perspectives on Artificial Intelligence in Times of Turbulence* (pp. 81–98). Theoretical Background to Applications. doi:10.4018/978-1-6684-9814-9.ch006

Sharmila, K., Kumar, P., Bhushan, S., Kumar, M., & Alazab, M. (2023). Secure Key Management and Mutual Authentication Protocol for Wireless Sensor Network by Linking Edge Devices using Hybrid Approach. *Wireless Personal Communications*, *130*(4), 2935–2957. doi:10.1007/s11277-023-10410-7

Shearer, E. (2021, January 12). *More than eight-in-ten Americans get news from digital devices*. Pew Research Center. https://www.pewresearch.org/short-reads/2021/01/12/more-than-eight-in-ten-americans-get-news-from-digital-devices/

Shelby, Z., Hartke, K., & Bormann, C. (2014). The Constrained Application Protocol (CoAP). *IETF RFC 7252. ISO/IEC. (2017). ISO/IEC 27001:2013 - Information technology -- Security techniques -- Information security management systems -- Requirements.*

Shiraly, D., Eslami, Z., & Pakniat, N. (2024). Certificate-based authenticated encryption with keyword search: Enhanced security model and a concrete construction for Internet of Things. *Journal of Information Security and Applications*, *80*, 103683. doi:10.1016/j.jisa.2023.103683

Shoukat, A., Hassan, M. A., Rizwan, M., Imad, M., Ali, S. H., & Ullah, S. (2022). Design a framework for IoT-Identification, Authentication and Anomaly detection using Deep Learning: A Review. *EAI Endorsed Transactions on Smart Cities, 7*(1).

Siddiqui, Z., Tayan, O., & Khan, M. K. (2018). Security analysis of smartphone and cloud computing authentication frameworks and protocols. *IEEE Access : Practical Innovations, Open Solutions*, *6*, 34527–34542. doi:10.1109/ACCESS.2018.2845299

Singh, P., Borgohain, S. K., Sarkar, A. K., Kumar, J., & Sharma, L. D. (2023). Feed-forward deep neural network (FFDNN)-based deep features for static malware detection. *International Journal of Intelligent Systems*, *2023*, 2023. doi:10.1155/2023/9544481

Siwakoti, Y. R., Bhurtel, M., Rawat, D. B., Oest, A., & Johnson, R. (2023). Advances in IoT Security: Vulnerabilities, Enabled Criminal Services, Attacks and Countermeasures. *IEEE Internet of Things Journal*, *10*(13), 11224–11239. doi:10.1109/JIOT.2023.3252594

Sohal, M., Bharany, S., Sharma, S., Maashi, M. S., & Aljebreen, M. (2022). A Hybrid Multi-Cloud Framework Using the IBBE Key Management System for Securing Data Storage. *Sustainability, 14*(20), 13561. doi:10.3390/su142013561

Somu, N., Daw, N., Bellur, U., & Kulkarni, P. (2020). Panopticon: A comprehensive benchmarking tool for serverless applications. *2020 International Conference on COMmunication Systems & NETworkS (COMSNETS)*, (pp. 144–151). IEEE. 10.1109/COMSNETS48256.2020.9027346

Sonia, R., Gupta, N., Manikandan, K., Hemalatha, R., Kumar, M. J., & Boopathi, S. (2024). Strengthening Security, Privacy, and Trust in Artificial Intelligence Drones for Smart Cities. In *Analyzing and Mitigating Security Risks in Cloud Computing* (pp. 214–242). IGI Global. doi:10.4018/979-8-3693-3249-8.ch011

Stallings, W. (2017). *Cryptography and Network Security: Principles and Practice.* Pearson.

Stellios, I., Kotzanikolaou, P., & Psarakis, M. (2019). Advanced persistent threats and zero-day exploits in industrial internet of things. *Advanced Sciences and Technologies for Security Applications*, (pp. 47–68). Springer. doi:10.1007/978-3-030-12330-7_3

Stojmenovic, I., Wen, S., Huang, X., & Luan, H. (2014). An overview of fog computing and its security issues. *Concurrency and Computation*, *28*(10), 2991–3005. doi:10.1002/cpe.3485

Strielkowski, W., Streimikiene, D., Fomina, A., & Semenova, E. (2019). Internet of Energy (IoE) and High-Renewables Electricity System Market Design. *MDPI. Energies*, *12*(24), 4790. doi:10.3390/en12244790

Štuikys, V., & Burbaitė, R. (2024). Methodological Aspects of Educational Internet of Things. In *Evolution of STEM-Driven Computer Science Education: The Perspective of Big Concepts* (pp. 167–189). Springer. doi:10.1007/978-3-031-48235-9_6

Subashini, S., Kamalam, G., & Vanitha, P. (2024). A Survey of IoT in Healthcare: Technologies, Applications, and Challenges. *Artificial Intelligence and Machine Learning*, 136-144.

Subha, S., Inbamalar, T., Komala, C., Suresh, L. R., Boopathi, S., & Alaskar, K. (2023). A Remote Health Care Monitoring system using internet of medical things (IoMT). *IEEE Explore*, (pp. 1–6). IEEE.

Sufi, F., Khalil, I., & Hu, J. (2010). ECG-based authentication. Handbook of information and communication security, 309-331.

Sumithra, A. (2016, March). A Smart Environmental Monitoring System Using Internet of Things. *International Journal of Scientific Engineering and Applied Science*, *2*(3), 261–265.

Sung, A. H., & Mukkamala, S. (2003) Identifying Important Features for Intrusion Detection using Support Vector Machines and Neural Networks. *IEEE Proceedings of the 2003 Symposium on Applications and the Intern*et.

Sun, G., Zheng, X., Li, J., Kang, H., & Liang, S. (2023). Collaborative WSN-UAV Data Collection in Smart Agriculture: A Bi-objective Optimization Scheme. *ACM Transactions on Sensor Networks*, 3597025. doi:10.1145/3597025

Sun, L., Jiang, X., Ren, H., & Guo, Y. (2020). Edge-cloud computing and artificial intelligence in internet of medical things: Architecture, technology and application. *IEEE Access : Practical Innovations, Open Solutions*, *8*, 101079–101092. doi:10.1109/ACCESS.2020.2997831

Sunyaev, A., & Sunyaev, A. (2020). Cloud computing. *Internet Computing: Principles of Distributed Systems and Emerging Internet-Based Technologies*, 195–236.

Sun, Z., Zhu, M., Zhang, Z., Chen, Z., Shi, Q., Shan, X., Yeow, R. C. H., & Lee, C. (2021). Artificial Intelligence of Things (AIoT) enabled virtual shop applications using self-powered sensor enhanced soft robotic manipulator. *Advancement of Science*, *8*(14), 2100230. doi:10.1002/advs.202100230 PMID:34037331

Suresh Babu, C. V., & Akshara, P. M. (2023). Virtual Threats and Asymmetric Military Challenges. In Cyber Security Policies and Strategies of the World's Leading States (pp. 49-68). IGI Global. doi:10.4018/978-1-6684-8846-1.ch004

Suresh Babu, C. V., & Srisakthi, S. (2023). Cyber Physical Systems and Network Security: The Present Scenarios and Its Applications. In Cyber-Physical Systems and Supporting Technologies for Industrial Automation (pp. 104-130). IGI Global.

Suresh Babu, C. V., Akshayah, N. S., & Janapriyan, R. (2023). IoT-Based Smart Accident Detection and Alert System. In Handbook of Research on Deep Learning Techniques for Cloud-Based Industrial IoT (pp. 322-337). IGI Global.

Suresh Babu, C. V., Simon, P. A., & Kumar, S. B. (2023). The Future of Cyber Security Starts Today, Not Tomorrow. In Malware Analysis and Intrusion Detection in Cyber-Physical Systems (pp. 348-375). IGI Global.

Suresh Babu, C. V. (2023). *IoT and its Applications*. Anniyappa Publication.

Susan, M. B., & Rayford, B. V. (2000). Intrusion detection via fuzzy data mining. *Proceedings of the 12th Annual Canadian Information Technology Security Symposium.*

Syed, N. F., Ge, M., & Baig, Z. (2023). Fog-cloud based intrusion detection system using Recurrent Neural Networks and feature selection for IoT networks. *Computer Networks, 225*, 109662. doi:10.1016/j.comnet.2023.109662

Tabrizchi, H., & Kuchaki Rafsanjani, M. (2020). A survey on security challenges in cloud computing: Issues, threats, and solutions. *The Journal of Supercomputing*, *76*(12), 9493–9532. doi:10.1007/s11227-020-03213-1

Taghavirashidizadeh, A., Zavvar, M., Moghadaspour, M., Jafari, M., Garoosi, H., & Zavvar, M. H. (2022). Anomaly Detection In IoT Networks Using Hybrid Method Based On PCA-XGBoost. *Proceedings - 2022 8th International Iranian Conference on Signal Processing and Intelligent Systems, ICSPIS 2022*. IEEE. 10.1109/ICSPIS56952.2022.10043986

Tanimoto, S., Hori, S., Sato, H., & Kanai, A. (2023). Operation Management Method of Software Defined Perimeter for Promoting Zero-Trust Model. *Proceedings - 2023 IEEE/ACIS 21st International Conference on Software Engineering Research, Management and Applications, SERA 2023*, (pp. 440–445). IEEE. 10.1109/SERA57763.2023.10197716

Tan, Q., Zhang, Y., Zhang, X., Pei, X., Xiong, J., Xue, C., Liu, J., & Zhang, W. (2014, May 21). A Hazardous Chemical-Oriented Monitoring and Tracking System Based on Sensor Network. *International Journal of Distributed Sensor Networks, 10*(5), 1–8. doi:10.1155/2014/410476

Tanwar, S., Bhatia, Q., Patel, P., Kumari, A., Singh, P. K., & Hong, W. (2020). Machine Learning Adoption in Blockchain-Based Smart Applications: The Challenges, and a Way Forward. *IEEE Access : Practical Innovations, Open Solutions*, *8*, 474–488. doi:10.1109/ACCESS.2019.2961372

Tawalbeh, L., Muheidat, F., Tawalbeh, M., & Quwaider, M. (2020). IoT Privacy and Security: Challenges and Solutions. *Applied Sciences (Basel, Switzerland)*, *10*(12), 4102. doi:10.3390/app10124102

Tayfour, O. E., Mubarakali, A., Tayfour, A. E., Marsono, M. N., Hassan, E., & Abdelrahman, A. M. (2023). Adapting deep learning-LSTM method using optimized dataset in SDN controller for secure IoT. *Soft Computing*, 1–9. doi:10.1007/s00500-023-08348-w

The Snort Project. (2013). *Snort User Manual.* Sourcefire, Inc.

Thilakarathne, N. N. (2020). Security and privacy issues in iot environment. *International Journal of Engineering and Management Research, 10*(1), 10. doi:10.31033/ijemr.10.1.5

Tiwari, M., Kumar, R., Bharti, A., & Kishan, J. (2017). Intrusion Detection System. *International Journal of Technical Research and Applications.*, *5*, 2320–8163.

Toth, P., & Toth, P. (2017). *NIST MEP cybersecurity self-assessment handbook for assessing NIST SP 800-171 security requirements in response to DFARS cybersecurity requirements*. US Department of Commerce, National Institute of Standards and Technology. doi:10.6028/NIST.HB.162

Tsouplaki, A. (2023). Internet of Cloud (IoC): The Need of Raising Privacy and Security Awareness. *Lecture Notes in Business Information Processing*. Springer. doi:10.1007/978-3-031-33080-3_36

Uddin, M. S., & Bansal, J. C. (Eds.). (2022). *Computer Vision and Machine Learning in Agriculture* (Vol. 2)., doi:10.1007/978-981-16-9991-7

Vadakkethil Somanathan Pillai, E. S. (2023). *Misinformation with sentiment.* GitHub. https://github.com/sanjaikanth/MisInformationWithSentiment

Varghese, A. (2015, June). Weather Based Information System using IoT and Cloud Computing. *Journal of Computing Science and Engineering : JCSE*, *2*(6), 90–97.

Veeranjaneyulu, R., Boopathi, S., Narasimharao, J., Gupta, K. K., Reddy, R. V. K., & Ambika, R. (2023). Identification of Heart Diseases using Novel Machine Learning Method. *IEEE- Explore*, 1–6.

Velmurugadass, P., Dhanasekaran, S., Anand, S. S., & Vasudevan, V. (2021). Enhancing Blockchain security in cloud computing with IoT environment using ECIES and cryptography hash algorithm. *Materials Today: Proceedings*, *37*, 2653–2659. doi:10.1016/j.matpr.2020.08.519

Venkateswaran, N., Vidhya, R., Naik, D. A., Raj, T. M., Munjal, N., & Boopathi, S. (2023). Study on Sentence and Question Formation Using Deep Learning Techniques. In *Digital Natives as a Disruptive Force in Asian Businesses and Societies* (pp. 252–273). IGI Global. doi:10.4018/978-1-6684-6782-4.ch015

Verma, R., Christiana, M. B. V., Maheswari, M., Srinivasan, V., Patro, P., Dari, S. S., & Boopathi, S. (2024). Intelligent Physarum Solver for Profit Maximization in Oligopolistic Supply Chain Networks. In *AI and Machine Learning Impacts in Intelligent Supply Chain* (pp. 156–179). IGI Global. doi:10.4018/979-8-3693-1347-3.ch011

Vimal, P. V. (2017). IOT Based Greenhouse Environment Monitoring and Controlling System using Arduino Platform. *2017 International Conference on Intelligent Computing, Instrumentation and Control Technologies (ICICICT),* (pp. 1514- 1519). IEEE. 10.1109/ICICICT1.2017.8342795

Vimalkumar, K., & Radhika, N. (2017). A big data framework for intrusion detection in smart grids using Apache Spark. In In*ternational conference on advances in computing, communications and informatics (ICACCI)*. IEEE. 10.1109/ICACCI.2017.8125840

Visser, J., Lawrence, J., & Reed, C. (2020, October 22). Reason-checking fake news. *Communications of the ACM, 63*(11), 38–40. doi:10.1145/3397189

Walczak, R., Koszewski, K., Olszewski, R., Ejsmont, K., & Kálmán, A. (2023). Acceptance of IoT Edge-Computing-Based Sensors in Smart Cities for Universal Design Purposes. *Energies, 16*(3), 1024. doi:10.3390/en16031024

Walker, M. (2019, November 19). *Americans favor mobile devices over desktops and laptops for getting news.* Pew Research Center. https://www.pewresearch.org/short-reads/2019/11/19/americans-favor-mobile-devices-over-desktops-and-laptops-for-getting-news/

Wang, X., Wan, Z., Hekmati, A., Zong, M., Alam, S., Zhang, M., & Krishnamachari, B. (2024). IoT in the Era of Generative AI: Vision and Challenges. *arXiv preprint arXiv:2401.01923.*

Wang, G., Nixon, M., & Boudreaux, M. (2019). Toward cloud-assisted industrial IoT platform for large-scale continuous condition monitoring. *Proceedings of the IEEE, 107*(6), 1193–1205. doi:10.1109/JPROC.2019.2914021

Wang, H., Xiao, Y., & Long, Y. (2017). Research of intrusion detection algorithm based on parallel SVM on Spark. In *7th IEEE International conference on electronics information and emergency communication (ICEIEC).* IEEE. 10.1109/ICEIEC.2017.8076533

Wang, Y., Cui, Y., Kong, Z., Liao, X., & Wang, W. (2024). Design of Public Transportation System Scheduling and Optimization in the Internet of Things (IoT) Environment. *Advances in Engineering Technology Research, 9*(1), 89–89. doi:10.56028/aetr.9.1.89.2024

Wang, Z., Goudarzi, M., Gong, M., & Buyya, R. (2024). Deep Reinforcement Learning-based scheduling for optimizing system load and response time in edge and fog computing environments. *Future Generation Computer Systems, 152*, 55–69. doi:10.1016/j.future.2023.10.012

Waqas, M., Kumar, K., Laghari, A. A., Saeed, U., Rind, M. M., Shaikh, A. A., Hussain, F., Rai, A., & Qazi, A. Q. (2022). Botnet attack detection in Internet of Things devices over cloud environment via machine learning. *Concurrency and Computation, 34*(4), e6662. doi:10.1002/cpe.6662

Wei, Y. Y. (2015). A Survey of Wireless Sensor Network Based Air Pollution Monitoring Systems. *Sensors (Basel), 2015*(12), 31392–31427. doi:10.3390/s151229859 PMID:26703598

Whig, P., Velu, A., Nadikattu, R. R., & Alkali, Y. J. (2024). Role of AI and IoT in Intelligent Transportation. In *Artificial Intelligence for Future Intelligent Transportation* (pp. 199–220). Apple Academic Press.

Will, N. C. (2022, April). A privacy-preserving data aggregation scheme for fog/cloud-enhanced iot applications using a trusted execution environment. In *2022 IEEE International Systems Conference (SysCon)* (pp. 1-5). IEEE. DOI: 10.1109/SysCon53536.2022.9773838

Wójcicki, K., Biegańska, M., Paliwoda, B., & Górna, J. (2022). Internet of Things in Industry: Research Profiling, Application, Challenges and Opportunities—A Review. *Energies, 15*(5), 1806. doi:10.3390/en15051806

World Health Organization. (2023). *WHO coronavirus dashboard.* WHO. https://covid19.who.int/

Xiong, J., & Chen, H. (2020). Challenges for building a cloud native scalable and trustable multi-tenant AIoT platform. *Proceedings of the 39th International Conference on Computer-Aided Design*, (pp. 1–8). ACM. 10.1145/3400302.3415756

Xu, R., Baracaldo, N., & Joshi, J. (2021). *Privacy-preserving machine learning: Methods, challenges and directions.* arXiv preprint arXiv:2108.04417. https://doi.org//arXiv.2108.04417 doi:10.48550

Xu, L., Zhou, X., Tao, Y., Liu, L., Yu, X., & Kumar, N. (2021). Intelligent security performance prediction for IoT-enabled healthcare networks using an improved CNN. *IEEE Transactions on Industrial Informatics, 18*(3), 2063–2074. doi:10.1109/TII.2021.3082907

Yahya, M., Breslin, J. G., & Ali, M. I. (2021). Semantic web and knowledge graphs for industry 4.0. *Applied Sciences (Basel, Switzerland), 11*(11), 5110. doi:10.3390/app11115110

YangG.PangZ.DeenJ.DongM.ZhangY.-T (2020).;Lovell, N., & Rahmani, A. M. (2020). Homecare Robotic Systems for Healthcare 4.0: Visions and Enabling Technologies. *IEEE Journal of Biomedical and Health Informatics, 24*(9), 2535–2549. doi:10.1109/JBHI.2020.2990529 PMID:32340971

Yanushkevich, S. N., Boulanov, O., Stoica, A., & Shmerko, V. P. (2008). Support of interviewing techniques in physical access control systems. *Computational Forensics: Second International Workshop, IWCF 2008, Washington, DC, USA, August 7-8, 2008 Proceedings, 2*, 147–158.

Yazdinejad, A., Dehghantanha, A., Parizi, R. M., Srivastava, G., & Karimipour, H. (2023). Secure intelligent fuzzy blockchain framework: Effective threat detection in iot networks. *Computers in Industry, 144*, 103801. doi:10.1016/j.compind.2022.103801

Yinka-Banjo. (2022). Intrusion Detection Using Anomaly Detection Algorithm and Snort. Springer. doi:10.1007/978-3-030-93453-8_3

Yoon, S., Song, J., Seo, G., Han, S., & Hwang, E. (2023). A Content-assisted Dynamic PUF Key Generation Scheme Using Compressive Autoencoder for Internet-of-Things. *IEEE Sensors Journal, 23*(15), 17572–17584. doi:10.1109/JSEN.2023.3285784

Yu, K., Jiang, H., Li, T., Han, S., & Wu, X. (2020). Data fusion oriented graph convolution network model for rumor detection. *IEEE Transactions on Network and Service Management, 17*(4), 2171–2181. doi:10.1109/TNSM.2020.3033996

Yunana, K., Alfa, A. A., Misra, S., Damasevicius, R., Maskeliunas, R., & Oluranti, J. (2021). Internet of things: applications, adoptions and components-a conceptual overview. *Hybrid Intelligent Systems: 20th International Conference on Hybrid Intelligent Systems (HIS 2020).* Springer. 10.1007/978-3-030-73050-5_50

Zaguia, A. (2023). Smart greenhouse management system with cloud-based platform and IoT sensors. *Spatial Information Research*, 1-13.

Zahid, A. Z. G., Al-Kharsan, I. H. M. S., Bakarman, H. A., Ghazi, M. F., Salman, H. A., & Hasoon, F. N. (2019, December). Biometric authentication security system using human DNA. In *2019 First International Conference of Intelligent Computing and Engineering (ICOICE)* (pp. 1-7). IEEE. 10.1109/ICOICE48418.2019.9035151

Zareen, M. S., Tahir, S., & Aslam, B. (2024). Authentication and Authorization of IoT Edge Devices Using Artificial Intelligence. *IFIP International Internet of Things Conference*, 442–453. 10.1007/978-3-031-45878-1_32

Zeinab, E. (2020). Ahmed, Hasan Kamrul, Rashid A Saeed, Sheroz Khan, Shayla Islam, Mohammad Akharuzzaman, Rania A. Mokhtar (2020). Optimizing Energy Consumption for Cloud Internet of Things. *Frontiers in Physics (Lausanne)*, *8*, 358. doi:10.3389/fphy.2020.00358

Zhang, D.-S., Song, W.-Z., Wu, L.-X., Li, C.-L., Chen, T., Sun, D.-J., Zhang, M., Zhang, T.-T., Zhang, J., Ramakrishna, S., & Long, Y.-Z. (2023). The influence of in-plane electrodes on TENG's output and its application in the field of IoT intelligent sensing. *Nano Energy*, *110*, 108313. doi:10.1016/j.nanoen.2023.108313

Zhang, H., Wang, J., Zhang, H., & Bu, C. (2024). Security computing resource allocation based on deep reinforcement learning in serverless multi-cloud edge computing. *Future Generation Computer Systems*, *151*, 152–161. doi:10.1016/j.future.2023.09.016

Zhang, J., & Tao, D. (2020). Empowering things with intelligence: A survey of the progress, challenges, and opportunities in artificial intelligence of things. *IEEE Internet of Things Journal*, *8*(10), 7789–7817. doi:10.1109/JIOT.2020.3039359

Zhang, L., Zhang, G., Yu, L., Zhang, J., & Bai, Y. (2004). Intrusion detection using Rough Set Classification. *Journal of Zhejiang University. Science*, *5*(9), 1076–1086. doi:10.1631/jzus.2004.1076 PMID:15323002

Zhang, Li, Q., Zhang, C., Liang, H., Li, P., Wang, T., Li, S., Zhu, Y., & Wu, C. (2017). Current trends in the development of intelligent unmanned autonomous systems. *Frontiers Inf Technol Electronic Eng*, *18*(1), 68–85. doi:10.1631/FITEE.1601650

Zhang, Q., Yang, L. T., Chen, Z., & Li, P. (2018). A survey on deep learning for big data. *Information Fusion*, *42*, 146–157. doi:10.1016/j.inffus.2017.10.006

Zhou, X., Xu, K., Wang, N., Jiao, J., Dong, N., Han, M., & Xu, H. (2021). A secure and privacy-preserving machine learning model sharing scheme for edge-enabled IoT. *IEEE Access : Practical Innovations, Open Solutions*, *9*, 17256–17265. doi:10.1109/ACCESS.2021.3051945

Zhu, L., Tang, X., Shen, M., Gao, F., Zhang, J., & Du, X. (2021). Privacy-preserving machine learning training in IoT aggregation scenarios. *IEEE Internet of Things Journal*, *8*(15), 12106–12118. doi:10.1109/JIOT.2021.3060764

Zhu, S., Ota, K., & Dong, M. (2022). Energy-efficient artificial intelligence of things with intelligent edge. *IEEE Internet of Things Journal*, *9*(10), 7525–7532. doi:10.1109/JIOT.2022.3143722

Zolanvari, M., Teixeira, M. A., Gupta, L., Khan, K. M., & Jain, R. (2019, August). Machine Learning-Based Network Vulnerability Analysis of Industrial Internet of Things. *IEEE Internet of Things Journal*, *6*(4), 6822–6834. doi:10.1109/JIOT.2019.2912022

About the Contributors

Amina Ahmed Nacer is a Post-doc at University of Lorraine. She obtained her Ph.D. from University Abderrahmane Mira of Bejaia (Algeria) in co-guardianship with University of Lorraine (France). She received his Master's degree in Services, Security and Networks from University of Lorraine in 2013 and in Networks and distributed systems from University of Sciences and Technologies of Algiers (Algeria). She obtained her Graduation degree in Computer Science in 2010 from the same university. Her current research activities are focused on Business Process Management, cloud computing, and security.

Mohammed Riyadh ABDMEZIEM is currently an associate professor at ESI Algiers (Ecole nationale Supérieure d'Informatique). Previously, he served as a postdoctoral fellow as well as a lecturer at University of Lorraine (Polytech Nancy), he was within Loria laboratory and member of Coast team for several years. He received his PhD in Computer Science from the University of Sciences and Technology of Algiers (USTHB, Algeria) in 2016. He has been qualified for "Maitre de conférences" positions by CNU (France) since 2019, and received his HDR in 2022. His research activities are focused on security, key management protocols, and distributed artificial intelligence. He managed to publish several papers at an international level in conference proceedings, books, and journals.

Adam A. Alli, completed a PhD. in Computer Science and Engineering at the Islamic University of Technology-Dhaka. He received his Bsc. in Computer Science(2002) at Islamic University in Uganda, Msc. in Computer Science(2008) at University of Mysore India. He also received a Postgraduate Diploma in Management and Teaching at Higher Education(2015) at the Islamic University in Uganda and a Graduate Diploma In ICT leadership and knowledge society(2013) at Dublin City University through the GeSCI program. He was Dean Faculty of Science at the Islamic University in Uganda from 2011 to 2016. He is senior Lecturer of Computer Science and Engineering at both Islamic University in Uganda and Uganda Technical College(UTC) Lira. He is a researcher, mainly working on AI, IOT standards and Big Data. He also has an interest in Knowledge societies, leadership, and Education research work

A. Sherly Alphonse has received her B.E degree from Manonmaniam Sundaranar university, India and M.E from Anna University, India. She has five years teaching experience in various prestigious institutions. She is a reviewer of various international journals. She completed her full time Ph.D at Anna University, Chennai, India. Her research interest includes image processing and facial expression analysis.

Bhuvaneswari Amma N.G. received a PhD Degree from the National Institute of Technology, Tiruchirappalli, Tamil Nadu, India in 2020. Currently, she is an Assistant Professor (Senior) in the School of Computer Science and Engineering, Vellore Institute of Technology, Chennai, Tamil Nadu, India. She has 12 years of teaching experience and 7 years of research experience. She has the credit of publishing 30+ research articles in refereed journals and international conferences. Her areas of interest include network security, machine learning, data analytics, and statistical methods.

Revathi.B Assistant professor Department of Artificial Intelligence and Data science, Jaishriram Engineering College Dharapuram Road, Avinashipalayam Tirupur Tamilnadu 638660 revathi.pec@gmail.com

D. C.V. Suresh Babu is a pioneer in content development. A true entrepreneur, he founded Anniyappa Publications, a company that is highly active in publishing books related to Computer Science and Management. Dr. C.V. Suresh Babu has also ventured into SB Institute, a center for knowledge transfer. He holds a Ph.D. in Engineering Education from the National Institute of Technical Teachers Training & Research in Chennai, along with seven master's degrees in various disciplines such as Engineering, Computer Applications, Management, Commerce, Economics, Psychology, Law, and Education. Additionally, he has UGC-NET/SET qualifications in the fields of Computer Science, Management, Commerce, and Education. Currently, Dr. C.V. Suresh Babu is a Professor in the Department of Information Technology at the School of Computing Science, Hindustan Institute of Technology and Science (Hindustan University) in Padur, Chennai, Tamil Nadu, India.

Schin Chaudhary completed his Graduation from MJPRU, and Post Graduation from AKTU, Moradabad, U.P. Currently Pursuing his Ph.D. in Computer Science and Engineering from Govt. Recognized University. Presently, he is working as an Assistant Professor in the Department of Computer Science and Applications, IIMT University, Meerut, U.P, India. He has been awarded as Excellence in teaching award 2019. He is the reviewer member of some reputed journals. He has published several book chapters and research papers of national and international reputed journals.

Smanathan Pillai is a Senior Systems Analyst for Visa Inc. with 18 years of industry experience. Sanjaikanth completed his bachelor's degree from The University of Calicut, India, and his Master's in Electrical and Computer Engineering (Software Engineering) from The University of Texas at Austin. He is currently studying toward a Ph.D. in Computer Science at The University of North Dakota. His expertises include application programming, automation, performance optimization, and data research.

Dr. Pawan Kumar Goel is presently working as an Associate Professor at the Department of Computer Science and Engineering, Raj Kumar Goel Institute of Technology, Ghaziabad, U. P., India. Before that, he worked for several years as an Associate Professor & H.O.D. CSE at Shri Ram Group of Colleges (NAAC A++ accredited institute) .He has more than 17 years of experience in the academics. He has earned degrees: Ph.D (CSE), UGC NET in CS, M.Tech., MBA (HR), and B.Tech (IT) and has authored more than 35 research papers in professional journals and conferences. He has authored and edited more than 5 books with reputed publishers. His research areas include Information Security, Wireless Sensor Networks, Machine learning, information retrieval, semantic web, ontology engineering, data mining, ad hoc networks, sensor networks and network security. He received a International Achiever Award 2023 by Gyan Uday Foundation, Kota Rajasthan, for contribution in the category of "Distinguished Teacher 2023, Educator of the Year 2022 Award by Namaste India Council of Educators on Teacher's Day, 5th September 2022, National Education Excellence Achiever award by Navbharat Rashtriya Gyanpeeth, Pune Maharashtra for excellence in education field on 20/03/2022, Certificate of Appreciation for I2OR National Award 2021 in the category of "Distinguished Teacher" powered by International Institute of Organized Research (I2OR), "Global Outreach Agricultural Award-2020" Established Teacher in Computer Science & Engineering during 5th Global Outreach Conference on Modern Approaches for Smart Agriculture (MASA-2020), He is a member of the Asia Society of Researchers (ASR), the International Association of Engineers (IAENG), IACSIT (International Association of computer science and Information Technology), CSTA(Computer Science Teacher Association), ACM (Association for Computing machinery), UACEE (Universal Association of of Computers & Electronic Engineers), SCIEI, Internet Society ISOC, India, Academy & Industry Research Collaboration Center (AIRCC), IFERP (Institute for Engineering Research and Publication).

Mnoj Gupta working as an Assistant Professor in the School of Computer Science and Application IIMT University, Meerut, U.P.

Wen-Chen Hu received a PhD in Computer Science from the University of Florida. He is currently an associate professor in the School of Electrical Engineering and Computer Science of the University of North Dakota. He is the general chairs of about 20 international conferences and has been the editor-in-chiefs of the Journal of Information Technology Research (JITR) since 2023 and International Journal of Handheld Computing Research (IJHCR) from 2010 to 2017. In addition, he has acted as more than 200 positions like editors and editorial board members of international journals/books and program committee members of international conferences. Dr. Hu has been teaching for more than 25 years at the US universities and about 20 different computer/IT-related courses and advising/consulting more than 100 graduate students. He has published about 200 articles in refereed journals, conference proceedings, books, and encyclopedias, edited more than 10 books and conference proceedings, and solely authored a book. His current research interests include (mobile) data research and applications.

Kssim Kalinaki (MIEEE) is a passionate technologist, researcher, and educator with more than ten years of experience in industry and academia. He received his Diploma in Computer engineering from Kyambogo University, a BSc in computer science and engineering, and an MSc. Computer Science and Engineering from Bangladesh's Islamic University of Technology (IUT). Since 2014, He has been lecturing at the Islamic University in Uganda (IUIU), where he most recently served as the Head of Department Computer Science department (2019-2022). Currently, he's pursuing his Ph.D. in Computer Science at the School of Digital Science at Universiti Brunei Darussalam (UBD) since January 2022 and is slated to complete in August 2025. He's the founder and principal investigator of Borderline Research Laboratory (BRLab) and his areas of research include Ecological Informatics, Data Analytics, Computer Vision, ML/DL, Digital Image Processing, Cybersecurity, IoT/AIoMT, Remote Sensing, and Educational Technologies. He has authored and co-authored several published peer-reviewed articles in renowned journals and publishers, including in Springer, Elsevier, Taylor and Francis, Emerald and IEEE.

Dr. Bhupendra Kumar completed his Graduation and Post Graduation from Chaudhary Charan Singh University, Meerut, U.P. and Ph.D. in Computer Science and Engineering from Mewar University, Hapur. Presently, he is working as a Professor in the Department of Computer Science and Applications, IIMT University, Meerut, U.P. He has been a huge teaching experience of 19 years. He is the reviewer member of some reputed journals. He has published several book chapters and research papers of national and international reputed journals.

Mgezi Masha, a dynamic IT specialist from Uganda, holds a diploma in Computer Science and Bachelor's degree in Information Technology from the Islamic University in Uganda and is currently pursuing a Master's in Information Technology Management at IUIU. Serving as an IT administrator and Lecturer at the university, Magezi excels in maintaining IT systems, backed by diverse experiences as an Enrolment Officer at the Electoral Commission and a Multimedia Trainer at Swiss Contact-Uganda. Proficient in CCNA, leadership, and project management, Magezi is not only a dedicated professional but also actively engages in various activities, demonstrating his commitment to continuous learning and personal growth. Navigating technology, leadership, and academia, he remains a versatile contributor to the world of information technology with a research focus on Media and technology.

D M. Sureshkumar completed his undergraduate in Mechanical Engineering and postgraduate in the field of Engineering Design. He completed his Ph.D. from Anna University, Chennai, Tamil Nādu, India.

R.Nagarajan received his B.E. in Electrical and Electronics Engineering from Madurai Kamarajar University, Madurai, India, in 1997. He received his M.E. in Power Electronics and Drives from Anna University, Chennai, India, in 2008. He received his Ph.D in Electrical Engineering from Anna University, Chennai, India, in 2014. He has worked in the industry as an Electrical Engineer. He is currently working as Professor of Electrical and Electronics Engineering at Gnanamani College of Technology, Namakkal, Tamilnadu, India. His current research interest includes Power Electronics, Power System, Network Security, Cloud Computing, Wireless Sensor Communication, Digital Image Processing, Data Mining, Soft Computing Techniques and Renewable Energy Sources. He is published more than 120 Research Articles in various referred International Journals and he is published more than 60 Books & Book Chapter in various referred international Publications.

D..BINAYA earned her B.E., from Anna University and she earned her M.E from Anna University. She earned her Ph.D. from Anna University in 2022 in the area of Artificial Intelligence. At Vellore Institute of Technology in Chennai, she is currently employed as an Assistant Professor in Senior Grade 1. Her research interest includes Artificial Intelligence, Machine Learning & Deep Learning, Recommender systems, Fuzzy Logic & Optimization Technique. She has proposed various novel information filtering algorithms for recommender systems and pattern recognition algorithms in image processing. She has published various papers in recognized international journals. She has published various book chapters on Application of Machine Learning in Agriculture, IoT, etc. She is a lifetime member of Institution of Engineers (India) [IEI].

Dr. Hamsa S Associate Professor Department of Electronics and Communication Engineering, Jyothy Institute of Technology Thathaguni, off kanakapura Road, Bangalore Urban Karnataka 560082 0000-0002-0454-4975

Rshid A. Saeed received his PhD majoring in Communications and Network Engineering, UPM, Malaysia. He is Professor since 2000 in SUST. He was senior researcher in Telekom Malaysia™, Research and Development (TMRND) and MIMOS Berhad, in 2007, 2010 respectively. Dr. Rashid has been published more than 140 research papers/tutorials/talks/book chapter on wireless communications and networking in peer-reviewed academic journals and conferences. His areas of research interest include computer network, cognitive computing, computer engineering, wireless broadband, WiMAX Femtocell. He successfully award 10 U.S patents in these areas. Dr. Rashid is a Senior MIEEE since 2001 and Member IEM (I.E.M).

Dr susanta Kumar Satpathy Professor Department of Computer Science And Engineering, Vignan Foundation of science technology and research, Vadlamudi, Guntur GUntur Andhra Pradesh 522213

Elmustafa Sayed Ali Ahmed received his M.Sc. in Electronics & Communication Engineering, Sudan University of Science & technology in 2012 and B.Sc. in 2008. Worked (former) as a senior engineer in Sudan Sea Port Corporation for 5 years as a team leader of new projects in wireless networks includes (Tetra system, Wi-Fi, WI-Max, and CCTV). In addition, he also worked as a senior lecturer and Head of Electrical and Electronics Engineering Department in the Red Sea University. Worked also as a head of marine systems department in Sudan Marine Industries. He is currently working as a project research specialists in the Sudanese defense industries. Elmustafa published more than 65 research papers, and book chapters in wireless communications systems and networking in peer reviewed academic international journals. His areas of research interest include, routing protocols, wireless networks and systems, Internet of Things (IoT) Applications, Underwater Communications, and Artificial Intelligence (AI) in wireless networks. He is a member of IEEE Communication Society (ComSoc), International Association of Engineers (IAENG), Six Sigma Yellow Belt (SSYB), Scrum Fundamentals certified (SFC), and Sudanese Engineering Council (SEC). ORCID ID: 0000-0003-4738-3216

Wasswa Shafik is an IEEE member, P.Eng received a bachelor of science in Information Technology Engineering with a minor in Mathematics in 2016 from Ndejje University, Kampala, Uganda, a PhD and master of engineering in Information Technology Engineering (MIT) in 2020, from the Computer Engineering Department, Yazd University, Islamic Republic of Iran. He is an associate researcher at the

Computer Science department, Network interconnectivity Lab at Yazd University, Islamic Republic of Iran, and at Information Sciences, Prince Sultan University, Saudi Arabia. His areas of interest are Computer Vision, Anomaly Detection, Drones (UAVs), Machine/Deep Learning, AI-enabled IoT/IoMTs, IoT/IIoT/OT Security, Cyber Security and Privacy. Shafik is the chair/co-chair/program chair of some Scopus/EI conferences. Also, academic editor/ associate editor for set of indexed journals (Scopus journals' quartile ranking). He is the founder and lead investigator of Digital Connectivity Research Laboratory (DCR-Lab) since 2019, the Managing Executive director of Asmaah Charity Organisation (ACO).

Nzeer Shaik Assistant Professor Department of Computer Science & Engineering, Srinivasa Ramanujan Institute of Technology (SRIT) Rotatrypuram Anantapur Andhra Pradesh 515701 Orchid Id: 0000-0001-5414-5289

Dr. Kewal Krishan Sharma is a professor in computer sc. in IIMT University, Meerut, U.P, India. He did his Ph.D. in computer network with this he has MCA, MBA and Law degree also. He did variously certification courses also. He has an overall experience of around 33 year in academic, business and industry. He wrote a number of research papers and books.

Vikas Sharma completed his Graduation and Post Graduation from Chaudhary Charan Singh University, Meerut, U.P. Currently Pursuing his Ph.D. in Computer Science and Engineering from Govt. Recognized University. Presently, he is working as an Assistant Professor in the Department of Computer Science and Applications, IIMT University, Meerut, U.P. He has been awarded as Excellence in teaching award 2019. He is the reviewer member of some reputed journals. He has published several book chapters and research papers of national and international reputed journals.

Saand Arun Yamgar is currently pursuing his B.Tech. Computer Science and Engineering with Specialization in Cyber Physical Systems from Vellore Institute of Technology, Chennai, Tamil Nadu-600127. His primary areas of research include Machine Learning algorithms and Anomaly Detection.

D. Tarun Kumar Vashishth is an active academician and researcher in the field of computer science with 21 years of experience. He earned Ph.D. Mathematics degree specialized in Operations Research; served several academic positions such as HoD, Dy. Director, Academic Coordinator, Member Secretary of Department Research Committee, Assistant Center superintendent and Head Examiner in university examinations. He is involved in academic development and scholarly activities. He is member of International Association of Engineers, The Society of

Digital Information and Wireless Communications, Global Professors Welfare Association, International Association of Academic plus Corporate (IAAC), Computer Science Teachers Association and Internet Society. His research interest includes Cloud Computing, Artificial Intelligence, Machine Learning and Operations Research; published more than 20 research articles with 1 book and 10 book chapters in edited books. He is contributing as member of editorial and reviewers boards in conferences and various computer journals published by CRC Press, Taylor and Francis, Springer, IGI global and other universities.

Index

K

L

M

N

O

P

R

S

T

V

Z

www.ingramcontent.com/pod-product-compliance
Lightning Source LLC
LaVergne TN
LVHW080633011026
849160LV00014B/1197